Mr. Apology

and Other Essays

BOOKS BY ALEC WILKINSON

MIDNIGHTS
(1982)

MOONSHINE
(1985)

BIG SUGAR
(1989)

THE RIVERKEEPER
(1991)

A VIOLENT ACT
(1993)

MY MENTOR
(2002)

MR. APOLOGY
AND OTHER ESSAYS
(2003)

Mr. Apology

and

Other Essays

....

Alec Wilkinson

HOUGHTON MIFFLIN COMPANY

BOSTON · NEW YORK

2003

FOR SARA BARRETT

AND

SAM MAXWELL WILKINSON

· ·

For information about permission to reproduce selections
from this book, write to Permissions, Houghton Mifflin Company,
215 Park Avenue South, New York, New York 10003.

Visit our Web site: www.houghtonmifflinbooks.com.

Library of Congress Cataloging-in-Publication Data
Wilkinson, Alec, date.
Mr. Apology and other essays / Alec Wilkinson.
p.   cm.
ISBN 0-618-12311-3
I. Title.
AC8.W597 2003
081—dc21   2003047837

Printed in the United States of America

Book design by Robert Overholtzer

MP 10 9 8 7 6 5 4 3 2 1

Several of the essays collected in this book were originally published
with different titles and in slightly different form. Three of the essays
were published in *Esquire,* two were published in *Rolling Stone,* and
two were published in *Vogue.* The rest appeared in *The New Yorker.*

CONTENTS

Part One

Cameos

HERE COMES HUGH in his truck, turning heads. Hugh Cosman in a 1953 Ford F-100, the special deluxe edition pickup, with the rounded fenders, and the clamshell hood stamped from one sheet of steel. The horn button on the steering wheel says 50TH ANNIVERSARY, 1903–1953. You lose that horn button and good luck finding another one. Other details: the boomerang-shaped ornaments on either side of the hood. Originally they were chrome, but when the truck was built the manufacturer wasn't putting nickel under the chrome, because nickel was a defense-appropriated material. Korean War. The chrome wore thin, so Hugh had his boomerangs sandblasted at a shop out in Roosevelt, Long Island, and then he painted them ivory, to match the tailgate lettering and the bumpers.

Hugh works at Treitel-Gratz, in Long Island City. Its card says:

CRAFTSMEN IN METAL FABRICATION

PRECISION PARTS

CUSTOM FURNITURE

DESIGN MODELS

Treitel-Gratz also makes sculptures for artists such as Isamu Noguchi, Barnett Newman, and Walter De Maria. Hugh is thirty-seven, and he went to Vassar, formerly a women's college, where they (still) don't offer courses in automotive restoration. In the chain of events that delivered the truck into Hugh's hands, it is likely that he occupied the role of guy D. Guy A has the truck parked in his barn or garage or out back on the lawn, and has always meant to do something about it — slap some putty here, a little paint there, maybe bang out a dent — but never has. Guy B sees it, or sees an ad, or knows somebody who knows about the truck, and he buys it, thinking he'll put a few hours into it and give it a new coat of paint and have a showcase piece of rolling stock. He does some slipshod patching of rust with strips of metal and pop rivets, sees how much more of a commitment is required, and puts the truck back on the market, turning it over to guy C, who thinks he'll devote several evenings and weekends to it, then realizes he's in over his head and throws a tarp over the truck and puts a For Sale sign on it, and in comes guy D. Years may have passed (Hugh's truck was last on the road in 1979, registered in Pennsylvania) and a lot of bad amateur work may have been performed on the truck by the time guy D gets hold of it. Hugh paid nine hundred for the truck, in December 1987. The ad that he answered described a West Coast rust-free truck. He says that the truck that came into his hands was "an East Coast rust-eviscerated vehicle."

Hugh began restoring his truck in the yard of his weekend house, in New Jersey. Then he brought it to the city, piece by piece, and worked on it at night in a corner of the shop at Treitel-Gratz. Eventually, every part of the body except the cab had been removed and brought to the city to be sanded or sandblasted or galvanized or painted. The bed he had rebuilt in poplar by a cabinetmaker.

Hugh's association with Treitel-Gratz provided him with garage space, specialized tools, and access to Frosty — that is, Forrest Myers, an artist, car restorer, and metalworker, whose support, knowledge, and philosophical example gave Hugh the kind of head start that most guys (guys A, B, and C, for example) lack. There is an aspect of friction, though, in Frosty's relationship with Hugh. Frosty's position is that Hugh's truck is a classical showpiece, not a beater. Some months ago, after enough mechanical work had been completed to allow Hugh to register his truck, he ran an errand in it, using the bed of the truck to carry lumber. Frosty's reaction: "He's making a *farm* truck out of it. He's throwing cinder blocks into the back, and hay bales, and I don't know what else. The last time I looked, there was *dirt* in the bed." Frosty does, however, approve of the care with which Hugh pursued the restoration. What Hugh really did was not simply restore his truck — he remanufactured it, duplicating all kinds of rotten sheet-metal pieces in stainless steel, so they will never rust again.

A few weeks ago, Hugh brought the truck to Oscar's Auto Body, on

Twenty-first Street in Queens, for painting. Parts of Hugh's truck have spent a lot of time at Oscar's. The fenders alone spent a year. While his truck was at Oscar's, the only contact Hugh had with it took place one night in a dream. Oscar does work for Hugh at a discount, when one of his painters is free. Normally, Oscar handles Jaguars, Bentleys, and Rolls-Royces. He doesn't have much extra time. Whenever Hugh paid a visit to see whether progress was being made on his truck, Oscar would give him a tour of the shop and explain why there were delays. He would point to the Jag that belonged to the orthodontist who drove straight on into a truck with its lift gate down. Or the Bentley with the door that stopped a bicycle messenger. Gradually Hugh's truck was sanded down to the frame and touched up with primer, until it looked like a person shaved and painted and waiting for surgery. Oscar used to cushion Hugh's disappointment at not having his truck finished by saying, "When you get this truck done, it will be one of those few."

Of all the new elements of his truck, Hugh takes the greatest satisfaction in his tailgate. In order to turn heads, the hood and the tailgate must be in top condition — must be cherry — because those are the two parts of the truck that people see first. Besides, everyone knows that the condition of your tailgate says a lot about the kind of person you are. So Hugh took pains with his tailgate. That meant painting the letters spelling FORD in ivory, then painting over them in vermillion, the color he painted the rest of the truck, and buffing the letters until the ivory reappeared. The dream that Hugh had about his truck involved the tailgate and the head of the New York Public Library. It took place shortly after he finished buffing out the letters. In the dream, he was standing in the shop at Treitel-Gratz, showing the tailgate to an acquaintance, who was a sculptor. The man studied the work. He rubbed his hand over the letters to feel how the enamel had been buffed to a texture that was almost like glass. He admired the richness of the color. He was silent for a moment, and then he turned to Hugh and said, "That's great. You did yours the same way Vartan Gregorian did his."

(1989)

The young man responsible for the slightly perceptible knot in pedestrian traffic at the northeast corner of Bleecker Street and Seventh Avenue is Jean-Pierre Fenyo, The Free Advice Man. He has a sign: J.P.'S FREE OBJECTIVE AND REALISTIC ADVICE ON AL-

MOST ANY SUBJECT. It also says, "Make no assumptions, please; not a religion, not a mystic," and "Not qualified to give medical or legal advice." Occasionally, to attract benefactors or patrons (he never calls them clients or customers), he has lain down in the middle of the sidewalk. Typically, though, he sits on a folding chair outside the Geetanjali Restaurant and waits for people to come to him. Now and then he will lean forward and say, "Good evening. I've got a problem, do you?" Or "Good evening. Financial, personal, marital, career — try me with one big problem." Patrons and benefactors used to sit beside him on a second folding chair. At night, The Free Advice Man would lock the heavier of the chairs to the No Parking sign on the corner and take the other chair home. A few weeks ago the heavier chair was stolen. Now he sets up his chair beside a concrete box concealing a pump outside the laundromat next door to the restaurant, and patrons and benefactors sit on the box. It is not as private or intimate. The Free Advice Man has dark hair, dark eyes, and dark skin. Recently he lived for two years in the Sudan. His face is heart-shaped, his chin is pointed, and he has an almost flawlessly sculptured nose. He is frail. If you ask him how old he is, he says, "I have been around the sun twenty-three times."

Mr. Fenyo has a flyer that reads, "New York's one and only 'Free Advice' guy may have the answer to your problem(s)." It also says that he has received media attention from places as far away as Ireland and the Philippines, and that his advice is based on "infinite realism," and that interviews and photo sessions are best scheduled for Wednesdays. Altogether, he has given advice to about six thousand people, only four of whom were dissatisfied. What happened is they failed to follow his advice. Despite his success, he says, "I do use disclaimers."

Mr. Fenyo would like to have a column in a newspaper. "Anything," he says, "to be known internationally as The Free Advice Man." He wears a whistle on a cord around his neck, for security reasons. He also carries a map of the city. "I don't like to spend too much time giving directions," he says, "but because there's such a demand, I do give them. Sometimes. I don't really consider it advice. It's directions. I like to make the distinction."

He also says:

"I'm accessible."

"My main tool is simplicity."

"I was born in Washington, D.C., and I lived there three years. With my parents, I moved every two or three years, all over Europe and Africa and the U.S. I've visited sixty countries and lived in seven, and I speak six languages. My mother is a retired professor of archeology, and my father is a professor of history. She dug up the past, and he just talks about it."

"I don't take anything for granted, except nothingness, and that's not much."

A characteristic exchange with a benefactor:

Young Man: "I just got out of school, and I'm staying in Poughkeepsie for the summer, and I have to go home in the fall. What do I do? I don't want to work. I never liked any job I ever had."

The Free Advice Man: "You don't have to have a job. You can have a career."

Or this:

T.F.A.M., to young woman standing before him reading his sign, "Hi, what do you do for a living?"

Young Woman: "Not much."

T.F.A.M.: "But what?"

Y.W.: "Acting."

T.F.A.M.: "Not doing too well?"

Y.W.: "I don't want advice about that. I already get too much."

T.F.A.M.: "Let me ask you a question. Are you invested in any stocks and bonds?"

Y.W.: "No."

T.F.A.M: "Good. Stay out of that. Got any land?"

Y.W.: "No."

T.F.A.M.: "Too bad. Get that."

When people tell him that they don't think they have any problems, he tells them that he thinks they do. He recommends that they go recline and reconsider. Something will come up.

The other evening, The Free Advice Man was sitting in his chair outside the restaurant. He held his sign in front of his chest. People passed in and out of his view on both sides. Some of them stopped and read his sign, but no one sat down, and if he spoke the people moved on. A black woman paused in front of him.

The Free Advice Man said, "Good evening. I've got a problem, do you?"

The woman said, "I'm my *own* analytical analyst," and walked away.

A man came by on a motorcycle that was elaborately decorated with twisted metal and looked like a piece of abstract sculpture on wheels. The man parked the motorcycle on the far side of Bleecker Street. The Free Advice Man picked up his chair and moved it across the street, next to the motorcycle. "This is fantasy, I'm reality," he said to someone admiring the motorcycle. He stood in the middle of the sidewalk, forcing people to walk around him. He held his sign slightly above his head, and waved it slowly, as if it were being moved by the breeze. In a moment, a woman walked by with tears streaming down her face. Unfortunately, The Free Advice Man was looking in the other direction.

(1987)

Embassy Pictures gave a party at the Tavern-on-the-Green following the screening of a movie that features the Rolling Stones in concert. Ahmet Ertegun was there, Bill Graham was there, Mary McFadden was there, and so was a man who told a nervous woman, "You call me about business. I will call you to see if you are all right on an emotional basis, but I will never, ever call you about business." Sam Holdsworth, the editor of the magazine *Musician,* was there, and Keith Richards, looking strange and unearthly, the way he always does, was there with his father and his son Marlon, and so was a woman who looked at Keith with his son and said, "Keith is so devoted to Marlon. Until a few years ago, he used to dress up as Santa Claus for him."

Mick Jagger was there, looking ideal. He wore a white shirt with a wing collar, a black jacket, and a pastel striped four-in-hand, and he worked the room like a politician at a fund-raiser in his hometown district, bending now to this ear, now to that, smiling across the room, and huddling at one table, then another. Some people told him they admired his performance in the film; others asked for and received autographs; still others found themselves completely unable to frame the simplest kind of sentence.

A tall black woman too handsome to be a model, wearing a blue shirt and dark pants and carrying a clipboard, was there attempting to keep order among a throng of photographers lurking in a small chamber outside the banquet room. The photographers had been promised a "photo opportunity" with the four members of the Rolling Stones attending the party. (As well as Mick Jagger and Keith Richards, Charlie

Watts and Ron Wood were there.) The photo opportunity was chaotic and brief, with as many pictures taken of the Rolling Stones in, say, three minutes as are taken of the average person to document his entire life.

During the photo opportunity, the tall black woman strode back and forth making remarks that were largely ignored: "Everybody take a step back. . . . *Please,* you're too close. . . . Gentlemen, if you can't behave we'll have to stop it. . . . Everybody, *five* steps. . . . Gentlemen, go somewhere else to resolve your disputes. I *mean* it. . . . I'll get security. . . . Gentlemen, you're too close, please! . . . Get *off* the table. . . . Ralph, would you get security."

Guests — people associated in one way or another with the business of popular music — ate Chateaubriand, veal piemontese, pasta carnevale, assorted cold poultry, fresh vegetables, salad, cheese, and fresh fruits dipped in chocolate. The Rolling Stones stayed just so long. Then bodyguards carrying coats appeared and escorted them swiftly to their car. A young man trailed after them saying, "Keith! Keith! We're friends?"

(1983)

In anticipation of crossing the Bering Strait in his taxi, Ioan Oprisiu intends to take a look at the strait this summer, while driving his cab to the Arctic Ocean. Oprisiu, who is Romanian, plans to visit a fare in Prudhoe Bay, Alaska. He picked up the man last fall in Manhattan and, after they talked for a while, the man, who works in the oil industry and has lived in Prudhoe Bay for twenty-five years, gave Oprisiu his card and invited him and his wife and two boys to visit. Driving to the Arctic Ocean will be the longest trip of the sixteen that Oprisiu has made in his taxi. He arrived by himself in New York nine years ago — his wife and two sons came four years later — and worked for a while in a restaurant, then got a hot dog vendor's cart, and then, as he says, "decided to go for a cab." To learn more about America, he began making trips of a week or so in his cab, each longer than the last, until he had reached the Pacific. "Unfortunately, a lot of people don't know what a great country this is," he says. "They fly. Everyone should have to make one trip across the country. The problem is, once you make one, you have to make two, and after that you can't stop yourself." The first trip Oprisiu made was a circle that included Boston, Albany,

Cleveland, Detroit, Chicago, Indianapolis, and Pittsburgh. On the way to Boston, a man flagged him down on the Cross Bronx Expressway. As it happened, the man wanted to go to Boston, where Oprisiu dropped him off, but only charged him twenty dollars.

Oprisiu is forty-two. He has black hair and a black mustache, and a round face. He generally wears cowboy boots, jeans, a Western shirt, a bolo tie, and a cowboy hat. "When I was thirteen, we had a carnival in my school, and my costume was a cowboy suit," he said. "Even my nickname for my father was the Sheriff. So Western passion probably came from there." Oprisiu is not the first member of his family to come to America. He had a great-great-grandfather who emigrated to Cleveland in 1905. When Oprisiu drove through Cleveland, he visited his ancestor's grave and bought him a headstone. "He never had one," he says.

Oprisiu has driven his taxi throughout the South and the Southwest, and up and down the West Coast. If you happen to occupy his cab and fall into conversation with him, you are likely to end up looking through his scrapbook, which he keeps beside him on the front seat and which features his cab parked in front of various landmarks. Oprisiu will say: "That's the Continental Divide and my son. The Grand Canyon, my wife. This is the desert, that's Hoover Dam, that's Santa Monica. This is Mexico — look at the machine guns the cops have, and that's just the regular ones. This is Oklahoma, the bombing place. This is Arizona — just to the left here is the Biosphere — and this is Arizona also, the biggest meteor crater, and this is Amarillo. They have a great steakhouse. Seventy-two ounces. If you order it, they put you up on a stage. You have one hour, and if you eat the whole thing you get it free."

Oprisiu has not yet decided how he will cross the Bering Strait. "Driving across the ice, I think, is not what I need to do," he says. "About seven years ago, there was a truck company in Italy that had a round-the-world trip for their trucks, so I know it can be done. They used a boat, I think, so, if it's possible for a truck, I guess a yellow cab can make it."

Oprisiu's ambition is not simply to cross the Bering Strait. He intends to drive from the strait to London and take a picture of his cab in front of Buckingham Palace. What he needs, he believes, is a sponsor. "Such a trip," he says, "it's not an easy one. Probably it's not going to demonstrate anything, but it will give me an idea of the many pleasures along the road." Oprisiu is now on his third taxi, which has a hundred and five thousand miles on it. He keeps his cab in excellent repair. He uses only original parts, and he doesn't let anyone else drive it. "In Romania, we have a saying," he says. "My car, my pen, my wife, I don't lend."

(2000)

Joel Hirschhorn, a fifteen-year-old senior at Stuyvesant High School, in Manhattan, talking about his paper "On the Distribution of Twin Primes," to which the attractive equation

$$E(n) = \frac{n}{\log^2 n - \log n \cdot \log \log n}$$

is somehow essential, and for which he was recently chosen as one of forty finalists in the Westinghouse Science Talent Search, a national competition among high school seniors:

"Two years ago, I was talking to a friend in the computer room at Stuyvesant, and he told me what twin primes were, and I started thinking about them. Primes are any numbers that can be divided by themselves and 1 but by no others, without a remainder, and twin primes are primes that are two apart — 3-5, 5-7, 11-13, and so on. I wasn't exactly sure I would do it for the contest, though. I was thinking about a few other things, too. For instance, I still haven't found anyone who knows if mice are colorblind. I asked around, but all anybody could come up with was an inconclusive study done in the early nineteen-hundreds — which is surprising, I think. I just read in *Scientific American* that they have discovered color vision in fish, and fish seem a lot more difficult to work with than mice, but I found out that for the competition you're not allowed to remove vertebrates from their environment, so I gave that idea up. I also thought about doing something on the Lyon Hypothesis, which has to do with genetics. That came up because a couple of years ago on a biology test the teacher asked for a reason for a particular thing to have happened, and I came up with an explanation that I later learned was the Lyon Hypothesis. My father is a research physician, and I asked him about it, and as he explained it I got interested, but I later discarded it because it would have been very complicated and so difficult to get results for that I might have put in all that time and not necessarily had anything to show for it — which is almost what happened anyway. I had a couple of other ideas, too, but I forget them now. Whatever they were, I guess I didn't think about them very long.

"I began in the spring of 1980, by counting twin primes. I didn't have a computer — just a programmable calculator, and that didn't have a printout, so I just had to sit there and watch it and wait and write down the answer when it arrived. Right away, it started to take about five minutes to come up with the next twin prime, and it got even slower as it went on, because of the nature of the problem. I didn't get past 150 before I decided it was useless, considering I was working up to eighty billion. So I gave it up for the moment. That summer, when I was fourteen, I went to a math program at Hampshire College, and one of the courses I took was about prime numbers, and that helped; and I also learned a little bit about computers. I began the project for real, then, last winter. I figured I'd better get an early start, so I wouldn't be frantic at the end, and it was lucky I did. I had some trouble. I got a computer, but I didn't write a really good program for a while, and I was getting the wrong data. The computer seemed to be *adding* wrong — which is impossible, I think, for a computer. I wanted the right data, so I checked back, and found the error, and revised the program, but I had lost some time — a lot of time, actually — and I didn't have all that much to begin with. Monday afternoons, I teach computers at the Village Community School; Tuesdays, I have a bassoon lesson; Wednesdays, the math team — I'm on it — has meets with other schools in the city; Saturday mornings are All-City High School Orchestra rehearsal, and after that I have my piano lesson. I study with Erna Jonas, on Ninety-sixth Street, and, along with other piano students, I play a concert once or twice a year at Carnegie Recital Hall or the Donnell Library. So Saturday is almost like a school day — except it's not, too. So, anyway, I've used up the spring, and now I'm into the summer.

"Then I had real trouble. This gets a little technical for a moment. It's not as important to understand what was happening with the mathematics as it is to know it went horribly wrong. As it is now, the first half of my project shows that there *is* a constant for predicting twin primes, and the second half shows how that constant works with my formula to predict the actual numbers. But from mid-August to the middle of November I was on a different tack — I was *expecting* the constant for twin primes to match the square of the constant for primes. It would have made a neat package. I was also trying to prove that the constant for twin primes approached 1, as the constant for single primes does. What's important to know, however, is that I was *counting* on it, I put all my hopes on it, and it turned out to be totally a red herring. And I spent three months trying to figure out what was wrong with my data that they didn't show what I wanted them to — I wasn't sure I had *enough* data. There was no one I could ask about it except the great mathematicians, so I went to the library at NYU and found a small reference to a source that was an article in a journal, and it suggested that the constant *definitely* doesn't go to 1, and I went, 'Oh, no.' That was supposed to be kind of the knockout punch of my paper. Instead, I had to suddenly cross out everything that had to do with 1 and the relationship to single primes. So it's mid-November, the paper's due in mid-December, and I'm suddenly back to mid-August. And not only that — I've suddenly gone from a whole paper to half a paper. The main problem was that once I found out that the constant wasn't 1, there either *wasn't* a constant, and then I had no paper at *all*, or there *was* one, but I might not find it in time, in which case I *still* had no paper. I was dismayed. So — for no reason except curiosity, I guess — I just thought I'd try my formula on the numbers starting at 80×10^9, which is eighty billion, and then down in intervals of ten billion to 70×10^9, 60×10^9, and so on. I ran them all at once, and as I read down the column a moment later on the printout I suddenly realized there *was* a constant. It wasn't 1, it was 1.255. It just hit me over the head: 1.255; 1.255; 1.255. All in a row. And then, just like that, I was back from half a paper to a whole paper again."

(1982)

Flipping is done in the South Bronx, in a vacant lot that flippers call the Garden, at 163rd Street and Prospect Avenue. It involves the performance of aerial maneuvers — flips and twists and spirals — above a pile of mattress springs. Kevin Jones and Terrence Ford are renowned flippers. Terrence is fourteen, and his ambition to flip was born in him about ten years ago, when his father used to pick him up and toss him into the air. After that, he jumped mainly on his bed until his mother enrolled him in a gymnastics class, and then he learned the maneuvers that are fundamental to flipping style. Kevin, who is fifteen, learned by watching other flippers.

"Every day is flip," Kevin says. "Jump and flip. Flip is like a drug to me, like a habit. I can't go a day without flipping." Kevin is slight and rangy and soft-spoken. He has almond-shaped eyes and a round face. Terrence is smaller. He smiles quickly, but is reserved in his manner. Occasionally, Kevin and Terrence compete with each other — they call this battling — but Kevin always walks away the winner, because he can perform a double backflip and Terrence can't.

At the moment, flippers are flipping in reduced circumstances. They launch themselves from six mattress springs piled on top of a box spring near the 163rd Street end of the Garden. The flipper performs his trick and lands on the crash pad — an intact mattress resting on a stack of four mattress springs. The mattress prevents the feet of the flippers from getting caught in the wires. In terms of equipment, the most favorable moment in the history of flipping occurred a year ago, when the flippers had three lines of mattresses and springs running nearly the length of a block. At the head of two of the lines were refrigerators. The flippers would launch themselves from the refrigerators and twist and flip and twirl like Slinkys down the rows of mattresses and springs until they arrived at the other end of the block. This golden period ended when a traveling revivalist set up his tent in the Garden and the Sanitation Department carried off the mattresses to clean up the area.

Flippers collect their springs from factories that restore mattresses — especially from Peters Mattress, at 165th Street. Terrence's father, a small, slender man with thick glasses, employs himself by scouting the neighborhood for discarded mattresses and selling them to the factory. Sometimes the factory discards the springs — you can rebuild a mattress only so many times — and these springs become flipping equipment. Kevin and Terrence and their friends drag them to the Garden. A set of springs lasts about six weeks, then begins to get lumps and depressions, which throw the flippers' trajectory out of kilter, and may sometimes make them land clear of the crash pad.

Beside the Garden is a row of ailanthus trees, and next to that is a red brick apartment building. One day, as Kevin is standing beside the crash pad, a window on the fourth floor opens and a young man's voice calls out, "Yo, Kevin, do a show for me!"

Kevin says, "That's my friend Jigga. His real name's Jamal. He's been working in a barbershop. He's someone who really started me flipping. He's old now, but he can still do it."

Kevin bounces several times on the launching pad, forces his arms hard to his side, and turns a somersault in the air. In the little slot of the window, two children stand between two women. One of the women holds back a curtain. All of them cheer.

Terrence is carpentering with his grandfather in a building that overlooks the other side of the Garden. He hears the noise and appears in a window. Kevin yells, "Yo, Terrence, come flip." In the meantime, Jigga arrives. He is twenty-three, small and lithe, and he wears a gold earring that spells his nickname. The women in the apartment window, it turns out, are his wife and her sister, and the children are Jigga's son and a friend.

"They want me to flip," Jigga says. Kevin smiles. Jigga says bashfully, "I don't flip no more." He takes some cassette tapes out of his pockets, though, and a comb, hands them to Terrence, who has just arrived, and steps onto the launching pad. He bounces several times, gathering height, and does a creaky version of a backflip.

"Hey, Jigga!" one of the women shouts. "You can do better than that!" Jigga smiles shyly. "Do a twirl!" she shouts.

"No twirl," says Jigga, bouncing on the launching pad. "I'm scared to hit the floor."

"*Jigga!*" yell the children.

Jigga performs another flip, this one more self-assured, but not stylish. Kevin steps onto the launching pad and does a double.

"*He beat you, Jigga!*"

Jigga flips once more. Quarters fly from his pockets. Terrence collects them. Jigga tries a double flip and misses the crash pad completely.

"*Boo, Jigga!*"

Terrence hands Jigga his tapes, his comb, and his quarters. Kevin steps onto the launching pad and begins to gather height. The mattresses creak. Terrence says, "You all watch what he's about to do." In the air above the Garden, Kevin turns his back to the apartment building, claps his hands to his knees, and revolves twice against the sky. A car stops. By the time Kevin lands, the driver is applauding.

(1992)

Ry Cooder, the virtuoso guitarist, who lives in Los Angeles, so dislikes performing that he is almost never seen onstage, but he was in New York last week to appear with the seventeen members of the Buena Vista Social Club, the band that he and the producer Nick Gold assembled three years ago in Havana from a collection of mostly elderly men and one woman. The record they made in

1996 — *Buena Vista Social Club* — has sold millions of copies around the world and has been certified gold in America; it won a Grammy in 1997. The band's principal singer, Ibrahim Ferrer, who is seventy-two, has a new record, and he and the pianist, Rubén González, who is eighty, are playing concerts in America and Canada, with the band behind them. A week ago last Thursday all of them attended a party in their honor at a restaurant in the Village; Friday night they played at the Beacon Theater in Manhattan; on Saturday they left for performances in Boston; and on Monday morning they came back to New York to appear on *Late Night with David Letterman*.

At the party on Thursday the bartender made drinks from lime and rum and mint. On the tables were candles, and trays filled with water on which gardenias floated. A number of the band's members sat shoulder to shoulder at a banquette along one of the walls. They wore coats and sweaters against the cold, and looked like men waiting for a bus, or their turn to bowl. At a table in the corner several of them played hands of dominoes. Ibrahim Ferrer made some remarks in Spanish and so did Rubén González. A translator said, "The two of them express that they don't have words to express how they feel, but they say that, because they are Cuban, they had to speak for five minutes."

The rehearsal for *Letterman* began shortly after four and ended around five. The show began taping at five-thirty. In the meantime Rubén González sat on a chair in a hallway outside the band's dressing room in the basement of the Ed Sullivan Theater, where the show is taped, and Ferrer sat on a chair in a small dressing room on the theater's sixth floor. González is thin to the point of being frail. He is a bit stooped and sometimes limps a little. He has small hands and feet, and his handshake is delicate. He often wears suits and looks like a figure of romance, a plantation owner perhaps.

Ferrer is taller and lithe and likes to dance, which he does as if the movement cost him no effort at all. His face is small and round and easily conveys pleasure. He usually wears a felt cap with a brim, the kind of felt cap that men who owned English sports cars in the forties and fifties often wore. He is a tenor, and his voice is a little gritty and warm and expresses emotion succinctly and without being sentimental.

Cooder and Gold were three days into making their record when Cooder felt that the combination of voices wasn't exactly right. "Isn't there anybody who can sing the bolero?" he asked. "Doesn't anybody have that romantic style?" In assembling musicians, Cooder and Gold had the help of a man named Juan de Marcos González. González said, "There's one guy, I have to find him."

"So Marcos went to where he knew Ibrahim was," Cooder says. "And he found him walking in the street — he had nothing else to do — and Ibrahim said, 'I'm not interested. I don't sing anymore.' He'd had a lot of disappointments and about five years before, he'd just given up singing, retired, he's making his living shining shoes. Marcos is a forceful guy, though. He says, 'This is interesting, you want to do this, we need you,' and Ibrahim says, 'I can't now, I've been shining shoes, I need to go home and take a bath,' and Marcos said, 'You don't have time for that.' When he arrived in the studio, you could see he was heavy, you just didn't know at what. This music really rests with the singing. It's required that someone can sing these songs so the music is illuminated, and Ibrahim is entirely unique. You wait years for someone like him to appear."

In his dressing room, Ferrer said that his new life as a celebrated singer arrived so abruptly and is so strange and surprising that it feels a little like a dream. "I feel exactly as if two lives had been joined together," he said. "My old one and my new one, and this new one is a good one." The only disadvantage he could think of, he said, is that now that he is a notable person everyone in his neighborhood in Havana comes over to his apartment, which is small, and wants to spend the day with him.

When the first royalties were paid for the record, Nick Gold went to Cuba with cash to distribute among the musicians. He arrived at González's house to give him his share while González was playing the piano. Gold had the cash in a satchel. González asked to look at it. Gold held the satchel open and González peered in at the dollar bills, then waved his hand. "Take it away," he said. In the theater basement someone asked him if he had actually made such a gesture. He smiled broadly. "I did do that," he said, "but it was a joke."

(1999)

My new best friend is Cash Money. Cash and I have become friends only recently. I don't know since when, exactly, but lately. A lot of people know Cash more intimately than I do and are going to feel that I have no business talking about him. But that doesn't bother me. What do we do together? Visit cafés, where the waiters make a quiet fuss over him, where he places one hand on the table, his nails curved so perfectly into arcs that it is as if a mathematician and not a manicurist had worked on them.

Within Cash's capacious and complex personality are all the virtues I have ever sought in any companion. He's exceptionally attractive, especially when he's had a night's rest, but even in that run-down condition he sometimes shows up in, his jacket torn and his lapels astray and covered with stains whose origins are uncertain, with a name or a small drawing somewhere on his front in blue ballpoint ink, like a tattoo, and him slightly withered as if he had been bossed by some friends into extending a party to celebrate the sale of, say, a fabulous painting, a Monet, a van Gogh, in which he had obscurely and deftly figured, even perhaps made possible, although he would never claim such a thing, he's more worldly than that. His company (I find) is soothing and quietly reinforcing of one's sense of well-being. He's as seductive as a beautiful dark-haired woman in her thirties whose manner conveys intelligence and sexual accomplishment. He's protective of confidences and willing to arrange the acquisition of any pleasure no matter how singular, showy, or demeaning. Even when you go slightly mad in the pursuit, he stays by your side, at least as far as your claim on his attention allows. Most people are unreliable anyway. You can know them too well. You can arrive at a period where you're privy to their secrets, you can hear their words in your head before they speak them, they bore you. With Cash, any failure of his to entertain you is really a failure of your own imagination. Sometimes, true, it's hard to get him on the phone. He's elusive. No argument there. He can seem unable to remember your name. All true. Sometimes he's aloof, but so is God.

Before I knew Cash I never cared about the Moneys. I met Cash in Jackson Hole in 1972 at the summer ranch of the family of some friends from Bennington. The rest of the year the family lived in Princeton. Cash would show up for breakfast at the long table in the ranch mess and drink coffee and eat bacon and eggs and pancakes without ever somehow being seen to actually put anything into his mouth, which would have been vulgar, while everyone talked about Bluebell or Charger or whatever horse they were going to ride that morning and gave instructions to the staff about what they wanted placed into their picnic hampers and where the car was to meet them with the hampers and so on. I discovered that everyone knew Cash to be the only rider sufficiently accomplished to manage Thunderbolt, so he never took part in the talk, and the horse was always saddled for him, a four-legged piece of distemper and misanthropy, waiting by the corral. Everyone seemed extremely fond of Cash — even the hard-bitten cowboys liked him and invited him to the bunkhouse to play poker; they called him Tin and Scratch, which amused him endlessly, and he always let them win. The ranch had been in the family for generations, and Cash had the best cabin, with a view of the Tetons, and over the doorway, like a waspy joke, the cow skull that Georgia O'Keeffe had found in a pasture. He wore beautiful tweed jackets that fit like an embrace and were a little frayed at the cuffs. His place was always set at the table with the ranch china and crystal and a tin cup for coffee, and the waiters served him first, although he waved them off cheerfully and sent them toward my friend's grandmother, and he always remembered the names of their children and had a little something for them, candy, I don't know what, something he took from his pockets.

In years after that I saw him various places. Once fifteen years ago on the beach at Sagaponack in front of a house that looked like the old TWA terminal at Kennedy, glass and steel with cables holding the whole sorry structure together and the cables looking as if they were about to snap. He was with a couple of guys in their thirties who were smoking cigars and slapping each other on the back and had those big phones that resembled the ones that guys in war movies used to have, and he looked desperately ill at ease. I hardly recognized him. I'm pretty sure I saw him another time on the deck of a yawl that dropped anchor late one evening in the bay off La Samanna — at least I thought I made out his high forehead, wide shoulders, and long form — but the light was failing, and no one came ashore, and the next morning the sailboat was gone and the horizon was as empty as a slate that had been wiped clean.

We had for several years a tentative friendship. The idea that women more easily become intimate with each other than men are able to is partly a feminist rant, but it is also partly true. I was a little uncertain of myself with Cash — his sporadic and solicitous attention I felt was partly a favor to my parents — and I was never sure what sort of conversation might interest him. On the other hand, I was also innocent, and protected myself by means of the invention that I was the only person on the face of the earth, a young man's defense. I got married — my parents added Cash to the guest list but he was abroad; he sent a cut-glass bowl I keep on a table beside my bed and fill with change. My wife and I moved to Manhattan, to a small cold-water flat, a walkup on Mulberry Street in Little Italy. Cracked plaster walls, windows looking out on a churchyard, and the smell of garbage rising from the sidewalk in the summer. Across the street was a storefront clubhouse belonging to some gangsters. On the occasions when Cash came slumming downtown, he'd bring an old bottle of Château Lynch Bages and sit in our small living room before taking up the pattern of his evening and say such things as, "No elevator, five floors, really you're a hero, kiddo." What surprised me was that he was fond of the gangsters. They'd invite him for an espresso or a grappa, whatever it is they drank together, and grin and slap him on the back and give him those little European hugs where you kiss the guy on both cheeks.

Over the years I fell out of touch with him. He didn't call and I was embarrassed to call him. I was trying to be a painter and no one seemed interested in my work, and I was getting a little old to pretend that I preferred living in a slum. I fell into feeling wounded and thinking of him as a fair-weather friend. Then he would invite me to lunch at the Gloucester House or the Racquet Club, buy me two martinis and a swordfish steak from Block Island and tell stories and ask if I was getting enough to eat and send me home in a taxi, and I would look out the window at the fabulous people of Midtown and think, what more really could one ask of a friend than that he devote himself, intensely, for a few hours to your well-being.

I know. I grew up. I no longer considered raffishness such a laudable trait. As I said, I always viewed Cash as a member of another generation, the kind of figure you occasionally see in the corner of a photograph depicting a lawn like a pelt leading to a big white elephant of a house in Greenwich, and it really surprised me, when I got over my shyness and diffidence, that he has a kind of ageless and almost permanently youthful quality that makes chronology seem irrelevant, and his own difficult to pin down anyway. He apprehends all there is to understand about history. Knows every card game — coon cane, peter pot, arcane versions of poker — and when to bet up the odds and when only a fool or a daredevil would. Never says where he's been, who he's been talking to. Everything's mysterious. The mark, I think, of a truly cultured person — someone with acquaintances all over the map, who's welcome anywhere and knows how to behave at a cockfight as well as at a dinner with three wineglasses and seventeen utensils. Someone who knows how to put you at your ease. Who supports your own best impression of yourself. When he's distracted or tired he seems disengaged and a little forbidding. Other times he's radiant.

Where this new infatuation is going, I can't say. I hardly see him frequently enough to be certain. Sometimes I'll sit there talking to someone across the table and think, Why can't you be Cash? I want to be just like him. When we're together, I study how he holds himself, his gestures and rhythms of speech, his manner of dressing, and the absence in it of any of the fussy preoccupation with clothes that seems so much in vogue. I think I was a moron for the time that I held him at some remove. I look for him everywhere, crossing streets, in the backseats of limousines, reflected in the windows of stores. It's an obsession, I know, a May to September thing, I suppose, ruthless and thrilling, but I'm not at all sure that I don't really like it.

(2001)

Think about Call Reluctance, a modern affliction. According to the cover story in the October issue of the magazine *Selling*, "Call Reluctance strikes men and women, rookies and veterans, and people in every selling field. It's as common as the common cold but a lot more deadly — it can kill a sales career."

Call Reluctance involves an aversion to using the phone to make sales calls, or to set up appointments for meetings. One man who had it said, "I had an actual fear of the telephone." Salesmen and saleswomen often catch Call Reluctance from one another. "Certain forms of Call Reluctance are highly contagious," the magazine says. A woman who had Call Reluctance says that an attack brought on "big purple hives" all over her face and that to conceal them she wore blouses with high collars and let her hair grow.

A person might think of Call Reluctance as a salesman kneeling in the dark, narrow lobby of a building with one elevator. It is late in the afternoon. The salesman has a sample case. He is leafing through a collection of business cards, trying to think if there is anyone in the neighborhood who will see him on the spur of the moment, since he couldn't call ahead. He *used* to call ahead, but one day he couldn't anymore. He would sit in his office at Rake's Progress Sales, the blinds drawn, eyeballing the phone, cracking his knuckles, exhaling deeply, then picking up the receiver. He would ask the woman who answered if she had time to see him and his new line. His wife has become frightened by this charade. When he says, "I think you'll be very excited with our new products. How about I bring them by tomorrow?" she says, "Harry, what's the *matter* with you?"

The answer used to be nothing, until, through some kind of casual contact — a handshake, one of the paper cups at the water fountain, the toilet seat, for Christ's sake, who the hell knows — he contracted Call Reluctance.

When he tries to use the phone, he breaks out into a fine sweat that bathes his body, making his face shiny in bright light. He feels like he runs out of breath before he reaches the end of what he has to say. He thinks, "If I can get through the door, I *know* I can sell them. I just can't make the *call.*"

In the dreary lobby now, he rises and drops a coin into the slot on the phone. The sound of the dial tone fills him with dread. The air feels heavy. He imagines humiliations, conspiracies at the other end of the line. His palms are damp and his fingers leave little smudges on the card he has been gripping so tightly that it is crumpled. He closes his sample bag and decides to get a drink and take an early train home. He'll make new calls tomorrow. Everyone will be gone by now anyway.

(1994)

Dependents

WHEN LARRY KING, the radio and television interviewer, turned sixty, on November 19, his agent threw a big party for him in Washington. The agent invited the President and the First Lady and the members of the Supreme Court, but they didn't come, although a number of other prominent people such as Alexander Haig and Tip O'Neill and Ed Meese and George Mitchell and Newt Gingrich and George Stephanopolous and Joseph Kennedy did. Larry was glad that they came — he appreciated the effort they had made to be there — but he didn't dance with any of them. The only man he danced with was Herb Cohen.

Larry and Herb have been friends off and on for fifty years — since they were boys together, in Bensonhurst, Brooklyn. When Larry talks to Herb, he often leans toward him, and sometimes he puts an arm around his shoulder. If they are eating and crumbs fall on Herb's chest, Larry brushes them off. The smile he displays when his eyes light on Herb is several degrees brighter than the smile he shows anyone else. More than once, Herb has been described as "the world's best negotiator," most recently in a commercial he made for General Motors which is being broadcast in California, before, he hopes, being shown to the rest of the country; if it does, he becomes richer. In 1980, he published a book called *You Can Negotiate Anything*, which was on the *New York Times* bestseller list for nine months and was a bestseller in Australia for three years. He was an adviser to President Carter and to President Reagan on terrorism. His favorite maxim is "I *care*, but not that much," by which he means that success in negotiating is partly a matter of not becoming too attached to a specific outcome. Herb and his wife, Ellen, have been married for thirty-six years. Larry got married for the first time before Herb did, and has been married often enough for any eight or nine ordinary guys. Herb is prudent and conservative with money. A number of women who have been married to Larry, or have dated him for any length of time, have suddenly changed tax brackets as a result of his consideration.

Herb lives in an apartment at the Watergate, and Larry lives across the Potomac River, in an apartment in Arlington, Virginia. They live only slightly farther from one another than they did as children. If one of them leaves a light on at night, the other can see it.

If in, say, 1946, you had appeared in Bensonhurst, on the corner of Eighty-sixth Street and Bay Parkway, and asked for Zeke the Greek, the Mouthpiece, you would have met a slightly fleshy, round-faced, big-headed thirteen-year-old with gapped teeth and glasses, whose real name was Larry Zeiger, later Larry King. "Zeke" sounded a little like Zeiger; "Greek" was thrown in for the rhyme. "He never shut up," Herb says, "so, the Mouthpiece." The Mouthpiece hoped to be on the radio. Standing on the corner, he would put one hand to his ear, the way radio announcers do. "Here comes a Dodge now, folks," he'd say. "A *big* Dodge with whitewalls, New York plates, man in a suit at the wheel and a woman with a hat beside him, yes!" At baseball games, he would roll up his program and talk into it as if it were a microphone.

Herb's nickname was Handsomo. He was small and compact, with a dark, asymmetrical face in the shape of a V. He had a wide forehead and dark wavy hair, and his nose was sharp and turned slightly to the right. His eyes were heavy-lidded and set wide apart, and had the brainy and disdainful look of a natural-born prankster. He met Larry in the principal's office of their junior high school, where they had been sent for offenses that neither recalls, although Herb thinks it was probably talking in class. Larry talked endlessly. He would see a movie that was an hour and a half long and take two and a half hours to explain it, Herb says. At times, he gave the impression of saying every single thought that crossed his mind. Herb tends to ponder more than talk. Up to the time that he found himself studying Larry from a chair in the vestibule outside the principal's office, he had been in the habit of causing trouble so as to bargain his way out of it. Once he met Larry, it became more diverting to him to get Larry into trouble. "We used to walk to school," Larry says. "The school was by an open field. Herbie had a way of calling dogs, and he'd point to me and they'd follow me into school. Herbie would say, 'Don't worry, I'll get you out of this.' And we'd go into class and the teacher would ask, 'Whose dogs are these?' and Herbie would say, 'Larry's.'

"One time in high school we were walking down the street, and there had been these robberies going on in the neighborhood, and a cop is watching us, and suddenly he pulls up and says, 'Hands against the wall, you look like the guys that did these robberies,' and Herbie says, 'They got us, they got us.' I start crying, I'm seventeen, and Herbie's confessing to open crimes."

At the age of twelve or thirteen, Larry, Herb, and some friends formed an outfit called the Warriors Social Athletic Club. A Warrior's signal possession was a reversible jacket, dark red on one side, with a white *W* on the chest, and white on the other with the *W* red. Over the left breast of the red side, each Warrior had his name stitched in loopy white-thread characters. Mostly, the Warriors walked around with their jackets worn red side out. White was considered to imply formality. One of the other original Warriors was Irving Kaplan, who had drunk a bottle of ink.

Herb: He had it in his hand, the teacher was harassing him, and he said, "If you don't leave me alone, I'm going to drink this bottle of ink and say you made me do it."

Larry: Waterman's blue-black.

Herb: When we first met him, his teeth were blue.

Larry: We need guys like this in the club, we said.

Inky, Larry, Herb, and the other Warriors had their quarters in the basement of a house belonging to the parents of a Warrior named Bernard Horowitz. Someone had once shouted at him, "Hey, Bernie," and he answered, "Who?" and the guy said, "What do you mean, 'Who?' I'm asking you a question," and he said, "Ha?" and so he was called Who-ha. The Warriors paid rent to his parents, Dora and Nathan.

Herb: This was an unfinished basement — there were coal bins down there. We didn't know how to go out and buy a sofa, but in our neighborhood were apartment buildings with furniture in the lobbies.

Larry: We furnished the club through thievery.

Herb: We regarded it as misappropriating a couch.

Larry: You'd walk in and tell the doorman you were here to pick up the couch for reupholstering.

Herb: You'd wear caps; it made it look better.

Larry: The super might show up and you'd say, "We got to get this couch back to the shop, give us a hand here," and he would hold the door for you. Nobody had said anything to him about getting the couch reupholstered, but you looked like you knew what you were doing.

Herb: You'd give him a pat on the back as you went out the door.

In their clubhouse, the Warriors smoked cigarettes, tried out wrestling holds on one another, talked big, did homework, and speculated about girls. Using paint that glowed in the dark, they painted on the floor the profile of an Indian warrior wearing a headdress. A Warrior who had lured a girl to the clubhouse sometimes managed to enlarge his experience of romance by asking if she wanted to see the Indian glow in the dark, then turning off the lights. "We were not too swift with girls," Herb says. Of all the Warriors, Larry and Herb followed sporting events the closest. They often left Bensonhurst for Madison Square Garden to watch hockey played by teams such as the Brooklyn Torpedos, the Sands Point Tigers, the Manhattan Arrows, the Long Island Sharks, the Rovers, and the New York Rangers. They also kept up with baseball, football, and basketball. Their preoccupation struck the other Warriors as juvenile and undignified. "To shut them up, we went into Woolworth's and bought a wallet," Herb says. "There was a picture in it of a beautiful girl, and on this picture we wrote, 'To Larry and Herb, my two favorite guys, you give me so much pleasure.' We named her Miriam Glick. It was right for that neighborhood. If we had given her a fancier name, it wouldn't have been convincing. So now, instead of saying, 'We're going to the Garden,' we'd say, 'We're going to see Miriam Glick,' and we showed her picture. She looked like Cybill Shepherd. These guys were drooling. They'd say, 'How come you're not bringing her here? She too good for us?' 'No,' we'd say. 'We're just going on a quiet house date.' 'Why do you keep this girl to yourself?' they'd say. 'It's perverse.'"

The Warriors threw their allegiance behind a boxer a few years older than they, who was working his way through the ranks of the city's fighters. He was an Italian from Bensonhurst, and the most efficient and murderous and well-built fighter they had ever seen. They thought he must be invincible. One night, he won a split decision from a black fighter at the Fort Hamilton Parkway Arena, but was badly beaten up, and it was the first time the Warriors sensed a world beyond the boundaries of their neighborhood that was mysterious and complicated and unsentimental.

Without Larry: Herb and Larry graduated from Lafayette High School in 1951. Larry found work delivering milk for a dairy, and Herb went to New York University. In 1953, out of boredom, he volunteered for the draft, and was sent for basic training to Fort Dix, in New Jersey, and then, less than a week later, in the middle of the night, to Camp Chafee, Arkansas. He was trained at Camp Chafee as a clerk-typist and then was shipped out. "I could have gone to Korea," he says, "but I was sent to Germany — luck of the draw." On his arrival, in Zweibrücken, he and the others were put in formation. An officer asked if anyone spoke French, and Herb, figuring he was staring at a Paris assignment, put his hand in the air; he had studied French at Lafayette. He took a French test that afternoon, and then he walked back to the barracks. In the meantime, everyone else had been assigned to Paris or London or Berlin.

"What they had in mind for me now was Bad Kissingen, Germany," he says. "I look on the map, I can't find it. Next morning, they put all of us on a troop train, which stops first somewhere near the French border, where nearly everyone gets off. 'Goodbye, Herb! Goodbye, Herb!' The train goes east and stops next near Frankfurt, where everyone else except me and one other guy leaves. 'So long, Herb!' This other guy asks to see my papers. He looks at them, looks at me, and says I'm no longer a clerk-typist. What I am now is a tank gunner, he says. I sit down. 'This has to be a mistake,' I say. 'I never had any tank training.' He looks at the paper again and tells me, 'That's what it says.' So I'm going to Bad Kissingen — Bad K, I come to learn they call it — and I'm a tanker. I'm going to be either driving a tank or firing a gun at one. And the train is going farther and farther east. Eventually, it stops and I get off. 'Best of luck, Herb.' Our assignment at Bad K is to patrol the Fulda Gap, and everyone knows that if the Third World War is going to start it will be by the Russians driving their tanks through the gap at Fulda, because that's the best flat pass they can drive tanks through into western Europe.

"For chums I have an outfit of guys from the deep, deep South — mainly Mississippi, Alabama, Louisiana, maybe some from Georgia. I am now running with army men who play music like 'Hillbilly Heaven'

— 'I dreamed last night I was in Hillbilly Heaven, Oh what a beautiful sight.' My roommate is fourteen years old. He lied about his age. He wets his bed. These are very volatile people, excessively devoted to kicking off the Third World War, and they make me nervous. We'd have breakfast and they'd say, 'Today we're going to get us a Commie,' and I'd say, 'What does that mean?' They'd drive up to the border and throw hand grenades over it and shoot at any shadow or leaf that moved. They blew up a German guard tower one time. I'm either going to die with these guys or get court-martialed, because I can't control them. Day after day, I'm watching what they do, and I'm thinking, Does the army know about this? And I guess they did, because eventually they added other outfits to ours, and with these other outfits came people from all over America, and they made us less warlike. Their new attitude added stability and was refreshing."

Herb was transferred then to courts and boards, the agency that conducted courts-martial. He spent his day in an office where no one bothered him. To make money in the evenings, he refereed basketball games among the servicemen. He was made coach of the battalion team, and his team won the battalion championship for Germany. "They love me now," he says. "We're on the map. I'm a miracle guy." He was appointed coach of the regiment's team and began traveling to games held all over Europe. The team lost to a much better team representing V Corps, but finished second among a large field. In the European tournament, V Corps lost its first game. Orders were cut for Herb to replace their coach. He led V Corps to the European championship. "I come back to Bad K and they immediately give me fourteen days R and R," he says. "Like I need it. And that's how I learned to ski." His career with courts and boards flourished. "I'm on top of the world," he says. "They want to court-martial people, they can't do it if I don't want to."

When it came time for Herb to leave the army, he was depressed. "I'm thinking, Never again in civilian life will I attain this kind of prestige and power and authority." He hadn't seen combat and didn't feel comfortable celebrating his return. To be certain that he could just slip quietly back into Brooklyn, he wrote his mother and father with the wrong name of his troop ship and gave an arrival time later than his actual one. He planned just to show up at their apartment. He wrote Larry with the correct name of the ship, but also gave him the wrong time, and asked him not to make a big deal of his return. During the years that Herb was away, Larry delivered milk and also worked for a package-delivery service. Occasionally he had dinner with Herb's parents. Herb's father would ask Larry what he planned to do with himself, and Larry would say that he wanted to be a personality on the radio. Herb's father would ask how he intended to accomplish that, and Larry would say he didn't know, he just wanted to be on the radio. Smacking Larry on the lapel, Herb's father would say, "What are you, another Arthur Godfrey? You got to go to school. You got to get a job." As Herb's ship approached its mooring in the Brooklyn Navy Yard, Herb could see Larry on the dock, with Herb's mother and father. "He had been making phone calls for weeks, checking the passenger list of every troop ship to arrive in New York harbor," Herb says. "And there he is now, standing behind the rope, waving like I had won the war."

Soon after Herb had arrived, Larry told him that he had got married while Herb was away. Herb asked why he had done that, and Larry said, "It was winter, and I didn't want to go out and stand on the corner anymore."

Without Herb: In 1957, someone told Larry that Miami was a good city for a person who wanted to find work in radio, because there were no unions, so he bought a train ticket to Miami. He was twenty-three and had never been farther from New York than Philadelphia. He took a room in a hotel and went from one station to another and eventually found work sweeping up at one of them. The manager told him that if he hung around long enough he would have the opportunity to go on the air. After hearing that, he hardly ever left the station. "I slept there," he says. His first day on the air was May 1, 1957. Half an hour before he was to go on, the manager called him into his office and asked what name he planned to use. Zeiger was too Jewish, the manager said; it didn't sound like show business. While the manager spoke, he turned the pages of a newspaper. He came to an advertisement for a liquor store named King's and said, "That's your new name. You're Larry King." Larry went into the studio and sat in front of the microphone and waited for the sign that said ON AIR to light up.

A song called "Swinging down the Lane" was playing. Larry faded the music and opened his mouth. Nothing came out. He brought the music back up. He took a deep breath and faded the music. He brought the music back up. "In that minute," he says, "I'm thinking, 'I can't do this.'

My mouth is dry, the palms of my hands are damp. 'All those years,' I'm saying inside, 'you were fooling yourself, you won't be any good at this. You can't be on the radio.' The door to the studio opened and the manager said, 'Larry, radio is a communications medium. Communicate!' And I said, 'Good morning, my name is Larry King. I just got that name fifteen minutes ago, and I'm nervous.'"

While Larry was working in Miami, Herb was raising a daughter and two sons in New York and working as a claims adjuster. He was learning to care, but not that much. He moved several times. He and Larry lost touch. From friends in Brooklyn, he would occasionally hear that Larry often talked about him on the air and wrote about their past in the columns he contributed to Miami newspapers. He was aware that Larry was becoming well known and wasn't sure how he would feel about hearing from him. "A lot of people like to live their lives forward," Herb says, "not looking back." In 1976, Larry's mother died in Miami. Herb's mother, who had also moved to Miami, saw the announcement in a Florida paper and went to the funeral. She saw Larry and showed him pictures of Herb and Ellen and their children, Sharon, Steven, and Richard. Larry called Herb, who was living in Chicago, and told him that the next time he was in Miami he should come and see him.

Herb and Larry both say that when they got back together "it was as if all the other years never happened." This is not the kind of remark that Ellen, who spent those years with Herb, likes to hear. Ellen is tall, with short, reddish blond hair, long legs, and a tiny waist. She grew up in Flatbush, a more prosperous section of Brooklyn than Bensonhurst. She and Herb met in the cafeteria of New York University, after Herb returned from the army. When Herb would call for Ellen at her parents' house, her father always had four cups of tea set out on the table in the kitchen, and he would ask Herb, "Which one tastes more like sugar?" He was trying to come up with a low-calorie substitute for sugar, and eventually he did: Sweet'n Low. When Ellen first met Larry, Inky, Who-ha, and the other Warriors, and Herb's other friends with Dick Tracy names like Noodles, Sheppo, Jim the Book, and Gutter Rat, she thought they were morons.

Ellen has known Larry for almost as many years as Herb has. She was the matron of honor at Larry's second wedding. She does not resent the intimacy between the two men, but she sometimes feels as if Larry has assumed her position.

"Every family event or gathering, you'd think Herb and Larry are the parents," she says. "I can't find a picture of Herbie and me."

If Herb raises his eyebrows, or purses his lips, or gives any other sign that he considers this remark an exaggeration, Ellen says, "What happened at Steven's bar mitzvah?"

"All the pictures at Steven's bar mitzvah are me and Larry," Herb says.

"What happened at Richard's?"

"What happened?"

"All the pictures are you and Larry. And Sharon's wedding?"

"Sharon's wedding is me and Larry."

Ellen once asked Herb, "Larry and I are drowning in the water, which one of us would you save first?"

"Give me the total circumstances," Herb said.

"*Which one would you save first?*"

"Well, I have known Larry for a *very* long time."

Larry believes that Herb's career as a negotiator began in the ninth grade, when Herb talked the principal out of suspending him and Larry and a friend of theirs named Brazie Abbate for an extravagant prank that got out of control.

Larry's version: We're in ninth grade — in the incorrigibles class. One of the guys in that class was Gilbert Mermelstein, whom we called Gil Moppo, because his hair was like a mop, all curled up. One day near the end of the winter, the beginning of spring, Moppo does not come to school. Myself, Herbie, and Brazie Abbate, who became a brain surgeon in Buffalo, or maybe a urologist in North Carolina, go over to Moppo's house to inquire. Gil Moppo's cousin is sitting in front of Gil Moppo's house. The shades are drawn, Gil Moppo's cousin looks forlorn. Gil Moppo, he says, has developed tuberculosis. Gil's father and mother have taken Moppo to Phoenix, Arizona, for the cure. And this was like March. Moppo they've taken to Arizona. "I'm going to Arizona tomorrow," the cousin says, "but before I can leave I have to go tell the school what happened to Moppo and have them transfer his records to Lafayette High School, because Moppo won't be back to junior high school." Herbie says, "Leave tonight, we'll tell them." The cousin says, "Would you do that for me?" Herbie says, "Go ahead to Arizona."

Herbie, Brazie, and I are then walking back to our corner. Herbie says, "I have an idea that could make us five dollars apiece to go to Nathan's." Nathan's was a very popular hot dog place about six minutes by car from the corner where we hung out. Brazie says, "What's your idea?" Herbie says, "We go into class tomorrow and tell them that Gil Moppo died." Brazie and I look at each other. "Now, they're going to call the house," Herbie says. "No answer, disconnect — Moppo's in Phoenix, Moppo's mother and father are in Phoenix with him, and his cousin is on the way, so it's not possible for them to check. We raise money in the class for flowers, we take the money down to Nathan's. Fifty cents apiece, there's thirty kids in the class. It can't fail."

Brazie says, "It can't fail?"

"They'll forget about him," Herbie says. "We'll be in high school when he comes back. Fifteen bucks, what the hell. Who will know?"

Herb's version begins differently: We would walk to school, four or five guys. We're in the ninth grade, junior high school, in a backward class, and the next year, with luck, we'll be promoted to high school. One day we're walking — me, Larry, and Brazie Abbate. Someone told me that Brazie ultimately became a neurologist, but we haven't seen Brazie in thirty-five years. We have lost touch with Brazie. In any case, along the way a guy comes up to us and says, "What's the story with Moppo, how come he's not in school?" Now, Moppo is a guy whose real name was Gilbert Mermelstein. He had curly red hair, like Harpo Marx, which caused him to pick up the name along the way of Moppo. The guy has a point. It's the middle of term, probably March, Moppo's been absent for two weeks, why isn't he here?

I said, "I don't know." They ask Larry, Larry don't know; they ask Brazie, he don't know. The guy comes back to me. "Hey, come on," he says. "You *know*." I shrug my shoulders. He says, "It's bad, huh? Come on, what do you know?" I have this rule — I don't know where I got it — I have a rule in life: if someone asks me something as many as three times, I feel an obligation to tell him the truth, but after telling him three times if he doesn't accept it I'm not telling him the same thing again. And I do this even to this day. I make something up. I tell him something outrageous. I figure he'll know it's an invention and give up. That guy asks me a fourth time, "Herbie, you really know what happened to Moppo, don't you?"

"Well, I don't want this to get around," I said. I lowered my voice. "You want to know what happened to Moppo? He's dead."

"He's what?"

I said, "Listen, we don't want this to get around. This is something we're not talking about, I've made my last statement, this is it."

The guy ran off. The three of us went on to talk about other things. About ten minutes later, we arrive at school. We get to homeroom and everybody's whispering. What are they whispering about? Moppo. We assumed it was because he hadn't been around for so long. In a little while, we heard it. What about Moppo? He's dead. I don't remember that I related this to what I had said. He had been a sickly type, and I guess it hadn't seemed impossible that he could have caught something and died. Anyway, we learned that Moppo was dead, and that the class had heard the news from a friend of Moppo's, but there was such confusion that we didn't know: how did it happen? People were speculating scarlet fever — that was going around. Maybe polio. The teacher went out and she immediately notified the principal, and the principal's office called Moppo's home and learned that the telephone had been disconnected and the family had moved.

Larry: We decide to carry out Herbie's plan, and we go into class the next day, and go up to our teacher, Mrs. Dewar — tall, slim, wore a wig. We say, "Mrs. Dewar," and we have our heads down, we look sad — me, Brazie, and Herbie — and we say, "Mrs. Dewar, Gil Moppo died." She says, "He died?" Moppo had been a sickly boy, so the news wasn't incredible. So as not to alarm the rest of the class, Mrs. Dewar calmly rises and goes out the door. We hear her footsteps going down the hall to the principal's office. The office calls Gil Moppo's house. Disconnected. The principal's office writes "Deceased" across Gil Moppo's card. Deceased. Accepted our word. We raised fifteen bucks, went down to Nathan's, had a ball. We think, End of story.

Herb: Larry always says that after we collected the money we went to Nathan's. Didn't happen. What happened was the teacher had the principal's office call Moppo's house and they heard that the phone had been disconnected. They wrote "Deceased" on his card. The teacher was shocked and said we ought to do something for Moppo. We never had anything like this, she said, Moppo was a nice kid. We as a homeroom should do something for him. At this point, Larry volunteered that me and him and Brazie would collect money and get something to commemorate Moppo. We spent Moppo's money, maybe some of it. All right, we spent it, it's true.

Larry: Two weeks later, the principal, Dr. Irving Cohen, asks to see the three of us. Herbie says, "Don't worry. We'll say that we heard from somewhere that Moppo had died, we sent the flowers to charity, but we'll give the money back. Don't worry, don't worry, don't worry." We get in the office. Dr. Cohen says, "Hello, Herbert. Hello, Lawrence. Hello, Brazie. Sit down. I want to tell you something."

Herb: At a faculty meeting, he had heard about what we had done in raising money to buy flowers for Moppo.

Larry: High schools in New York City got all the attention in the press for their sports teams, he says.

Herb: Junior high schools got none.

Larry: To draw attention to the school, they were going to have a big assembly.

Herb: The Gilbert Mermelstein Memorial Award.

Larry: Given to an outstanding ninth grader.

Herb: He had called the *Times*.

Larry: As I look back, that was the moment to have said, "Doc . . ."

Herb: It is now the morning of the Gilbert Mermelstein Memorial Award.

Larry: Being held with the whole school on hand in our spacious auditorium, which faces Eighty-fourth Street and is also the left wall of the punchball court.

Herb: Larry, Brazie, and I are sitting on the stage.

Larry: To our right is this huge, huge plaque.

Herb: And above us is a banner across the entire back wall saying, GILBERT MERMELSTEIN MEMORIAL AWARD.

Larry: The *New York Times* guy is in the front row, with a photographer.

Herb: The chances were that Moppo hadn't died. I didn't know for sure what had happened to him, but it was not likely that he had died. We didn't know how to use the phone book, and I didn't know for sure where he lived. We didn't really know how to find out what had happened.

Larry: We're in our full suits, with ties.

Herb: Dr. Cohen is going on about the virtues of Moppo. "Moppo's gone, but Herb and Larry," etc.

Larry: The plaque is up, the banner.

Herb: And Larry is not being stoical. He's having a breakdown. Brazie is saying, "Screw it, I never wanted to be a doctor anyway." I appear to be the most calm, but really I was dying.

Larry: Unbeknownst to us —

Herb: Moppo returns to school. He had had TB or scarlet fever or maybe asthma, and it required him to go to Tucson or Phoenix, someplace with a dry climate — at that time Arizona had a dry climate — and he recovered.

Larry: Made what has come to be known in Arizona tubercular circles as the most dramatic recovery on record.

Herb: Came back that day.

Larry: But he came a little late.

Herb: He does not know about the assembly.

Larry: He went to his homeroom and no one was there.

Herb: He runs into a janitor in the hallway or someone who tells him that everyone is at an assembly.

Larry: There are two ways to come into the auditorium.

Herb: One is through curtains at the side of the auditorium.

Larry: And one is through big brass doors at the back.

Herb: Now, what happened next all happened very fast.

Larry: There's this crash —

Herb: And the doors swing open.

Larry: The first thing Moppo sees is his name, Gilbert Mermelstein, up in lights.

Herb: And the second is "Memorial."

Larry: The kids in the back see Moppo, and right away they know the whole bit: Herbie, Larry, and Brazie made up the death, they took us for fifteen beans, Moppo's still alive.

Herb: Laughter starts spreading from the back of the auditorium to the front.

Larry: Dr. Cohen, who wouldn't know Moppo if he saw him, looks up from his speech and puts on his glasses.

Herb: He peers at Moppo and says, "Who is that?"

Larry: Herbie stands up on the stage, cups his hands over his mouth, and yells, "Moppo, go home! You're dead!"

Herb: I panicked.

Larry: Moppo slams the door and runs home.

Herb: Dr. Cohen turns and looks straight at us —

Larry: And says, "I'll see the three of you in my office."

Herb: "Immediately."

Larry: He storms off the stage, the place is in a panic. Herbie's saying, "We'll handle it, don't worry."

Herb: Larry is saying, "This is it. We're dead. We will all drive trucks for the rest of our lives." And Brazie's looking at me and saying, "I didn't even say anything, this was your idea." So we're breaking down. We are not a solid group anymore.

Larry: We're walking down the hall to the office and the *Times* reporter is saying, "You guys faked a death? And the guy comes back on the day . . . ?"

Herb: We leave the reporter in the vestibule outside Dr. Cohen's office.

Larry: Dr. Cohen looks at the three of us in his office, and he says, "You are suspended from school. You're not graduating. Not this year. Not next year, or any year after that. If it were in my power — and it might be — I would send you to Rikers Island and put you at hard labor until you were eighteen, at which time we would have no further control over you, but at least we would have you there until then. You have pulled the most despicable act I have ever seen in a schoolroom." Brazie and I are staring at the floor, and suddenly Herbie says, "Wait a minute, Doc. You're making a big mistake for you."

Dr. Cohen says, "What did you say?"

"You're really going to kill yourself if you do this," Herbie says.

Dr. Cohen says, "What do you mean?"

Herbie says, "It's true we're not graduating this year, and maybe not ever. We'll do manual labor for the rest of our lives, maybe work in factories doing the worst and most hopeless of all possible jobs. But what about you? If you suspend us, there is a hearing before the Board of Education. That's automatic. At the hearing, we'll get suspended, no doubt, because we did a terrible thing. But one of the questions the Board of Education is going to ask you is, you took the word of three thirteen-year-old boys who told you that someone was dead? Shouldn't you have checked?"

"We did check," Dr. Cohen says.

"You made one phone call," Herbie says. "Shouldn't you have done more than that? You made one phone call, and the operator said the phone was disconnected, and you wrote 'Deceased' on the card? We have a bad disciplinary track record already, and we come in and tell you that a kid is dead, and you make one phone call? And then you give us an award? Doc, we may be suspended, but you're out of work." He pauses to let this sink in, and then he says, "Why don't we forget the whole thing, and ask the *Times* guy not to print it."

Herb: Dr. Cohen agreed not to suspend us, and we talked to the reporter and said that what we had done was stupid and we were returning the money, and he agreed it was really more of a *Daily News* kind of story, and we went to Moppo's house that afternoon to try to explain what had happened, but to this day I don't think he really understands how we could have said that he was dead.

Larry: It shook him.

Herb: For a while after that, the big joke was always, "Moppo, what are you doing here? You're dead." Or, "Moppo, you're not looking too good. I think you're going to die."

Larry: It is now the end of the story. Graduation day, we're lined up to get our diplomas. The way it is arranged, Moppo is in front of Herbie in the procession. Dr. Cohen is reading the students' names on the stage and giving out diplomas. He reads, "Gilbert Mermelstein," and Herbie pushes ahead of Moppo and says, "I'll take it, Dr. Cohen. He's dead."

Not long after Larry's mother died and Larry met Herb's mother at the funeral and called Herb in Chicago, Ellen and Herb had a reason to be in Miami, and Larry invited them to the radio station. Herb appeared on the show, and Larry told the Gil Moppo story. Gilbert Mermelstein called the station. He was living somewhere in Florida. He said, "Larry, you'll never guess who this is." Larry spoke to him for a few minutes, then handed the receiver to Herb.

Herb said, "Moppo, go home. You're dead," and hung up the phone.

(1994)

Elmore's Legs

ELMORE LEONARD, the writer of sleek and authentic novels about criminals, has never much enjoyed doing research. His earliest books were written in the fifties and involve cowboys and bandits. Leonard has always lived in Detroit. To describe a canyon or a butte, he consulted the magazine *Arizona Highways*. When the market for Westerns disappeared, in the sixties, he relied on a newspaper reporter he knew who covered crime. "I don't like to research," he says. "I like to write." Nevertheless, for the last fifteen years, whatever part of the verisimilitude of his novels is not the result of his imagination is the result of legwork. Not his legs.

Leonard's legman is named Gregg Sutter. He lives part of the year in Michigan but mostly in Hollywood, Florida, a popular destination for tourists from Quebec. Along Hollywood Beach, two-story flat-roofed motels alternate with apartment buildings that look like file cabinets. Sutter came to Florida four years ago, to do research for Leonard, and likes it well enough, although sometimes, he says, he feels rootless there, and he still has Michigan plates on his car. He lives in a one-bedroom apartment with a lot of books and electronic and video and computer equipment. When he gets up in the morning, he stands his bed against a wall to make more room.

Sutter is forty-five. He is tall and large-boned, he has dark shaggy hair and small features, he stoops a little, and he has a shuffly walk. He frequently tucks his chin down and to the right and looks back at you with eyes askance, a form of shyness. His manner is somewhat measuring and aloof. "I'm very charming when it comes to librarians," he says, "but I don't have any charm otherwise. I put it all into that."

Sutter's name occasionally appears in newspaper and magazine sto-ries about Leonard, whom his friends call Dutch, usually because Leon-ard has raised it. A friend of mine saw it in a profile of the author and suggested I call him. When I asked Sutter what he was working on, he said that when Leonard had finished *Out of Sight*, his thirty-third novel, he had intended to write about the fashion industry. He expected the book to include the Mafia and sent Sutter to New York to look around.

"I walked the fashion district for a few days and took the usual as-sortment of photos," Sutter said. "Dutch is very visual. I do a lot of pan-oramas — picture, picture, picture, then tape them together. Mean-while, I thought about the wholesalers, was that interesting? Or the buttonmakers? The guys pushing racks? I went to the New York Public Library and ran the clips for Mob stuff, but it turned out they had a lot less to do with the industry now than they had even ten years ago. I picked up the ancillary crime stuff — the Svengali of Greenwich Village — and then I got the call. 'It's getting to be too much like work. We're doing the Spanish-American War.' Meaning that in one day I'm going from reading fashion retailing guides and talking to better-dress guys in the Woolworth Building who've spent forty years in the trade, and thinking, How am I going to get a handle on this, to the Span-Am War and bandits and buffalo soldiers and runaway slaves and race riots and thinking, Hey, this is all right."

I asked Sutter if I could come see him and maybe visit some of the places and people who had figured in his research, and he said sure. I stayed in a Holiday Inn next door to his building. In Palm Beach we drove down a sand road through trees along the border of the golf course at the Breakers Hotel and looked at the golf holes I had seen on a map Sutter had drawn for Leonard to use in plotting the kidnapping of a wealthy guy in *Riding the Rap*. We drove up Worth Avenue, where Sutter once made a videotape at a rally of Nazis and bikers because he thought that such an event in such a place contained sufficient irony to appeal to Leonard. *Rum Punch* begins, "Sunday morning Odel took Lewis to the white power demonstration in downtown Palm Beach." We visited Mike Sandy, a bail bondsman whom Sutter interviewed to pro-vide Leonard with material for his character Max Cherry, the bonds-man in *Rum Punch*. We sat in a courtroom in West Palm Beach pre-sided over by Judge Marvin Mounts, the outline of whose life suggested to Leonard his character Judge Bob Gibbs in *Maximum Bob*, and after

Mounts had given probation to a weeping woman in an assault case whose husband had once pointed a shotgun at her and her children, we went into his chambers, where he showed us old, glossy, black-and-white evidence photographs of car wrecks and death scenes and an enigmatic image depicting a tabletop-size hole in the ground and a man standing next to it and what appeared to be, a foot or so down in the hole, a piece of metal. "See that," the judge said. "That was a murder case we had one time. The man had argued with his wife, and he didn't mean to, but it ended up with his putting his hands around her neck and strangling her, and then he put her in the trunk of her car and drove it downtown here and parked it overnight, and the next morning he thought better of it and picked up the car and drove north near Tallahassee to the farm he grew up on, and he went into the bush on a back part of the farm and dug a deep hole and buried the car with her in the trunk — you're looking at the roof right there — and we never would have known what happened to her if he hadn't got a guilty conscience, and here's what she looked like when they took her out of the trunk. Pitiful."

Sometimes while driving we listened to the tape of an interview Sutter conducted for *Out of Sight* with a man who had escaped from more prisons in Florida than anyone else. *Out of Sight* revolves mainly around a convict named Jack Foley and an ex-convict named Buddy. As the book opens, Foley is engaged in breaking out of the Glades Correctional Institution, in Belle Glade, Florida. Leonard modeled the prison break on an escape made from Glades in 1995 by five Cuban prisoners who dug a tunnel under the prison fence. Leonard decided that Foley would lure a prison guard into the prison chapel, jump him for his clothes and hat, then follow the Cubans through the tunnel, and that Buddy would be waiting with a car in the prison parking lot.

When the Cubans leave the tunnel, they run, are chased and shot at, and two are killed. Dressed as a guard, Foley walks.

That a con might remain in possession of his nerves during a prison break was suggested to Leonard by this interview. "You're getting ready to escape and you're scared," the escape artist said. "Your adrenaline's flowing, and you can reach a point where you're too scared to move. You're immobile. When people romance breaking out of prison, man, they don't romance *that*.

"To move, you got to master your terror. How do you do it? The way to control your emotions is to act. You *act* cool, you going to *be* cool. I *walk* to the fence, I don't run to the fence — I don't run and crash and frantically climb that fence. I walk up like my attitude is 'Fuck it, man. Ain't no big thing.' And when I come down the other side, I don't haul ass and run, either. That's *panic.* Soon as I hit the ground, I walk. Man, I *stroll.* And when you hit those woods, hallelujah, God damn, that's a wonderful feeling."

In January of 1981, Leonard needed someone to read newspaper files and thought of Sutter, who had come to see him the winter before. Sutter and a friend had been trying to start a magazine called *Noir* and wanted to interview Leonard for their first issue. When Leonard called, Sutter was working on the engine line at a car factory, an experience he hopes might someday become part of a novel, "a Nathanael West on the line," he says. He was also writing for magazines and newspapers about topics such as making movies in Detroit, beer, prairie architecture, and novels by Elmore Leonard.

Sutter's own ambitions as a novelist he is content to defer. "I may not yet be successful as a writer," he says, "but I am successful as Elmore Leonard's literary researcher. What I do contributes to the work of a man I think is a great writer, and I feel privileged to be a part. I'm like someone who leads an archeological dig, then turns the findings over to someone who knows what they mean. Where I get satisfaction is in knowing that these stray bits I collect will be used in making something large and original and valuable."

Except inadvertently, Sutter does not supply Leonard with material for characters. "He makes the bad guys up," Sutter says. The response that Sutter works hard to produce is delight. Sutter values Leonard's allowing him to pursue what he feels intuitively will be interesting, and he doubts that he could work happily for any other writer, especially one who would simply give him lists of material to retrieve. Devotion, above all, is what Sutter feels for Leonard. "Life being a series of tests of loyalty," he says, "some of which I have already failed, I am here for the long run. If Dutch ever had a reversal of fortune, I would be there." The only disappointment I have heard Sutter describe was when I mentioned how pleased I had been by a scene in *Out of Sight.* Sutter said, "I envy people who get to read him for the first time and have all the thrills. By the time the books are finished, I'm too familiar with the story to do that."

For *Rum Punch,* Leonard asked Sutter to find a bail bondsman who would explain how bonds were written. The man who wrote the majority of bonds in West Palm Beach, where the courts are, wouldn't talk. Asking questions of other bondsmen and using the yellow pages, Sutter found a half-Lebanese, half-Sicilian former FBI agent named Mike Sandy.

Sandy has an office down the street from the courthouse, with a sign on the door that says PRIVATE, and one afternoon Sutter and I stopped in to see him. When we arrived, he told us to step around the ceiling tiles on the floor. "Water damage," he said.

We looked at some Remington prints of Indian warriors and cavalry soldiers that Sandy bought at flea markets, then we consulted a catalog to see what they were worth, then I asked Sandy, as Sutter once had, about writing bonds, and that led to a description of the anxieties involved in a bondsman's life, and he said, "Here's what happened to a bondsman in town. For years, one of his clients was a Colombian who brought him cases. We'll say the Colombian's name is Pedro Lopez. Very reliable. Suppose the bond's two hundred and fifty thousand, Lopez brings two hundred and fifty thousand, counts it out, then counts out the twenty-five-thousand-dollar premium for the bondsman. No collateral, no complications, cash business. Arrives with boxes and chests of money like it was the Captain Kidd days.

"One day an individual Lopez has paid for doesn't show up in court. Lopez comes into the bondsman's office, says, 'We don't want you to pay this bond,' and picks up his money.

"A few days later, Pedro Lopez is found floating in the bay off Key Biscayne. There's two pieces to him. Top and a bottom. The bondsman gets a phone call from someone saying, 'Pedro has fallen on a serious accident, please be at such and such bar at eleven tonight.' The bondsman's concerned. He's *innocent* — he's done nothing out of line that he can think of — but these people are Colombians. He shows up at the bar, with his brother. Why his brother? I don't know. The bartender greets him by name. The bondsman's lived all his life in Miami — he's never seen this guy, he's never been to this bar — but the guy knows his name. True story. Gregg and I both know the bondsman. Bartender points to a table in the corner and tells the bondsman and his brother to wait. Bar's dark.

"Time passes, music plays, maybe some people come and go. Eventually three Colombians walk in and join the brothers at the table. One man talks, another interprets, and the third says nothing at all. Third guy has a mustache. The one talking tells the bondsman that Mr. Lopez developed a problem the other night, he fell on a power saw. In his apartment. Bondsman nods. First time he's heard what happened. He's listening closely. He's sweating a little. He's thinking, Why am I here? 'But before he fell on the power saw,' the man says, 'he told us that you returned only a hundred and fifty thousand of the two-hundred-and-fifty-thousand-dollar bond.'

"When the bondsman hears this — which isn't true — he doesn't say, 'He's lying,' he doesn't say, 'There's been some mistake,' he doesn't say, 'I don't know what you're talking about.' He stands up and says, 'An hour. We'll make some calls. My brother will wait here, and I'll be back in an hour with the money. Forty-five minutes, let's make it forty-five minutes. This table in forty-five minutes.'

"The Colombian says, 'No, no, sit down, we want you to know that after Mr. Lopez fell on the power saw, we found the money. That's not why we called you here.' Bondsman sits down. We asked you to meet us so that we could demonstrate the faith we have in you by introducing the man you and Mr. Lopez have been working for.' They'd brought the heavyweight, you see. Show of confidence. This is ten, nine years ago, maybe. The man talking points to the third man at the table who hasn't said a word and never does: Pablo Escobar. True story."

Chronology: Sutter was born in Detroit, in 1951. The hospital was later torn down to make way for a Cadillac plant. He went to Catholic grade school, and in 1969 he went to Oakland University, in Rochester, thirty miles north. "My first major was behavioral science," he says, "which I still don't know what it is. I hooked up with all these worldly East Coast Jews from Teaneck and Weehawken who knew blues and jazz, and I didn't; they were the kind of guys who'd hole up in a room and play eighteen different versions of 'Billy's Bounce,' by Charlie Parker, and not only know which one had the reed squeak but exactly where it was. I took a lot of guidance from this crew, and eventually it would lead me to Elmore Leonard.

"First, though, I fell into film history. I thought of myself as a cine-Marxist, sit around the apartment and talk about the Revolution and watch movies. I wrote about Cuban revolutionary posters and Nazi cinema, and got a degree in history, never thinking about what I would do the day after I graduated. Which, it turned out, was work in a factory. First making cables for welders, then at Chrysler, on the engine line. In *Out of Sight*, when Buddy describes to Foley his experience on the assembly line, the experience he is describing is mine. That's about all the good that came from that."

Sutter thought that he was going to be laid off, so he quit and, through an ad in the paper, got a job doing publicity for the Women's Symphony of Detroit. "Then I became editor of the *Grapevine Gazette*, the magazine of the Detroit Metropolitan Bar Owners Association," he says. "Sad little stories about bar owners and liquor commission violations. Then I and a friend, Russ Rein, started a magazine in Ann Arbor called *Art Beat*, which folded after four issues, when we ran out of money." For a while, Sutter felt he was at a loss, then a friend got him a job, in January of 1976, with Norman Levy Associates, an industrial liquidator.

"We'd go into a shop — a lathe shop," he says, "for example — assign a book value to everything, scrub the machines with kerosene to make them shiny, paint the lettering on the tires of any rolling stock, and send in a photographer with an assistant to wave sheets behind the machines to give the picture an opaque background for the catalog.

"We held two auctions — a seven-day one and an eleven-day one — to liquidate a factory in Lansing belonging to Diamond REO, a custom truck maker, and then I stayed on supervising the cleanup crews, making sure the place didn't burn down, and just generally losing myself in this dead factory — thirty-seven acres of rooms of mahogany dies for fenders, and piles of documents that no one thought were valuable enough to do anything with except leave behind. I spent so much time reading documents and opening drawers of desks in otherwise empty rooms that after a few months I decided to pocket my per diem and give up my apartment, and I moved into a back office. Months passed, the last copper wire was pulled from the wall, and the wrecker ball was ready to swing. Even after, I would sneak in and explore the tunnels and passageways the wrecker ball exposed. It gave me a sense of peace, some kind of vengeful working-class feeling, I guess, to witness what I thought of as one version of an end to the Industrial Revolution.

"I had been training as an appraiser, but what I wanted to be was a setup man — the guy who sets up a factory for an auction. I did a tidy job on a titanium-processing plant in Indianapolis and left with my head up, but the commute was too rough, and I quit.

"Working on Diamond REO, I had done a report on the factory for the fire marshal in Lansing, and he set me up with an interview at Oldsmobile. I was full of myself, full of experience and obscure knowledge, and I thought, They'll make me a foreman. But they didn't. I started on the line on August 22, 1977, the week after Elvis died.

"It was exciting in some ways: I loved the harsh, nervous sound of hundreds of air drills working at once, like gunfire, and the big ocean-liner-like procession of the line, but it was also my life going down the drain. For a while, I was an extra man — meaning I didn't have a specific task — and they had me unload boxcars of tire rims, or do transmission fluid top-off, because it was a disgusting job and you came home smelling of diesel fuel and transmission fluid. Or I wrote the job number with a grease pencil on the sides of tires as they came by — what's called tire run — or I was on air cleaner, which I liked especially because I had a table for my stock where I could set up a novel. I'd get several air cleaners ahead and try to read two pages before a car was in front of me again. How far ahead I got depended on how fast the line was running; on a fast day it was fifty, sixty cars an hour.

"Working air cleaner is when I got really interested in hardboiled fiction — Woolrich, Chandler, Cain, pulps, all the tough-guy writers of the thirties. I read Elmore Leonard then, *Fifty-two Pickup* when it came out in paperback, and because it was about Detroit it deeply addressed a feeling I had of being stuck in a permanent backwater. Here was someone writing about streets that had always seemed inconsequential and overlooked by everyone else, and suddenly weren't. Instead of feeling isolated from the rest of the world, I now felt like you could be anywhere, as long as you're brilliant. I read everything of his I could find. All his books about Detroit had something in them that elated me, even if it was just the description of a Near East Side bungalow with a Blessed Virgin birdbath in the backyard.

"The period of the year when the factory is converting the line to accommodate the new year's models is called changeover. Usually you get two weeks off. Changeover at the end of 1979 is when I looked up Elmore Leonard in the phone book and called him."

Sutter said that he was flying to Detroit to meet Leonard at his house to go over material for *Cuba Libre*, the book on the Spanish-American War, and he said I could go with him. He picked me up at my hotel, and we stopped at a used-book store called John K. King's so I could look

for some old Leonard books and Sutter could see if he could find anything on Cuba. He didn't expect to — he had been to King's a few days
before — but he wandered into a back room and came out with two
copies of volume 1 of a book called *The Island and Her People*. It was
published in 1899 and was the size of an atlas, and it had a lot of photographs of things such as sugar estates and boats in Havana harbor.
Sutter bought both copies. While he stood at the counter, waiting to pay
for them, he said, "If it was between me and another guy for this book,"
he said, "there would be blood."

Leonard lives in a suburb north of the city. As we drove through the
town's leafy streets, Sutter paused in front of a red brick house and said
that Leonard had lived in it until ten years ago, and then he turned onto
a street of much larger houses and said, "See if you can pick out where
he lives now," and I pointed to a chateau-looking place behind a hedge
with a big rug of a lawn and awnings on one side and was surprised
when he turned into its circular driveway.

Leonard answered the door. He was a small-framed man, in a T-shirt
and jeans, with gray hair and narrow shoulders, wiry and slightly
stooped.

We sat in his living room. I asked how the book was going, and he replied, "I'm on page 9." He said it begins with a saddle bum shipping
horses from Galveston, Texas, who arrives in Havana harbor two days
after the *Maine* has blown up and sees the buzzards worrying the sail-
ors' corpses and wonders what has happened. "The dialogue is different," he said. "I can't swing with it yet, and I don't know what obsceni-
ties they used."

He said that the details Sutter gives him mainly "enrich a scene, give
it some color." I asked if Sutter's work had ever changed the course of a
book and he said, "Not exactly, but one time I was interested in getting
some background on Perfirio Rubirosa, a Dominican playboy who
married a couple of wealthy women — he was killed in a sports car one
night in the Bois de Boulogne — and I had a character like that in *Split
Images*, in 1981, so Gregg got me a magazine that had a piece about
Trujillo's daughter, who was married to Perfirio — she was the first wife.
I was reading that, and I turned the page and here was a picture of a
squad of marines walking down a street in Santo Domingo and I
thought, That's my next book — one of these guys goes back fifteen or

sixteen years later to walk his perimeter and meets this girl sniper who shot him. That became *Cat Chaser* — cat chaser was the squad's radio identification."

While I was writing that down in my notebook, Leonard and Sutter began talking about the business of shipping horses, and Sutter showed him a copy of a handwritten ledger he had found among the archives of a horse museum in Texas. The ledger recorded the transactions of a freight company and had entries for the cost of feed and other details of a shipment of horses to Cuba. Then Sutter laid *The Island and Her People* on a coffee table and said, "Look what I got." Leonard leaned forward in his chair and rested his elbows on his knees and said, "Oh, my God, oh, look. Look at this." He turned each page slowly and sometimes shook his head. Sutter sat beside him, smiling slightly. It was clear that he drew pleasure from Leonard's proximity. Leonard had examined about half of the book's pages when he leaned back and said, "This book, I can't believe it. A *picture* book of the period." He looked at Sutter and said, "This is all I need — I don't know how you found it — I can get everything I need out of this." Sutter slumped and let out his breath. "Don't say that," he said. "That's the last thing I want to hear."

(1996)

Perfect

L ET'S SAY WE'RE at a drag strip somewhere in the petroleum wilderness of the republic, watching funny cars, a peevish and irascible species of hot rod. Funny cars resemble regular cars, but the front wheels are farther from the back wheels than they usually are, so the body is longer; they're called funny cars because they look peculiar. They make a numbing amount of noise, they travel at spectacular speeds, flames shoot from their tailpipes, and they frequently explode. One funny car races another down a quarter-mile track. The race lasts five seconds. It takes longer for the cars to come to a stop than it does for the race to be run. For companions under the sprawling blue big top of the American sky, we have big, fat, jiggly guys wobbly on beer. We have guys in T-shirts decorated with the names of fishing-tackle shops or the rescue squads of small towns or with slogans such as KICKIN' ASPHALT. We have middle-aged women as skinny as lizards in tank tops and jeans. We have fathers carrying sons on their shoulders. We have among us so many billed caps that seen from a hill beside the track we look like a flock of ducks.

Funny cars don't so much leave the starting line as detonate. The engines make a sound like a chain saw the size of a backhoe. Flames spray from the cars' exhaust pipes, and the ground shakes. Track grit and pieces of balled-up rubber thrown up by the tires rain down like ash. Blue smoke from the wheels mixes with black smoke and dust from the clutch and green smoke from the nitromethane that the cars burn as fuel. Your teeth rattle, your chest feels like someone has his knee pressed meanly upon it, the exhaust pricks your sinuses, your eyes water, and you can hardly breathe. The shapeless, smothering sound feels lunatic and malign. Your skin seems to be shouting at you. Then suddenly the battering air stops vibrating. The cars and their collection of assaults have vanished. Silence rushes past your ears like wind.

A while ago I developed an enthusiasm for funny cars. I learned that they are the most rancorous, malevolent, thuggish, and unmanageable rolling stock in the world. I learned that they are much more difficult to control than top-fuel dragsters — the long, pointy, needle-nosed cars with the tiny front wheels. "Top-fuel dragsters want your respect," a driver named Ron Capps told me. "Funny cars demand it." I learned that a funny car goes 100 mph in a second; 250 mph by the track's three-quarter mark — by which point the resistance of gravity has flattened the driver's face — and 300 mph by the finish line; the record is 312 mph. I learned that each of a funny car's eight cylinders delivers an amount of horsepower approximately equal to the entire horsepower of the kind of car that races in the Indianapolis 500. I heard one driver describe a funny car as a "six-thousand-horsepower beast that wants to kill you," and I heard another one say that driving a funny car is like being "strapped into a grenade and shot down the track."

I also learned that the sport has been dominated for six of the last seven years by a flamboyant and indefatigable racer from Southern California named John Force, who used to drive trucks, who bought his first funny car partly with money raised by selling a home organ that his wife had won on *Let's Make a Deal,* and who, since 1990, has won every world championship but one — he placed second in 1992. Force has raced funny cars for more than twenty years. In the decade and a half before he won his first championship, all he did mostly was burn up, crash, and lose.

Force is forty-eight years old. He is not that tall, and he has a small potbelly — a "tub," he calls it. He has a round face, clear blue eyes, a brown mustache, and brown hair as straight and thick as a horse's mane. His smile reveals a shapely row of teeth, like fence posts, which he says are his best feature. Having polio as a child left him with one leg a little shorter than the other, and when he is tired he favors the shorter leg slightly. The scars on the backs of his hands and between his fingers are the result of sweat having come to a boil during the occasions when he has occupied his car while it was on fire. He has undoubtedly driven more cars that have exploded than anyone else in the world. In addition to fire, he is afraid of heights, electricity, and elevators. He is as restless as a child. He talks almost constantly. Furthermore, he drinks a lot of coffee, which appears to work on his mind as a purgative: words come out of him then in torrents. He will often say, "Anyway, the point is . . . What's the point? What are we talking about?" He almost never arrives anywhere on time. He's exceptionally generous. One of his brothers came to work for him not long ago. At the end of his brother's first day, Force gave him a raise, and shortly after that Force gave him a car. Force says that he is not especially devout but that he often feels the presence of God. Early in his career, he occasionally raced at tracks that were dangerously fogbound. "I'd drive into those fog banks," he says, "and suddenly it was like God cleared them up. I know how that sounds, but after you've been on fire as much as I have, you'll get religion." He likes country music and is given to bouts of sentimentality. "Put me in a corner of a little pub in some small town or a bar in Kansas City," he says, "and sing me some song about the corn don't grow, and I'll cry all night." His mother says that Force is her dumbest child (she has five) but that he is also her richest.

Force spends more time at drag strips or on his way to or from them than he does at his home. Sitting in his trailer in the pit at a racetrack, he says, "This is my backyard. I live in this house, in this town, at the end of this street." He and his second wife, Laurie, a tall, handsome woman with brown hair, have three daughters, the oldest of whom is fourteen. They live in a house on a hill in a town on the eastern outskirts of Los Angeles. Force says that when he moved to the town, it was "all orange fields and oil wells." Now it is mostly high-tension wires, shopping centers, and Spanish-style houses. Force also has a daughter from his first marriage; she runs his office. When his and Laurie's girls were younger and Force would return from a long trip, their mother would say, "Come see your father," and the girls would run to the television.

Adapting himself years ago to the deprivations of a nomadic and anxious profession, Force began living in a world of his own making. "I can't hardly go back into the real world now," he says. "You're gone for so long, you don't know how to go home anymore. Where I feel at home is in the Dallas airport at midnight. I know where I am; I know where I'm going; I know where everything is. You go home, you know that someone's getting ahead of you. You sit there and fear that you'll lose."

As belligerent and menacing as funny cars are, they are also a type of ephemera. The stresses their engines contain are so acute that they can run at top speed for only six or seven seconds before they blow up. Funny cars are built by hand. Each car costs about $175,000. To make working on the engines easier, the bodies detach from the chassis; the bodies are made from fiberglass and weigh about as much as the hull of a small sailboat. At any given time, there are probably forty funny cars in the country, a pair belonging to each of the approximately twenty men who drive them professionally. Force has four; the second pair, the ones he no longer drives, are used by his teammate, Tony Pedregon.

During the five seconds that a funny car takes to travel a quarter mile, it consumes approximately $3,500 in parts. An engine costs between $8,000 and $10,000; a driver uses about twelve in a year. A new one might last half a run, or it might last twenty races. It sometimes happens that an engine blows up, is replaced, and the new one blows up. Funny-car drivers say that if you want to become a millionaire by racing funny cars, start with two million.

To pay mechanics and for parts and shops and planes and hotels, a driver needs sponsors. The pool of merchants willing to back race cars is small, and most prefer "roundy" cars — the drag racers' term for cars that circle a track. Sponsors pursue successful drivers, which for most of his career Force was not. According to Force's brother Walker, who works for him, Force's manner of recruiting sponsors was to appear in their stores and say, "I'm John Force. How'd you like to sponsor my race car?"

"Ninety-nine times out of ten," Walker says, "they said no." Force became adept, however, at persuading businessmen who had never been to a drag strip that the sponsorship of a funny car was the underutilized detail in their marketing strategy. His first sponsor was a Los Angeles stereo store. The store had engaged a clown to hand out balloons. Force asked the manager how much he paid the clown. The manager said, "One fifty a day." Force said, "For one hundred fifty dollars, you can have a race car, and I'll buy the balloons."

Force believes that the two most important components of a racing career are winning and pleasing your sponsors. "You got to run good," he says, "and you got to carry the signs." He goes to extravagant lengths to ensure that a sponsor has more than one opportunity to congratulate himself for backing a funny car in the first place. "You give Force ten dollars," one of his sponsors told me, "and he gives you eleven dollars' worth of service." For a while, Force received money from Wendy's. When a woman who had been hired to appear as Wendy didn't show up at a franchise in Montreal where Force was displaying his car, he put on the blue-and-white dress and red-haired wig and stood in front of the restaurant and said, "Don't worry, John Force will be here in a minute."

The bulk of Force's expenses are now met by an arrangement with Castrol, but he began his racing career with money he earned by driving a truck. When the cash ran out, he drove trucks again. "You couldn't go to the bank," he says, "because the bank wouldn't lend you." Whenever money came into his hands, he applied it to racing.

"One time in 1976," he says, "I was leaving for a race in Sacramento and blew up the truck transmission and needed transmission fluid. I pulled into a gas station off the freeway, and it's around eight-thirty at night, dark, and the guy was a foreigner, an Iranian maybe. He's about to close — maybe he's Turkish — and when I told him I needed transmission fluid, he ignored me. He didn't understand what I meant. I said, 'Aw, hell, I'll get the stuff myself,' and went looking for the storeroom. He's busy turning out lights and locking doors. It's pitch-dark out, raining — did I say that? — and I'm feeling around the shelves with my hands, looking for oil in the dark.

"All of a sudden I hear a truck pull up. I look out a window, and it's an armored truck — like a Brink's truck — and I think, This is a rough area to be picking up money so late at night. The Iranian guy's standing on the apron, reading the pumps — maybe he's Spanish — and he doesn't even probably remember I'm back there. Maybe he thinks I went to the bathroom. Anyway, he had already pulled the gate across the front window, and I see the lights on the gas pumps go out. I'm running my hands over the cans like I can read the labels with my fingers, and next thing I hear is a chain slinking up behind me in the dark.

"The Brink's truck wasn't picking up money — wasn't no money in sight. What it was, really, was a truck dropping off guard dogs for the night. The one creeping on me in the pitch-dark had a hounds of Baskerville head big as a football. I raised up my arm to protect myself, and his jaws closed down over it. Noises come out of me then like I didn't even know I could make. With my other arm, I started slugging him, and I drug him through the storeroom door, trying to find help. I was so panicked that I lifted him right off the ground — they're trained not to let go. The handler heard me screaming, and he came and yelled at him, and he wouldn't let go, and then he started beating on him, too. I don't remember how he finally got him off me, but when he did, I just lay down on the pavement in the rain and passed out.

"Few weeks later, when it came time for the settlement, I went psychological and said I didn't date girls anymore because they reminded me of dogs, and I took the fifteen hundred dollars that they gave me and used it to buy one of my race cars."

Anything traveling 300 mph on the ground wants to fly. The wheels of a funny car remain on the pavement because the tailpipes point up in the air. The thrust of the exhaust coming out of them presses downward. On either side of the engine, there are four pipes, each attached to a cylinder. If a cylinder fails, a commonplace occurrence, nothing comes out of the tailpipe attached to it. You have four cylinders working on one side of the engine and three on the other. The car turns violently toward the weaker side.

Another obstacle to getting a funny car to the finish line is traction. On their way to the starting line, funny cars pass through a tire bath, a trough worked into the track, which rinses grit from the tires. Any object between the tire and the track might cause the wheel to spin; while the wheel spins, the driver loses time. The drivers then conduct a sprint of, say, a hundred or two hundred feet. This is called a burnout. The burnout heats a compound in the tires, which makes them sticky.

After the burnout, the cars back up to the starting line, where there is a pole called the Christmas tree — a collection of lights divided into two vertical rows, one for each lane. At the top are two yellow bulbs that light up when the cars arrive. Two yellow bulbs beneath them light up when a laser determines that the cars' front tires are positioned properly for the race to begin. A starter presses a button, and three amber lamps the size of stoplight bulbs light up; then almost immediately a green one lights up, beginning the race. Force tries to cut the amber — to leave, that is, before he sees the green, but not so soon that he is disqualified for a false start. Getting out of the hole is how drivers describe the feeling of leaving the starting line. Funny-car races are often won by the first driver out of the hole. Not infrequently, the losing driver records the faster speed. Force's reactions at the starting line consistently rank among those of the Top 5 drivers. In his trailer he has an electronic device the size of a calculator that has a Christmas tree on it, and he practices obsessively with it between races. "Funny-car driving's not a brute strength sport," he says. "It's technical. Your muscles deteriorate, not your reflexes."

Funny cars are prone at the start of a race to an excessively violent vibration called tire shake, caused by folds developing in the tires; the tires actually drive over themselves. Drivers subjected to severe cases of tire shake sometimes lose vision until it subsides. The process of achieving traction drivers call hooking up. Not hooking up, they say, is like driving on marbles.

If a driver has too much trouble hooking up, he'll quit. While the tires spin, the engine revolves wildly and, if not subdued quickly, will blow up — that is, grenade, as in, "Sucker grenaded on me halfway up the grandstand." When a funny-car engine grenades, you've got junk; you can't fix any of it. A driver can try to hook up by slowing the wheels with the hand brake, or he can feather the accelerator. This is called pedaling. A peculiarity of funny-car racing is that because of how much it costs to send a car down the track, there is no such thing, really, as a practice run. A race is over in five seconds. During the course of a year, a driver with a full schedule might make, say, a hundred passes down the track. Which means that he will spend between 400 and 500 seconds racing — more than six minutes, that is, and fewer than nine. Ten years of racing will give him an hour and a half of experience. The one run out of five when the car goes straight down the track the way it should is hardly an occasion for learning at all. The people who knew Force as a young man agree that he appeared unsuited to racing. Henry Valasco, one of Force's first crew chiefs, says, "He had no ability. None." Bob Fisher, who has been a member of Force's racing team during much of Force's career, says, "I'm not saying that he has natural ability, because he wasn't that good to begin with, but he improved it and improved it to where, years ago, he could pedal so efficiently that people thought we had illegal traction-control devices." Officials searched Force's car at the finish line on dozens of occasions and never found anything. Several videos of Force have been produced; they are displayed among the plastic funny-car models, key chains, and T-shirts at racetrack concession stands. The explanation for why Force's buttocks briefly appear in one of the tapes is that a driver whom Force had just beaten began screaming that Force had a traction-control device concealed in his pants.

Excellence at pedaling is a matter of a driver's having a sensitivity for the tolerances and tendencies of his car. When Force is concerned that his feel for his car is impaired by fatigue or anxiety, or by the arrival of bad luck, he will say, "Oh, man, I ain't got no feet."

Fundamental American archetypes intersected to produce the solitary, romantic, migratory, and daredevil elements of Force's nature. His mother, Betty, is from Broken Arrow, Oklahoma. She went to Los Angeles in the thirties, during the period of Dust Bowl migration, and lived in a Hooverville, the name for the shantytowns around the country inhabited by people made homeless by the Depression. His father, Bill, who was also known as Willie and as Harold, came from Ohio. The family name derives from France and used to be La Force. Force has three older brothers, Walker, Louis, and Tom, and an older sister, Cindy. As teenagers and as young men, Louis and John built cars together, and Louis later drag-raced trucks as Diesel Louie. Walker is retired from the Los Angeles County Sheriff's Department and now oversees contracts and endorsements for John. Tom is retired from a job with an aluminum manufacturer, and Cindy is the manager of a credit bureau.

Force's father drove trucks. He hauled hay for a circus (Force: "I used to say he hauled elephants, but really he hauled hay"), and occasionally he delivered cattle to John Wayne's ranch outside Phoenix, but mainly he transported redwoods for logging companies throughout Northern California and the Pacific Northwest. His family went with him to wherever he found work. For a while they lived in a school bus fitted with bunk beds; when the bus went around a corner late at night, the children sometimes fell out of bed. For a while his father felt that having his own truck would give him some independence, so he bought a dump truck, and the family slept on mattresses in the dump truck's bed. When it rained, he strung a tarpaulin above them. If no one had work for him driving a truck, he and his wife and the older children would pick strawberries beside other migrant workers in California's San Joaquin Valley.

"We were very itinerant," Force says. "My friends would be bored in their yards in California; we'd load up and move to Oregon." One year, Force sat in classrooms, surrounded by strangers, in ten different schools.

The logging trucks were so big that they were forbidden to use the public roads and could travel only the dirt roads between the woods and the mills. The roads ran past the camps. Several times a day, the truck that Force's father drove came into view of his family's yard, trailing dust. Force loved the immense proportions of the trucks and had a romantic impression of his father's occupation. He would stand by the roadside and wave to his father. "He was just a skinny little kid with a bum leg, covered with dust, waving to his dad," Walker says.

Another of Force's childhood preoccupations was football. He loved wearing a helmet and shoulder pads. When he was ten, his family was living in a logging camp beside an Indian reservation in Northern California. The boys on the reservation played flag football, without equipment. To play in a league that used helmets, Force hitchhiked several times a week to a team in another town. "Just putting on a helmet, you feel more powerful," he says. "You can run into walls; you can tackle; you can do anything. Big old shoulder pads, you become a big man."

When Force was a teenager, his father moved the family to a trailer park in Bell Gardens, an area of Los Angeles. Their trailer had two rooms. Force slept on a couch in the front room and often fell asleep with his parents sitting on his legs, watching television. "To understand my fascination with cars," he says, "you got to know that when you live in a trailer house, you don't have your own room. You don't have big family parties, because there's nowhere to put everyone. You eat your dinner on a TV tray outside on the patio, which is really just a piece of the parking lot with an awning over it. I wanted a car so I had a place to put my football helmet and my schoolbooks."

Force bought his first car when he was a freshman in high school — in California at that time you could get a license at fifteen. He and his friends returned pop bottles for gas money to drive to the beach, where they surfed. He was constantly replacing the steering wheels and the gearshift knobs or tinkering with the suspensions to make the cars look like race cars. His father regarded Force's absorption with hot rods as frivolous. John and Louis once spent a day removing the gearshift from the steering column of their mother's car and replacing it with a stick shift. The first time that his father reached for the gearshift on the steering column, he got so angry that he sawed John's surfboard in half.

By his sophomore year, Force was quarterback for the Lancers at Bell Gardens High School. The team played nine games a year. He graduated in 1967 with a record of twenty-seven losses. "He could throw a football a hundred miles," says Walker. "He'd stand in one place and send everybody long, but nobody could catch the thing."

Force briefly attended East Los Angeles Junior College. When he tried out for the football team, the coaches asked what was wrong with his right leg. "They noticed that when I ran a lot, I would stumble," he says. Force threw so often and ran so infrequently that once, when he forgot his cleats, he played a game in his street shoes. "I had a great football arm and a polio leg," he says. "Eventually I had to get something to do my running for me, and that was a race car."

After college, Force drove trucks. He hauled money for the Wells Fargo Bank — loading bags of coins until his hands hurt, and if you broke a bag the police shut down the street until all the money was accounted for — and he drove for a tannery. "I hauled hides out of the Bay Area," he says, "that you'd stink for two days after you delivered them."

When Force was twenty-one, he applied to the Los Angeles County Sheriff's Department, where Walker was working. "There again, I had a dream of wearing a helmet," Force says. He got an audition but "flunked the inkblot test."

Force went back to trucking. At night, he and Louis built hot rods in Walker's garage. "They'd promise not to start them," Walker says, "because of the noise, and when I left for work, they'd crank them up." Experimenting, they put an unlikely engine in a car or installed the engine sideways. They replaced the transmission in one car with a chain — like on a motorcycle — in order to transfer power directly to the wheels instead of through gears. "It was the quickest car off the line," Walker says, "but the chain couldn't take it. After about the third pass, it'd blow up."

Force got married and divorced, and in the early seventies he met Laurie, his second wife, at a wedding in which he was the best man and she was the maid of honor. "On one of our first dates," she says, "we were motorcycle riding and he asked me if I liked to go to the races, and I thought he meant horses." The first race that she saw Force take part in was stop sign to stop sign on a side street, because he didn't have the license he needed to drive at a drag strip. "He hit a curb that was two feet high," she says, "and flipped over and landed upside down on some railroad tracks, and I thought, Oh, so this is racing, huh?"

Force had an uncle who drove a funny car called the *L.A. Hooker*. For part of the year, he raced in Australia, which is where, in the fall of 1974, the *L.A. Hooker* fell off its trailer. The uncle decided that he'd had enough of racing. He shipped the car back to California and sold what remained of it to Force, who paid for it with his tax refund.

Force repaired the car, took it to a drag strip, and asked if he could bring it to the starting line and have some pictures taken of it — he still had no license. The owner let him park beside a well-known driver named Mickey Thompson, who was running a solo race — that is, a race against the clock. In the pictures, Force is wearing his helmet, his car is running, and his hands are on the wheel, and unless you know the circumstances, you would assume that he was about to race Thompson, whose car appears in the foreground.

In December of 1974, Force left for Australia with the *L.A. Hooker* and two friends who agreed to serve as mechanics. His uncle told him that he needed a nickname, so he had a car painter write BRUTE FORCE on the sides of the car and paint a fist clenching lightning bolts. When Force showed the Australians the photographs of him and Mickey Thompson, they thought, If he's raced Mickey Thompson, he must be all right. Running on junkyard parts and sharing hotel rooms with his mechanics — flipping a coin to see who got the bed, and when they ran out of money altogether, sleeping in the truck that they hauled the car with — Force made it from one race to another. Hoping to persuade someone else to pay for his meal, he would sometimes say that he was Don Prudhomme or Kenny Bernstein, the dominant funny-car drivers of the period, who were back in America.

At Force's first race, some reporters asked whether he would perform a burnout, and while he was obliging them his car caught on fire. The next night, after the burnout, he couldn't get the car into reverse to return to the starting line. On his second run, he lost control of the car before the finish line and ran off into a field. On his third run, he made it to the finish line but the throttle stuck. He caught fire, and the engine, his last, blew up. He came to rest in a pasture where cows were grazing and thought, My career is over. As it happened, he had crossed the finish line traveling slightly more than 200 mph, the first driver in Australia to do so. The next morning he saw his name in a newspaper headline. As a national-record holder, he was given help by promoters and was able (barely) to finish the season. After four and a half months, he went back to California, in April 1975.

"I came back here and raced clean into 1982 without winning nothing," he says. "I figured I wasn't put on this earth to win."

The words *fiery* and *ill-fated* often appear in newspaper articles written during the early years of Force's career. On his first run after returning from Australia, he caught fire. "I came back to the States," he says, "got a new body on the car, raced at Orange County, California, and it put me in the burn center — I got no hair and no eyebrows."

Funny cars explode for a variety of reasons: a gasket tears, the crankshaft fractures, a crack opens suddenly somewhere in the engine. What ignites is the oil, which sprays everywhere. If the engine grenades and the car crashes, and the car's body is thrown clear, the driver is in a more fortunate position than if the body remains in place. Then he is enclosed in a burning vault going 300 mph, with the end of the track approaching. Funny cars stop by means of two parachutes. The cars also have hand brakes. Fires frequently incinerate the lines to the parachutes, or the parachutes themselves, before they can be deployed. A drag strip is a half mile long — a quarter mile to race and a quarter mile to stop. Nearly all drag strips were built when a fast funny car went, say, 200 mph. A quarter mile is not enough room for a hand brake to stop a funny car going more than 240 mph. Tracks sometimes string nets at the end of the pavement; others have sand pits.

A funny-car driver wears a jumpsuit called a fire suit, which is made of layers of fire-resistant material. The suit burns off a layer at a time and prevents the fire from working its worst effects for about a minute. Under his helmet, he also wears a fireproof hood with slits for his eyes. Walker Force says that for a driver in a fire suit, sitting in a burning car is about like "sitting with your head in a fireplace."

After emerging from a burning car, Force searches for a television camera. He believes that a car on fire makes the best sort of background for an interview. He once escaped from a burning car and heard someone yell "Cut!" because the camera was out of tape. The cameraman replaced the tape. Force jumped back into the burning car and came out again. Sometimes after crashing, he makes enigmatic pronouncements. Once, in Memphis after a showcase crash, he said, "I saw Elvis at a thousand feet."

When I want to show someone a performance that I feel is emblematic of Force, I play a tape of a crash he had in 1992. In the minds of many people, it is the most arresting crash in the history of funny-car racing. Force's car caught fire at the finish line. He crashed into the guardrail, and the body flew off. The chassis spun 180 degrees, as if it were on a lazy Susan, then traveled backward down the track. Then it spun forward again. The front wheels striking the dirt at the end of the track raised clouds of dust that enveloped the car. When the wind cleared them, the chassis was revealed to have tipped to one side. Force's feet emerged first. He crawled free of the car and rose to one knee. Members of a rescue crew arrived and helped him to stand. A television announcer held a microphone toward him. Force, grinning extravagantly, said, "Bitchin', huh? Is this live?"

Force always asks, "Is this live?" because he wants to be careful not to use any profanity. Off-color remarks might cause his interview to be censored and prevent the names of his sponsors from being broadcast. No matter how spectacular the wreckage he has just emerged from, Force mentions his sponsors, which is more self-possession than most people could summon after wrecking a car. Occasionally, the crash that Force has survived has been so unnerving to witness that the cameramen and the reporters are shaken. Force says, "Is this live?" and they think he is saying, "Am I alive?" Weeping, they shout, "Yes, yes, you're alive! You're alive!" This is aggravating to Force, who just wants to mention his sponsors and get shed of the interview so he can find out what went wrong with his car.

Force races from February to November. As a rule, he flies to California every other week on Monday, spends Tuesday and Wednesday with his family and attending to business at his shop, and on Thursday he flies to the next race. He has his headquarters in a flat-roofed two-story concrete building the size of a small factory. It used to be a Japanese-car dealership. He calls it "my little concrete chateau." On display in the showroom are two funny cars that he no longer drives, a Dodge Viper, a Harley-Davidson, and several dozen trophies. Force refers to the showroom as the museum. The Viper and the motorcycle have hardly any miles on them. "They don't go nowhere," Walker says. "He don't have the time." Force figures that they might as well be on display. The showroom is not open to his fans, but several times a day cars slowly circle the parking lot, and people stop and peer through the smoky windows at the drowsy interior.

Force has twenty-eight employees. When the phone rings, it is answered, "Force Racing." In the bays where the dealer serviced cars, Force has his shop. Adria, his eldest daughter, works in an office behind the showroom, and Walker has an office upstairs. Force has an office next to the showroom floor. He has a big black leather chair and a black lacquered desk with two tiers of round slots on either end. The design was his own idea. Contracts and mail that require his attention are put in the slots on the left, and when he has disposed of them he transfers them to the slots on the right. The desk is on a raised platform. Force sits at the elevation of a judge. One day not long ago Walker put papers in front of Force and asked him to approve publicity photographs and the designs for a new jacket with Force's name on it. Then Walker handed him a contract. While he read it, his lips moved.

"What does 'fruition' mean?" he asked.

"Going to happen," Walker said. "Like fruit in the trees."

"Let me put the words in here," Force said, picking up a pen. "It's. Going. To. Happen."

Walker showed Force a list of the cars that Force has driven over the years, taken from the Internet. The list needed to be corrected. While reading it, Force asked about a young man who had been interviewed for a job.

"You going to hire him?"

"Thinking of it."

"Careful hiring a guy that big and strong that can kick your butt in the parking lot if you fire him," Force said.

Walker handed him a list of appearances scheduled by the public relations firm that represents him, and Force, feeling that he already had a sufficient number of distractions from racing, reluctantly agreed to them. To me, Walker said, "He can't say no. There's so many times he was starving, he thinks it's like a dream, and it can all go away."

Force put the list in a slot on the right-hand side of his desk. "Someday I'm going to jump the Grand Canyon in my funny car," he said. "I don't know why — some sponsor'll suggest it, and it'll be all that's left, the last thing to do. We will have made all kinds of preparations, built a ramp, everyone will be there, helicopters, I'll be all ready to go, big burnout, then we'll launch it, and just about the time the thing's falling two feet short of the other side, I'm going to be thinking, This was a bad promotion."

I asked Walker how he thought Force would be regarded after he retires.

"As a guy that tried and tried and failed for years and years and years and years and never give up on himself," he said.

"Where do we go from here?" Force asked.

"Into the history books," Walker said.

Force raised his eyebrows.

"There's no question in my mind," Walker said. "He'll be the most famous man in drag racing."

Force said, "Then everyone will ask, 'Why did he jump the Grand Canyon?'"

One day, I got to Force's shop before he did. He arrived with a briefcase and coffee in a Styrofoam cup. He was wearing a polo shirt, jeans, and high-top sneakers. He wears basketball sneakers, he says, so that his polio ankle doesn't cave in, and it annoys him that people often ask why he dresses like a teenager. As he came through the door, he said that he had some business to attend to, "and then I'm going to lie down and sleep for two days."

After Force spoke with Walker, Force and I drove in his new Lincoln, a lagniappe from Ford, one of his sponsors, to meet some members of the local government so that he could describe the plans he has for his property (a quick-lube center, a doughnut shop, maybe Johnny's 300 MPH Diner, a waterfall, multiple pennants). He wanted to see if there was any opposition, and there wasn't. Then we went to Krystal Koach, a limousine builder, so that Force could buy a limousine to take him to the airport and to ride in when he wants to go to restaurants and drink beer with sponsors. The Lincoln had a phone system that responded to a user's voice, but it hadn't been programmed yet to recognize Force's voice. He tried it anyway.

"This is John," he said.

"Name, please," said the system.

"It's me," Force said.

"Repeat, please."

"John Force, funny-car champ."

"Once more."

"Don't you follow drag racing?"

"Name not recognized."

"You don't know me," Force said, "but you will," and dialed his office. He was buying a gold watch for Austin Coil, his crew chief, to commemorate their years together. Adria answered. He asked if the jeweler had delivered the watch, and Adria said he had. Then she put Coil on, and he said he'd seen the watch and liked it. "Is it the one you want?" Force asked. "I never said I wanted it to begin with," Coil replied, "but it's a beautiful watch." Force said then that his arm was bothering him. The week before, in Dallas, he had crossed the finish line first and put out his parachutes. Behind him, the other driver crashed into the guardrail and was knocked unconscious. His car kept going and hit Force's car and drove it into the guardrail, too. Force never saw him coming; funny cars don't have rearview mirrors. He wasn't badly hurt, but he was knocked out briefly and he bruised his arm, and now, he said, it was tingling. "Where?" asked Coil. "Shoulder," Force said. "Those are bad symptoms," Coil said. "You better get a doctor to take a look at you." Force said he would. "And if you think you're going to die," Coil said, "pay for the watch before you tip over."

"Listen how they talk to me," Force said, hanging up.

Then he said, "First thought I had when I hit that wall in Dallas was: My eyesight come back."

"Eyesight?"

"I hit my head last year," he said, "and afterward I couldn't read my checkbook. When I crashed in Dallas, my vision got better like you snap your fingers."

When we got to Krystal, we walked around the showroom and into the factory with John Beck, Krystal's vice president, then out into the white California sun to the parking lot, to look at some cars that were waiting to be delivered.

Force opened the door of a white Lincoln, stooped and put his head in, then stepped back. "I don't really need the little starry lights on the ceiling," he said.

"Fiber optics," Beck said. "That's an option."

Force opened the back door of a longer white Lincoln and got in, and Beck and I got in with him. "Could we build a seat in the middle that spins?" he asked.

"A fishing seat," Beck said. "Problem is the seat belt law."

Force decided to bring the limousine back to the concrete chateau and park it in the museum so that he could see what it looked like beside his other rolling stock. He drove and I sat in the back. Maneuvering the big, lumbering car seemed to amuse him. He found a country music station on the radio. He raised and lowered the window between the cab and the front seat. He started to sing. I remembered his telling me that for nearly the first ten years of his career, he would finish a day's racing, then stay up all night driving the truck that hauled his cars from one track to another. As a child, Adria had sometimes gone with him. In the dark, on the long straight roads through the Texas Panhandle, he once sat her on his lap and put her hands on the wheel, and told her to tell him when a curve was coming up. Then he leaned his head back and shut his eyes and went to sleep.

At a stoplight, a woman in the next lane looked over at him. Her look was opaque. She might have thought he was attractive; she might have thought he was a car thief. The windows between them were open. He turned toward her and shouted, "Just give me forty acres and a mule." She blanched. The light changed, and her car sped off, without her knowing, of course, that she had just decisively disposed of the world champion funny-car racer.

I asked what he had in mind for the future, and he said that he intends to race hard for ten more years and accumulate enough money to ensure that his family will be safe from ruin if something happens to him. He said that a newspaper columnist once wrote that he had a death wish, and the judgment bothered him. Force said that when his father died of cancer, he had been with him in the hospital and had held his hand.

"Losing a parent — you fear it all your life," Force said. "I always thought about death as a big black hearse limousine coming for you, and I was afraid of it. My father left his body to the UCLA Medical Center, in case they could learn anything from it, and we notified them, and about an hour after he died, they showed up in a cocoa-brown Chevy Malibu. A guy stepped out and said, 'How are you doing?' But this is about how your whole life you're wrong. A brown Malibu come to pick up my dad, and all my life I thought it would be a black hearse. Anyway, the point is . . . What's the point? What are we talking about?"

"Your death wish."

"I got a death wish? I don't think so. I got a wish to race cars to the very end. The day they tell me I'm too blind to see, I'll go to the dirt tracks where they'll take me with no license."

I asked if he ever thought about the turn his life might have taken if he had passed the inkblot test and become a policeman.

"Not really," he said.

"Other than the helmet, what was the attraction?"

"Saving people," he said. "But I'm too emotional. I had a temper, and I would fight a lot. I'm very motivated to make things happen now."

"Doesn't really seem like you, anyway," I said.

"Policeman?"

I nodded.

"Wasn't," he said. A Travis Tritt song began to play on the radio. Tritt and Force are friends, and Force appears as himself in one of Tritt's videos. Force turned up the volume. "I wish I was a singer," he said. "I got no voice, though. I just kill a tune. I was on the stage with Travis one time and they didn't even let me hum."

He seemed bruised. For a moment, he simply listened to the song. Then he shrugged. "Ah, well, it don't matter anyway," he said. "The thing of it is, I'm perfect as a race car driver."

(1997)

Spy

I F JIM DUNNE were a figure in a certain sort of fiction, he would
have an office in a neighborhood of pawnshops and stores selling
rebuilt and secondhand car parts. A stairway (not an elevator)
would take you to his place — this is not a street-level activity he's engaged in. At the end of a dimly lit hallway would be a door with a panel
of frosted glass, and on the glass would be written JIM DUNNE, C.S.P.

Dunne takes photographs of cars that are two or three years from being brought to the market and in the meantime are being kept hidden.
He will not say where he finds them. I asked him once where he had
taken a photograph of a car that had snow on it. We were in a restaurant. He said, "Canada." I said, "Yeah, but where?" and he started tap-
ping the fingers of his right hand on the table and said, "Northern Canada." I said, "I know, but I mean, where?" He picked up his fork,
examined it, put it back beside his plate, looked across the room, and
said, "There's a road up there that crosses the country east to west, and
there's civilization along it for about half a mile on either side. Why
don't we talk about something else."

Some of the cars in Dunne's photographs are being developed for the
future, and some are cars already for sale — the new Mustang, say — to
which changes are being made. The manufacturers call the cars prototypes. They are assembled mainly in small shops around Detroit; there
may be only a few in existence; each may have cost several hundred
thousand dollars; and all are dismantled after undergoing a series of
tests. Dunne's pictures of them appear each month in *Popular Mechanics;* they illustrate his column, Detroit Spy Report. Dunne will not
trespass to take a picture, and he does not wear any disguise more com-

plicated than a hat, but he works surreptitiously. Often, the first time an automaker knows that a picture has been taken of his years-in-the-making, totally sequestered, if-this-works-we-all-become-millionaires car is when he sees it in Dunne's column.

Dunne is sixty-six. In a hotel lobby, he is likely to pick up a newspaper and peer around the edge of it at the rest of the room. He is about five foot ten, with narrow, sloping shoulders, big forearms, and thick hands. The expression on his face is solemn, slack, and opaque, and it hardly ever changes. It is as if as a younger man he had tried out a variety of expressions and settled on this one. He has chalky blue eyes and hair that is short, white, and as thin as string on top. In moments of abstraction, he sometimes runs a palm across the top of his head. He does this so deliberately that it looks like a mannerism from the kind of Japanese theater in which an actor takes fifteen minutes to rise from a seat on the floor. It is the slowest gesture I have ever seen anyone perform. Once, I stepped on an escalator as his hand began crossing his pate, and I rode to the top before it reached the far side.

Dunne is divorced. He has two grown sons and five grown daughters, and he lives by himself in a brick house with a yard, in a suburb of Detroit. He keeps the house very clean. There are more rooms than he can use, and there is a composed and orderly feeling of solitude to the place, as if no one had been in any of the rooms for a while. In the basement is a television with a chair in front of it.

For a week each fall, Dunne takes a cottage on Cape Cod, and every day he goes bluefishing. His manner is genial but reserved. He falls into conversation easily with waitresses and barmaids. As an icebreaker, he offers to read their palms. I spent a day with him once in Detroit, and we had lunch in a Polish bar. I got up to go to the bathroom, and when I came back the barmaid was in my seat. Her palm was in Dunne's hand and he was saying, "You're too focused. People ever tell you that?" "All the time," she said. "What are you so focused on?" he asked. "I just wish I knew," she said.

Dunne invented the occupation of car-spy photographer about thirty years ago, when he was writing about cars for *Popular Science*. He had beforehand been in the army, then attended the University of Detroit, then been a parts runner for a secondhand-car lot, then sold construction equipment, then become a writer at a trade magazine called *Auto-*

motive Industries. He realized that if he waited for the press conferences the automobile manufacturers held to announce new cars and used the photographs they gave him, the cars would already be on the market by the time he was able to publish the pictures. He borrowed a camera from his sister-in-law and managed to take pictures of the styling changes being made to the 1966 Corvair. His editor published the pictures without saying anything about them. Dunne wrote the editor that he had hoped for a response, and the editor wrote back, "The pictures were electrifying. Get more."

Perhaps two or three other people in America devote themselves to taking car-spy pictures. In addition, there is a small collection of people who every once in a while see something peculiar and happen to have a camera with them. A classic shot of this kind is of a sporty future car by the side of the road, with a highway patrolman next to it, writing a ticket. Sometimes these photographers send the picture to Dunne and ask him to sell it for them. Dunne refers to them as one-timers. He gets a few hundred dollars for most pictures, but every so often he gets a great shot of something desirable and it ends up on the cover of a car-buff magazine such as *Road & Track* or *Car and Driver.* This happened, for example, in 1981, when Dunne was the first to photograph the 1984 Corvette and sold the photo to *Car and Driver.* Dunne tells people that the check went a long way toward paying a year's tuition at the University of Michigan for one of his daughters.

Dunne isn't really interested in photography. He considers himself a writer. He believes a photograph is what the people who invented photography thought it was: a factual document. A Dunne photograph is the final step in an elaborate engagement with the automobile industry. A car is proposed, models are made, prototypes are built and secretly tested, then someone slips up and Dunne gets a picture. The photograph is proof of his having overcome the obstacles that the carmakers put in his way.

A typical Dunne photograph is of a car by itself with a snowbank or a guardrail or a piece of pavement behind it. The car is not always in focus. Dunne may be the highest-paid photographer in America who isn't good at focusing his camera. Often he can get no closer to the car than a few hundred yards, so the texture of many of his photographs is grainy. Obstacles sometimes intervene. A faint gray crosshatching occasionally appears in the foreground, and this is the chainlink fence that Dunne took the photograph through. Dunne's manner of working is sometimes described as grab shooting. Grab shooting involves taking a picture of a car from the roadside or from another car. One or both of the cars might be moving. Dunne's favorite grab-shooting maneuver is the billiard shot, which requires two moving cars and, for fun, some traffic. Driving with one hand, Dunne trains the lens on the image of the car in his side-view mirror. Speed blurs the background, which he likes because then no one can tell where the picture was taken.

People often think that Dunne has confidants at the carmakers who tell him where a car will be at a certain time and that this is how he gets his pictures. This is not the case. Dunne is simply methodical. He goes where he believes the cars will be and by means of persistence finally crosses paths with one. In years past, he would trespass on the carmakers' premises, but he has reformed and now considers the suggestion that he would trespass in order to take a picture an insult to his resourcefulness and integrity.

"Number one," he says, "I don't have to do that; number two, it's like going into someone's house when you're not invited; and number three, it's against the law. Well, maybe number one, it's against the law."

Dunne will not sell his photographs to a carmaker. When one calls asking for a picture of a rival's car, Dunne tells him where the picture was published. Sometimes the carmakers enlarge their competitors' pictures and put them up on the walls in their war rooms.

Dunne's favorite professional maxim is "Never tell a lie," by which he does not mean "Always tell the truth." Dunne is proficient at isolating a facet of the truth and guilelessly presenting it as a full confession. I once listened to him talking on the phone to someone at a Volkswagen factory. He had called to find out the location of a secret testing facility. At the end of a silence during which I assume he was asked why he wanted the address, I heard him say, "I need to know for my job."

Twenty years ago and more, Dunne used occasionally to trespass on the carmakers' premises. He says that he hated doing it and that anxiety over being caught made him so nervous he couldn't sleep for nights beforehand. He never tried to conceal his appearance, but he used props. "Nowadays, people walk around with nametags, and you have coded door locks, and it's impossible to get in anyway," he says. "But back then, all you needed was a white dress shirt with the sleeves rolled up, a tie, some dress pants and dress shoes, a plastic penholder in your shirt pocket, and a clipboard."

In the early seventies, Dunne worked often with Jerry Flint, a columnist at *Forbes* who was Detroit bureau chief for the *New York Times* from 1967 to 1973. In bowling alleys, Flint met people who worked in the car business, and from one of them he learned the route to the secret research facility at the Chrysler factory. "Dunne and I would go in around lunchtime," Flint says, "and Dunne would have his camera under his coat. We got the clipboard, the sleeves rolled up, we're talking to each other, and past the guard you go. To get to the secret plant, you went through the factory and the rail yards next to it. You came to a door and opened it and there you were. We'd been several times before and had got great pictures — I'd block and Dunne would shoot. I mean, I'd stand so that someone couldn't see him, and he'd take his picture. I suppose we should've figured out that Chrysler would see the photographs and sooner or later guess what was up, but we didn't, and so one day we're in the secret plant and we go through the door and bang, we're surrounded by six guys. Everyone had a badge. We didn't have a badge. It's embarrassing, and, more than that, I'm thinking, I'll lose my job. I mean, when they hire you at the *Times,* they tell you to get the story but they don't tell you to go into someone's factory and take pictures of their secret designs. So this is it, there goes the job. It's really only a formality now. And maybe there's jail involved, too. One of the six guys looks at me and says, 'Who are you?' My feet are stuck in place and I can't move my jaws. Without a second's hesitation, though, Dunne looks right at them and says, 'We're from publications.' I turn and look at him, and he says, 'Downtown.' Which was true! We both had our offices downtown in those days! And you could see these guys look at our clipboards and sleeves rolled up and Dunne's poker face, then look at each other and relax, and one of them says, 'Well, jeez, publications, you guys should have your badges, because we've been having a lot of trouble here with people getting in and taking pictures.'"

Over the years, a reliable place for Dunne to take a picture has been from the top of a hill overlooking a straightaway inside the General Motors Proving Ground in Milford, Michigan. In various circles in Detroit, this hill is known as Dunne's Hill. About fifteen years ago, General

Motors planted sixty tall fir trees to conceal a few test tracks that could be seen from the top of the hill, and these trees are known as Dunne's Grove.

A car being tested is the kind most likely to end up in Dunne's column. Ford, Chrysler, and General Motors perform the bulk of their tests on their proving grounds in Michigan, but some tests involve extremes of climate that they haven't got the capacity to produce. The engineers want to know, for example, if their car will start after being cold-soaked — that is, after being left out all night at, say, twenty-five below zero — or if the air conditioning will work in the desert in August if the car has been running for an hour. As a rule, the companies go south in the summer and north in the winter. They carry their cars aboard trucks that look like moving vans and have phrases such as SPE-CIALIZED AUTOMOTIVE TRANSPORT written on the side of them. All three companies have proving grounds in Arizona, but to drive their cars any distance, they have to use roads outside their gates.

To prevent someone like Dunne from getting photographs of their cars, automakers surround their test tracks with chainlink fences, high walls, courses of trees, and flowering hedges. They drape their cars with cloths. They conceal details such as the door handles with tape. They paint half of a car black and half of it white to make it difficult for a photographer to settle on an exposure. They build false trunks and fenders from fiberglass. They stretch a strip of vinyl, called a bra, across the headlights and grille or one called a diaper across the taillights. Dunne describes a car with an excessively altered appearance as "dirty." Sometimes he gives a photograph of a dirty car to an artist he knows, who removes the bra and diaper and adds details that he believes resemble the ones the company is hiding.

Sometimes Dunne is able to find a vantage from beside the company's fence, but the company's security patrols often run him off before anything valuable shows up. Dunne has partly solved this difficulty by buying property adjacent to the Chrysler proving ground in Wittmann, Arizona. He noticed the property because the chainlink fence that runs for miles along one side of the proving ground doglegs around a rectangular patch of desert about four hundred feet wide and a thousand feet deep. An access road leading to the proving ground's track runs within about twenty feet of the far end of the fence, and Dunne had occasionally taken pictures through the fence. He called a real estate agent whose name appeared on a sign saying ACREAGE FOR SALE that was stuck in the ground nearby. He faxed the agent a drawing, and the agent said that the land belonged to Chrysler. Dunne said he didn't think so. The agent discovered that the land was part of an estate sale. Two days after Dunne bought it, someone from Chrysler called the agent. *Automotive News,* a trade periodical, ran a story about Dunne's buying the property. The reporter quoted Dunne as saying about the people from Chrysler, "I'm going to get me some boots and a hat, and when they come round, I'll just say, 'Howdy, neighbor.'"

When Dunne goes to the desert, he usually stays for two days. What he wants to see is there, or it isn't. I went to the desert with him not long ago. We drove from Phoenix to Beatty, Nevada, about 375 miles along roads where Dunne knows that engineers test cars. On the morning of the day that Dunne arrived in Phoenix, he had had laser surgery on his nose and there were scores of small circular hemorrhages the color of eggplant on it. The hemorrhages were painless but they looked strange.

We had breakfast at a café near Chloride, Arizona, and then sat in the shade of an abandoned motel and watched cars leaving the Chrysler proving ground. They came out at intervals of about one a minute and took the ramp onto the interstate. All of them were painted black and white, and all of them had bras or diapers or both. Some were towing trailers. On the front doors of each was written, in black letters on a yellow background, MAKE SURE YOU HAVE THE CORRECT VEHICLE. The cars were too disguised to be useful to Dunne. He doesn't take a photograph of anything that he isn't pretty sure he can print. If the driver tells the engineers he's around, they don't send out any more cars.

We saw tails of dust rising from the desert at the foot of some hills several miles away — cars on the dirt oval in the proving ground, Dunne said — so we left the paved road and drove down a two-wheel track through the desert, then parked. Dunne put a cap on and carried his camera in a small duffle. We scared up a jackrabbit and stopped to see if any creature was living in a collection of sticks and mesquite branches that looked like a little tepee. The heat was so forceful that I felt as if the sky were shouting at me. I followed Dunne toward the top of a rise. As we got closer he said, "This will tell the story when we get up there." When he got there he said, "Nope," and kept walking, and when I got there all I could see was the next rise, about a hundred yards away.

There was a constant dry wind. Dunne kept stopping to remove burrs from his socks. As he did, he said, "We're almost there." When I stopped to write on my notepad, insects with wings like crinoline lit on the paper, then were blown off by the wind. The heat warmed the water in the bottle that I carried in my hand. Crossing a shallow gully, Dunne put up birds whose wingbeats were so fast they sounded like shuffling cards. From a book I had seen at the airport in Phoenix I knew that there were scorpions and rattlesnakes all through the territory, and it made me nervous that I couldn't see any. I felt that every place I looked for them was two or three inches to the left or right of where I would have known to look if I had grown up around there. Standing atop the next ridge, we could see the far turn in the track and the fence around it and the hills like pyramids in the distance, but there was no more dust. The wind made a noise like the wash from a fan. We walked back to the car, scuffing pebbles along the dry bed of a creek. A bird with a call that sounded like a zipper followed us, landing in the branches of one mesquite tree after another. "I don't know if it's my imagination," Dunne said, "but people treat me nicer with this nose."

North of Las Vegas, we left the highway for a dirt road that had looked on the map like a shortcut to Death Valley. We ended up driving in the desert longer than we expected to, so when we came to a whorehouse with a sign on the door that said, COME ON IN, THE PARTY'S INSIDE, we stopped for directions. A stocky middle-aged woman stood behind the bar. Dunne said, "We're lost," and she said, "You ain't lost, sugar, you're right at home!" It was early in the afternoon. A thin old man with skin like dry saddle leather was sitting at the bar, and in the center of the room a dark-haired, thick-waisted woman wearing shorts and a halter top was standing on a chair, hanging party decorations from the light fixture in the ceiling. Dunne said, "When's the party?" and she said, "Seven-thirty." The old man nodded and said, "That's a fact." Then the woman at the bar told us to stay on the road we were on until we came to the blacktop and then turn left.

In Death Valley, Dunne drove through the parking lot at Zabriskie Point to see if any prototypes were cooling down, but none were. He said that the long, sulfurous ridges of rock reminded him of loaves of bread. We drove down to the floor of the valley, and I got out of the car to see what it was like. I felt as if I were standing under a waterfall of heat. I got back in the car and into the air conditioning, which made the skin on my arms and face tingle as if I had been slapped. Dunne drove through the parking lot of the hotel and general store in Furnace Creek. He saw some people standing around a car at the far end of the lot and said, "This might be something," but it turned out to be a family unloading its luggage. In Stovepipe Wells, the next town north, we stopped for water. Dunne saw a brand-new BMW in front of the general store and said, "Whew, finally!" All of the car's windows were open, which I guess meant that the driver wasn't allowed to use the air conditioning. He was wearing a short-sleeved shirt, shorts, socks, and lace-up shoes, and he was sitting with the door open and his feet on the pavement. He was a little heavy and his face was red. On the seat next to him was a computer, about the size of a case of liquor, attached to some wires and tubes running under the dashboard. I asked if this was a new car he was testing, and he said, "Yah, ve testing."

"You brought the car over from Germany?"

"Yah."

I asked what kind of test he was doing, and he said, "Ve cool it down ten minutes, then ve go again." I asked what happened to the car when they were finished in Death Valley, and he said, "Ve put it on an airplane and take it to Finland, then ve test again." Then he wouldn't answer any more questions. We got in our car and left. Dunne said, "Damn, he's going to remember this nose."

That night, we stayed in Beatty, Nevada, across Daylight Pass from Death Valley. We tried to get rooms at the Stagecoach Hotel & Casino, the Exchange Club Motel, and the Burro Inn, which Dunne said was the best place in town, but they were full. We ended up in a motel called the El Portal, where we had to pay in advance and where the picture on my television worked but the sound didn't. Every second or third car in Beatty was a BMW, and there were German engineers standing around them with their hands in the pockets of their shorts. Their faces and shins were sunburned. It was as if the town were a famous destination for male German tourists. I saw the engineer we had seen in Stovepipe Wells step from a car outside a room at a motel and take off his shirt. His arms were red and his stomach was white. We had dinner early, we drank beer, and I played a slot machine; then we agreed to get up at five-thirty and make a pass through Stovepipe Wells and Furnace Creek on the way back to the airport in Las Vegas.

The next morning, we counted seventeen cars in the parking lot of the Exchange Club Motel, thirteen of which were BMWs. Some had shrouds spread across their dashboards, some had computers in the front seats, and some had jugs of water in the backseats to approximate the weight of passengers. The jugs had seat belts around them. Each car had a number discreetly painted in white on the back of the side-view mirror, which made me think of the signs at the Chrysler proving ground that said, MAKE SURE YOU HAVE THE CORRECT VEHICLE. Dunne stopped behind one of the BMWs and said, "Is that gas cap smaller? It's closer to the front than the others. Those taillights are different, they're blacked out. They're blacked out! We've got a new car!"

He took a baseball cap from his camera bag and walked toward the car with the cap over his camera so that he looked like a man concealing a gun. I held back the branches of a bush in front of the car and Dunne took a picture. Then he looked to his left and suddenly started walking fast back toward our car. "Someone's at the window," he said. "I saw the curtain move." I stared at the curtain but didn't see it move. When we got back in the car, Dunne clapped his hands and said, "Oh, that was sweet."

We stopped outside town and watched a truck watering the roads of the Bullfrog Mine; then we drove over Daylight Pass and pulled into the gravel lot of a low, flat-roofed, shacky-looking motel in Stovepipe Wells. Dunne stopped the car beside a young man in shorts and a T-shirt and sandals who was lifting a suitcase for a very attractive young brown-haired woman and loading it into the trunk of a small foreign car. An older man was standing next to them, and beside him on the gravel was a camera bag.

"Car spies," Dunne said.

"Sorry?"

"See the camera bag?"

It looked to me like the camera bag of someone who believed that the more equipment he owned, the better his pictures would be.

"I'm going to ask them some questions," Dunne said. He rolled down the window. "Where's the best place to get a shot of scenery around here?" he said.

The young man said, *"Pardone?"*

Dunne said, *"Italiano?"* The man grinned.

Dunne said, *"Roma?"*

"Pisa," said the young man. He said that he worked in a bank and that the best place for pictures, according to his guidebook, was Zabris-kie Point. He was telling Dunne how to get there when Dunne abruptly said, "All right, thanks," and rolled up the window. Then he said, "Damn, I should have said Hans Lehmann" — the name of a man who has a car-spy agency in Europe — "and waited for the reaction."

Dunne drove around to the back of the motel, where there were two Volkswagens with bundles of wires running from their engines, across the parking lot, and through a window into one of the rooms. The cur-tains in the window were drawn. We got out and were careful not to scuff the gravel, and Dunne got down low and took a few pictures look-ing up into the headlights. Then we got back into the car and drove to Las Vegas.

On the way, we passed a place in the desert where Dunne had once taken a photograph of the same Corvette that appeared on the cover of *Car and Driver*. General Motors was changing the body of the Corvette for the first time in fifteen years, and the editor of the magazine had told Dunne he would kill to have a picture of the new car. Dunne found one in Death Valley. Each day, it would leave the garage with a pair of chase cars carrying parts in case the Corvette broke down, and they would go so fast that Dunne couldn't catch them. He didn't want to hang around the garage, because the engineers might see him and not bring out the car at all. He recalled a small airport north of Las Vegas offering sightseeing rides. At the airport, they had a helicopter. Dunne explained to the pilot what he wanted to do.

Early the next morning, Dunne and the pilot flew over to Death Val-ley, and when the Corvette arrived they drew several miles ahead of it and landed beside the road. "We were blowing up all kinds of dust," Dunne said. The Corvette appeared and the driver pulled over and got out to look at the helicopter. Dunne jumped out. The driver saw him and ran for the car. He had left the door open, which wasn't the shot Dunne wanted. When he got in and closed it, Dunne took the picture.

(1997)

One Green Dog

YOU COULD SAY that the Grateful Dead was a willful, remorseless, evanescent and arcane, infidel, raucous, and occasionally clumsy inside joke, and you got it or you didn't, but either way it's gone, one extravagant means of making noise in the world disappeared and no more easily replaced than Charlie Parker or Elvis or Bill Monroe or John Coltrane. No other luminary rock-and-roll band was as supple, as tribal, as ardent in pursuit of spontaneous invention, less shy of fumbling, as rarefied or complex in its musical and lyrical references, as deft at storytelling, less greedy, or more indifferent to the embrace of the popular culture. Everyone knows that the effort didn't always succeed. There were setbacks and fallow periods. The veneration surrounding the musicians was simple-minded and tedious. It reduced Jerry Garcia, an extravagantly gifted, haunted, and charismatic man, to something resembling a cartoon figure — Uncle Jerry, Captain Trips. Only the eleven members, four of them now deceased, know truly what being involved in the endeavor was like — it amounted to an intimate freemasonry — and how fragile it was.

Garcia died in 1995, and since then four of the band's members — Bob Weir, Phil Lesh, Mickey Hart, and Bill Kreutzmann — have toured occasionally as members of the Other Ones, which relies on the Grateful Dead's repertoire. In addition, Weir, the surviving guitarist, has toured assiduously to establish a following for Ratdog, a band that began as a collaboration between him and the bassist Rob Wasserman. Ratdog covers songs from Weir's solo career, songs from the catalog of rhythm and blues, and, at the insistence of promoters, a number of songs by the Grateful Dead. Weir was not keen to accommodate them

— he regarded it initially as living off the past — but on reflection he became aware that he "wasn't yet ready to give some of the material up." Ratdog travels by bus. Weir is one of the least spoiled men who ever enjoyed acclaim. He has never been pretentious about what restaurants he eats in or who makes his clothes or who cuts his hair or where he takes his vacations. He shed the opulence and prerogatives of rock-and-roll stardom as easily as someone sloughing off a coat. Ratdog plays at smaller halls and at lower volume than the Grateful Dead did. Weir's voice has been easier to hear and has become richer and more assured. For a few years he was the band's only guitarist, and the responsibility made his playing — always eccentric — more agile and inventive.

Weir was the youngest member of the Grateful Dead, and the others frequently treated him as if he were slower and less sophisticated than they were, as if he were a kid. For years the band engaged a sound engineer who didn't care to listen to Weir play guitar. The engineer reduced the volume of Weir's contribution until, at times, he was nearly inaudible. "I was definitely low man on the totem pole," Weir says, "especially at the beginning. And for a long time, I just had to shut up and take it." Of the reward in the next world for his tolerance of being the band's most put-upon member, he says, "Another star in my heavenly crown." Sue Swanson, who has known Weir since they were high school students and who attended the second rehearsal of the band that was to become the Grateful Dead — no one was allowed in to the first — says about him, "He's gracious and compassionate, and he's got a heart of gold. Being the kid whom everyone teased, he had to defend himself all the time, but he's matured a great deal, and I don't think he's going to play the fool anymore."

Weir is fifty. He used to look like a girl; now he looks like a rancher. As a young man, he was hollow-cheeked and wiry, but he has thickened slightly, his hair is shorter, and his slotlike mouth has turned down at the corners, so that if he's tired or distracted he looks grumpy. When he is engaged by the turn of a conversation, he listens with exceptional attentiveness. This heedfulness is perhaps the result of being dyslexic. His dyslexia is so severe, he says, that sometimes when he looks at trees on a hillside, they shift from one place to another. Throughout his childhood the condition went undiagnosed; he realized he had it about fifteen years ago, when he heard someone describing its symptoms. As a boy he assumed that everyone found reading as difficult as he did. What his classmates learned from books, he derived from what he heard. He listened carefully to his teachers so that he could repeat what they'd said, with sufficient elaboration to sound thoughtful. When a phrase struck him as notable, he retained it, especially if it was ornate.

The vigilance and fierce resolve required to absorb what he hears is also apparent in Weir's character, in the form of an exquisite antipathy toward authority. He avoided being drafted into the army by visiting his draft board dressed as Cochise, an Apache chief; also by having been arrested for possession of marijuana. He received his first draft notice shortly after the arrest. "With a shaky hand and a tearful eye," he says, "I had to write the draft board saying that until the matter was resolved and my innocence established, I was, regrettably, unable to serve." He was acquitted, drafted again, then arrested again. He wrote another letter, insisting on his innocence, and after that the draft board left him alone. Weir continued to correspond with the draft board, however, sending it bricks, stones, sticks, tree limbs, tree stumps, pieces of lumber, packets of gravel, masonry shards — "anything I could get into the mailbox," he says — under the impression that the draft board was obliged to retain any correspondence from a citizen.

By nature, Weir is skittish and balky and not easily drawn into conversation that is revealing. He usually says no more than is necessary, and his way of letting a person know that an exchange is at its end is to say less and less until he is mostly responding by answering Yes, No, or All right, as if the effort of speech had worn him out. A person who spends any time with him becomes aware that his attention has different degrees of acuteness and that sometimes he appears to withdraw himself altogether. It is as if he had been stunned. His friend John Barlow, who has known Weir since the two were classmates in high school and who has written the words to many of Weir's songs, says, "Bobby has a lot of internal weather. He gets cloud-bound." Weir's aloofness never seems arrogant, but there are periods of silence when the air seems rigid around him.

Weir's manner is considerate to the point of courtliness. Some years ago, a woman who was a friend of his from childhood became pregnant by a man she didn't intend to marry. Weir offered to marry her and pay to have the baby delivered in Switzerland so that the child could have a Swiss passport and avoid serving in the American military. Sue Swanson once threw water balloons from the roof of the house the Grateful Dead occupied in San Francisco during the late sixties; when the police arrived, Weir said that he had thrown them, and was arrested in her place.

Weir was not an accomplished musician when the Grateful Dead began, but he developed one of the most artful, unorthodox, and self-effacing styles of guitar playing in rock-and-roll. Its hallmarks are lyric asides and cunning contrapuntal remarks that suggest a line of melody traveling through the map of the chord changes. The patterns of his attack and the structure of his accompaniments have elements of orchestral music and of jazz, especially the left hand of a jazz pianist, especially the left hand of McCoy Tyner, who was a member of the John Coltrane Quartet. Thousands of people have played guitar in rock-and-roll bands, but no one else has thought that it might be played the way Weir has played it. Using a commonplace object with a specific tradition differently from how everyone else has used it is an indication of a singular mind.

Weir grew up a "silver-spoon kid," he says, in Atherton, a prosperous suburb south of San Francisco, near Palo Alto. He was the second of two boys adopted by Frederick and Eleanor Weir. His older brother, John, joined the army when Bob was sixteen. John is now a long-haul trucker and lives in the East Bay; Bob sees him only occasionally. Two years after the Weirs adopted Bob, they had a daughter, Wendy, an artist with whom Weir has written two children's books.

Frederick Weir was an engineer with his own firm in San Francisco. "My Dad went to Annapolis and came out at the beginning of the Second World War," Weir says. "From the time he left port on his first commission to the time he got back, he was seasick. They got him well and sent him off again, and this time the seasickness nearly killed him. I think he met my mom while he was recovering in the hospital in Seattle.

"I had a pretty regular growing up, I guess. When I was nine or ten, my parents decided that the richest child is poor without the gift of music, and bought a piano and gave us all lessons. I wanted to play the piano, but I hated 'The Bluebells of Scotland,' and, being dyslexic, I couldn't read the music anyway."

As a student, Weir was nomadic. He was suspended or removed or expelled from school on at least eight occasions — twice from elementary school, twice from junior high school, and four times from high school. "If there was a snowball fight or a prank happening somewhere," he says, "and you got to the bottom of it, I was probably there. I just couldn't help myself."

His parents sent him for his sophomore year to a boarding school in Colorado called Fountain Valley, where his roommate was John Barlow. "He was a strange, goofy kid," Barlow says. "He's not a troublemaker as much as he's just different from other people. He was definitely then, as now, marching to his own drummer, and it may not be a drummer at all."

Weir and Barlow once rolled the pages of three months of the *New York Times* into balls, which they tossed over the transom of a room belonging to a boy who was away for the weekend, and when the boy returned and opened his door, the paper flew toward him like shrapnel. Weir emptied a bucket of water on Barlow while he was sleeping under an electric blanket. The blanket delivered Barlow a stunning shock. (Weir: "I didn't know it was an electric blanket.") They dressed as cowboys and chased each other up and down the halls with cap pistols. Years later, an airline banned the Grateful Dead after Weir fired a cap pistol in the vicinity of a ticket agent; among the other musicians he was known as Mr. Bob Weir Trouble. Barlow recalls that Weir liked to play guitar in the tiled showers for the echoing resonance. His one other passion was football. "I developed a mean streak," Weir says. "I just loved to play. I was flipped out about football."

At the end of the year, Fountain Valley gave Weir what he calls "the old toe" — that is, they informed the Weirs and the Barlows that one or the other of their sons could return, but not both. Barlow went back. "The difference between you and Mr. Weir," Barlow says the school told him, "is that you know right from wrong, and we're not sure that he does."

Barlow is descended from a family that settled in Wyoming during the nineteenth century. The summer after Weir went to Fountain Valley, he left home without telling his parents and got a job as a hand on the Bar Cross Ranch, which belonged to Barlow's mother and father. Barlow spent part of the summer at the ranch and the rest of it at summer school. Weir rode on a roundup, mended fences, put up the hay crop, and lived in the bunkhouse with the cowboys. Barlow's father noted that Weir did poorly with repetitive work, so he assigned him what Barlow says is the "most random task in the hayfield: scatter raking." Scatter raking required Weir to drive a tractor hauling a rake. The rake collected whatever hay the harvester had missed. When the rake was full, Weir was to dump the hay in front of a piece of machinery called a hay sweep, which carried the pile to the haystack. Barlow describes his father as an employer of last resort and says that decades of superintending ranch hands — that is, misfits and drunkards and solitaries — had accustomed him to eccentric and unpredictable behavior. Even so, Weir struck him as an exotic. He frequently found the tractor that Weir had been driving stuck between trees in a windrow or spinning its wheels in a ditch. The explanation was likely to be that Weir had seen an old rusted tool in the grass and had abandoned the tractor to examine it, or perhaps had jumped off to follow the progress of an eagle pursuing a field rat. The tractor had simply kept going.

"My father's diaries for the period are pretty funny," Barlow says. "He liked Bobby — it was almost impossible not to — he just didn't know what to make of him."

At the end of the summer, Weir returned to his room at his parents' house. He enrolled for his junior year at the only school that never kicked him out, Pacific High School, "a school for arty types," Weir says.

On the New Year's Eve of 1964, Weir and a friend were walking around Palo Alto when they passed the music store where Weir gave guitar lessons, mostly to high school girls, and heard someone playing a banjo. Weir knocked on the door, which was opened by Jerry Garcia, who was waiting for a student. Weir reminded him what night it was. The two of them picked the lock on the door to the room where the instruments were kept and played for several hours. As they were leaving, Weir says, "Garcia suggested that we had enough half-talent to form a jug band."

At first, Weir's mother would drive him to the music store — he didn't have a license — so that he could rehearse with Garcia. I asked Weir if, after school, he used to bring home Garcia, who was five years older than he was and living in a car. "A few times," he said. I asked what his mother and father made of Garcia, and he thought for a moment and said, "They would have preferred me hanging out with kids my own age."

Weir's parents felt that Pacific High was too permissive, so they enrolled him in Menlo Atherton High School, which kicked him out. When the suggestion of military school arose, Weir says, "I made it plain that if they ever wanted to see me again, they could give that up." His parents arranged a place for him next at the Drew School, in San Francisco, which Weir described as "a private school for well-heeled little maniacs at the end of the line."

Weir's attendance at Drew was episodic. "I would work with the band until closing time, at two," he says, "then get up in the morning at six to ride the train to school, and, needless to say, I missed a few classes." His schooling nearly ended altogether when the band was playing at a club near San Francisco, and a guy from Salt Lake City approached them with an offer to work as the house band at a bar in Utah. The offer, though, fell through. Wendy, Weir's sister, says that by now Weir was often staying out all night. "He would have dinner with my other brother and my parents and me," she says, "then go out, and we'd see him again when he came home in the morning as we were having breakfast. Finally our mother said, 'This is not the way our family operates. If you're going to keep this up, you'll have to move out on your own.' And he did."

During 1966 and 1967 — that is, when Weir was nineteen and twenty — the Grateful Dead occupied a converted rooming house at 710 Ashbury Street, in San Francisco. For a while, Weir's roommate was Neal Cassady, who had been the model, ten years earlier, for Jack Kerouac's character Dean Moriarty in *On the Road*. Cassady loved to drive around the city, and sometimes Weir would accompany him. "He'd go fifty-five or sixty miles an hour without ever stopping for a red light or a stop sign," Weir says. "One hand would be on the wheel and the other on his girlfriend beside him, and at the same time he had a way of punching the buttons on the radio so that the voices would appear to be having a conversation with each person in the car.

"He was about five feet eleven and a little wiry; he had a look that was something like a young Paul Newman, a Denver cowboy type," Weir says. "There were a few minutes during each day when he was more or less human, and then, as the day progressed, he would get more and more revved up, and by the end of the day or the evening or well into the night, he would be carrying on conversations with two or three people at a time. Some of what he said was kind of crazy sounding: he used to tell people that he was having to pay back in this life for indiscretions he'd committed as the Al Capone of Mars. He usually spoke in rhymes. I can't remember anything of it — it all went by so fast — but he used to come to our rehearsals and kind of rap along with us, and some of it might have been incorporated into lyrics. I had read *On the Road* as a teenager and it had hardened my resolve to be done with any other form of respectable life. I don't want to say that he was a saint, because that's not what he was, but being close to him was like being close to the sun. He looked like God to me."

Weir's bed was briefly a couch in the living room. The paper bag he kept at the foot of the couch contained nearly all his possessions. From time to time, his parents would visit, usually on Sunday afternoons, and ask if he wanted to come home.

Weir lives north of San Francisco, in a house in the hills he bought twenty-five years ago with money he inherited from his parents. The house is made mainly of redwood and cedar. It is built into the side of a steep hill and looms above the road that goes past it. Through windows in the living room, you look into the branches of trees. Beyond the trees are a valley and more hills, and in the distance are grass-covered hills that rise like waves: the Marin headlands. Above his garage Weir has a recording studio, where he has worked on his own records and where the Grateful Dead occasionally recorded — the neighbors complained about the noise.

Briefly, Weir and Garcia owned a house a few blocks from where I live in New York. Shortly before Garcia died, a For Sale sign was hung by the front door. A while ago I noticed that it had come down. I asked Weir if he had sold the house. We were sitting on a deck by his front door. It was a hot day, and a carpenter was banging nails at a house across the road.

"Yeah, it's history," he said. He had told me once that he and Garcia bought the house with the intention of using it together. I asked whether this had been part of a strategy to separate Garcia from the people in California who supplied him with heroin, and Weir said, "No, we were going to hang and have some fun. We rebuilt the penthouse as a sort of bachelor's duplex because we were both solo at the time. He was in good shape. It was when he was having his show on Broadway, around Thanksgiving of '87, and I was in New York for some reason. We were talking and I said, 'I could spend some time here,' and he said he could, too, and I said, 'I've got some nickels in my pockets, let's buy a house.'"

When Weir says, "I'm not grieving for Garcia," or, "I carry his memory with me," or that he is "fulfilling a promise" by continuing to play music, and that Garcia's death was "something I have learned to accept" and that acceptance is "just one of the lessons of life," I feel more the presence of his immense stubbornness and resolve than I do the workings of a timeless psychic process. He is resistant in any case to confession. "Even when he's hitting on all four cylinders," Barlow says, "he's not the most emotionally revealing person in the world."

Wendy Weir says that someone wishing to comprehend her brother's habitual disengagement must not undervalue the defenses an adopted child embraces. Barlow says, "You have to understand, he was born outside of everything. Outside of his family, outside of the rest of the world in some sense with his dyslexia, and even, at times, unable to find a meaningful role for himself at the core of the organization that was central in his life. He was always the kid."

Weir's mother and father died three weeks apart from each other, in 1971. His mother had been ill for some years with cancer. It was a relief to her, Weir says, to have lived long enough to see that her son would be able to support himself.

Ten or twelve years after his parents' deaths, Weir endured a period of insomnia that ended finally when he fell asleep early one morning. He dreamed then that he was a child in their house. He and his brother were in his brother's room, looking at the bed, in the center of which, under the sheet, was a lump. Weir, the bolder of the two, grabbed the sheet and pulled it back, and the lump turned out to be a stillborn child.

Weir's phone rang then and woke him. A young woman from his office said that she had on another line a woman who had called from a town east of San Francisco, saying that she was Weir's mother. Weir spoke to her. It was clear from details she knew about his adoption that she was who she said she was. As a condition of giving him up, she said, she had promised not to contact him as long as the Weirs were alive. Even after she read in the papers that both had died, she had struggled over whether it was proper to call.

Weir had no idea of his background. She told him that she had been living in Tucson, Arizona, when she discovered that she was pregnant by her boyfriend, and she had gone to San Francisco to deliver the baby and arrange for its adoption. She never told her boyfriend the reason for her leaving. She didn't know what had become of him, where he was or even if he was still alive. A private detective whom Weir engaged eventually found him. He had retired from the service as a colonel and had raised four sons, one of whom, a musician, had recently died from cancer. Remarkably, he lived about ten miles from Weir.

The detective gave Weir his father's phone number, but Weir did nothing with it for some time. Then he took a deep breath and dialed the number. He figured that he had about fifteen seconds before his father might hang up if he didn't come to the point, so he rehearsed several ways of introducing himself. "My name is Robert Weir," he eventually said, "and I live in Marin County, and I have some information that might be of interest to you. But first I have to ask you a few questions. Did you ever have anything to do with a woman named" — and he gave the name of his mother — "who lived in Tucson nearly fifty years ago?" His father said yes and then grew very quiet. "I don't know how many children you have," Weir went on, "but you might have one more than you thought you did." On hearing the news, Weir's father said, "Give me a second here." Then he said, "The only Robert Weir I know of plays guitar with the Grateful Dead," and Weir said, "Well, that would be me."

On the day a few years ago when Weir told me this story, I asked whether he saw much of his father, and he said, "We had dinner last night." His mother has since died. Then I asked whether his mother had given him a name when he was born, and he said that she had. I asked what it was, and he said, "It doesn't really feel right to go into that."

In June 1995, a couple of months before Garcia died, I heard the Grateful Dead play at the Meadowlands, in New Jersey, and after the concert I rode back to the band's hotel in New York with Weir, Mickey Hart, and Vince Welnick. To get clear of the traffic around the stadium, the band's car followed a police car with a flashing red light. I had never had a police escort before. To Weir and the others, of course, it was routine — the kind of courtesy the governor extends to dignitaries who make the state and its citizens a lot of money — but I couldn't overlook the radiant feeling of privilege or the sight of the flashing red lights reflected in the rear windows of the cars in front of us.

The conversation among the musicians revolved mainly around how much fun the three of them had derived from playing that night for thousands and thousands of people. I felt, somewhat morosely, that I had never in my life had as much fun as they were describing. And, of course, this had been a night more or less like any other in the career of a band that played more often than any other band. The night had been unusual, though, because a speaker blew in Jerry Garcia's amplifier, and so he passed several minutes playing notes that no one could hear, fiddling with the knobs of his guitar and throwing malevolent glances in the direction of the guy who was trying to patch him into another part of the sound system. As it happened, the band was playing "The Other One," Weir's swirling, vampy jam written in 1968. In Garcia's absence, Weir and Phil Lesh, the bassist, had stepped forward and played with terrific force and momentum, and I couldn't help feeling that part of the pace and exuberance was the result of Garcia's having been forced to lay out. Mickey Hart said something about whatever drug it was that Garcia had taken that night — I didn't recognize the name. Vince Welnick asked how much he had taken, and Hart told him. "Jesus," Welnick said. "That'd kill a normal person. Half that's toxic." They all laughed. "Anything less, he wouldn't even feel," someone said. Hart said he had fought with Garcia all night to keep the tempo from flagging, and they laughed some more. Near the end of the concert, during a lapse in a period of improvisation, Garcia had stepped to the microphone and had sung, rather plaintively, the chorus to the calypso that goes, "Matilda, Matilda, she take the money and run Venezuela." It had been a peculiar and unsettling moment — his voice was thin and mournful and so without artifice as to seem almost childlike.

Wendy Weir says that when her parents died, Garcia became a father figure for her brother, and that when Garcia died, Weir found himself adrift. Part of what has helped restore him, she says, is the relationship he has begun with his actual father.

From a diary: June 1996, Bob Weir at Louise M. Davies Symphony Hall in San Francisco, eight or ten people in the audience attending a rehearsal of *Apartment House 1776* and *Renga*, two pieces by John Cage, being played simultaneously as part of the program of "An American Music Festival," put on by the San Francisco Symphony, with Michael Tilson Thomas conducting. On the stage are the San Francisco

Symphony Youth Orchestra, Michael Tilson Thomas, and, occupying folding chairs by the footlights, what's left in town of the Dead — in addition to Weir: Mickey Hart, Phil Lesh, and Vince Welnick. Bill Kreutzmann, the other drummer, is living in Hawaii, skin-diving mostly, and couldn't be persuaded to return for the performance. A few days earlier he consented to taking part in a sit-down held at the Grateful Dead office to discuss the band's business, but once that had been disposed of, he got back on a plane.

Under the gauzy indoor light, Weir, the bashful cowboy, the artless pretty boy, the goofy, football-playing *sensitif,* is fingering his chin and peering at the score, which sporadically requires him to make "new music"–style contributions — tics and twitches and noodly little gestures of sound. He's baffled, really, but he's trying. The score consists of curving lines and shapes and geometric figures that Henry David Thoreau drew in notebooks — sketches of plants, scratchy little calligraphic bird tracks, animal tracks, and various squirrelly subjects such as cracks in pond ice. Cage transferred the drawings to music paper, arranged them into groups, and divided the groups among the orchestra. Michael Tilson Thomas had the idea that parts could be given to electric guitar, bass, keyboard, and drum synthesizer, which made it possible to engage the Dead. The musicians have been instructed to play their idea of what the figures they've been assigned represent — it's a conceit — and Weir is puzzling over how to respond; he's got drawings that look like star clusters and crawling snakes and creatures you see under a microscope, and nobody's said anything to him like, "Uh, Bob, this figure at the top here, the little blob with the feelers coming out of it — I guess it looks a little like a virus, huh? — that actually represents, in a funny way, a C-sharp ascending lentamente to a G-natural, and the rhombus two measures ahead is an E major 7, pianissimo," so he's waiting for his cue and squinting at the squiggles on the paper. To his left and a little behind him is a kind of altar built from four large televisions on which appear a number that identifies for the orchestra the section of the piece being played. There are thirty-eight sections; Weir's parts are brief and appear in only a few of them. During the approximately forty minutes of full-bore, roundhouse, swing-for-the-fences cacophony, he will play for a total of, say, two minutes, maybe less. The rest of the time he will simply sit there, an icon of the popular culture at rest.

In the balcony are instrumental soloists — a drummer, a violinist, a young woman playing a piccolo — and on the stage there are also four singers, who stand, two on each side, to the left and right of the Dead. A white man sings Sephardic music, a black woman sings a slave song, a white woman sings a Protestant hymn, and an American Indian man sings a chant and beats a skin drum he holds in his hands. Each singer is performing a fragment of music that Cage assumed was heard in America in 1776. Sometimes the singers overlap, and always they sing against the grain of the orchestra. "Come go with me to that land where I'm bound," sings the slave, and at the same time the Indian goes, "Hey-ah, way-ah, hey-ah, hey-ah." This sort of chaos, of course, is close to the hearts of Weir and his companions, but the first run-through of the pieces is shrill and ragged, and the electric instruments sound tinny among the warmth of all the brass and wood. Thomas stops the orchestra. He is tall and thin, middle-aged, with dark hair and a narrow, boyish face. He pensively holds a finger to his lips, then turns to the soloists in the balcony. In the empty hall, pitching his voice just above a whisper, he says, "Have the courage to play softer."

The soloists and the singers and the Dead and the orchestra begin again, and this time, over the course of the next half-hour, there are moments of striking beauty and great clamorous authority, and the effect of all the lavish discordance and the subtle observations is beautiful and complex and moving.

The audience for the performance the following night will consist partly of blue hairs from the list of symphony subscribers and partly of a hopeful posse of the sweet, bland, disengaged kids who followed the itinerary of the Grateful Dead as a calling. Drawn by the first opportunity in nearly a year to lay eyes on Weir and the others, these polite, aimless zealots will cheer and applaud when the Dead appear from the wings, as if they draw a kind of runic sustenance from the musicians' presence, as if the sight of them were a balm. The music, though, confuses them. They exchange looks. They refer to the program. They shuffle their feet and finger their hair. It sounds nothing like the Grateful Dead, and the Grateful Dead are no more important to its success than the singers or the Youth Orchestra or the lady in the balcony with the piccolo. Afterward, the lost and dispirited will gather in the chromium darkness in front of the hall, on Van Ness Avenue, and try to decide whether the experience had been broadening or unsettling. Or worse, designed to make sport of them in some abstruse way.

Weir, on his way home, will stop at a club in Marin County and play guitar until early in the morning with musicians who invite him on-stage. Beforehand, though, backstage at the symphony, someone will re-fer to the poor perplexed pilgrims, and Weir will smile and say, "I think it's a safe bet that none of them had any idea what they were walking into."

The idea that the members of the Grateful Dead might play with each other again was suggested in December of 1997 by Bruce Hornsby. Kreutzmann declined. Hornsby had toured with the Grateful Dead. His occupying the position of keyboard player left no room for Vince Welnick, who now has his own band anyway, the Missing Man Forma-tion. Weir thinks that one of the reasons he and Lesh and Hart were willing to take up Hornsby's suggestion is that "it wasn't Bill or me or Mickey or Phil who raised it," he says. "We're too used to not taking each other seriously."

Instead of the Grateful Dead, the band members call themselves the Other Ones. In addition to Hornsby, Weir, Lesh, and Hart, the Other Ones includes John Molo, the drummer in Hornsby's band; David Ellis, the saxophone player in Ratdog; and guitarists Mark Karan and Steve Kimmock. During most of May, Weir and the Other Ones rehearsed six days a week, working "more hours than your average fireman," Weir says. Running through material for the new guitar players was occa-sionally fatiguing for Weir. "I feel like I'm singing the life out of these songs," he said. "The Grateful Dead never did much rehearsing, so there was always room to preserve the excitement."

One evening after a rehearsal, Weir was sitting at a table in a Japa-nese restaurant in a shopping mall in the town in Northern California where he lives. He was having dinner with the actor Woody Harrelson, whom he calls Young Woodrow. When Weir arrived at the restaurant, Harrelson was sitting by a window and writing with a pencil in a note-book. He put the book away, and they ordered sake. Weir noticed that the sunset looked dramatic and suggested that they go outside and ob-serve it, so they left their seats and crossed a parking lot and stood be-side an inlet of San Francisco Bay. They discussed surfing, which Weir took up seriously about twenty years ago, and a remote beach they had been to in Costa Rica that had exemplary waves and no one around to compete with you for them. Weir decided, somewhat sheepishly, that the sunset hadn't been quite as striking as it had appeared from his seat. They went back in and had some miso soup and more sake and some vegetable sushi. Weir's girlfriend, Natascha Müenter, a kindergarten teacher, a sleek, dark-haired, olive-skinned young woman, arrived with their infant daughter and a friend, had dinner, then left, taking Weir's car.

Two of Weir's friends showed up also and insisted that he accompany them to a club. Weir said, "No, it's a school night. I want to be home by ten-thirty."

"Come on," Harrelson said. "We'll have you home by twelve . . . thirty."

Weir was dependent on them for a ride home, so he finally shrugged. "Natascha will probably hit me with the frying pan," he said, "but it's a hero's way to go."

His friends kept him out later than twelve-thirty, and the next day he was late for the rehearsal, which was meant to start at eleven. He arrived around noon and spent six hours working through material inside the big high-ceilinged studio in the old Coca-Cola bottling plant that the Grateful Dead bought just before Jerry Garcia died. In the front of the warehouse are offices for various business ventures involving the Grateful Dead. In these areas, the part of the building where the musicians rehearse is referred to as the Boys' Club.

The band auditioned a series of guitar players before hiring Kimmock and Karan. They began with Stan Franks, a jazz and funk guitarist from the East Bay who had been suggested by one of their managers. Franks had been only peripherally aware of the Grateful Dead. The idea of selecting a guitarist distant in tone and musical background from Jerry Garcia appealed to all of them. Each day for several weeks, Franks took home tapes of Grateful Dead performances prepared for him by one of the Dead's engineers. At night he absorbed the arrangements of dozens of songs he had never heard before, and during the day he devoted himself to finding a place among the ensemble while also deciphering the multiplicity of musical references the band members share. "It's one thing for the Grateful Dead to quote Stephen Foster," Weir says, "and another for the Grateful Dead to quote Charles Ives quoting Stephen Foster, and another for someone else to try to take that all in, I guess."

The band, with Franks but without Hornsby, who was engaged

somewhere else, or Dave Ellis (honeymoon), spent much of one day rehearsing "Corrina," a song Weir wrote that has a strong percussive and modal feel that lends itself easily to elaboration. Their exchanges with each other were concise: "We need to keep chasing this for a while, key of D," or, "There's two ways of playing this — lyrical or toothy — you can move back and forth between them." No one made any remarks about anyone else's playing. Occasionally the band would stop and Weir or Lesh would say, "Teach Stan that line that Jerry used to play there." Weir was wearing a pair of sandals made from what looked like the kind of twine you wrap heavy boxes in, and Franks said, "Now I know what to do with all that extra rope I got around the house."

John Molo's drumming has a lithe, vibrant, and perhaps more linear feel than Kreutzmann's, which makes the music less atmospheric and more orderly. The textures of Weir's guitar, Lesh's bass, Molo's drums, and Hart's succinct and intelligent embellishments wound in and out of each other so deftly and offhandedly and with such vigor that it seemed to me as if the music itself were breathing and had a life of its own.

I was impressed by their applying themselves so diligently to finding new ways of handling familiar material, by their responsiveness toward each other, their inventiveness, their belief that form would emerge from a context that was still unfocused, and their faith in music as a means of invoking an intensified and elevated version of experience. This is what I was thinking. What I was doing was standing in a corner and keeping my mouth shut. I was obliged by arrangement not to make any remarks or talk to anyone while the rehearsal was in progress. Weir had once told me that while there were "a lot of unspoken agreements among the Grateful Dead, there were a lot of unspoken disagreements, too." What, beyond the obvious, had sustained him and the others, I didn't ask. A few days later, though, I came across a sentence by Oliver Goldsmith, the British writer from the eighteenth century, which seemed apt. Goldsmith wrote, "Innocently to amuse the imagination in this dream of life is wisdom."

(1998)

Bruisers

Y OU'RE AT a hockey game, watching a hockey fight, and you're no one — Mr. No One, Señor No One, account vice president at the Nada Advertising Agency, 1 Billion Madison Avenue, New York. Bob No One selling cereal in a suit of a cunning Italian weave. You have shoes made from the skin of a reptile, an apartment with a view of one of the picturesque but filthy rivers that flow past the city, a Land Rover, and a special way of wearing a fedora with the brim rolled as if it were the brim of a cowboy hat. You like wine. You're in agency seats with some cereal guys from Battle Creek, Michigan, and, to demonstrate the fineness of your feelings, you're shaking your head and saying that such displays of brutality are juvenile and coarse and the reason hockey will never amount to a major-league attraction in America, word up, memo to the commissioner, signed, Robert No One.

But forget you, Bob. Most people whose interest in hockey is peripheral believe that the fighting is deplorable. They regard it as undignified, unsuitable as an example to children, and lowering to the image of Sport. A blight, a sideshow, a carnival event. Thuggish, discreditable, boorish, indefensible, crude, degrading, and superfluous. Perhaps, except superfluous.

A hockey fight is not a dispute between two soreheads settling a grievance that has festered between them. Hockey fights are impersonal. They are not conducted by athletes who dislike each other. Two *teams* may dislike each other, and a fight may break out among their players, but only if one of them provokes it. Fighters rarely confront each other more than once in a game. They have been called on to resolve a dispute and are no more likely to revisit the matter than lawyers are to open a settlement. They may participate in other disputes, but these will involve new complaints.

What partly accounts for the disengagement is the regard that fighters have for any player who will fight. Hockey is a roughneck prairie pastime imported from the Canadian frontier. Its code of behavior insists that a player be responsible for his conduct. If he torments other players with his stick, he is certain to be reproved. The admonishment will arrive in the form of an assault by a player of threatening stature. If the offender is a player of commonplace ability who declines to defend himself — if he falls to the ice, say, and puts his hands over his head, what is called turtling — he might be harassed until he quits the sport. If he is a gifted player, someone will defend him. If he has honor but is overmatched, he will grab his opponent's arms and press his forehead against the other player's chest; such a defense is difficult to penetrate — he ties. If he can defend himself, he will be given some degree of respect, although he will probably learn to modify his behavior so that he doesn't have to defend himself to the point of distraction. If, however, his only hope of making his living playing hockey is to be irritating, he will persevere. All sports feel congenial toward athletes who are tough and mean-spirited and will never quit or back down. Even chess.

The other explanation for the disengagement is that the disputes that fighters are called on to settle don't usually begin with them. A hockey fight is proof that the players' confidence in the structure of discipline intended to ensure an orderly unfolding of a game has collapsed. The event that brought about the fight was not the one that caused the players to drop their gloves and dance. It happened earlier. Perhaps a player of questionable skill roughed up the other team's star. The offense may have been observed by everyone watching the game, or it may have been taken in only by the players and the referees and linesmen, or only by the players. In any case, the infraction was overlooked by the referees or else was insufficiently addressed. The players have excused it — perhaps what was intended as a permissible check turned into a knee-on-knee collision because the star shifted direction suddenly and the slower player couldn't get out of the way.

On any hockey team, only a few players fight. Some are too small for it, some have no inclination toward it, and some are too talented, too important to their teams, and too rich to expose themselves to gratuitous roughhousing. Typically the players who fight excel at no other component of the sport. Of a game's sixty minutes, such players are likely to take part in only five or six. After noting a second or third infraction, a coach may tap the shoulder of his assassin, meaning, simply, your turn on the ice. The avenger does not need to be told to rebuke the offender; he has seen the offense. He will seek out the troublemaker, or someone of his stature if the troublemaker is not on the ice. He will not seek out a player who does not fight. That would be unsporting.

Incivility toward another team's star is not the only cause of hockey fights. Other reasons (briefly): Two teams are playing a game following one in which the winner assumed the lead easily and then handled the loser roughly; early in the new game, the losing team's sergeant at arms might start a fight so as to encourage the other team to behave more considerately. A fight might also break out at the end of a one-sided game if the losing team wants the winner to know that, despite the score, it will not tolerate liberties being taken against it. To establish himself, a physical player new to the league will taunt a player whose reputation for fighting is acknowledged. If the new player wins, he advances himself. If he loses, he demonstrates that he had the courage to challenge a fearsome player. If he loses decisively, he will have to try again. Some players are signature players for their teams — your captain, perhaps, or your best player. Treating them rudely, especially on their home ice, is cause for a dustup. A fighter protecting the well-being of his smaller and more skillful teammates is serving as a kind of insurance, a way of doing whatever a team can to allow its best players to take part in a game without fear of a knucklehead's hurting them or causing them to play with the self-conscious distraction of caution.

In addition to the severity of the provocation, whether or not a fight occurs has something to do with the score. In a close game, insults are not necessarily addressed. Players have memories. They can wait for another occasion. Also, certain fighters are sufficiently feared that simply having them take the ice can pacify an opponent. Hockey is a game of intimidation, and fighting is a means of answering a threat. A straightforward way to win a hockey game is to make your opponent lose heart. A team of big players, especially big, fast players, will force another team's most talented defenseman to handle the puck a lot. When that defenseman is on the ice, the bigger team will carry the puck to the middle of the rink and shoot it into the corner on the side of the ice that the defenseman patrols. A race for the puck begins, with the defenseman aware that a bruiser is bearing down on him. The defenseman gets leveled a few times. It occurs to him to let the bruiser get the puck first. I'll get it next time, he thinks.

I admire the courage of hockey fighters. I dislike hearing them referred to as goons. Such a term is inaccurate and disrespectful. Claiming a place on the roster of a National Hockey League team is, to me, a singular and impressive accomplishment. I admire the willingness of these players to accept sore hands, black eyes, split lips, cuts to their cheeks and foreheads, concussions, and injuries to their shoulders in return for paychecks substantially inferior to the ones converted into Mercedeses and Bentleys and restaurants by the players whose honor and well-being they defend.

Fighters menacing enough to intimidate other fighters are as uncommon as goal scorers are. The most punishing fighter in the National Hockey League is generally conceded to be Tony Twist, who plays for the St. Louis Blues. Twist is six feet one inch tall and weighs 245 pounds. His shoulders are so broad that his name on the back of his jersey looks like an abbreviation. A fighter who is held in some regard by other fighters might fight twenty or thirty times in a season; Twist fights about fifteen times. One reason he fights only occasionally is that he doesn't get on the ice that often. He is not a swift or shifty skater. Understand, if he were to take the ice at your rink, he would be the greatest skater you ever saw at close hand, but compared with the most accomplished players in the world, he is cumbersome. This means that his usefulness is limited to circumstances in which his difficulty in catching other players, traveling with the pace of the action, and taking part in the game, is not a liability. If he skated faster and with greater coordination, he would be rich. After the stars, the most significant players on a hockey team are those who have the size, speed, and strength to pursue and claim the puck, or those who can punish the other team for having it. Hockey is not yet the employer of glandular freaks that football and basketball are, but it is eager to be. The only example of a skillful player as big as Twist is Eric Lindros, a forward on the Philadelphia Flyers. Lindros is six feet four and weighs 236 pounds. Players say that Lindros is so big and skates with such speed and determination that the blades of his skates make a sound against the ice that is different from the sound made by any other player. When your back is turned and you are headed into a corner to retrieve the puck, you can hear him bearing down on you. Players able to control the puck deftly are said to have soft hands. "Hands of stone" is the epithet most often applied to players whose hands are clumsy. Having hands of stone means Twist does not, as he says, "take the ice to score a goal or tie the game up."

The other explanation for why Twist fights infrequently is that players visiting his arena in St. Louis, or welcoming his team into their own, often realize that hockey needn't be played antagonistically. You can have just as much fun being polite. No fighter in the league is susceptible to fear, but none of them fights Twist without anxiety. Twist is bigger and probably stronger than any other fighter in the league. He punches harder than anyone else. He is ill-tempered. Some coaches tell their players not to fight him. He might hurt you; he might beat you severely. You are unlikely to defeat him.

If you are standing on the ice in hockey skates and you throw a punch as hard as you can at someone and you miss him, you will fall down. That is why hockey fights begin with the players grabbing each other's jerseys. Balance, to a large extent, determines how forcefully a player punches. If you have no balance, the force of your punch derives from the strength in your arm. Balanced fighters throw with the force of their bodies moving forward. Twist has terrific balance. Many fights, though, become wrestling matches. The most accomplished fighters are trying to maneuver their opponent into the line of their fists. Some players try to rock their opponent back and forth, so that they can hit him while he's moving toward them. Some players just try to grab their opponent's stronger arm and hold on. They will try to prevent him from throwing punches and either attempt to upend him, which is difficult to do against Twist (weight, balance), or press him against the boards or in some manner subdue him so that the linesmen can step in and separate them. To prevent being neutralized in this way, some fighters wear jerseys several sizes too large. When their opponents grab the jerseys, they get fabric.

Twist's attitude toward fighting is efficient and remorseless. "I'm not a grabber," he says. "I'm out there to throw. If I get in a fight, I want to hurt you. You can hit me, but I'm going to hit you harder. That's the scenario. I want you next time to see me coming and think, It's probably not worth it. When people grab me, I think, What have we accomplished here?"

The fighter I have most enjoyed watching is Joe Kocur, who plays for the Detroit Red Wings. Injuries in hockey fights are uncommon. Most of a fighter's body is protected by equipment. The part of a player's face that is exposed is approximately the size of a slice of bread. Fighters in the NHL have been practicing fighting for years. They know how to tuck their chins or turn their heads or lean back in order to avoid being hit anywhere but on the helmet. While it is unusual for a fighter to be hurt in a hockey fight, it has not been unusual to be hurt fighting Kocur.

Kocur is thirty-three. He is six feet tall and weighs 205 pounds. He has a small, round face, high cheekbones, a gap between his two front teeth, and a mischievous and obscurely defiant expression. Kocur was raised on a grain farm in Saskatchewan. He is of a physical type described in hockey circles as a hay baler — that is, he has the rounded, sloping shoulders of a farmer. He is exceptionally strong. Between 1991 and 1996, Kocur played for the New York Rangers. Colin Campbell, a former coach of the Rangers, says that when he once asked Kocur what his strength derived from, Kocur said, "Slews." Slews are small, shallow ponds among the fields of a farm. To avoid driving through the fields and packing down the soil, tractors and trucks drive along the edges of the fields on bands of uncultivated land called headlands. The headlands are usually bordered by irrigation ditches. As a boy, Kocur would be assigned by his father to clear the headlands of rocks, which meant picking them up and tossing them into the slews and ditches. Kocur was a teenage player of modest promise when he got into one of his first fights. Everyone in the arena noted that when Kocur hit the other player, the player fell down.

Kocur's manner of fighting is distinct. Whereas most fighters try to throw as many punches as they can, Kocur wants to throw only one. He tolerates being hit while waiting for the opportunity to launch his right hand, which comes from somewhere down by his hip or from behind his shoulder. As a junior-league player, Kocur once hit an opponent so hard that the player was knocked unconscious. He remained standing because Kocur had him by the jersey. As a professional, Kocur broke an opponent's cheekbone with a punch; the player retired for a year. Kocur broke another player's jaw. According to Campbell, the helmets that players wear are "built to stop .44 Magnums. Hitting one with your fist is like hitting a concrete wall." Tony Twist once threw a punch with such force that it dented a player's helmet. Campbell says that he once saw Kocur hit a player with such power that he cracked the player's helmet and gave him a concussion. Kocur developed a reputation in the NHL as the only player capable of knocking someone out with one punch. People used to say about Kocur, "When Joey hits people, they stay hit."

Between 1985 and 1991, the year Kocur was traded to the Rangers, he played in Detroit with a guy named Bob Probert, who was regarded for more than a decade as the most successful fighter in the NHL. Any young player wishing to prove himself as a fighter had to dance with Probert. Even more so than Kocur, Probert is a legitimately skilled player — one year he played in the all-star game. Probert and Kocur's most gifted teammate on the Red Wings was Steve Yzerman, the team's captain. Kocur described his responsibility to the Red Wings as "keeping flies off Stevie." Probert and Kocur were intimidating partly because they seemed only halfway under the control of their coach and partly because they had the habit — perhaps Kocur more than Probert — of picking fights with players the other had fought earlier in the game. Sportswriters referred to Probert and Kocur as the Bruise Brothers. Probert's fights were often long and rancorous. In the *Hockey Scouting Report* covering the 1990–91 season, Michael A. Berger wrote, "Unlike teammate Joe Kocur, who remains relatively calm during a fight, Probert loses control." Kocur's fights were shorter. Often he hit someone and the player fell down. In *Bad Boys,* Stan Fischler's book about hockey fighters, a player answers a question about how he had done fighting Kocur by saying, "It was OK. I came out of it alive."

Opponents who wanted no part of Kocur's right hand would grab his arm and duck and try to hold on. Kocur would try to free his arm. The patter of television announcers describing these fights would consist of remarks such as, "Davis has got ahold of Kocur's right arm, and he's not going to let go. Kocur's trying to get his arm free — Joey's a big-time heavyweight in this league, and if he gets that right hand — *Jesus and Mary, look out, he's got that arm free— Mayday. . . .* Well, Davis'll know better next time."

The consequence to Kocur of such an incautious style has been a right hand that has been described as looking like a homemade tool. The actor Jeff Daniels, a friend of Kocur's, says that Kocur's hand is a "blunt object with fingernails." Kocur's hand has been cut and stitched so many times that the skin on the back of it can no longer be gathered. It's as shiny and smooth as a piece of linoleum. Some of the scars are small and white, like the marbling in a piece of meat, and some wind back from his knuckles like trenches. One of the longer scars is the result of incisions made to repair a tendon that had split, and another is the result of surgery to control a staph infection — Kocur had cut his hand on an opponent's teeth, and the doctor sewed the cut without cleansing it thoroughly. The infection became so virulent that doctors considered amputating his arm from the elbow. Kocur's hands are always cut, and they always hurt. When he fights, he becomes so involved that he isn't aware of the pain, but afterward he is.

In 1996, Kocur felt he had become incidental to the fortunes of the Rangers and asked to be traded. He was exchanged for a player on the Vancouver Canucks. Kocur played eight games, and during the summer the Canucks let him go. He joined a minor-league team in San Antonio, played five games, and left. He ended up playing in an amateur league in Detroit. Halfway through the season, the Red Wings gave him a contract. He played the rest of the season and figured in the Red Wings' winning the Stanley Cup. He fights rarely now. "I'm not supposed to go looking for trouble anymore," he says. "I'm just here if things get out of hand."

Kocur is far from the most graceful skater in the league — he has the agility of a file cabinet — but he is better than many and is so strong that he is valuable to the Red Wings as a player who can slow down the other teams' belligerent and talented players. I asked Campbell whether he thought that Kocur was still as highly regarded for his ferocity. "Everyone's sure Joey's got one more punch," Campbell said, "and no one wants to be that last punch."

(1998)

Another Green Dog

S
EPTEMBER ARRIVES and Ry Cooder goes to Cuba, in 1996, to make a record with some African guitarists, but as it happens the Africans can't leave Africa — they've lost their passports or they can't obtain visas; exactly what occurred even Cooder's not sure, it was all very sudden. He rides from the airport in a taxi past buildings in pale colors, past motorcycles with eight people onboard, past the loopy trucks from Russia that haul semitrailers resembling moving vans, except that the trailers have windows and seats and carry passengers because the country doesn't have conventional buses, and right away he's happy to find himself amid such tranquil festivity, and then he's in Havana — a picturesque and singular American at large, a man who Walter Hill, one of the directors for whom Cooder has scored movies, says is "the most talented person I've ever known," who is not simply "a singer or a guitarist or a folklorist or a collector of indigenous musics or a rock-and-roller or a bluesman but a very great artist who uses all these things to make the material of his own music," a traveler now at a loss in the landscape of fascinating rhythms and tricky chord changes. His eyes take in palm trees, old Studebakers and Lincolns, decrepit buildings, streets in deep shadow, the ocean and the wide-open tropical sky. The clear blue air smells vaguely of gasoline. He smokes cigars as big as hammers that last all day and make the inside of his head feel like a fabulous nightclub.

Cooder is fifty-two. He is tall and big-boned. He has black hair, a wide and pleasingly proportioned face, and dark eyes. Lenny Waronker, the record executive who signed Cooder to his first contract, in 1969, describes Cooder as a young man by saying, "Of course he looked tremendous," and he pretty much still looks tremendous, does yoga and is the picture of rude health. Cooder, though, seems indifferent to what he looks like. From having walked behind him to tables in several restaurants, I know that he is the sort of person whose arrival in a room people notice. This is partly because he has a head-bobbing walk that makes the movement appear to be a collection of gestures he is still practicing, but it is also because he is strikingly handsome. He has never, though, put an especially flattering picture of himself on the cover of any of his records. On most of them his features are obscured, or the lighting is unsympathetic, or he is making a goofy face, or there is no picture of him at all. Cooder is averse to self-promotion. He has never changed the color of his hair. He has no tattoos. He has never appeared in a beer commercial, or made an arrangement to wear the clothes of a specific designer, or connived with a press agent to be photographed in the company of a famous actress, or released photographs of how he looks sitting around his house or ones that reveal his body or that portray him engaged in lewd activities, and it is unlikely that he will — it is difficult to persuade him to have his photograph taken at all. The photographs of him that best reveal the warmth and complexity and depth of his nature have been taken by his wife, Susan, to whom he has been married for almost thirty years.

By temperament Cooder is diffident and retiring. He is more apt to find fault with himself than with someone else. He worries a lot and is subject to unbidden apprehensions and is pleased to observe that his son, Joachim, who is twenty and plays drums, seems to worry about nothing at all. He has a versatile and agile intelligence, and he reads a great deal, and his talk is expansive and idiosyncratic. Walter Hill describes Cooder's conversation as verbal jazz. "It's very poetic," he says. "There's a kind of circularity to it." If you ask Cooder how he happened to record a certain song, "Hey Porter," for example, by Johnny Cash, he might say that what makes modern American music different from the music of other cultures is the jukebox and that before World War II, during the jazz band era, that is, musicians made records to promote their performances, so that people would come to see them — records were novelties, almost — radio hadn't yet embraced regional music, and there weren't that many radio stations anyway. After the war, people developed the habit of going to bars and cafés and feeding the jukebox, and if you were a musician and wanted your record to be chosen from among the fifty offered, you had to come up with something conspicuous and memorable, and so the music of the period — Johnny Cash, say, with "Big River" or "Hey Porter" or "Ring of Fire" — was very poignant and microcosmic in its compression of experience, the best songs were honed to something that resembled miniature masterpieces — proof of this was that nothing else was going to come into your mind while you're listening to them — and meanwhile everyone was working to get a hit, even Howlin' Wolf, even Muddy Waters, and these great records were made in very informal settings, hotel rooms sometimes, and the offices of record companies where the employees pushed the furniture to the walls at the end of the day and set up microphones, and so the records had a warmth and informality that has surely been lost, because at a certain point technology overtook sentiment — bound to happen, there was so much money involved — and so you began to hear more of the equipment used in making the record and less of the music, more of the science and less of the feeling, and you can't go back now, no, you can't, you sure can't, and the only time you can perhaps is to a place like Cuba, where they still have beautiful music and not so much of a technological society.

Cooder went to Cuba with the producer Nick Gold. Making a record in Cuba was Gold's idea. Cuban music has its origins in strains of African music, and Gold thought something worthwhile would undoubtedly come of having Cooder and the Africans play with Cuban musicians. Without the Africans, there's nothing to do but start auditioning Cubans and asking the whereabouts of musicians Cooder knows from records. Twenty years earlier, as part of a cultural exchange, he was briefly in Cuba with some American jazz musicians. He brought home a wagonload of records and a tape someone gave him of a performance by a musician playing a type of twelve-string lute called a *laud*. Cooder found the music in Cuba deeply alluring — he loved the seductive and intricate rhythms, the concise and lyrical melodies, and the music's capacity to succinctly express emotion — but he says, "I was too young and uncertain to know what to do about it; I couldn't just go up to someone and say, 'Let's record,' so I went home and thought about it for twenty years." Occasionally when he met someone familiar with Cuban music, he played him the tape of the *laud* player and asked if he knew who it was, but no one did.

Cooder doesn't like to perform. He would rather play music in a recording studio than in public, with the result that he has probably been seen onstage less often and by fewer people than any other popular musician of his stature. More than ten years have passed since he appeared on tour to promote one of his rock-and-roll records. Seven years ago he played a series of concerts with Little Village, whose other members were John Hiatt, Jim Keltner, and Nick Lowe. In 1998, with a collection of Cuban musicians and Joachim, he performed at two concerts in Amsterdam and one in New York at Carnegie Hall, all of which were sold out. Rather than occupy a position at the front of the stage, he sat near the back, on a folding chair, beside Joachim.

Cooder withdrew from performing partly because he doesn't like leaving home; partly because there are areas of the world, especially northern Europe, where he feels an unease that is close to dread; but mainly because onstage he feels exquisitely self-conscious. "I don't like being watched," he says, "and I don't like being an entertainer. You get up there and it's all so loud, and the stage is so big, and how you do is all so critical, and I thought, I can't stand there one more time and say, 'Ladies and gentlemen, and especially you ladies . . .'" Furthermore, once a show was over he tended to become despondent. "I felt like a withered balloon under a chair on the day after a birthday party," he says. "People who love the applause should have it, but I don't care for it."

Very few people hear Cooder play guitar anymore. He lives in Santa Monica, California, and mainly he plays by himself or with only a few people present, in a recording studio (usually somewhere in Los Angeles) or in the practice room he has at home in what used to be the garage. Joachim has a friend named Sunny Levine, who mixes records in the bedroom he occupies in his parents' house in Pacific Palisades, the next town north from Santa Monica. Recently Joachim asked his father if he would play guitar on a song that Levine was working on, and Cooder said that he would, so one afternoon I went with Cooder to Levine's room, which had a view out a sliding glass door of the roofs of Pacific Palisades and beyond them the ocean, and Joachim and a friend of his sat on the bed, and Cooder sat on a chair in the center of the room, with his back to the view, and untangled guitar cords and plugged himself into a small amplifier and put on some headphones and tinkered with his guitar until he got it to produce the swampy, raspy, low-down, growly tone that he wanted. Sunny set up a microphone by the amplifier, and for Cooder's benefit we listened to the song, which was a trancy, ethereal dance tune with a guy sort of half singing, half whispering a refrain that went more or less, "I used to love you," something, something, "but that was enough for me," and Cooder said, "Uh-huh . . . that's nice . . . well, all right, I can do something on that." He recorded three takes, each lasting several minutes. On the first, he played a restrained and sinuous figure involving two dense chords. On the second, he played a rhythmic and piercing tenor line that had a slightly Indian feel to it. On the third, he added a series of steplike bass figures. He started beating time with his foot, and then he closed his eyes, and his head began moving from side to side and back and forth like a bird's, and his knee rose higher and higher until his foot was pounding on the floor, and he was frowning and flinching and wincing, and he looked like a holiness preacher at a tent revival, and I felt like I was sitting in the amen corner.

Cuba: Cooder and Gold have no simple time organizing the musicians. Nearly all of them are elderly — the oldest is eighty-nine — and one of them Cooder hoped to find is dead. Few of them have phones, and most people in Cuba, he learned, don't answer the phone anyway. "Down there when the phone rings," Cooder says, "it's like a dog barking — no one pays any attention." After a few days, Cooder and Gold have chased down and invited and talked from retirement a collection of suave and spry and elegantly accomplished men and one woman, nearly twenty altogether, and they set up shop in Old Havana in a studio called Egrem, which is on the second floor of a sprawling, rickety, wooden, and termite-ridden apartment house. Egrem belongs to the government. It is hardly used anymore and has been allowed to dilapidate. Water leaking from apartments above has soaked the tiles on the ceiling. When the tiles dried out, they shrank, and some of them fell off and others hang loose, but something about the age of the walls and the shape of the room is sympathetic, and anything recorded here sounds warm and natural and true and has the breath of life, and later, in California, when Cooder plays back tapes of music recorded at Egrem, he sometimes says, "You can hear the room, can't you?" The tape machines at Egrem are old and over the years have been repaired with whatever materials were at hand — "It's real dime-store engineering," Cooder says — and he and Gold send to Mexico City for parts, and they're almost ready to make a record. What they need is a singer. Someone suggests Ibrahim Ferrer, who is seventy and two years earlier, having no work, completely gave up the idea that he was ever going to sing again, but he's graceful and thin as a reed and moves like a cat, and his voice is fit.

Among the musicians Cooder hires is Barbarito Torres, who is considered the best *laud* player on the island. Cooder plays Torres the tape, and Torres's eyes open wide as umbrellas and he says, "How did you get that?" Cooder says, "Twenty years ago" and "present from someone" and "kept it all this time," and Torres says, "It is me, when I was a young man."

After a Havana hangout that no one remembers the exact location of anymore, Cooder and Gold call the record *Buena Vista Social Club,* and the rest of the story is perhaps sufficiently familiar that I needn't add that the record sells millions of copies and wins a Grammy, and as a result every agent and promoter and performer in America sees dollar bills when he looks at the map of Cuba, and in February 1999 the *New York Times* prints an article ("More Americans Going to Cuba as Performers") that fails to mention Cooder and instead says that seventy country-and-western and rock-and-roll acts and Burt Bacharach and Jimmy Buffett and MTV are all going to Cuba, most of them together, and you might think that a life on an island, even a hard life on a semi-impoverished island, with palm trees and sugarcane and the smell of diesel fuel and raw sewage in the air, and the ocean and the wide-open tropical sky, such a life, bereft of seventy American pop acts and Burt Bacharach and Jimmy Buffett and MTV, is not an existence a person would necessarily rush to describe as one of deprivation, but even if Cooder thinks so he is far too gracious a person ever to say such a thing.

Under his own name, Cooder made eleven records from 1970 to 1987, and then he quit making them. The records consist of songs he found beautiful for one reason or another. Some of the songs are so primitive in their structure that they are hardly songs, and some are so complicated that they would tax the capacities of most popular musicians. The records include songs he wrote; songs from the catalogs of blues, soul, rhythm and blues, rock-and-roll, rockabilly, and jazz; Hawaiian songs; cowboy songs; drifter, tramp, and hobo songs; Mexican songs; American songs from bygone times, especially the Depression and the Dust Bowl era; pop songs, gospel songs, folk songs, and songs from the Caribbean. They represent a variety unexampled in the repertoire of any other popular musician. "The biggest inspiration I had," he says, "was to take *norteño* soul music and fuse it with Mexican music. It was my great big idea to do that. I was listening to *norteño* stuff — accordion and rhythm and boleros. This is the seventies. You got a culture that is centered around northern Mexico and the border and southern Texas, people who got across the border but didn't go far. They play this music with an accordion, which was brought to them by Germans that worked on the railroads, and so they play these polkas, but in a Mexican style." Cooder learned to play the accordion well enough that he could go to San Antonio and teach songs to the accordion player and band-leader Flaco Jimenez and then come back to Los Angeles and teach them to the singers he worked with, and finally he got Jimenez and his band and the singers together in Los Angeles to make a record he called *Chicken Skin Music.*

The rhythms of Cooder's arrangements are distinctive and highly eccentric. He describes them sometimes, especially the earlier music he recorded, as having the feel of "some kind of steam device gone out of control," or as having "a weird teapot effect, like the lid's about to blow off." Such a keen sense of the divisions and stresses of rhythm were inspired partly, he says, by listening as a young man to a record of brass music made by a group of black men who had found in a field the instruments belonging to a regiment of Civil War soldiers who had dropped them when they fled an engagement. No one had taught the men how to play the instruments, and they had arranged the music to suit their own ears. If you happen to be unfamiliar with the sound of a typical Cooder arrangement, one way I can think of to describe it is to say that when Cooder was a young man, he was brought into the studio to assist the Rolling Stones in recording their album *Let It Bleed,* and one day he was playing guitar, goofing around, clicking this and popping that, and Mick Jagger came dancing over and said, "Oh that's very interesting, what you're playing; how do you do that? You tune the E strings down to a D, and you put your fingers there, oh, I see, and you pull them off quickly like that, yes, that's very good," and Cooder showed him the whole thing — he was young, he didn't know that sometimes you got to keep your stuff indoors — and the next thing he knew, the Rolling Stones were picking up royalties for "Honky Tonk Women," which sounds precisely like a song arranged by Ry Cooder and absolutely nothing like any other song ever arranged in thirty years by the Rolling Stones.

·　·　·

The first of Cooder's ancestors to arrive in America, around the time of the Revolution, came from the Low Countries — that is, the area including Holland, Belgium, and Luxembourg. He spelled his name Kuder, and one of his descendants married into a family in Ohio named Ryland.

Cooder grew up in Santa Monica. His father went to World War II, then, with a GI loan, bought a house on a hill above the Santa Monica airport. Cooder was an only child. As a boy, he often had trouble sleeping. In the middle of the night, from the window of his bedroom, he aimed binoculars at the planes landing and taking off and at the people on the night shift coming and going from a factory where aircraft were built. The activity suggested a world at one remove from his own — men and women who worked while the rest of the world slept — and he tried to imagine what they did. When he was about four, his parents gave him a radio. "The guy on the air would tell the time and give the ads brought to you by whoever," he says, "and it was reassuring." Part of Cooder's apprehension derived from an accident he had when he was three. He was fixing a toy car with a knife, and the knife slipped and entered his left eye. For a year after that, he says, "all I remember is sitting in dark rooms and going to hospitals and seeing doctors. A kid can't foresee anything like that, and once it happened it seemed as if the sky could fall in, as if at any time something can go wrong in a big hurry, and forever." He was eventually fitted with a prosthetic eye. His left eyelid occasionally droops, which makes him look sleepy.

One night in the year after the accident, when Cooder was four, he was lying in bed in the dark on his back. The door to his room opened. A friend of his father's, a violinist, came in and laid something on his stomach. Cooder asked, "What's this?" and the man said, "It's a guitar."

Throughout his growing up, Cooder kept mainly to himself. He rode his bike to the ocean. He liked to visit the airport because "it was quiet and peaceful, and the little planes looked like toys." Sometimes he took the bus to the beach or down to Venice, where the oil wells were. "To me that was heaven," he says. "It was messy, and it looked like the desert." When he got a driver's license, he liked to drive downtown and look at the old buildings, whose appeal for him was strong but obscure. "It's empty enough to where you could like something in there," he says. "I just don't know what it is, I'm sure I don't."

He didn't care for school. "It was like something I thought I'd never

survive," he says. "Like it was Devil's Island, and I was each night making one more mark on the wall, crossing off the days." By the time he
was sixteen, he played guitar well enough that he was working as a side-
man in recording studios. When he was eighteen, a producer engaged
him to help the legendary figure Don Van Vliet, who performed as Captain Beefheart, make his first record, *Safe as Milk*. Van Vliet's outfit was
called Captain Beefheart and His Magic Band. Cooder was taking the
place of Van Vliet's guitarist, who had suffered a nervous breakdown.
Van Vliet lived in the desert. Cooder would drive out to rehearse with
the band. Occasionally the guitarist would appear at a rehearsal and
Van Vliet, whose manner with the members of his band was imperious,
would order him to return to his room. One day the guitarist showed
up carrying a loaded crossbow. "The first thing I thought," Cooder says,
"is that he's going to point it at me, since I'm taking his place, and the
next thing he's going to hiccup and shoot me." Van Vliet ordered the
guitarist to put down the crossbow and go back to his room. Cooder
finished the record and then decided to enroll at Reed College in Portland, Oregon, where he lasted only a year. "I liked the trees, I liked nature, I liked being up in Portland," he says, "but once you've recorded
with Captain Beefheart and looked down the barrel of a crossbow, you
might get a little bored in college." While he was in Oregon, he kept getting calls to return to Los Angeles and contribute to various records.
Finally, he had missed enough school that he was summoned by his adviser, who asked him to explain the absences. Cooder described what
was involved in playing on sessions. The adviser asked, "Do you get
paid?" Cooder said, "Last time I played about a week and made five
thousand dollars." The adviser recovered himself and said, "What are
you doing here?" and Cooder said, "Well, it was kind of my parents' idea."

Many rock guitar players consider their guitar to be an accessory to
their appearance. They match its color to their outfits. They have guitars made in novel shapes. They have flags painted on them, or maybe
the insignia of a liquor company. They have the necks and bodies inlaid
with mother-of-pearl dragons or death's-heads or devils or snaky patterns of geometric figures. Cooder's guitars are homely. He plays guitars
that a lot of musicians would be embarrassed to be seen with. He cares
about how a guitar sounds, not how it looks. He plays guitars that look
as if he bought them at a yard sale on a trailer lawn in Arkansas where

the lawn wasn't grass but pavement and the only other things for sale on the floppy little card table set up for the affair were some not thoroughly washed jam jars and glasses, a few pieces of cheap pewter flatware, a drink box without a lid, some filthy children's clothes, and a fan whose blades don't turn anymore and whose motor (you would discover when you got it home) makes a bad smell when you plug it in.

Most of Cooder's guitars are built for him from parts obtained from other guitars. He has an affection for the sound of guitars that no longer exist. A person can examine a photograph of, say, Robert Johnson, or some other historical figure holding a guitar, and try to determine what company made it, but the guitar in the picture might not be the one the musician played on his records. It might have belonged to the photographer, or it might have been rented as a prop for the occasion. Even if the guitar in the photograph was the one the musician played, it was undoubtedly a cheap guitar that likely ended up stolen or pawned or changing hands in a card game and by now the strings have pulled the neck out of line or someone left it in a basement that flooded or ran over it while backing out of the garage.

When Cooder finds a guitar with a sufficient number of companionable qualities, he sends it to a guitar builder and repairman on Staten Island named Flip Scipio. Describing Cooder's collection of guitars, Scipio says, "He has a *few* vintage instruments, but he also has things that seem to be out of the trash can. There's a certain kind of music he wants to play where you need cheap instruments. You can't use a thirteen-thousand-dollar guitar to play a song that was recorded in a hotel room in Chicago in the fifties by a blues musician who bought his guitar at Sears." Cooder says, "Everything I got is irreplaceable, junk though it may be."

Cooder is not attempting merely to reproduce the sound of cheap, old guitars. He is obsessed with finding a sound that is resonant and authentic to his ear and that frees his mind from thinking about anything else when he's playing. Scipio says that Cooder is "always looking for the big note, the sound that makes all the inhibitions fall away." Not having the sound that he wants frustrates him the way not having a sufficient grasp of the grammar and vocabulary of a foreign language frustrates a traveler abroad who has something important to communicate about what he is feeling.

Cooder is receptive to intuitions and impulses and the texts of dreams. As a young man he dreamed one night that he was lost in the jungle. "You could see the sky through the tops of the trees," he says, "but that's about all you could see. Everywhere else you looked was just the trees. I knew that if I kept on walking, I would probably come to a place where I could see where I was, so I continued and eventually found a little clearing. By now it was night, and I thought I would lie down and get some sleep, and just as I did I heard this *crash, crash, crash* coming through the jungle, and out jumps Curtis Mayfield, from the Impressions, looking like a savage, with the war paint on his face and his chest and the bone in his nose and the necklace of teeth and a spear in one hand and a shield in the other and the black-rimmed glasses he wore. He had this guitar strung on his back, and the guitar was made out of bark and leaves and branches and snakeskins, and it had barbed-wire strings. I said, 'Whoa, so that's it, that's the secret — the barbed-wire strings.' He said, 'If that's what you think is the reason for the sound, then I can't help you,' and he turned around and disappeared back into the jungle. I had that dream twenty years ago, and I never forgot it."

One night Joachim's band was playing at a club in Hollywood, and I went with Cooder to see them. The band has eight members — two sisters who are singers, and six guys who, among them, play drums and percussion, guitar, lap guitar, violin, accordion, trumpet, and trombone. Joachim has known the younger of the sisters since they were classmates in the seventh grade and performed together in the school's talent show; she sang and Joachim played drums. The girls are tall and slender and have dark hair and big dark eyes and sharp cheekbones — not long ago a movie star offered to keep one of them — and from time to time Cooder's lawyer is occupied making phone calls to executives in the record business who would like to separate them from the band. The lawyer, Cooder says, instructs the executives "to stay the hell out of Dodge."

Speakeasy plays music like Cooder played during Joachim's childhood, which is to say, some rhythm and blues, some ballads, some rockabilly, some car songs, and some country songs. Cooder sometimes helps them with arrangements and teaches the guitar player parts.

Cooder and I arrived at the club early and drank two margaritas. There was a stage at one end of a dance floor, and a bar to one side.

Cooder said that the place was similar to clubs he had played during the early days of his career, when he traveled with a guitar and a mandolin and performed by himself. "I used to love to come to these places early," he said. "Arrive and watch the waitresses set up and lay out the napkins. It was a nice, quiet time." Before long, he grew nervous, though. He began to pace. Then he sat down and tried to keep still. He went and talked to the soundman, because they usually only know how to set up microphones for heavy-metal bands, he said, and his son's band was more complicated than that. Joachim arrived, and I heard Cooder tell him, "The song's too slow."

"Still?"

"Give it a bit of a groove tempo. It'll still feel down, but it won't be so down," he said, the way another kind of father might say, "Quit chasing the ball. Don't swung until you get the pitch you really want."

Several bands were on the bill for the evening, and Speakeasy had been engaged to play first. While the members were setting up their instruments, Cooder sat at a table near the back of the room and said to no one in particular, "See how good I'm being — I'm just sitting here." He was especially anxious because Eliades Ochoa, who played guitar on the *Buena Vista Social Club* album, was in Los Angeles making his own record and had said he would come hear Joachim. Ochoa arrived with his girlfriend, who had an oval face and long shiny black hair and wore a T-shirt and a full, pleated skirt. Neither she nor Ochoa speaks English. Around eight-thirty, the two beautiful sisters stood in the center of the stage, and the boys stood on either side of them, like parentheses, and the girls sang like angels and the boys played wonderfully while Cooder ran up and down the stairs to the sound booth, making suggestions.

Afterward we helped Joachim load his drums into his car. Then we drove Ochoa and his girlfriend to their hotel in Hollywood. Eliades wanted a cigar, and Cooder tried to find a place where he could buy one. "What we need is one of those yuppie places with fancy cigars," Cooder said, and he thought of one, but when we arrived it was closed. Eventually we pulled up in front of a convenience store next door to their hotel, and Cooder sat double-parked in the car, and I went in with Ochoa and his girlfriend and stood with them in front of a glass cabinet filled with cigars that I felt sure would only disappoint someone from Cuba. After a lot of discussion with his girlfriend, Ochoa bought two cigars, and I followed them back outside. Cooder had parked the car and was walking toward us. The evening was a little cool, and he was wearing a blue duffle coat, like a boarding-school boy. Ochoa was wearing jeans and a shirt and cowboy boots and a straw hat in the shape of a cowboy hat. He is short, and Cooder towered over him. The three of them stood talking. Cooder doesn't speak Spanish, so the talk was mostly gestures and a few words, with Cooder leaning toward Ochoa as if he were addressing the brim of Ochoa's hat. Cooder thanked him for coming to hear Joachim. They all nodded. Cooder seemed fatigued by having seen to all the details of the evening, among them their comfort. For a moment the three of them stood there — an exotic American, a notable Cuban, and a woman for whom "Señorita" seemed the only proper form of address — three figures on the Hollywood pavement, awash in the shimmering light that was a mixture of the light from the streetlamps, neon, car headlights, and the illumination from the windows of the big hotel. Cooder patted Ochoa on the shoulder, and then Ochoa and his girlfriend started walking toward the hotel, Ochoa rocking from side to side on the worn heels of his boots, like a small boat in heavy weather. Not until the crowd on the street had absorbed them did Cooder turn toward his car.

(1999)

Ms. Ramos

HERE IS SOPHIA in Iowa. That would be Sophia Ramos, twenty-six, a rock-and-roll singer from the South Bronx, a Puerto Rican, a Latina: sultry Sophia who sings with Psychotica, a rude and cacophonous band from New York. Psychotica represents a segment of American popular music called glam rock — that is, glamour rock. A lot of makeup is involved. Sophia and Psychotica have just been onstage in Des Moines at two in the afternoon, the first band appearing on the slate of big-deal bands that will shatter the clear blue air until late at night at the Iowa State Fairgrounds, under the banner of the Lollapalooza tour. Now Sophia and the band are on their way to sign copies of a CD consisting of four songs, two of them from their first album, released at the end of July. They pass (mainly) white boys and girls, the everywhere boys and girls of America, the boys and girls in Des Moines who look exactly like the boys and girls in Los Angeles and Boston and Natchez and Cleveland and Fairbanks, because they all take their way of dressing from MTV. The everywhere boys and girls have noses and eyebrows and ears and navels pierced with pewter studs and little hoops the color of old spoons, and they have tattoos, so many tattoos, how did anyone in America ever live without four or five tattoos before? Creepy fire-snorting dragons and dripping daggers and tombstones and wizard figures with blazing-red eyes, so many tattoos that the everywhere boys and girls look like comic strips walking, it's quite beautiful in its way, a sauntering little pageant of cartoons. Among them strolls copper-skinned Sophia, untattooed, wearing a shiny burnt-orange nightie. You could call it a shift, but in the trailer that serves as Psychotica's dressing room, rummaging through her suitcase, she held up the shift and said, "Shall I wear the nightie?" and Patrick Briggs, Psychotica's lead singer, who performs in a skintight silver jumpsuit that constricts in the heat and makes him feel like a sausage in its casing — "It's good, though," he says, "because it makes me really irritated and angry before I go on" — and who sometimes stands onstage with his arms at his sides and looks from the audience like a pair of tweezers, said, "Sure."

On this blistering day of sullen farm heat, the needle on a thermometer worn on a string around the neck of a white boy like a piece of jewelry reads a hundred degrees. The expressions on the faces of the everywhere kids are flat and abstracted, as if they had just been yelled at. The band they're listening to is playing so loud that the sound stirs the surface of a glass of water on a table in a room a hundred yards from the stage. Three white boys wearing shorts and no shirts stop Sophia, and one of them asks for an autograph. He extends his arm and Sophia writes with a black felt-tip marker on his biceps.

Sophia is double-jobbing with Psychotica. She does not appear on their album. The young woman who does left the band, and Patrick, whom Sophia knew because both have spent years on the same sweaty circuit of clubs in New York, asked Sophia to take her place for the tour. When Sophia signs a copy of Psychotica's CD, she does not sign her name, she signs "Sophia's Toy," the name of her sinuous, stage-demolishing (and currently unsigned) band in New York. By appearing across the country with Psychotica and by signing "Sophia's Toy" on hundreds if not thousands of CD covers and concert programs and scraps of paper, she hopes that she will make an impression that will help her when her band has a record of its own.

Sophia is small and compact — "I don't have that long-legged thing," she says. She has a narrow face, with a strong, dimpled chin; she has a long, finely drawn nose, shapely lips, and dark eyes; and she has thick black hair curled as tightly as springs. She favors, gratuitously, push-up bras; "I don't know why, really," she says, "but I don't wear makeup, except sometimes onstage, so I have to do something for effect." A man who sees Sophia onstage strutting in a leather bustier and tiny shorts, one hand gripping her crotch, her head bobbing back and forth, and her tongue making snaky movements through her lips, is likely to conclude that she is more serious and strenuous fun than he feels comfortable with. In private, however, Sophia is reserved and a little bit shy.

As Sophia stands under the open furnace of the Iowa sky, a slight breeze lifts the hem of her nightie. The Iowa boy who has asked for her autograph turns to his friends and raises his eyebrows in a hubba-hubba manner. On his arm, in indelible ink, Sophia writes, "Pussy Power, Sophia's Toy." The boy reads the inscription, looks at her, looks at his friends, and backs up. Sophia walks. Between her and the boys, the shoulders of the everywhere kids come together like closing doors.

Sophia formed Sophia's Toy in 1992. Before that, for four years, she sang (regrettably, she feels) with a club band in New York called The Crunge; and before that, when she was seventeen, she and the singer Michelle Shocked had an act called the Brolk Sisters, named for a combination of "broke" and "folk." After The Crunge, Sophia resolved that her next band would include the best musicians she could find. She wanted, she says, a band that would "leave holes in the stage." The obstacle lay in persuading accomplished musicians, who would likely be older than she was, to work with an unknown singer. "I didn't want anyone taking over my project," she says, "so I figured I could get the best players and also maintain control if I paid them — 'Here's your money, see you at the next gig' — they couldn't give me any lip." Renting space to rehearse, paying the musicians, and sending out a mailing whenever the band played would cause her to lose money, but she hoped that eventually the musicians would regard her highly enough to give up being side-men and share the risk that she was assuming.

To pay the band, underage Sophia tended bar in Chelsea at a club called Spoodeeodee, now defunct. One night at Spoodeeodee, she heard Michael Ciro, a guitar player, chicken-scratching with a funk band, and the next night she heard him as a soloist with a rock band and asked if he was interested in working with her. Sophia and Ciro formed a Memphis-style blues band called Sophia and Her Sexual Overtones and be-gan writing songs together. What they wrote, however, wasn't suitable for the blues clubs — it was rock-and-roll. They decided to give up play-ing blues and instead play the music they were writing. This is also when they changed the band's name to Sophia's Toy.

She gave up bartending and began hustling work as a singer wher-ever she could find it. A friend who sang with a band of Russian musi-cians at weddings and nightclubs in Brighton Beach had a conflicting obligation one night and asked Sophia to take her place, and the band liked her so much that they hired her, too. The band's repertoire included sappy American pop songs — Whitney Houston and Mariah Carey sorts of things — and Russian and Jewish folk songs that Sophia learned from tapes the musicians gave her. She sang with the Russians every weekend she didn't have a job with Sophia's Toy. The clients in the nightclubs were mostly Russian gangsters who dressed extravagantly ("Versace *down*," Sophia says) and spent slaphappy amounts of money on food and vodka and cognac. When they requested a song, they tipped the bandleader twenty dollars. One of the occasional members of the band lived in New Jersey, and on nights when he played, he drove Sophia home — she lives in Manhattan, on the Upper West Side, in a tiny studio with one window, a bed on the floor, a desk against one wall, and a standing lamp with a broad fringed shade; on the door is a photograph of a redneck with a shotgun and under the photograph it says, "You Will Be Shot." She usually arrived at her apartment around three. All other nights, she rode the subway.

In December of 1993, Sophia's Toy signed a recording contract with an established label, Epic, and made a record during February and March of 1994. Sophia quit the Russian wedding band. Because she is Puerto Rican, people often tell her that she should sing in Spanish, which she finds exasperating because it suggests to her that the person she is speaking to believes that her appeal is limited. Halfway through recording the album, the man from Epic who had signed the band asked if she had noticed that there were a lot of Spanish television stations broadcasting in the city (there are two); she asked if he watched them. He said no, and she said, "Exactly."

Not long after that, in June of 1994, the same executive invited Sophia and Michael Ciro to a breakfast, where he told them that Epic had, unhappily, decided not to release the record. "He told us that the company felt there was no market for female rock-and-roll singers," Sophia says.

For a time, she felt lost. "It opened up all these old childhood wounds about failure and being different," she says. "It made me feel that my difference — my being a woman, my being Puerto Rican — was a curse, something that was going to hold me back forever." The feeling lasted almost a year. Finally, she says, "I just accepted and embraced my difference. I came to feel that it was the very thing that makes me shine. What else could I do?"

Without a record to represent on a tour, Sophia's Toy was confined to the circuit of dingy clubs it had been making for the last two years. Sophia went back to singing with the Russian band. "I don't really like to tell what else I do for a living," she says. "It's not cool." If you persist, she will say, "All right. I'm a jingle singer." What people call her for is scoring — that is, improvising around the score — and screams.

In the hope of leaving the club circuit behind and getting another record contract, Sophia took the job with Psychotica, even though she is only a peripheral performer and is being paid less than she has ever otherwise been paid for a job on the road. The first stop on the Lollapalooza tour was in Kansas City. As I stood backstage, beside her, looking at the crowd and listening to the announcer saying, "Welcome to the Lollapalooza 1996 tour," and hearing the crowd cheer, and then the announcer saying, "Ladies and gentlemen, the passion and pageantry that is Psychotica," I said, "Are you excited?" and she said, in a way that did not imply a complaint of any kind, "I wish it was my band."

Sophia was born in 1969. Her mother and father came to New York from Puerto Rico; Sophia is first-generation Nuyorican. Her father was a super in the building the family lived in. He saved his money, borrowed some more, and bought a building of his own, which he eventually sold; he then moved back to Puerto Rico. He and Sophia's mother were divorced when Sophia was three, and Sophia and her two older sisters were mainly brought up by her mother, who, according to Sophia, was excessively strict. Except to attend school, Sophia was rarely allowed to leave the house. To have a social life, she became a Pentecostal Christian. She was six. At church, she sang hymns and engaged in ecstatic experiences such as dancing in the spirit and speaking in tongues.

In school, she says, she was always very different from her classmates. Being a born-again Christian, she wore skirts. She also wore thick glasses, and although she was Puerto Rican, "I was an Afrocentric one," she says. "I mean, I had this hair. Most of the other Puerto Rican kids, they were not having me." Furthermore, she didn't speak Spanish. Her mother asked Sophia and her two older sisters to speak English at home, so that she could learn. Although Sophia speaks Spanish now, she spoke it so poorly then that the other kids ridiculed her when she used it, so she gave it up.

When Sophia was twelve, she began talking very loudly in class and constantly replying, "What?" to her teachers, which annoyed them until one of them suggested to Sophia's mother that Sophia have her hearing tested. The doctor discovered that fluid had collected in Sophia's ears and that she had lost 40 percent of her hearing. He said she needed an operation. The night before it was to take place, Sophia's grandmother took her to one side and said, "Listen, why are you going to make your mother spend all this money for an operation when you know God can heal you?" The grandmother took Sophia and her mother that night to see a Puerto Rican evangelist who was said to have "the gift" — that is, he was believed to be an agent through whom God heals. "It was a church in the Bronx called John 3:16," Sophia says, "after the verse in the Bible that begins, 'So God loved the world.'" When the evangelist finished his sermon, he asked the men and women who had come to be healed to approach the altar. Perhaps four hundred people were in the church. Two hundred stepped forward — people in wheelchairs, people missing limbs, people hobbled by rheumatism and arthritis, blind people who found their way to the altar by placing their hands on the shoulders of people who led them. Fear is what Sophia mainly felt. Being healed, she was certain, would depend on the steadfastness of her faith — and what if she didn't have enough?

Her grandmother stood behind Sophia and put her hands over Sophia's ears, and Sophia's mother put her hands on Sophia's shoulders, and the congregation began praying and shouting and testifying, and suddenly everything got louder. "My grandmother looked at me and I didn't say anything — I was just soaking in the sound," Sophia says, "then my grandmother said, 'You're healed, right?' And I said, 'Yes.'"

The next day, at the hospital, the doctor who was to perform the operation checked her ears and found nothing wrong. He asked Sophia what had happened and she said, "Jesus healed me." He went and got another doctor, and the two of them in turn got a specialist who examined her, then shrugged and said, "Jesus healed her." Two years later, at fourteen, she left the church, because, among other things, she couldn't believe the minister when he said that women who wore pants were going to Hell.

Where Sophia is sitting while she tells me this story is in my rental car on her way from Kansas City to Des Moines. It is night. Flat deep-blue fields and windrow stands of trees slide past the windows. Sophia is slumped in the front seat. She looks tired. We will talk for an hour or so more and then I will drop her off at a hotel on the outskirts of Des Moines where the band has stopped to ask directions to their own hotel, a Best Western or a Motel 6, one of those dreary roadside places with polyester sheets and dead air and plate glass windows you can't open, where she will share a room, as she will every night of the tour, with Enrique Tiru, a member of the band, a cello player. She will take a shower and get to bed late and be awakened early to ride in the van to the state fairgrounds.

Before all that, while we are still driving, she will tell me that when she was a teenager she sometimes stayed away from home for a couple of days and that her mother almost always found her. "'Cause why?" she will say. "Because I came to her in a vision." Her mother wouldn't know the name of the person Sophia was with, but she would begin calling Sophia's friends and saying that she knew where Sophia was, she just didn't know the number, until one of the friends felt sufficiently uneasy to give her the number. "Finally one day in the spring when I was sixteen," she will say, "my mother had had it with me. I came home from a Van Halen concert at one in the morning and my mom was like, 'If you don't play, blah, blah, blah, by my rules, blah, blah, blah, or I'm going to put you in a home.' So over the next few years I lived with my boyfriend here and there. Sometimes, for a few weeks or a month, we squatted in the East Village — no heat, you have gas, hot water, and electricity, and you can open the oven or buy electric heaters when it's cold. I'd scour the Dumpsters for books and magazines and lay them on the sidewalk on Astor Place and sell them for whatever I could get, and the cops couldn't stop you because it's the First Amendment. For a while I had a job in a clothing store, but I didn't really have the clothes. I waitressed a little and got fired for spilling things, I rolled posters in the gift shop of the Metropolitan Museum, then I got a job as a performing artist in the afterschool program in Brooklyn, which I liked a lot, but I lost it because Michelle Shocked asked me to come to Los Angeles to sing on her album, and they wouldn't give me the time off, so I quit."

When I find her the next morning, in Psychotica's trailer, she will be asleep on a couch. No one else will be in the trailer. She will open her eyes, and I will say, "I'm sorry, I didn't realize you were sleeping. We can talk later," and she will say softly, not quite awake, "Give me a minute."

Five young men are members of Psychotica. Patrick Briggs, a handsome, intelligent, mischievous, and effortlessly charismatic figure, is the leader and singer. In the section of the Lollapalooza program devoted to Psychotica, Briggs says that the band formed at a club he runs called Squeezebox. The program quotes him as saying that Squeezebox is "notorious for being sexually ambiguous — a pseudo-glam melding of punk, new wave, drag queens, rockers, and all things New York." The other members of Psychotica are Ena Kostabi, who plays guitar; Buz, the drummer; Tom Salmorin, who plays bass; and Enrique Tiru, the cellist. Mostly Sophia sings a kind of second lead vocal, some harmonies, and a ballad with Patrick, if ballad is the correct word for a song with a slow tempo played at a volume that is audible at half a mile.

Here are Sophia and Psychotica in their trailer, preparing to take the stage. The trailer has a large front room, with some couches, and a smaller room in the back that is cooler. Black plastic has been taped over the windows to keep out the sun. It is one in the afternoon. Patrick is applying makeup in front of a small round mirror. He is tall and thin, with an alert and angular face. Both sides of his head are shaved. Down the middle of his crown, Mohawk style, is a three-inch-wide strip of long hair. He has applied a clay mask to his hair, which is blond, so it is now a kind of dull blue, a blue you sometimes see in frescoes. To the sides of his head he is applying three-inch strips of orange electrical tape so that he can spray his hair with silver paint and not get any on the part of his head that is shaved. Across his eyes, nearly to where his hair begins, like a pair of wraparound sunglasses, is an inch-high orange strip, and down the center of each eyelid is a silver line.

Sophia, looking through her suitcase, says, "Should I wear leather?"

Patrick says, "You bet. For the farm boys."

She takes a leather bustier from the suitcase, holds it in front of her, then drops it. "Too hot out for this," she says. I ask her about something I heard, that she had auditioned for the musical *Rent*, and she says, "I did. In November. Patrick called and said, 'Listen, you should audition for this play, it's called *Rent* — it's by this Jonathan Larsen guy.' I did the audition, and they asked me when I could start rehearsal, but our schedules collided — I was going to Amsterdam to see about a possible tour for my band, so I couldn't do it."

Patrick says, "Henry, tape me. I can't turn around, my neck hurts." One of Patrick's trademark stage gestures is to fling his head from side to side very quickly. His hair flies back and forth and it's very dramatic — also, apparently, painful. Henry gets up from his mirror, where he's applying eye shadow, and comes over and presses strips of orange electrical tape to the sides of Patrick's head. "My favorite thing is to go to a hardware store and cut loose," Patrick says. "I always find great things to use for the show, like orange electrical tape."

Sophia raises her eyebrows and, looking into a mirror, begins applying eye shadow. "Anyway, two weeks before I left for Europe," she says, "I did a showcase for Virgin records. They flew a woman in from L.A. to see us. After the showcase, she said that she was going to fly us to L.A. to begin negotiations for a record deal. I get back from Europe first week of January, and she hasn't called."

Patrick picks up a can of silver spray paint, stands up, and steps outside to spray his hair silver.

"So meanwhile, the people from *Rent* call and say that they're recasting *Rent*," Sophia says. "They remembered when I was coming back. They say, 'Jonathan really loved you' — he was still alive — 'a lot of good things are happening, we're getting good press,' but nobody says anything about the play going to Broadway; no one knew yet that it would. The thing I want most to work out is my band — I want that more than anything else — so I get on the phone to Virgin and find out what they're thinking, because I have this play I can do, I tell them, and if I'm not doing anything with Virgin, I want to do this play. Virgin doesn't know for sure what's happening, but the *Rent* people want my answer, so I had to call them and say, 'I'm waiting for this deal,' which means I turn down whatever chance I had with this play for a second time."

The trailer door opens and Patrick comes back in. His hair is silver. "Once I covered myself with glow stick," he says. "You know, that stuff that glows in the dark if your lights go out, and you can't find your way?"

Sophia says, "How did you know it wouldn't make you break out in a rash?"

"I called the company," he says. "I always call and say, 'Will this make me grow a third eye?' Like this silver spray, I called them. They asked why I would spray myself with it, and I said, 'It's the only thing that will give me that chrome look.'"

Sophia bends toward the mirror. Across her lips she runs a dark, nearly black lipstick and says, "Anyway, the whole thing with Virgin falls through. And then, of course, even worse, Jonathan Larsen dies."

The door from the back room opens and Tom, the bass player, walks in. Among his tattoos is a line of flame climbing his upper right arm. He takes Patrick's mirror. Sophia and Patrick look at him aghast. Sophia says, "I would *never* touch Patrick's mirror."

Tom says, "Me and Patrick go way back."

Patrick says, "Not that far back."

To me, Sophia says, "So I blew it." She runs her fingers through the hair on the top of her head, trying to make it stand up. "So, now, dig this," she says. "I get a call in March from the casting guy at *Rent*. He tells me, 'I want to know if you're available, because we're auditioning for understudies and I remember Jonathan loved you.' So I go, I audition — I treated it like rock-and-roll, not like some actor audition. I sang well and really *felt* that I was the character. Even though it was only an understudy's role, I was excited and hopeful, and the director hated me. He just *hated* me."

I am still trying to think of something to say to make her feel better when the door opens and Nite Bob, the road manager, puts his head in and says, "Five minutes to showtime, ladies and gentlemen."

The night before Sophia left New York to join the Lollapalooza tour, Sophia's Toy played for the door with four other bands at Brownies, a dim bar in the East Village. It was supposed to be a performance like any other: the bustier, the shorts, the sass; the captivating state of happiness involved in playing electric instruments, the slightest gesture of your fingertips eclipsing the sound of everything else around you; the momentary forgetting that membership in a rock-and-roll band is frequently the equivalent of an entry-level position for a career in table busing or carpentry or furniture moving or clerical help, maybe the civil service; the anesthetic and short-lived amnesia concerning the catalog of a musician's misfortunes (deceptive and bullying club owners; inept, corrupt, and rapacious promoters; bad food and piss-poor pay; and, in Sophia's case, being a Latina doing a mainly white-girl thing). It was supposed to be show up, play, and get paid, but it went awry. The trouble began around nine-forty-five, when the soundman, a thin, pallid, and nervous young man, approached Sophia on the sidewalk outside the club and said, "You guys go on in five minutes." Sophia had been under the impression that her band was to set up at ten-thirty. Ten-thirty was what she had printed on the nine hundred announcements she had sent out (costing her three hundred dollars), and ten-thirty was what she had told the A and R man from Atlantic Records she'd invited to hear the band.

To the soundman Sophia said, "We were told ten-thirty. Our drummer just got here."

"I don't care what you were told," he said. "You're on the list for now."

"What's on the list is a mistake," Sophia said. "They told us to be ready at ten-thirty."

"I got five bands," the soundman said, "and I can't keep running the show back. The stage has been clear for ten minutes." Sophia stood in front of him with her arms folded across her chest. She looked over his shoulder and said nothing. "I can't deal with start times," the soundman went on. "I can only deal with finish times. You guys are *finished* at five after eleven, so you *better* set up."

By the time Leslie Ming, the drummer, had found a parking space and brought his kit into the club, it was ten-thirty. It would take fifteen minutes for him to set up his drums and for Michael Ciro and Eddie Martin, the bass player, to put their amplifiers in place and tune their instruments, which would leave twenty minutes for the band to perform, instead of the forty-five they had expected.

Sophia and Michael and Leslie and Eddie began playing at ten-forty-five. Sophia spent the first few minutes of her performance shedding her indignation by making obscene and menacing gestures toward the soundman.

At the end of the fourth song, the soundman appeared at the edge of the stage. Standing in front of Sophia, he held a finger in the air and mouthed the words, "One more." Sophia shook her head. He persisted in waving his finger, and she ignored him. He tugged on her microphone cord, the way you might tug on the leash of a disobedient dog, and thrust his finger in front of her once more. The cords on his neck stood out.

The band played a fifth song. Sophia ended the song and started another. While she was singing, the soundman turned off her microphone, and she seemed to lose control of herself. On one wall of the stage was a sign that said BROWNIES in white letters on a black ground. Sophia pulled it down. She ran to the front of the stage and knocked the monitors to the dance floor. Then she ran to the far corner of the stage and began shaking a column of speakers that was standing on top of a table. Someone in the crowd yelled to Michael, "Man, you better go get her!" Michael ran over and put his hand on her arm.

The soundman came to the stage and demanded the microphone. Sophia said, "Don't say two words to me." The soundman retreated. He came back with two big guys and stood behind them. Sophia glared at them. Seconds went by. Everyone was watching her. When she was sure that Michael and Eddie had packed their guitars and Leslie his drums, she made a lewd and extravagantly showy gesture, and, with the crowd clapping and laughing and calling her name, she surrendered the microphone.

The soundman refused to pay the band. Michael tried to get the money from the woman at the door, but she said she had been told not to give it to them. Michael said, "Who told you? Go get him." She left, and he turned abruptly and walked outside. "It's probably two hundred bucks," he said. "Who cares?"

Sophia was standing on the sidewalk with five or six women friends. "Every time I play in the East Village, something bad happens," she said.

Perhaps twenty-five people stood on the sidewalk in front of the club — enough so that anyone who wanted to pass had to step into the street. A black man, a member of one of the other bands on the bill, appeared in the club's doorway and said in a loud voice, "Where's Sophia? Sophia, where you at?" Everyone turned and looked at him. When he saw Sophia, he strode toward her. Towering over her, shouting at the top of her head, he said, "Don't even talk to me. I don't want to hear one thing. Nothing. I've been wanting to do that for *years,* and you did it before me, and that's the *only* reason I hate you. Girl, you are ready *now.*"

(1996)

Sophie's Guernica

THE IDEA OF MAKING a copy of Picasso's *Guernica* as Matisse might have done it was suggested to Sophie Matisse by her dealer, Francis Naumann. Naumann is a bit of an art-world wise guy. He was the curator of "Making Mischief: Dada Invades New York," at the Whitney Museum, in 1996, and he is also an authority on Man Ray and Marcel Duchamp, who happens to have been Sophie Matisse's step-grandfather; Duchamp married Alexina Matisse, known as Teeny, after she was divorced from Pierre Matisse, Henri Matisse's son.

Naumann is fifty-four, and Sophie, who is Matisse's great-grand-daughter, is thirty-seven. They have known each other for almost twenty years, ever since Naumann paid a visit to Teeny Duchamp at her house in the country outside Paris. If you ask Naumann and Sophie how they met, they tell different versions of the same story. Naumann, who was then an art historian, says that it was raining, and he was picked up at the train station by a svelte and alluring dark-haired young woman (Sophie), and while they were driving to Teeny Duchamp's she turned to him and said (provocatively, he thought), "Are you the adventurous type of art historian?" Before he could answer, she veered off the road and headed through some trees into a field, where the car bogged down to the axles, and they had to dig it out. Sophie's account includes no erotic subtext. She says that she was spending the summer at her grandmother's house and was often sent to the station to fetch the art-world types who made small, pious pilgrimages to see Duchamp's widow. On the way was a shortcut — a tractor path that was barely visible between trees. Having found out what her passenger did, Sophie liked to ask whether he or she was the adventurous version. There was almost immediately an impact as the wheels left the pavement, and then the critic or the curator would be bumping down a rutty old road that could only partly be made out. "People would arrive at the house all shaken up," Sophie says. "They had started out excited about meeting Teeny Duchamp at her house in the country — a perfect art-critic day! — and now they can't stop worrying about the ride back to the train."

In January of 2002, Sophie, who lives in New York, had a show at Naumann's gallery, Francis M. Naumann Fine Art, on East Eightieth Street. The show, her first, consisted of twenty-one deft reproductions of modern and Old Master paintings by, among others, Degas, Hopper, Vermeer, and Grant Wood, from which Sophie had removed the people or, in the still-lifes, some of the objects. Without the figures, the paintings were spooky and unsettling. One critic described them as "pronounced statements of absence." The first painting from which she removed a figure was the Mona Lisa. Sophie is married to the French pop artist Alain Jacquet, and one night in 1997 they were looking at a book of variations made from the painting, including Duchamp's version of the Mona Lisa, with a mustache, an image that Sophie remembers from her childhood. Turning the pages, she suddenly thought, What if the Mona Lisa just got up and left? Her version of the painting has the hills in the background and the river running through the lowland, and in the foreground the balustrade that the Mona Lisa was standing in front of. Sophie called the painting *The Monna Lisa (Be Back in Five Minutes)*. Naumann first saw it on display in the vault of a bank in TriBeCa. Because the real painting is probably the most valuable painting in the world, Sophie thought it would be funny to show it in a bank vault. To attach it to the metal wall, she glued magnets to the frame. The show at Naumann's gallery also included her version of her great-grandfather's *Goldfish*, without the goldfish in the bowl on the table, and a version of Picasso's *Woman in the Mirror*, without the woman. To Naumann, the noteworthy thing about the Picasso was that without the woman the painting looked like what he calls "a very austere, Nice-period Matisse"; that is, a Matisse painted between 1918 and 1930, when the artist lived at a series of hotels in Nice.

Last September, Naumann decided to close his gallery and do more writing. He called Sophie and told her, and then he called a friend they had in common, an artist named Mike Bidlo. Bidlo told Naumann that he should give Sophie another show before the gallery closed, and he mentioned that if he did so during the winter it would coincide with the "Matisse Picasso" exhibition at the Museum of Modern Art. When Naumann hung up, he looked absently at his largest wall and suddenly realized that it was roughly the size of *Guernica.* "My first impulse," Naumann says, "was that if I want to combine Matisse and Picasso, I was just on the phone with the Matisse."

Initially, Sophie didn't see how the painting could fit her practice of removing figures. She was surprised that Naumann suggested *Guernica,* because she had been looking at it lately in books, as a result of 9/11. (She has never seen the actual painting, which hangs in Madrid.) She had been on the street when the first plane passed above her, and she watched it crash into the tower. Given a moment to reflect, she decided that she would love to try painting the Picasso.

Matisse and Picasso — Sophie pronounces it "Pee-casso" — were rivals of a kind. Gertrude Stein once said that they "became friends but that they were also enemies." In the Matisse family, vestiges of their rivalry remain. When Sophie told her mother that she was planning to paint *Guernica,* her mother said, "You mean that horrible painting with all the ugly figures?" Her father, who is a sculptor and an inventor, came to New York a few weeks ago, and she brought him to her studio, in TriBeCa. They talked about the Matisse-Picasso show, and her father said, "If I never see another Picasso, it won't be the end of my life." Sophie said, "You're in for a surprise." He looked at her sketches and studies, and she thought that she was going to receive a lecture, but instead he asked her, sympathetically, "What's it like drawing the Picasso line, after living with the Matisse one all your life?"

Like indulging in a forbidden thing, she thought but didn't say.

Sophie grew up in Cambridge, Massachusetts. Her father, Paul, was brought up in New York — his father was the dealer Pierre Matisse. He went to Harvard and met her mother, Sarah Barrett, in Boston. Nearly all the other branches of the family are in France. Because no one in Sophie's family talked much about her great-grandfather, she regarded him as an enigmatic figure. As a little girl, she occasionally saw her last name on the walls of museums, from which she concluded that it must be significant. A woman who worked with her mother once took her and one of her three older brothers aside and said, "Tell me the truth, are you really related to Matisse?" She said no, and her brother said yes. Mostly when she asked her father about Matisse, she felt that her question was diverted. Teeny Duchamp spoke fondly of Matisse. "She'd tell me what a wonderful man he was," Sophie says. "She said that sometimes if she had a problem with Pierre, her husband, she'd talk to Matisse about it. If I managed to get my father to talk about him, though, you might sometimes think he was a monster. One of the few stories I remember was of his being a child in a restaurant with Matisse and having a waiter who took himself to be a comedian. The guy did what he could to provoke a response from the great man, and when it finally arrived it was delivered in the most virulent tone. My impression is there just wasn't a lot of room with him for anybody else."

The family's reluctance to discuss Matisse left Sophie feeling excluded from something essential to her identity. Also obscurely deficient. A real Matisse either would have been let in on the secret or wouldn't have had to ask in the first place. In her studio, she has a photograph of Matisse taken when he was in his sixties. His fingers are cupped as if they were holding a cigarette. "That hand I noticed a long time ago," she says. "My grandfather had hands like that, too — squarish fingers, thick and long, but not skinny, and the nails are flat. I would look at my hands and think, The knuckles are like his, the fingers are the same." She also remembers looking often at a portrait of her father drawn by her great-grandfather, which hung in the living room of her parents' house. She can draw the portrait quickly from memory — a child's face with a round jaw and hair like waves in water. The ability to reproduce her great-grandfather's supple and shapely line seems to have been passed on to her the way a striking quality of temperament or a cast of mind might persist in another family. The features of the drawing that engaged her most were the nose and the eyebrow. The eyebrow crossed over the left eye, then turned down and formed the nose, like a backward seven. "I looked at it partly because it worked so well," she says, "but also because it broke rules, and that's always interesting for a child."

When Sophie was thirteen or fourteen, she needed money for something, and to raise it she made a series of little Matisse paintings. "Everyone loved them, because they were reminiscent," she says, "but I did it, I think, to establish a connection I felt I wasn't allowed to have."

As a grown woman with her own child — she and Jacquet have a daughter, Gaïa, who is nine — she thinks that her father was probably reticent about his grandfather because he wanted to spare his children from being fussed over for reasons having less to do with them than with the person doing the fussing. "I wouldn't have wanted him to do it differently," she says. "It preserved a kind of innocence. It's confusing, though, to unravel what the legacy really means for me, and I still haven't quite figured it out."

In 1987, when Sophie was in her early twenties, having attended a year of art school in Boston, then worked for a year with her father on his projects, she decided to move to France, because "it seemed like the door to the world." After staying for a while with her grandmother, she went to Paris with the intention of enrolling at the École des Beaux-Arts, where Matisse had studied. As a child she had made trips to France with her mother and father, but she didn't speak French. The French museum officials she met at her grandmother's would ask her questions, and when she couldn't reply they would make those clucking sounds the French make and say, "C'est incroyable," which embarrassed her. She learned enough French to present a portfolio to the admissions committee at the École des Beaux-Arts, and with the intervention of an aunt who knew which professor would be receptive to the figurative work she was doing, she was accepted.

She discovered immediately that she couldn't draw very well. In high school she had avoided drawing classes because she felt that a Matisse ought to know how to draw without needing help. She had always been accomplished at making copies of drawings and photographs, and she thought that was all there was to the matter. In Paris she learned that drawing from the figure required entirely different skills. She worked hard, though, and eventually became adept. Meanwhile, she lived a life apart from the French students. "I was this lost, naive person with this famous name, and people projecting onto me all sorts of things," she says. "Much of it was anger, not only because I had a name they would have killed to have but also because there was a kind of indignity involved in the way I appeared to uphold it. I was an American, and I didn't speak French, and I couldn't draw for beans, and I'd wear skirts that looked like they were made from burlap, and I had holes in my pants and in the soles of my shoes. I looked like the refugee I in some senses was. The only thing that protected me from their scorn was that I was so withdrawn. I would sit in my room and listen to music and think about things that made me feel good — my own name in a museum and my work on display, or about being glamorous, anything that took me away from where I was."

Because she didn't speak French proficiently, she didn't know for sure what the professors were saying when they evaluated her work, but she nodded and pretended to absorb every word. To earn a degree, she had to take classes in art theory and history, but she couldn't read or write French well enough (she is also seriously dyslexic). In her third year, the head of the school summoned her to his office and told her that it was unfortunate, considering her name, that she hadn't worked harder, and that the school could no longer offer her a place. All she could manage in French was to ask if there was anything she could do, and he said there wasn't. By this time, though, she had met Jacquet and was beginning to travel among the people he knew in the Paris art world, so leaving was not an intolerable disappointment.

Sophie is the only descendant of Matisse who is a painter. His daughter tried painting but destroyed her work because she felt unable to escape her father's influence. As a student in Paris, Sophie began making paintings so modest that they hardly look like paintings. They were mostly done on the pages of her engagement calendar: color studies and abstractions and sometimes a drawing about the size of a baseball card. Because no one ever saw them, she felt free to do anything she cared to. The colors in the earliest paintings are somber, but as the years go by they grow brighter and more like the deep blues and reds and yellows and greens in her great-grandfather's work. In 1993, she and Jacquet had Gaïa, and Sophie stopped painting to raise her. In 1996, they moved to New York, and in 1997 she painted the Mona Lisa.

Sophie began with a literal idea: to paint Picasso's painting as Matisse might have done it. This presented her with two issues: what forms he would have used and what colors. *Guernica* depicts figures that Picasso imagined to be suffering during the bombing of the Spanish town of Guernica by the Fascists, with the help of the Nazis, in 1937, during the Spanish Civil War. From left to right, these figures include a woman on her knees who is weeping and holding in her arms a child whose arms and head hang lifelessly. Behind her is a bull with an impassive expression, which some critics say represents the bestial nature of the Fascists and some people say represents Spain. Picasso said it was a bull. Above the shoulder of the bull is a bird, and below the bird is a fallen soldier. Above and to the right of the soldier, more or less in the painting's center, is a horse with a deep wound in its side. Above the horse a light bulb hangs from a reflecting shade. Approaching the horse is a woman staggering in shock, and above her another woman leans from a window and holds a lamp to see what the terrible commotion is about. At the far right is a woman who seems to be falling through the air. In the background are buildings in flame, so the setting seems to be outdoors, but the electric light also suggests a room. It is a painting of horror and anguish, and Picasso intended that it shame the Fascists for the massacre.

Sophie began work on studies of the painting on September 15. She made photocopies of a reproduction of *Guernica* from a book Naumann gave her, and began coloring them with gouache, a delicate paint that has a texture like fine cloth. In the first ones, the shapes were mostly black, and these were followed by ones in dark blues and blacks and reds. A few are all reds and greens; one is of nearly fluorescent yellows and greens, and one is a broad arrangement of blues and reds and greens and violet, and doesn't really work.

As soon as Sophie finished one study, she began another. Some were done quickly and some deliberately. After she had made about a dozen small studies, she began using larger sheets of heavy paper, and then she made two versions of the painting on canvas that are about six feet long and three feet high. None of the studies were definitive in the sense that she felt she had managed a version of the colors that she would want to reproduce on a larger scale, but several had elements that she liked. She worked on the color studies and on drawings and the paintings for three months, which put her up against a deadline to finish the painting in time for the opening at Naumann's gallery.

No matter how hard she tried to interpret Picasso's figures in drawings, she felt unable to find satisfactory equivalents in Matisse's work. Finally she made a large drawing in pencil using only figures derived from looking at Matisse. The woman with the dead child on the left-hand border became a Madonna-like figure looking down at her child. The woman with the lamp appeared slightly annoyed at having been disturbed, and the projection of her face forward into the drawing made her look like an ornament on the hood of a fancy car. Sophie could find no counterpart in Matisse's work for the falling woman, and mostly she is smudged out, as if she were a ghost. The most compelling figure is the horse. Sophie drew it somewhat naturalistically, coiled in pain and shock, and it is somehow collapsed and transcendent at the same time. It looks more like a figure from mythology than like a horse on a battlefield. After she completed the drawing, it occurred to her that Matisse had never drawn such figures, or depicted such emotions, partly because he believed that art should be restful. (He once said, "I believe my role is to provide calm. Because I myself have need of peace.") She realized that it was not possible to compel such figures into being, and so she decided that she should reproduce Picasso's — that they were simply too formidable to alter.

None of these resolves conformed to Naumann's idea for the painting. "My instinct was to do what a comedian would do, where he assimilates the voice and appearance of someone more famous than he is," he says. When Naumann went to Sophie's studio in December, he saw, among the studies, one in which she had used découpage — cutouts — as Matisse often did. The tail on the bull was a seaweedy species of Matisse imagery, and above the woman with the lamp were scatterings of leaves like the ones he sometimes used. As Naumann looked at the study, he found that for the most part he was unable to tell where one artist left off and the other began. There were places where he thought Sophie had been too faithful to Picasso, and he made some drawings of his own to show her how to make the figures closer to what he imagined Matisse would have done.

Over the next few days, though, Sophie lost her enthusiasm for the idea. "I thought it would be interesting to have a painting where you would think, Matisse/Picasso, Matisse/Picasso," she says, "like those drawings where you look at a vase and see two faces in profile, but when I tried to bring it off it turned into an exercise." She decided that what she really wanted to do was to make the Matisse part of the project hers and her sense of color, and not her great-grandfather and his.

Naumann told Sophie that she should paint the painting any way she wanted to and that he had only tried to help because he thought she was stalled. "The truth, however, is that I saw it as a defeat," he says, "even though really it's kind of a victory. The statement that these two artists are stylistically incompatible is a more interesting one to make. A comedian can stand up and pretend to be Burt Lancaster, but we know that Matisse and Picasso are extremely different and difficult personalities that in this case refuse to intertwine. If you can still make it work, though, you win. What's winning? If I can stand in front of the painting and see Matisse and Picasso at the same time."

Growing impatient to paint, Sophie gave up working on the studies just before Christmas. She bought canvas at an art store in SoHo, stood on top of a dresser in her studio to tack it up on the wall, and spent two days applying two coats of gesso. Sitting on the floor, she began drawing in the lower left-hand corner and worked along the bottom to the right corner. Then, sometimes standing and sometimes kneeling, she drew from right to left across the middle of the painting. She drew the images along the top while standing on the dresser, then on a stepladder, which she found in the hallway outside her studio. By the third day, she had left a trail of pencil shavings and pencil lead across the base of the painting. She kept a large photocopy of *Guernica* on the floor beside her, or picked it up and folded it lengthwise into thirds, like a man reading a newspaper on a crowded train, so that she could concentrate on a specific section. At one point, she stood against the far wall and looked at the drawing and said, "Sometimes you get the feeling of something, and sometimes it's just a struggle, and I don't know why."

Gouache is too delicate to use on a painting that has to be rolled up to be moved, and enough oil paint to cover a canvas the size of *Guernica* would cost thousands of dollars, so Sophie decided to use acrylic paints, which are mixed from pigments, and which she had never used before. First, she applied black in the areas where Picasso had used black. Then she mixed a bright yellow. She held the photocopy in one hand and a brush in the other. She leaned forward, put the brush to the canvas, stopped, looked at the study, then slowly moved the brush forward again. "This is the most nerve-racking time," she said. "Getting started. There can be disappointments."

She painted the horse first, using green, blue, orange, red, and purple, applying paint that had a texture like honey. The colors were bright and wet in the light, but they dried hard and flat, especially the reds and blues. As the days passed, she applied layers of color over them in slightly different shades, and the reds got warmer, and the blues went from looking like paint on a wall to being like water you were staring into. The horse proved so difficult that she stood back from it one day and said, "I'm just going to try to keep going with something else. I'll come back to that later." She turned to the figure of the falling woman.

One day, the phone rang and she told the caller, "I just put the color up on a wall next to the falling woman. We're looking kind of heavy and flat and uninteresting, but it'll be fine. It'll be just fine."

One of the last figures she handled was the staggering woman. The woman has a shawl on her back, and when Sophie painted the shawl a deep red and gave it a border of black wavy lines, it turned out to be the single detail in the entire painting that could have come from either Picasso or Matisse.

As Sophie painted, she was aware of the vibrant and, for her, nearly illicit quality of Picasso's brawny line. She was also apprehensive about whether Naumann would like the finished painting. (He saw it on January 13 and liked it enormously.) Or whether anyone among her family or friends would say, as some of them did after her first show, "It's wonderful, Sophie, but when are you going to do your own work?" — not understanding that her depiction of a signature painting by the painter most different from her ancestor was a means, however indirect, of gaining the ground she needed to work entirely from her own imagery. In addition, there was the practical matter of learning to use the new paints to best advantage. During the first week in January, she ran out of the medium the pigments are mixed in, and had to go back to the store, Guerra Paint & Pigment, in the East Village, where she had bought them. She had been taken there by a friend from the École des Beaux-Arts who lives in California and paints murals for rich people. The friend was visiting the city over Christmas. Sophie had told her that she didn't know what paints would give her the lush texture that gouaches provide, and her friend had said that acrylics would, and that she knew where to get the best ones, assuming that the store, which she hadn't been to for years, still existed.

It was cold the day Sophie went back to the paint store, and she wore a big warm coat and one of those Asian wool hats that have flaps that come down over the ears and strings of yarn to tie them under the chin. Guerra Paint & Pigment occupies a small storefront on East Thirteenth Street. There is a counter facing the door and some shelves behind it with plastic bottles of pigments. Along the walls on either side of the counter and up to the ceiling are little swatches of paint colors that look very much like the newsprint on the horse in *Guernica*. When Sophie came through the door, the owners, a young man and woman, recognized her as the cheerful and charming woman who had asked a lot of questions and bought lots of pigments and not enough medium even though they told her she needed more, so they were not surprised to see her again. She told them that she loved the paints, and asked how to mix this or that color so that it would be more glossy or less glossy and how to thin the medium and so on. She handed over her credit card. The woman said, "Ah, a Matisse. You must be a great painter." And for a moment Sophie's face looked uncertain and childlike, as if someone had said something thoughtless to her. She said simply, "I hope so."

(2003)

The Gift

LAST SPRING, shortly before Paul Simon began rehearsing his band for a tour of Europe, he wrote three fragments of music — the first to occur to him in a year and a half. It was as long a dry period as he had ever been through. I went one night to a baseball game with him, and going home in his car he said, "The melodies have started to come. It's a relief."

Songwriters sometimes describe the sensation of songs arriving nearly intact. Simon has had this experience (the shower, "Still Crazy After All These Years"), but not often. His talent is more the patient and painstaking kind than the ecstatic. Songwriting, he says, is "trial and error repeated almost endlessly." A song usually takes him three months to finish. When he concludes a body of work, he tends to think that he has depleted his resources and that they won't be replenished. "I always feel that the situation is serious," he said in the car. "I'm in a vacuum, it's a dearth, and then there's something — a few notes, a phrase — and I say, 'I guess there's something,' but it's so small that I don't even know whether to count it."

Simon regards writing songs as the effort to find form for sounds he hears in his head. "Maybe ten, fifteen years ago," he said, "I realized that what I was fascinated with, couldn't explain, was sound — that you can't really say why a combination of sounds is moving or feels really good and right — and the whole game was: Can I get the sounds in my head on tape?" His driver brought the car to a stop at a light. Simon looked out the window. "I should get ready to work," he said softly. "You go into training — you play more, think more, listen more — instead of fretting over why you're not hearing the melodies."

To rehearse, Simon put the new work aside. The last time he did that, three years ago, he had five songs under way when he left them to prepare for a tour with Bob Dylan. Several months passed, the tour was over. Visiting a friend in New Mexico, he listened to recordings of the songs — he hadn't yet written any words — and was very pleased. Then he realized that he no longer felt any vestige of the impulse that had supplied them.

"I thought they had come from an inspired place," he said, "and I was just furious with myself for interrupting the work. What a fool I'd been, I thought, because I had just arrogantly assumed that the inspiration would return when I wanted it to. Then I thought, God, I have to get the rest. Because five tracks is only half an album. Of course five songs is half an album, but what if the point was: This was a level of joy in creating that you always hoped to attain. You think the experience involves ten because you need ten for the marketplace. Maybe you should just appreciate the experience, maybe that was the point, and there won't be any more." He sighed. "Anyway, another couple of months went by. I just had to wait."

The feeling of joy eventually returned. Many of the lyrics uncharacteristically came to him so quickly that he felt as if he were "taking dictation." After he had recorded the songs, on *You're the One,* released in 2000, he took the tapes to Los Angeles and played them for the executives at his record company. "They were nice, respectful — it's a great honor and so on — but they didn't actually understand," he said. "Or at least I thought they didn't understand. That record was hypnotic, in its way, and they were thinking more about 'speed and impact.'"

On his way home, Simon stopped at his friend's house in New Mexico, and while he was there the company's response began to unsettle him. "I thought, Why am I so desperately wanting to enter the marketplace? And then I said to myself, with a couple of synaptic leaps that I'm leaving out, 'You're just a big liar. And I know what the lie is.'" The voice reprimanding him had the tone of an Old Testament figure. "'This is Judgment Day, and there's no defense,'" it announced. "'I'm going to tell you a deep truth, and you're going to listen. You made this thing that you received partly as a gift, and you took it immediately to the marketplace without sufficiently appreciating it. And when you intuited that the marketplace wasn't going to accept it you knew right away that you had no business taking such a thing there. The gift was the point.'"

Simon paused. "It got worse," he went on. "'You don't like that?' the voice said. 'Then atone. Be a better person. You're lucky that this didn't occur on your deathbed, so that it would be the last thought you had.'"

Several weeks went by before something in him relaxed and he thought, You exaggerate. You were born with a talent and you worked hard at it, and the result gave people a lot of pleasure, and no matter what you did that was wrong, you can't throw that out. You didn't do it to give people pleasure. You did it to see if you could make the sounds in your imagination come out on tape.

The insight was followed, even so, by the year and a half of drought, during which Simon couldn't listen to anyone's music, especially his own, and he felt that he might not write any songs again.

Simon is less nomadic than musicians often are. What keeps him mostly at home is his wife, the singer Edie Brickell, who is from Texas, and their three young children. Nevertheless, he travels frequently. Last spring, he and his family spent ten days in Jamaica; he went to London for a week to visit Harper, his oldest son, from his first marriage, who plays guitar in a rock-and-roll band; he went to Memphis to meet Joseph Shabalala, the leader of Ladysmith Black Mambazo, the Zulu singing group that appears on Simon's 1986 album *Graceland;* he went a few times to his house by the ocean at the eastern end of Long Island; he made trips to Connecticut to see how the contractors were doing in renovating a house that he was moving to in the fall so that his children could have a life in the country; and he and his wife went to Venice to celebrate ten years of marriage. The rest of the time, he kept to a fairly regular schedule. He took the kids to school, then came home and worked with a physical trainer for two and a half hours; then he played guitar, then sometimes he picked up the kids. He has, of course, no material incentive to work. His offspring will be prosperous for generations. He is like the rich painters who have ranches or islands or palazzi and spend their days looking at sketches and patterns of clouds out the window or reading and staring at canvases. The time passes in a manner that is both leisurely and anxious. Eventually he tells himself, "You've got to go to work. Try this, try that, it's not fun. Who said it was going to be fun? Go to work."

When Simon went to Memphis in May to meet Shabalala, I went, too. Shabalala wants to build a museum devoted to South African music, especially the kind he heard as a child on a farm; he is now sixty.

Ladysmith Black Mambazo was performing near Memphis, and Simon thought that visiting the Delta Blues Museum, in Clarksdale, Mississippi, about an hour and a half south of the city, might suggest to Shabalala a plan. Simon also wanted to visit a health clinic in Clarksdale to which he gives a lot of money through the Children's Health Fund in New York, a charity he started with his friend Dr. Irwin Redlener.

It was raining when Simon and I left New Jersey in a small jet he had rented. When we got to Memphis, one of those jeeplike cars that make you feel as if you're seeing everything from the perspective of a man on horseback had been delivered to the terminal for us, and Simon drove. Leaving the airport, he took a wrong turn, and we wandered briefly before finding the tall buildings on the horizon.

Heading toward them, Simon described his last trip to Mississippi, some years back. "When I was recording with the Muscle Shoals rhythm section," he said, "we did this song called 'Take Me to the Mardi Gras,' and we wanted to get a Dixieland marching band for it, but we didn't want to go all the way to New Orleans. We were in Alabama, so we found this band and decided to meet them halfway, in Jackson, Mississippi, at a studio called Malaco Sound. When we get to Jackson, no one knows where Malaco Sound is. I pull into a gas station and ask, 'Does anyone know where Malaco Sound is?' and a guy leaning on the register with a toothpick in his mouth says slowly, 'Tell you what. See that there road?' I turn around, look at the road, say, 'Yeah, OK, I see the road.' 'Take that there road till you reach a golf field,' he says. 'Go past the golf field about a quarter mile, then turn left and come back.' 'OK,' I say. 'In a quarter mile make a right turn,' he says. 'That's the road for Malaco Sound.' I said, 'Why don't you just make a left turn after you pass the golf field?' And he took the toothpick out of his mouth slowly and started nodding and said, 'You could do that, too.'"

When we got to our hotel, Shabalala was sitting in the lobby, at a table by a fountain. He was drinking tea. He is a small, sturdily built man, with a round, open face. He and Simon hugged each other, then the three of us went out and got in the car. Shabalala had brought a tape of South African women singing traditional farm music, without accompaniment. For several of the songs, he had written parts for Ladysmith Black Mambazo, whose ten members are men. The first song, a hymn, was sung in Zulu. Instead of progressing in the stately manner of a Protestant hymn, it advanced like a spiritual, with hesitations in the phrasing and silences between the verses. Six or eight women took part. Their voices were pure and unadorned, and the singing was deeply felt. The men's voices entered unexpectedly after what I took to be the first verse, answering the women's, and the contrast between the two registers and textures was thrilling. "I don't know what I can do with it," Shabalala said. "I hope I can do something. I'm still working on it."

We passed shabby little shopping malls with discount stores and stores selling car parts; several pawnshops, a burial ground next to a junkyard, the Crystal Palace roller-skating rink; and then, as if a piece of stage scenery had been pulled into the wings, we were driving among crop rows that ran on either side of us to the horizon. The road was so straight that it seemed to have been taped onto the fields. The next song was a work song, Shabalala said. Along with the singers, he whistled sharply now and then, like a man calling cattle. "I never heard you do that," Simon told him. "It's a good sound for you."

"There was a young man on the farm where I made the recording," Shabalala said. "He was playing a five-string guitar and whistling, and he reminded me that I did that when I lived on a farm."

We arrived at the museum — a warehouse beside some railroad tracks — around lunchtime. The director, Tony Czech, led us past glass cabinets with guitars and photographs, walls with displays of records, and a room that contained the shack in which Muddy Waters was born. Simon is often regarded uncharitably by musicians who don't know him. The impression they have is that to make *Graceland* he went to South Africa, bought some records, came home and wrote lyrics, cheated the South African musicians out of royalties, paid up only when called to account, and finally walked into the sunset with boxcars of cash. Anyone who had the idea could have made a fortune from it, they think, and Simon just had it first. I wanted to know what Shabalala thought, so, at a moment when Czech had Simon's attention, I asked Shabalala when he and Simon had first met.

"Paul came to South Africa in 1985," he said. "I was on tour. When I called home, my wife tell me that Paul Simon want to talk to me. 'Are you kidding?' I say. 'How can I go to New York? He's a New York guy.' She say, 'No, he's in Johannesburg. He's waiting for you.' But I was in doubt. How does he know me? So I take a car to Johannesburg and somebody lead me to the studio, and I find many people waiting and Paul leading an audition. When I come in, he stop everything and he say, 'Joseph, I hear that you are on tour. I'm Paul Simon.' And I think, Is this him? There are people supposed to talk to Paul, but not me. He say, 'I love to work with you. I am a fan of Ladysmith Black Mambazo,' and the way he say it, it was like music, like he was singing it. I discovered in his eyes this man is full of music. And I say, 'To work together, what is it about, are there songs?' And he say yes. I say that we should work together, but I didn't know how. 'Are we going to blend together? The accent is so different.'"

On *Graceland,* the song "Diamonds on the Soles of Her Shoes" begins with Ladysmith Black Mambazo's voices. I asked whose idea that was. "Paul ask me, 'Joseph, can you please bless this song?'" Shabalala said. "He play it for me, and I listen and said, 'This song is OK.' He say, 'I still need your blessing,' so I write five lines in Zulu."

I asked what they are in English.

"He sing, 'She's a rich girl, she don't try to hide it, diamonds on the soles of her shoes.' So I answer what he said. 'It's not usually so,' I say, 'but now we see girls that can afford to maintain themselves.'"

Tony Czech brought us to a stop in front of a glass cabinet that had in it a National steel guitar — a guitar, that is, with a body made of steel. He opened the case and took the guitar out and handed it to Simon. Simon stood on one foot and balanced the guitar on his raised knee and played a couple of simple blues figures, the way any kid in a guitar store would, and then he moved his hand high up on the neck and played a descending line, a succinct, self-contained remark. He gave the guitar back and had his picture taken with Czech and the cashier at the gift shop; then he bought some CDs — among them one by the blues singer and guitarist Robert Johnson, because Shabalala had never heard him.

From the museum, we drove to the health clinic, where we walked through the halls with the director, a woman named Aurelia Jones-Taylor, and doctors and nurses came out of doorways to look at Simon, and a little girl in the waiting room raised her head from her mother's lap to see what the disturbance was about. Then Jones-Taylor took us to lunch at a place called Abe's BBQ. After lunch, Simon and Shabalala and I made the trip back to Memphis listening to Robert Johnson. I drove and Shabalala sat in the backseat, humming along and every once in a while shouting softly, "Yeah!"

The next morning, Simon and I flew home through turbulence, and neither of us felt so well when we landed. That night, Simon was traveling to London to visit his son. As Angel Aponte, his driver, was taking us back to the city, I asked about some lines in "Darling Lorraine," a song on *You're the One* in which a man and a woman meet, court, marry, squabble, make up, and then the woman falls sick and dies. The narrator, whose manner is evasive, is named Frank. "All my life I've been a wanderer," he sings. Then, "Not really, I mostly lived near my parents' home." Describing Lorraine's death late one night in a hospital bed, Simon sings, "All the trees were washed with April rain / and the moon in the meadow took darling Lorraine." The lines are the song's emotional peak, and so mysterious and poetic that I wondered how they had occurred to him.

"It could have been the heavens, I guess, but I used the moon," he said. "My apartment's across from the Sheep Meadow, in Central Park, so that's there. 'Trees being washed,' a ritual of death — washing the deceased — but because it's April it gives you a feeling of the sadness. 'April is the cruelest month,' sadness. It wasn't winter trees, it was the moon in the meadow that had a kind of hopefulness to it that seemed to work."

A few years ago, Simon was on *The Oprah Winfrey Show* to promote his Broadway musical, *The Capeman,* and Winfrey tried to coax him into saying that he regarded himself as a genius. (She failed.) I asked if the exchange had felt awkward. "I never thought of myself as an artist until I was in my forties," he said, "and then it was only as a personality type. I thought I was a bright guy, real smart. I could figure stuff out.

"I was good at things. That's what I thought, but there were periods when I couldn't explain what I wrote. I don't think I'm special, and I never did — I didn't think, I'm twenty-one and I've written 'The Sound of Silence.' When I wrote 'Bridge over Troubled Water,' I thought, That's better than I usually write. As decades go by, you're grateful for the talent you have, but there's a time when you just put away your feelings and work. Whoever is sitting at the top of the heap, that's a genius," he said disdainfully. "Anyway, I wasn't ever sitting at the top."

He paused. Then he said, "As you get older, you're looked at differently. Now I'm 'legendary.' It means that kids don't listen to you as much as you might like, you're not talking about what they're interested in, and even if you were, they wouldn't be listening to you any more than kids want to listen to their parents."

He shrugged. "Actually, these observations form an internal dialogue of very little consequence, because you're going to do what you're going to do anyway. The question I have, though, is when you can create something as complicated rhythmically and thematically as 'Darling Lorraine,' how do you measure the quality, especially since the earlier work was enormously popular? I can still put together 'Darling Lorraine' or 'You're the One.' It won't mean as much as 'Graceland' or 'Bridge over Troubled Water.' Those songs had an effect on people's lives. 'Mrs. Robinson' or 'Still Crazy After All These Years' or '50 Ways' — they're in the culture. If the work isn't part of the popular culture, is it as meaningful? Even though there are examples of posthumous recognition, for the most part a song's a hit or it's gone."

The phone in the car rang and Simon answered it. He listened for a moment, and then, his voice full of affection — he was speaking to his wife — he said, "Ten minutes. We're on the West Side Highway."

About a week after Simon got back from London, and shortly before the rehearsals began, I met him at his office in Times Square, where he played a CD he had made of the two fragments he had written — he hadn't yet written the third. One of the tracks was a slow shuffle based on the descending line he had played at the Blues Museum, and the other was a briskly rising arpeggiated figure, a series of simple chords — a guitar practice pattern that he had adapted. The playing was skillful and intricate, and I asked why when he performed he let other guitarists play the more complicated parts. "I can't play and sing," he said. While I sat and listened to the shuffle, Simon stood behind me and sang nonsense syllables and every once in a while added a line. "Hell yeah, I'm angry at myself, can't blame no one else, so I'm angry at myself," is the only one I heard clearly.

After a few minutes, he turned off the disk and sat down. "That's the beginning," he said. Then he asked, "Do you mind if I play the guitar? I feel more comfortable with a guitar in my hands." From a closet, he got one and sat down and played the figure he had played at the museum. "It could go a lot of ways," he said. "If I added a blues harp, it would sound blues. I could add an acoustic bass. My son Harper thought it might sound good without a bass at all — a guitar record, which I haven't made in years."

He put the guitar down. "A lot of it anyhow is just slogging away," he said. "The first tracks, when I came out of the studio, I was ambivalent. I went through, first, denial — I don't think it's good, but maybe it's good and people will like it. Then I get to, I don't care what people think, it's no good. I have to find somebody to help me fix it, because I don't know what to do." He leaned forward and put his elbows on his knees. "I was thinking, I don't know who's going to help," he said, "and when I get over being annoyed I'll take out everything that I don't like, then I'll revise it. I worked with Vincent Nguini, the guitar player in my band, and Steve Gadd, the drummer, and we fixed the guitar part and the drums, and now it's right. There's still a section that needs to be improved, and I could easily fool with the bass and play with the sounds of the record, making the arrangements richer, which at least I have a theory about how to do, but since I'm going out on the road again, and the rehearsals are about to start, I'm going to leave it."

I asked if I could hear the songs once more, and he said sure. "Do you like it with the singing, or no singing?" he asked.

I said I liked the singing.

He turned the disk back on and began to sing quietly. Out of the corner of my eye, I watched him dancing, with his feet in place and his arms and shoulders moving in an angular way, as if he were a figure in a hieroglyph.

Simon is the size of a jockey, except that instead of being wiry he is barrel-chested and muscular. His hands are small and thick; they look like paws. His expression is habitually solemn, and it always has been. As a toddler, he smiled so rarely that his parents called him Cardozo, after the Supreme Court Justice Benjamin Cardozo, whose manner was pointedly grave. When he went as a child to candy stores to buy comic books, people would say, "What's the matter?" and he always thought, Why do they ask me that? His gestures are minimal and understated, and so is his manner. His sentences trail off and are completed by a slight extension of the chin, a mild widening of the eyes, a delicate shrug. His band members know that the remarks "I don't think so," or "Yeah, but . . . ," delivered with no special inflection, amount to an emphatic dismissal. The extravagant subtlety of his manner and movements must once have been a refinement, an awareness that a small man making flamboyant gestures or talking too loudly might look comical. Onstage he is subdued. He tends to raise his arms and wave his hands wanly — and he probably shouldn't. He has never been very comfortable with his appearance. A friend of his told me that he won't look at a photograph of himself. When I asked Simon if this was true, he said, "Yeah," then added, "Actually, it's better if you do look, because then you can do something about it."

He prefers reading poetry — especially Blake, Yeats, and John Neihardt — to fiction. Fiction writers "are in the world of the imagination," he says, "and I'm in the world of the imagination, so it's too much." He also likes to read "science for the layman, because I was never any good at science and I'm curious about it now." Growing up, he was a good baseball player, and is surprised that even though he no longer takes part in the sport he sometimes dreams that he is drawing a walk, or can hit major-league pitching, or is standing in the outfield and can't pick up his feet. "It can go either way," he says.

Fifteen or twenty years ago, he realized that he could recall nearly every piece of music he had heard as a child, and that some of it had found its way into his songs, however obscurely. John Lennon once told him that the BBC didn't play rock-and-roll when he was young, but Radio Caroline, the pirate station in the English Channel, did. "It was so far away," Simon told me, "that the signal would come and go, and the texture of it was something he said he always tried to get into his records." The rhythms of Elvis Presley's version of "Mystery Train" turn up again and again in his own writing, he said, each time differently.

As a singer, Simon is an adept and imaginative phraser, an ability he developed to compensate, he says, "for not having a big voice." What limits most songwriters' melodies, he believes, is the reach of their voices, so he takes singing lessons to extend his range. He says that he knows intuitively when a melody is right, but that he is less confident of his lyrics, which he sometimes asks friends to review. Among his contemporaries in popular music, perhaps only Paul McCartney is his peer as a writer of melodies, just as Bob Dylan and, maybe, James Taylor are his only peers as a lyricist. Writing, as John Cheever somewhere remarks, is not a competitive sport, and songwriting isn't, either. When Simon observes that he wasn't "at the top of the heap," he means that no one ever made a fuss over him the way people did over Dylan and the Beatles. The greatest difference among them, as far as I can tell, is that they matured at different times of their lives. Dylan and Lennon and McCartney did most of their memorable work as young men. Also, as young men they were innovators. Simon became an innovator as an older man. The careers of Dylan and McCartney seem circular, in that they both return to forms they have already made use of. Simon's career seems linear, in that he takes up styles and genres, then discards them, a pattern that he says he learned by observing the career of Miles Davis, with whom he was friends.

All of these artists are musical opportunists. Dylan used Nashville-style country music to present a startling version of himself in the same way that Simon later made use of South African music. As a younger man, Simon sometimes felt overshadowed by Dylan's larger reputation. Dylan's hobo persona, his subversive quality, and his contempt for authority were charismatic. A lot of people made fun of his voice, but nearly everyone agreed that the songs were compelling. Next to him, Simon and Garfunkel seemed polite, studious, and eager to please — college boys. The best of their music was pretty to listen to and sometimes, as with "Bridge over Troubled Water," had emotional force. Dylan's songs made a person feel powerful. Since *Graceland,* though, comparisons between Simon and Dylan no longer sensibly apply or take into proper account the distinctive merits of two maverick artists.

Simon's close friend Lorne Michaels, who has known him for thirty years, told me, "Since I met Paul, he's been saying that he's getting out of show business." When I asked Simon if that was so, he said, "I always ask myself when I start something, 'Is this what you want to do?' I recorded when I was fifteen or sixteen, and the record was a hit. So I was in show business. I was in the world of records at a very young age. I was already becoming what I am. Basically, what I'm doing is an idea conceived by a thirteen-year-old. And I often think, You can review that idea, because it was a thirteen-year-old who thought it up. And I do review it, but I still like it."

Simon is sixty-one. He was born on October 13, 1941, in Newark, New Jersey, but he grew up in Kew Gardens, Queens. He lived with his father and mother and younger brother in an attached house in a row of identical houses. His father, Louis, who is no longer alive, sometimes drove into the wrong driveway. "How you supposed to tell these places apart?" he would ask. Simon's mother, Belle, was a schoolteacher, who quit working to bring up Simon and his younger brother, Eddie, a former musician; he now helps handle his brother's business. Louis Simon was a professional musician; he played the upright bass. For a while, he was a member of studio bands that worked for the television personalities

Arthur Godfrey and Garry Moore. Simon and his brother would occasionally stay up late so that they could see their father when the camera showed the band. Louis also led his own bands, and for twenty-five years he had a job on Thursday afternoons at Roseland, where the other band on the bill played Latin music. When he was in his fifties, he grew tired of the musician's life and went back to school. He got a doctorate in linguistics and became a professor at City College.

In grade school, Simon heard Arthur Garfunkel, the son of a traveling salesman, sing at a school assembly. Observing the impression that Garfunkel's performance made on everyone, he decided that he wanted to be a singer, too. In the sixth grade, they were in *Alice in Wonderland* together — Garfunkel was the Mad Hatter, Simon was the White Rabbit. Simon's father gave him a guitar and showed him some chords. Simon used to sit in the bathroom with the lights off and turn on the water and play; he liked the reverberation against the tiles. The first lines of "The Sound of Silence" ("Hello darkness my old friend / I've come to talk with you again") invoke the experience. By the time Simon was twelve or thirteen, he was writing songs and he and Garfunkel were singing together. They were fourteen when they began looking up record companies in the yellow pages and trying to arrange auditions. Most of the companies were boss-and-a-secretary outfits in the Brill Building, at 1619 Broadway, where Simon now has his office. One day in 1956, when they were fifteen, they were recording a demo and a man named Sid Prosen, standing in the hallway outside the studio, heard them and signed them up. As Tom & Jerry, they recorded a song they had written called "Hey, Schoolgirl," and Prosen released it on the Big Record label, with a song of Simon's called "Dancin' Wild" on the B side. The magazine *Cashbox* picked "Hey, Schoolgirl" as its Sleeper of the Week and said, "This debut by the vocal duo looks as if it is going to make a strong bid to give the boys and the Big Label an initial high chart run. On the 'Hey, Schoolgirl' session, the stuff of which hit teen pressings are made, the up-tempo 'Hey, Schoolgirl' has its setting in the classroom. Tom & Jerry, with some vocal resemblance to the Everly Brothers, get the tune off invitingly. 'Dancin' Wild' is a lively issue highlighted by the twosome's bright harmony."

Prosen paid Alan Freed, the most popular disc jockey in the city, to play the record, and it sold a hundred thousand copies. For nine weeks it was one of *Billboard*'s Top 100, and in New York it was in the Top 10.

Tom & Jerry performed "Hey, Schoolgirl" on *American Bandstand,* and the show's panel of three couples gave it a score of 95, saying that it was great to dance to. (Simon: "Actually, I noticed when they said that, it wasn't.") He and Garfunkel were sixteen when the record came out and, because both had skipped grades, they were seniors in high school. "*American Bandstand*'s other guest was the manic rockabilly singer Jerry Lee Lewis. When Garfunkel and Simon went into the dressing room, Lewis was leaning into the mirror and combing his hair. He ignored them, and they found him daunting. "I think it was the tough blondness of it," Simon told me. "All the tough guys I knew were Italian. He looked dangerous." Some of the money Simon made he saved, and with the rest he bought a red convertible.

After "Hey, Schoolgirl," Tom & Jerry released "That's My Story," which went nowhere. Neither did the two or three records that came after that. They stopped recording. Using names such as Jerry Landis and Tico and the Triumphs, Simon continued to make demos. He also made a record by himself, without telling Garfunkel, which Garfunkel regarded as a betrayal, and for several years they didn't speak to each other.

Simon went to Queens College, where he had a teacher who persuaded him to major in English. ("Otherwise," he says, "I wouldn't have known what to do.") He graduated in 1962 and went to Europe and sang on the street. After a few months, he came home, and the next fall he went to law school at Brooklyn College, and more or less flunked out. Crossing a bridge in Kew Gardens, he met Garfunkel, who was now an architecture student. They began singing together again and eventually, in 1964, made a record called *Wednesday Morning, 3 A.M.* On it are some folk songs, a Dylan cover, and five songs that Simon wrote, including a version of "The Sound of Silence" on which Simon plays acoustic guitar and another musician plays the upright bass.

The record sold only a few thousand copies, and Simon went abroad again, this time to England, where he worked as a folksinger. While he was there, a producer added electric guitar, electric bass, and drums to "The Sound of Silence," without telling Simon. A few weeks later, performing in Denmark, Simon came across a copy of *Cashbox.* The record was No. 59 on the magazine's chart, with a bullet, meaning that it was rising quickly. Simon told himself, "My life is irrevocably changed." He went back to America. Garfunkel was living with his mother and father.

Simon moved into his old room in his parents' house. There wasn't really anything for them to do. In those days, musicians toured mostly with revues, and they weren't members of any. One afternoon, they were sitting in Simon's red convertible, listening to the radio, when the disc jockey played "The Sound of Silence" and said, "No. 1, Simon and Garfunkel," and Simon said, "That Simon and Garfunkel, they must be having a great time."

They made five albums and then, in 1970, they split up, partly because Garfunkel wanted to act in movies. In 1981, they played a reunion concert in Central Park that was attended by half a million people. They considered making another album. Simon was recording the songs for what became *Hearts and Bones*. Garfunkel wanted a copy when Simon was done so that he could add his own parts, but Simon wasn't willing to allow him that much control. They gave up the project, and the record, which was released in 1983, became Simon's first commercial failure. When he went to South Africa a year later, to pursue an enthusiasm for African music, he felt that no one was paying any attention to him at all.

The mature period of Simon's work — the songs that use more complicated structures and rhythms and are written without regard for whether they will be hits — began with *Graceland,* the record he made in South Africa. During this time, he stopped writing songs in a conventional manner — that is, by using a guitar or a piano to compose a melody to fit lyrics, or to write lyrics while he played the melody. He abandoned it partly because what he knew about music theory had outgrown what he knew about the guitar. "The amount of information I had as a player hadn't kept up with the melodies and chord structures I could think of," he told me. Also, he said, "what I discovered while making *Graceland* was a deeper understanding of rhythm. With most music, I just knew it wasn't there — this doesn't have a groove, there's no pocket, it doesn't make you want to move. It could be loud and fast, like punk, but it doesn't make you want to move. The big learning experience from the African musicians, and especially the guitarists, was how do I break down a rhythm and understand its workings, what its effects are derived from, how I might reproduce them, instead of writing something and thinking, That's a good groove. I hope I get another one."

With *Graceland*, Simon decided that he would make rhythm the most important consideration and that he would handle one element of a song at a time. He would begin with what he calls "a rhythmic premise," find music on the guitar to accompany it, record the combination, and, while listening to it, come up with a melody. Finally, he would write words to fit the melody. "If I have the guitar down on a track," he told me, "I can sing a counterpoint to it, I can sing in syncopation. Along the way, I'm going to compose partly intellectually and partly intuitively. I've had people say to me over the last few years, 'Why don't you write the way you used to?' and I don't know what they mean. They imagine me sitting in a room with a guitar, strumming a melody."

Simon's next album, *The Rhythm of the Saints*, which was made partly in Brazil, was the result of a conversation he had with the Latin musicians Eddie Palmieri and Tito Puente. "I met them at a club downtown called S.O.B.'s," Simon told me. "I went to hear some African bands, it was '87, and they said, 'Well, look, you can't just make one album and leave and turn away. You have to go on now. You've gone to South Africa, which is for voices, but now you have to go where the drum is, to West Africa and Brazil.'"

"Diamonds on the Soles of Her Shoes," the last song written for *Graceland*, ends with the South African group Ladysmith Black Mambazo singing to the accompaniment of West African drums. By putting them together, Simon had made a bridge, unconsciously or not, to *The Rhythm of the Saints*.

"The other thing that contributed to my going to Brazil was that Milton Nascimento — the Brazilian musician — asked me to do a duet. He said he'd send me a couple of songs he was working on — he wanted me to write the words. This was 1988. He sends me two songs, and I pick one. I didn't know what to do, though, because I don't know who I am. He just gave me the 'la la la.' I couldn't imagine what to say, because am I speaking as Milton or am I me? He's Brazilian. If I'm speaking as me, then what am I doing with someone else's music? He sings in a higher register than I do, so to get the sense of it I began to sing a line of harmony underneath his. Anyway, I'm getting nowhere.

"The days go by, so now here comes the week we go to L.A. I'm at the hotel. Milton says, 'What have you got?' I say, 'All I got is I sing along with you on the harmonies.' So I know I'm never going to get it. I think, I'm just going to get on a plane and go home. Then I think, You can't, you have to at least go to the studio and say, 'I'm sorry.' At the studio, Milton writes me out the words phonetically, and I sing them in Portuguese. They say it sounds good. And, well, anyway, there it is. It's done.

"After the session, we're standing in the parking lot and I say, 'I'm thinking about doing an album about drums, drumming as it goes from West Africa to Brazil to the Caribbean to Cuba and into New Orleans.' Milton says, 'I'll help. You come to Brazil, and I'll set you up with musicians.' So I go, in 1989."

The idea that he might write a Broadway musical came to Simon while he was touring in South Africa to promote *Graceland*. As he performed with Ladysmith Black Mambazo and Miriam Makeba and Hugh Masekela, he felt that the pattern of their duets resembled the comings and goings of characters in a show that didn't necessarily have a story but had a theme, and that if he saw such a performance in a theater he might like it.

The Capeman involves two murders committed in New York in 1959. A sixteen-year-old Puerto Rican named Salvador Agrún stabbed two Irish boys in a gang fight. The people who saw the fight said that the killer wore a black cape. The newspapers called him the Capeman. It took the police three days to find him, and when he was arrested he was defiant. A photograph of him in custody appeared on the front page of the *New York Daily News*, with the headline DON'T CARE IF I BURN, SNEERS SLAYER OF TWO.

The Capeman is written as if it were meant to be heard on the radio. Instead of the action's unfolding through exchanges among characters, the plot is conveyed mostly through songs. One of them begins, "It was the morning of October 6, 1960 / I was wearing my brown suit / Preparing to leave the house of D" — D being detention. Simon wrote the story and some of the words with the poet Derek Walcott. Simon feels that he probably wrote the story as if it were a song, and Walcott wrote his part as if it were a poem. The difficulties that the show experienced are well known — it was one of the more prominent Broadway failures of the decade — but they unfortunately overshadowed the music, which is superb. One way of thinking about *The Capeman* is that neither Paul Simon nor Derek Walcott is the equal as a dramatist of Paul Simon the songwriter. Another is to acknowledge the problematic nature of the material. The murders take place in the first act. Nothing that happens after — what became of the Capeman, whether he had an encounter with Saint Lazarus or only thought he did, whether he was cursed from childhood, whether his joining the Church was sincere — is as dramatic.

The *Times* reviewer described *The Capeman* as a "sad, benumbed spectacle," which "registers as one solemn, helplessly confused drone." The show closed after sixty-eight performances. My own feeling is that the evening contained one compelling moment — an exchange in a church, during which the Capeman's mother meets the mothers of his victims, asks to be forgiven, and is rebuffed — but that otherwise the narrative was too dreamy, surreal, and diffuse for Broadway. The production probably would have been better received had it played at, say, the Brooklyn Academy of Music, where it wouldn't have had to satisfy Broadway expectations. Simon thought that in order for the show to have the authority he wanted it to have he needed the Latin stars Marc Anthony, Ruben Blades, and Ednita Nazario, who were happy to put their other work aside to appear on Broadway, but who he thinks would not have responded to the enticement "Play in Brooklyn!"

Simon was among the investors who lost money on the show. His face during rehearsals was ashen, and his expression was grim. He put on weight from eating out on so many nights, and Marc Anthony, who played the young Salvador Agrún, got him smoking, which he hadn't done since he was a teenager. When he sat across from Oprah Winfrey, he could see in her eyes that she thought he looked a lot older than he had the last time she'd seen him.

The rehearsals for the European tour were held in a room above a rim-and-tire store near the West Side Highway. Simon had engaged eleven musicians — a drummer, a percussionist, a bass player, two guitarists, two keyboard players, a trombone player, a saxophone player, a trumpet player, and a singer to sing in his stead when he needed to listen closely to the band. A second percussionist would be joining them in Europe. Simon has a very intelligent band: there are no charts, every musician remembers his parts, even though since the last tour, a year earlier, he may have worked with dozens of other musicians playing music from all over the world. (For example, Jamey Haddad, one of the percussionists, had just returned from a festival of sacred music in Morocco.) Simon's band is so accomplished, he says, that leading it is like "driving a really expensive race car: if you have the touch, it responds, and if you don't it goes everywhere."

The band's first chair is occupied by the drummer Steve Gadd, who has recorded and performed with Simon for roughly twenty-five years. He is responsible for the strutty little military figure on "50 Ways to Leave Your Lover," which, after the drum part in "Wipeout," is perhaps the most widely recognized piece of percussion in popular music. A year ago, Gadd was touring with Eric Clapton, so Simon had to make do with another drummer; he was an excellent drummer — no one gets through the door without having superlative chops — but Simon felt that the band missed Gadd's authority. To compensate, the musicians augmented their parts until the arrangements became too elaborate for Simon's ear. As a tour progresses, musicians, either from enthusiasm, nerves, or inclination, tend to play more. A lot of what Simon hoped to do in rehearsals was strip away parts. "There's always a lot of clutter," he said. "After a while, it gets a little rococo."

The rehearsals began at noon. The room was large and painted black and had windows on two sides. Simon would run through a song from *You're the One* called "Old," which starts with his playing a briskly repeated pattern of simple chords, and the band would join him, and almost immediately he would wave his arms and say, "Does it start like that, with everybody?" Someone would sheepishly say no, actually it starts with the drums, and they would begin again. Or he would address one of the horn players: "You don't have to play the whole phrase. Leave out notes. It's that thing of tricking the ear into hearing what's not there." Or say to a keyboard player, "Drop two notes now and then. Play the shadow of it, so that we don't get too accustomed to it." Or tell the saxophone player, "Growl it, but stick it into the blend. Let's see if it works," and when the horn player did what Simon wanted Simon shrugged and said, "Too staccato. Lazy it up."

One day, he had an idea for a section toward the end of "The Coast," from *The Rhythm of the Saints*. The lyrics describe a funeral in "the harbor church of St. Cecilia." On the record, the section passes without any elaboration, but a part for a brass trio had lately suggested itself to Simon. After he taught it to the horn players by singing it to them, and they played it a few times without satisfying him, he said, trying to be helpful, "My original idea was that it was supposed to sound like a Salvation Army band. Or maybe New Orleans." He sat down on a folding chair and tipped the front legs off the floor. He was wearing a T-shirt, jeans, and a baseball cap, and the gesture made him look like a testy schoolboy. The horns played the section again. It still didn't strike him as apt. He walked over and sang into the ear of the trombone player. The musician, who was taller, bent to him as if he were listening to a secret. The musicians tried again, and this time Simon told them, "That sounds fine to me." The entire band played the song from the beginning, but when they came to the new part Simon waved his hands and said to the trombone player, "I think you come in too soon. And you should come in with a big slide."

"Go Dixieland, man," someone said.

Simon shook his head. "It's a funeral procession," he said.

The band had been at work, with a short break, for about six hours. "You're actors at this point," Simon told them wearily. "You're playing guys in a funeral procession. You're not you, you're just guys."

Then he sat down. "I don't know what's happened," he said. "Everything seems to have fallen apart." The musicians offered explanations. Simon stood up and listened to them. Then he turned his back to them, sat down again, and began absently playing his guitar.

To the last rehearsal I attended Simon brought his nine-year-old son, Adrian, a skinny little bristly-haired, redheaded boy. Adrian went around the room talking to all the musicians and having them show him things. His father stood at the front of the room, drinking coffee. The band worked through "The Coast" again. Simon had written a new guitar part for himself and wanted to try it out. "Fourteen years I've played this song," he said, "and I finally figured out the guitar part." Then they moved on to "Slip Slidin' Away," which has a part for a vocal quartet. Simon collected Jay Ashby, the trombone player, Tony Cedras, one of the keyboard players, and Mark Stewart, the second guitar player, to run through it with him. The three of them stood in a half circle, facing Simon, to sing. Cedras is a tall, thin South African with dreadlocks to his waist. He held a cardboard coffee cup in one hand and tapped time on the bottom of it with the fingers of his other hand. Stewart has long red hair, which he piled on top of his head and held in place with a chopstick, like a geisha. The other musicians sat in a lounge outside the room, having the conversation they always seemed to have, about computers. Adrian sat among them.

Two and three at a time, the musicians filed back into the room. Simon was at the microphone, ready to begin. When Adrian appeared, Simon said, "Adrian, what are you doing? You OK? You're not smoking, are you? 'Cause that is the smokers you're hanging with." Adrian grinned and went off to sit next to Jamey Haddad, the percussionist. The song took quite some time to work out. Adrian came over and lay down on the floor by his father, his head resting against a speaker. He sang along, grimacing like a blues shouter on the high notes. "Slip Slidin' Away" includes the lines

> I know a father who had a son
> he longed to tell him all the reasons for the things he'd done.

When it arrived, Adrian fell silent and looked up into his father's face. Haddad knocked over a cymbal, which fell to the floor. Simon stopped singing, and the band came to a halt. "That's nice," he said. "It's different. It's unusual." He took a sip of coffee. "Keep it," he said, putting down the coffee cup, "but make it sound like an accident."

Later that evening, I talked to Simon on the phone. "I didn't get much sleep last night," he said. "The words are starting to come — they woke me up at six. Usually when the words come in the middle of the night I think, I'll remember that, but I thought this time it was important to get up and write them down. And when I actually woke up I didn't remember any of them. I don't know what they are, probably not important." I could hear him turning pages.

"After I put the pen down and went back to bed, more came," he said. "In fact, the story came. I don't know the whole thing, and I don't know if it fits anything I'm writing. To me, it's an example of nothing but that the process has taken hold. It's waking me up — which is a good sign."

Then he said that he had written a third piece of music. "It feels like it has fallen into a title," he said. "The rhythm of the notes is exactly 'Once upon a time,' a slow descending line. Whether it's called that later, I don't know. It's usable now. The story had a guy like the guys I knew when I was growing up in Queens. So my mind is going click, click with these rhymes, and I can see every scene."

He paused and then said, "Anyhow, I wake up and I say, 'So I was born in the city of Newark, but as soon as I could talk I expressed a preference for New York' — Newark, New York, a rhyme. 'So I'm a talker-slash-New Yorker. I'm meeting a guy from Queens. Not a borough with a great name, blah, blah, blah.' I don't know what this is all about. 'Terrorists and tumors,' I don't know, terrorists and tumors and I have rumors, tumors — I became stuck for a rhyme' — and then I thought, Oh, no, no, no, I have baby boomers. I figure this guy's going to get on the cell phone, and he's going to hear a voice — it's going to be the voice of God — so the language will have to change. I'm not sure how I'll do it, but it's an interesting story. Maybe it won't be an interesting story, who knows?"

The extension he keeps for his family and his closest friends began to ring. "I have to take this," he said. "It might be my wife calling."

While I waited, I thought about the man hearing the voice of God on his cell phone, and the reprimand that Simon had received from the Old Testament figure. When Simon came back on the line, he said, "Anyway, it involves that device of letting the mind go effortlessly into a character and then turning at an unexpected point. So it's begun."

Because I asked him to, he read some entries from his lyric book. "This is from my books for You're the One," he said. "Here's a line: 'The ocean and the atmosphere, clouds on fire, pay dirt, dancing DNA, wake up, don't sleep, get out of the way.'

"'Star quilt,'" he continued. "That became 'quilt of stars.' 'If I was a guitar I wouldn't play that song' — didn't use it. 'Sage and sweet grass' — used it. 'Guru in the morning, bored by the afternoon, fool by sunset' — nope."

I asked what kind of book he wrote in.

"A loose-leaf binder," he said, "so I can tear the pages out. People always give me these hand-bound leather books, and I can't ever write in them. They're too perfect. It's a presumption to try."

When Simon and his wife got back from their trip to Venice, he and I and Angel Aponte went to the game at Yankee Stadium. Simon seemed subdued. In the car, he handed Aponte a CD, a recording of him playing a slow and spare chordal figure — the third fragment.

"It's beautiful," I said.

"It took me all day."

"It's so clean."

"That's what took me all day. Anyway, I wanted to get one more tune started before I went out on tour, and this is the one."

It was a cool, windy evening and every now and then programs and newspapers blew across the infield. Simon took a liking to a little Latino boy who was sitting with his mother in the row in front of us. She looked to be about twenty-five. When Simon heard the boy ask for some ice cream and his mother say she didn't want to leave the game, Simon told her, "I'll go." She appeared not to know who he was; at least, she hadn't paid much attention to him earlier, except to give him the smile a mother gives a mild-looking guy who is being nice to her child. Simon and the boy left and were gone longer than the errand seemed to require. The mother turned in her seat to look for them. Aponte said, "It's all right," and she, not especially reassured, said, "I only have the one." When they got back, Simon told her that the ice cream machine closest to our seats was broken, so they had gone to another. A few people approached Simon and asked if he would sign their programs or let them take his picture, and he said, "Can we do it after the game?" At the end of the game, the crowd pressed in upon him so avidly that no one could get a picture anyway. When someone asked for one, he said, "Oh, I don't really like pictures. Do you?"

Outside the stadium, Simon's car had been delivered to the curb. While we were waiting on Frederick Douglass Boulevard for a light to change, I turned to ask Simon a question and was brought up short when his arm shot to his armrest and his tinted window began lowering. He stared straight ahead, his face composed in its customary deadpan expression. I had no idea what he was doing. Next to us was a small car with all the windows open. The driver was a man who looked West Indian; at least, he had long dreadlocks, and so did the man next to him. Each of them had an unlit cigarette between his lips and neither of them moved. They paid no attention to us, and Simon appeared to be paying no attention to them. Then I realized that he was listening closely to the music coming from the speakers in their car. It sounded like single-chord reggae in a minor key, but the singer chanted more than sang, and the melody was mournful and Eastern-sounding.

"Jamaican," Simon said. Then, "Maybe it's not Jamaican. It's almost Arabic-sounding." His head moved slightly with the rhythm. The light changed, and the other car took off ahead of us. Simon hummed the melody. "It really had an African sound to it." he said. He raised his window. Then, his tone downcast, "I understand that sound — the pulse — you got to go out and dance. More people probably want to do that than listen to me explore the further ranges of my songwriting."

"Well, anyway, you're past the crisis point," I said. "The work's under way."

"I would say so," he said. He hummed the melody softly. He looked out the window. "There's nothing you can do if you don't have the confidence," he said. "You really have to believe it. And when you believe it's extraordinary — well, even if it isn't, just the pleasure of belief . . ." He completed the remark with the slightest of shrugs.

(2002)

Facing the Shooter

IKE RICHTER, the young goaltender for the New York Rangers, has a large, square face, like a detective in a comic strip. The bloodlines in his family run to two types: long-boned and thin, and compact and sturdy. Richter is the latter. He has sloping shoulders and broad hands. He is about five feet ten, and husky. He looks bigger in street clothes than he does in his uniform, because the padding he wears on his chest and shoulders is so bulky that it makes his head look small. When Richter is wearing regular clothes, one notices a wide back, thick legs, and shoulders that seem to descend from his ears. A crescent-shaped scar in the center of his forehead contracts when he lowers his head to think, as he usually does before answering a question. The scar is the result of a shot from a teammate which struck his helmet two years ago, during the warmup before a game. Richter's manner is cheerful and generous and cooperative, but guarded. It is not in his character to be introspective. There is a boyishness to his face which suggests that he hasn't yet grown into his circumstances — those of a big-time athlete in the world's biggest sports town — and also suggests an openness that is not actually part of his nature.

In June 1985, at the age of eighteen, Richter was selected by the Rangers in the second round of the annual draft of amateur players. He had graduated from high school two weeks earlier and had decided to attend the University of Wisconsin instead of Harvard. Richter is the youngest member of a large family — he has two brothers and four sisters — and his father had been ill, so there was little extra money for tuition. Wisconsin offered a full scholarship, with the expectation that Richter would play for their hockey team. For years, Richter, growing up in Flourtown, Pennsylvania, a suburb of Philadelphia, had privately nurtured the ambition to play in the National Hockey League, and he felt that the program at Wisconsin, which offered more games than Harvard's and a more single-minded atmosphere, would better prepare him to get there. That no one from suburban Philadelphia had ever done so didn't deter him.

It has always been a commonplace in hockey that a singular type of person is drawn to occupying the goal. Goalies have traditionally been thought of as men who nurse grievances, cherish slights, startle easily, brood, and suffer nervous complaints. The annals of hockey include at least one goalie who became nauseated and threw up before games. On occasion, he would leave the ice to be sick, then return to the net. Sometimes, asleep on an airplane, he would suddenly kick one foot to the side, as if he were stopping a puck. Ulcers and insomnia have been prominent among goalies. A goalie named Wilf Cude was habitually so tense on days when he was to play that once, at lunch, he threw a steak at his wife, because she asked how a particular goal had got past him. The steak hit the wall behind her, and before it reached the floor he had decided to retire.

Part of the anxiety a goaltender endures is a result of the signal responsibility of his position. A goalie is the only player who plays the entire game, and he is the only player whose lapse of concentration can almost surely guarantee a goal to be scored. He is also the only player who cannot win a game. All he can do is lose one, help preserve a lead, or keep his team in a game that is close. People unfamiliar with the complexities of hockey are more likely to blame a goalie for a goal than any other player, even one whose defensive error may have allowed the person who scored to be unattended. A goaltender once described the pressure all goalies experience by saying, "What other job do you know of where, when you make a mistake, a red light goes on behind you, and fifteen thousand people call you a jerk?"

Richter does not throw steaks. The streak of the exile is strong in him, though. Among his teammates, he is a rarefied species. Young men from Canada still fill the majority of positions on the rosters of National Hockey League teams. While it is no longer exceptional for a professional hockey player to be an American — perhaps one in every five or six is — what nearly all the other Americans have in common is that they grew up in cold climates. Like the Canadians and the Europeans they play alongside, they were raised within the context of a sport that was played widely by children in the towns where they lived. It is not unusual for professional hockey players to have played next to more than one teammate since childhood, and many professionals have played with or against one another, or have heard of one another, or have had friends in common for years before they begin making their living from hockey. In a back room of the house where Richter grew up is a corner with pictures of Richter on teams he belonged to as a child. Each year, several faces are subtracted — boys whose interest was eclipsed, or who no longer played well enough to keep pace with the speed at which Richter was advancing. Richter had the isolated childhood of an athletic prodigy. He played for teams whose members were drawn from ever widening circles of territory. By the time he was sixteen, he was tending goal for a team sponsored by the Tropicana Hotel and Casino in Atlantic City, eighty miles from his parents' house. Playing games on weekends, the team traveled as far north as Boston. As the years passed, the pictures on the shelf in the corner of the house featured fewer and fewer boys from Pennsylvania and the states around it, until Richter, at sixteen, was seated among players exclusively from Massachusetts and New Hampshire and Minnesota and Michigan.

Growing up in Philadelphia, Richter developed indefatigable habits of work to overcome his having so little time on the ice compared with boys raised in northern hockey towns. His obsession with hockey caused him to spend long periods of his childhood by himself. Richter's mother says that he was a simple teenager to raise, because she always knew that he would be home Friday night, preparing for Saturday's game. "I was fairly shy," he says. "In some ways, having so much to do was a relief for me. I never went to a prom. I never had an ordinary growing up. I always had a series of tasks in front of me — to do well in this camp, or at that tournament. When one has been accomplished, there was always a second on the horizon. One after another, they got me through my childhood."

At summer hockey camps Richter attended as a boy, he met coaches who told him that the best competition was to be found at private schools. In the eighth grade, Richter drew up an estimate of how much money his parents spent on electricity for him to watch television and use lights in the house, and of how many showers he took and what it cost to buy and heat the water and to wash his clothes, and of the expense of the gasoline his family used running him back and forth from practices and games, and of the food that he ate, and tried to convince his parents of how much money could be saved if he were at boarding school with someone else looking after his needs. His parents were unmoved. Eventually, though, they sent him for senior year to Northwood prep, in Lake Placid, a small school known for the quality of its hockey teams.

Richter is accomplished more than gifted. He has extraordinary speed in his feet and his hands, but so do many goalies. More remarkable is his ability to play his position intelligently. As a boy, Richter learned the technical aspects of goaltending, and he devoted himself to perfecting them. He has a tireless desire to better his game. John Davidson, the Rangers' television announcer and a former goalie, says that what distinguishes Richter from the approximately forty-five other goaltenders Davidson observes each season in the National Hockey League is the intensity of his resolve to make himself more proficient. Richter's determination is unusual in someone who has progressed as far as he has. His habits of work are a tenacious response to a permanent feeling of deficiency — of being set back, of having an obstacle to surmount — and the success he has had with them is clear. In his first full season in the league, he was a finalist for the Vezina Trophy, given each year by the league's general managers to the goalie they regard as the best. Even so, there is a solitary and lonesome quality to him, as if he still felt his separation from the kids he grew up with, who were going to movies while Richter did situps and jumping jacks and sat on his bed at night writing entries in the notebooks he kept to record his performances.

Fear preys less on the minds of goaltenders now than it did in the past. The equipment they wear is better designed and more substantial than it used to be; the position is less painful and dangerous. A goalie is the most cumbersomely attired figure in sport. He is also the player in a hockey game least likely to be injured by the puck. The first modern goalie to wear a mask in public was Jacques Plante, of the Montreal Canadiens, who put on a mask on November 1, 1959, at Madison Square Garden. He had been using a mask in practice and in warmups, but his coach would not allow him to wear one in a game. The coach felt sure that the eye slits on the mask were too small to allow Plante to see the puck clearly and, in particular, prevented him from seeing a puck at his feet. Moreover, the coach believed that the mask made Plante less fearful and therefore less alert and less effective. By November of 1959, in the course of tending goal, Plante had broken his nose four times and his cheekbones twice, had fractured his skull, and had received more than 150 stitches, without anesthetic, from trainers in locker rooms to close cuts on his face. Eight minutes into the game that night, the Rangers' star right wing, Andy Bathgate, released the puck from his backhand. The puck hit Plante in the face and opened a cut by his nose. Plante fell to the ice and was taken to the dressing room. Hockey teams then employed only one goalie. Each home team kept on hand a man willing to take the ice wearing an injured goalie's equipment. Often the replacement goalies were men with day jobs and a sideline interest in hockey. The Canadiens didn't want to use the replacement, so Plante returned after twenty minutes, with seven stitches and wearing the mask. He had refused to go back to the net without it. Before he was hurt, he had made two saves, and then he made twenty-five more. The Canadiens won, 3–1. After the game, Plante told reporters, "My head was hurting and I swallowed a lot of blood. I wasn't in any condition to play, but with the mask — well, I felt a little easier."

When he retired, Plante wrote an instructional book for goaltenders. "People say I was afraid when I started to use the mask in 1959," he wrote, "but I ask them, 'Would you call it brave if you jumped out of a plane and didn't wear a parachute?'"

It wasn't only the lack of a mask that compromised goalies. The padding they wore to protect their chests and arms and shoulders and hands was not thick enough. They frequently lost nails on their hands and feet and had bruises all over their bodies. During the 1960s, players routinely began taking exaggerated swings at the puck in order to send it faster toward the net — a slap shot. A forward would carry the puck into the opponent's end, and if he saw no clear opportunity for a successful shot he might draw his stick back above his shoulder, lean his weight into his swing, and bounce the puck off the goalie's shoulder, or his chest, or his head. The next time the player found himself in a similar position, he might repeat the theatrical arc of his swing. The goalie would flinch, slightly; his shoulders would rise, slightly; the blade of his stick would lift off the ice, slightly. And the player would send the puck underneath it. This kind of manipulation made goaltenders resentful and morose.

Richter says that often he doesn't see the shape of the puck coming toward him — he sees the streak and knows what direction it's headed in. He says that the puck doesn't hurt when it hits him — that the padding he wears protects him — but I have noticed bruises and welts on his body, and I have once or twice seen him wince when he takes off his equipment. Occasionally, a bruise will nag him all season, because it keeps being hit by the puck. Jacques Plante writes in his book that if you are the sort of person who worries about being hurt you are not cut out to be a goalie. I have never seen a goaltender, though, who doesn't try to get out of the way of a puck winging toward his head.

Richter says that a goalie is more likely to be hurt in practice than in a game, because there are so many pucks on the ice and not every player checks to be sure he has his goalie's attention before shooting. Also, Richter says, few of his teammates are able to control the elevation or the path of the puck once it leaves their sticks. When they wind up and airmail the puck to him from fifteen or twenty feet away, many of them have no better idea of where it might go than anyone else. Moreover, professional hockey includes a motley assortment of personalities, and there is always the teammate who finds headhunting diverting.

A player with a heavy shot can send a puck toward a goalie at a hundred miles an hour. A few players can shoot it even more forcefully. The verb that hockey players use in describing the velocity of a player's shot is "bring." The proper reply to the question "Who shoots the puck hard?" might be, "Well, I guess Al MacInnis can bring it, eh?" Assuming that no opposing players are standing in front of the goalie and intentionally blocking his view, or that a puck being brought to him has not struck any of the thicket of sticks that have been thrust in its path, the goalie is expected to stop the puck. A goalie defends a space six feet across and four feet high. In the course of a game, he will usually face between twenty-five and thirty shots. They will come at all speeds and from all directions, and in all sorts of sequences and intervals, and mostly with very little warning. The puck will strike all parts of the goalie's body. The shots that miss the net make a sound against the boards or the glass behind him like a rifle shot, or a slamming door. The ones that solidly strike the posts of the goal make a sound like someone clanging a wrench against a piece of plumbing pipe. Hockey is a raucous Canadian prairie attraction moved indoors, and it looks chaotic and formless, but it isn't. It's just fast — the fastest team sport in the world. If it were possible to freeze players in the midst of a game and trace their paths, their trails would indicate a plan as plainly as if they were steps on a ballroom dance floor. There are plans of attack and there are plans of defense. A goalie on a team with a feckless defense may face forty shots in an evening, and more is not out of the question. Richter once faced sixty-two, and saved fifty-nine, a Rangers record.

Watching Richter at work — that is, isolating him from the activity of the rest of the game — involves as many moments of boredom as it does to be Richter at work. In any game, he will pass a fair amount of his hour keeping track of the puck at the far end of the rink — "like a fan," he says, except his attention is not diverted by the hot dog vendor, or the drunk with the air horn behind him, or the figures on the out-of-town scoreboard. Richter will actually take part in very little of the game, but the parts he is involved in will be among the most important. As devoted as he is to staying on his feet and facing the puck — what is called "squaring yourself to the shooter" — he will spend a good amount of any game on his back or his stomach or his side, sliding this way and that, lunging toward a player who has carried the puck past his leg, stretching furiously to cover as much of the goal as he can. Because of the nature of the surface he plays on, he can't always be where he would like to be. Once he is down, it isn't easy to get up. He wears thirty-five pounds of equipment. As the game advances, his clothes and the pads he wears on his legs absorb water from the ice and from his body and grow heavier.

Richter is a little bit shorter and far more muscular than goaltenders usually are. With his large thighs and classically modeled upper body, he is more like a defenseman. The strength he is able to call on from his legs is at the center of his game: it allows him to move quickly from one side of the net to the other and to drop to his knees and get back up several times in the space of a few seconds. A lot of goals in hockey are scored on a goaltender who has fallen to the ice in making a save and hasn't been able to right himself fast enough to face a second or third attempt. This rarely happens to Richter. Goalies who rely more on their reflexes than on an ability to position themselves strategically move more after the puck has been shot. Richter moves more *before* the puck is shot, and when he is on his game he finds himself always where he wants to be. This forces a shooter to attempt a shot or a pass more complicated than the one he had planned, since the only parts of the net available to him are the corners.

To a shooter, a goalie looks like a piece of geometry. The best shooters see triangles — between the goalie's legs, between the goalie's leg and the side of the net, between the goalie's arm and the side of his body. Shooters will usually send the puck toward the center of an opening. The smaller the opening, the more difficult it is to aim for the center. The kind of battles that take place between a goalie and a shooter are rarely apparent to people in the stands. If a goalie is able by quickness and cunning to restrict a shooter's opportunities so that the shooter sends the puck wide of the net, or buries it in the goalie's pads, or passes instead of shooting, or loses possession of the puck without having taken any shot at all, most people in the stands will believe that the shooter fumbled a chance, not that the goalie gave him nothing to shoot at or forced him to try more than he could manage.

The style of a goalie who is adept at performing the technical movements of his position, who excels at calculating the intricacies of the angles available to a shooter and instantly reducing them to their least promising form, who can move with great speed in any direction, from any posture, and who has learned to let his body rather than his reflexes carry the burden of his work, will appear very unflamboyant. Since he is not likely to be caught out of position, he is not likely to be making the kind of diving, lunging saves that draw a crowd to its feet. It may seem as if the shooters were always sending the puck into his body. On his best nights, he may look as if he were facing an opponent who cannot manage an effective attack. He will demoralize opponents, and depending, of course, on the team in front of him, he will probably win far more often than he loses. A goalie who does this well is likely to be compared to Mike Richter.

For part of November and all of December 1989, Richter lived at Wally's Motor Inn, on the outskirts of Flint, Michigan. The view from his window was of a field with tires in it. Through the walls of his room came sounds representing the full catalog of human nocturnal behavior. Most of his neighbors were solitary men. Fistfights occasionally broke out among them. Wally's premises included a truck stop, and Richter ate most of his meals at the truck stop's restaurant, which was open all night. Often he fell asleep to the sound of diesels idling in the parking lot. Half a mile from Wally's was the rink where Richter practiced and played with his teammates on the Flint Spirits, at that time the minor-league affiliate of the New York Rangers. He was twenty-three. When he wasn't at the rink, he was usually in his room at Wally's, reading books on nutrition and fitness and positive thinking.

Richter's father had died in September of 1985, a few weeks after Richter had begun his first year at Wisconsin. When his mother called to tell him that his father had passed away, he was so at a loss that he said, "Are you sure?" He went home for the funeral. His father had rarely been sick, and his death cast a pall over the house. After the services, Richter returned to school and the familiar, timeless world of hockey practices and training and traveling and games. Obscurely, he felt that as long as he remained in Wisconsin he could put some distance between himself and what he felt about having lost his father, and to some extent he did. What he really felt about his father's death was waiting for him at the end of the school year, when he returned to Philadelphia and a house that seemed utterly changed without his father's being present. At some point, he found himself saying, "Enough tears, enough sadness — my life has to go on." Richter thinks that his father, a businessman, never thought much of the idea of hockey as a career, and it pains him that his father has not been able to see his successes.

Richter left the University of Wisconsin in 1987, late in his second year, for the team being assembled to represent the United States at the Olympics. At the end of a year and a half of preparation, Richter and his teammates arrived in Calgary, played a week and a half of boisterous, daredevil hockey, and finished seventh in a field of twelve. Richter and his agent felt that it was time that he came to terms with the Rangers. Before the Olympics were over, Richter agreed to a two-way contract — that is, he was to be paid one amount if he played for the Rangers and another if he played for the farm team. The Rangers had two capable goaltenders in Bob Froese and John Vanbiesbrouck, so they assigned Richter to their minor-league franchise, which at the time was in Denver.

"The assistant coach met me at the airport in Kalamazoo, where the team was on a road trip," Richter says. "I practice one day and play the next, and I say, 'OK, I'm in the pros now,' because I'm excited, but it turns out I'm in Kalamazoo for a month. There's some reason the team can't play in Denver — arena's booked, I guess. We played five games in eight nights in one stretch, then six in nine in another, but it's OK, I'm in the pros, and I'm playing a lot of hockey. Still, it's different. I had been through college hockey, where you play two games a week and travel by plane and stay in nice hotels, and I had played with the national team, where you travel by air and every time you turn around someone is trying to do something for you or give something to you — 'Can I get you something to eat, Mr. Richter? Are you comfortable with that chair?' In addition, everywhere the national team played we were the home team. We went into the Spectrum, in Philadelphia, and played the Flyers, and the crowd was cheering for *us*. In the minors, you are just one player among many. You visit Saginaw, Flint, Muskegon, Peoria. The fans were ruthless, because they were mad about the Olympics — no miracle on ice. And even though I'm playing a lot of hockey, and I'm still excited, some part of me can't help noticing that I'm traveling by bus now, and that the players are all different ages, and some have gone as far as they ever will and are thirty years old and holding on to a job that is paying them maybe forty thousand a year — better, still, than anything the world outside has waiting for them — and some are my age but know that the team has no plans for them, and that the future is likely to be a version of the present, but again, they at least have a job doing what they love. But even so, regardless of any of that, all of us are putting on wet equipment from the night before which no one has washed.

"As the days go on I begin to see that the team is also made of Western Hockey League players and Quebec League players, and the western Canadians don't particularly care for the Quebec guys, who feel the same way back, but if there's anything they both agree on it's that no one really likes United States college players. The Canadians think the United States players are taking jobs from Canadian kids, and that the Americans don't have the same fire for the game that Canadians do. Also, they think that Americans aren't tough enough. Someone told me soon after I got there not to wear anything like a sweatshirt with a college emblem, because that would be considered inflammatory.

"So it begins to dawn on me that I really do feel a letdown being sent to the minors. That year, 1988, was the last year of the Russian hockey

ALEC WILKINSON ✦ 170

team's true period of greatness, so I had been playing against strong competition, and even if our team hadn't distinguished itself at the Olympics, we had played well. You go to the minors and it's not something you dream of when you're young. Of all the fantasies I entertained about playing professional hockey when I was growing up, I honestly can't recall one that involved taking the ice in an arena that was half empty for a minor-league team where people in the stands shout unspeakable insults, which you hear on the ice. The team pulled itself together, though. We finished in first place in the division on the last day of the season.

"The next fall, Froese and Vanbiesbrouck came into training camp still established as the Rangers' goaltenders, but I played well in the exhibition season, and I was thinking that the Rangers would keep me around, but they didn't, and I was devastated. After I got the news, I went back to the locker room and told a few people, and they were saying, 'Don't go, don't go,' but I didn't see any point in refusing to report.

"I came back to Denver, and this time no one is at the airport to greet me. I'm eating lunches in *Denny's*. All the good players had been traded. I'm in a complete funk. We were going to get creamed — you could see it clear as a road map. We had a lousy team, and I was going to get shelled. We started the year with games where it would be five to nothing at the end of the first period. The year before, the team had been very tough; not only did we win games but we had some punishing physical players. They were all gone, though, and the guys on the other teams would remember how they'd been pummeled the year before, and they'd take it out on this team and just beat us up. We had a road trip that lasted a month, because the rodeo came to town. I looked at the schedule, and there were seventeen games away. We made the playoffs but we didn't win a game. I was called up then to the Rangers for the playoffs. The team was down three games to none to the Pittsburgh Penguins in the first round, and Phil Esposito, the general manager, who had fired the coach with two games to go in the regular season and had taken over as coach, put me in goal to start the fourth game. It was a desperate tactic — the team was demoralized and things were more or less hopeless — but I looked at it as an opportunity to steal the game. Which I didn't. Pittsburgh scored three goals in almost no time, and although I settled down after that, we still lost the game and went home for the season. David McNab, the Ranger scout who had first spoken to me, when I was a teenager, and who was partly responsible for my being drafted, called me and said, 'Congratulations, you're the only goalie in history to lose the playoffs for two Ranger teams.'

"The next fall in training camp I worked as hard as I could. Vanbiesbrouck and Froese were still ahead of me, but I began the year in New York. The Rangers had a new coach, Roger Neilson. By November, though, he had grown tired of trying to play three goalies. Also, it was hard for me to get time in the net in practice. It wasn't my place to ask Froese or Vanbiesbrouck to step aside, and I had to find time wherever I could, piecemeal. Mainly I was just sitting and not practicing, so they decided to send me down once again — this time to Flint, where the team had moved. Roger took me aside and said, 'It's tough; you're a good young goalie, but you're not getting the chances here.' Then he said, 'The bad news is you'll take a pay cut to play in the minors' — and I'm thinking, *A pay cut, I'm going from a hundred and twenty thousand to twenty-five thousand* — 'but,' he says, 'the good news is that Flint's not really a bad place, and you'll have a chance to play, and maybe some other team will pick you up.' I just felt my chest constrict, because I had been drafted by the Rangers and really wanted to play for them, and I hadn't even really had the chance, and here we were talking about leaving.

"So now I'm living at Wally's. I didn't want to move into a house or an apartment, because that was a step toward a permanent stay, and I wanted to be ready to be out of there, should the phone ring. The Rangers were playing an exhibition game against a traveling Soviet team on New Year's Day of 1990, and I had been told that I would be called up for the game. I began to get some sense from my coach, though, that maybe the Rangers had changed their minds and didn't really want me to come, and I felt like I was being manipulated, and didn't like it and got angry and said I was going. My girlfriend had come to Flint for New Year's, and I knew I was going to miss the team party, but I also knew I could go to New York, play the game against the Soviets, and be back in Flint in time to play the game on the schedule for the day after New Year's.

"I get to La Guardia. It's New Year's Eve. There's no one at the airport to meet me. It's Sunday night, dark, a pouring-down rain. No cabs, because they're all in the city taking people to parties. I finally get one of those vans that take you to the city and stop every ten minutes along the way. I had just enough cash to pay the fare. I hadn't brought any money, because I'd expected someone to be at the airport to meet me. The Rangers had reserved a room for me at a hotel by Madison Square Garden. I'm carrying my goalie equipment into the lobby, and the bellhop asks if he can help me, but I don't have any money to tip him, so even though I'm practically falling down and had barely made it through the revolving door, I say, 'Oh no, that's fine, I can get it.' All I had was a credit card and my bank card from Flint. I couldn't see, I'm so hungry. The hotel's room service was closed for the night. It's New Year's, and probably everyone else in the city knows you want to be on the twentieth floor or above to get away from the noise, but I'm from Flint and they give me a room on the fourth floor. I go out on the street and start walking around, looking for someplace I can eat with my credit card, but everything's closed, and the places I find open don't take credit cards. I'm standing in the coffee shops looking at the desserts in those turning display racks and those cabinets with the mirrors behind them. I come back to my hotel room. I had half a granola bar in my suitcase, and I eat that. Everyone in the world is drunk and is outside my window shouting and tooting those little tin horns. I had a glass of water and went to bed.

"The next morning, I walk over to the Garden, but it's locked. I go to a diner, where there's this old Greek man behind the counter, and I say, 'Hi, my name's Mike Richter, I'm a goalie in the Rangers' organization.' I tell him he can take my credit card, my bank card, my license — whatever he wants — but can I order some food and promise I'll pay him back? He said, 'Order what you want, we'll deliver it to your room, and you better pay me back.' So I had some ham and eggs and some toast and I felt better, and I go over to the Garden, and we lose, three to one, but I play OK. After the game, I take my shower and pack up my stuff and find the team guy who's supposed to get my ticket back to Flint, and tell him I'm in a hurry because there's a game back there and I want to be home in time to play. I figure the Rangers don't really want me around anyway, so I don't want to be there. Besides, my girlfriend is back in my room at Wally's. The guy goes to talk to Roger, the coach, and he says, 'Better have him hold off.' So I call my girlfriend at Wally's and give her the news, and get a ride to the Ramada Inn up in Westchester, where the Rangers have a room for me. Then I went with the team on a road trip in January and when I get back they put me in a hotel in

Armonk, and after a few weeks the real-estate agent who rents most of the players their places says to Roger, 'What about Richter? Don't you think you should get him a house? He's at the hotel,' and Roger says, 'Jeez, is he still there?'

"So I get a house, and I'm playing at Madison Square Garden. I lose my first game, then I play seven in a row without losing and get named the league Rookie of the Month, and I'm really excited, and I never see Wally's again."

One day I showed Richter an arresting picture of himself from the *New York Daily News*. The photograph appeared on the back page of the paper — that is, on the front page of the sports section. It took up most of the page — it was the biggest picture of Richter I have ever seen — and it showed him making a bell-ringing save on the shifty Philadelphia player Rod Brind'Amour, who had skated in alone on a breakaway. Richter looked like one of those soldier dolls whose legs and arms have been twisted into unnatural positions. His legs were split and his arms were flung to the sides like wings. His left arm was behind him, and his right arm held his stick so that the blade defended the triangular space between his legs.

Richter was living by himself at the time, in a house with five bedrooms and maids' quarters, in a neighborhood of big houses by the golf course of the Westchester Country Club, in Rye. He had rented the house in the fall with two other players, and both had been sent to the minors early in the season. The house was cold and enormous and drafty and dark. The only evidence in it of Richter was some cereal boxes in a row on the counter in the kitchen, a few books and pictures in the room where he slept, and a closet with his clothes. The house was on the market. People would arrive with real-estate agents and walk through it without Richter's knowing they were coming, or would be there while he was away and leave lights on in parts of the house he didn't often visit, and he would find them several days later.

Richter likes to use props when he talks. In a restaurant, he will collect anything at hand to depict a hockey player. "Say you're a forward," he will begin and start shifting the salt and pepper shakers and the sugar packets around as if they were cards in the hands of a monte dealer. At home, he liked to answer questions about goaltending by standing in front of the fireplace.

"That save was right near the beginning of the game," he said. "We were on a power play. Brian Leetch had carried the puck into the Philadelphia end and lost it. A Philadelphia player knocked it back up against the boards, a pool shot, and it came to center ice, where the only player was Brind'Amour. Everyone on our team was in the Philadelphia end — they'd been trapped by that quick clear — and they hadn't even started back by the time Brind'Amour got the puck. I skated about ten feet forward so that I could reduce the angle he had on the net, but I couldn't get out as far as I wanted, because he was traveling full speed, and I had to stop and begin traveling full speed in reverse to stay with him. I want always to be a barrier in front of him, with no holes, if I can help it, so that he has no way to shoot through me. The most difficult place to protect is the space between your legs. When you're in position, your knees are bent and your feet are apart, so there's a gap between your shins, called the five hole — the corners of the net are one, two, three, and four. For all the other saves, you make your body explode to reach the puck, but with the five hole everything is moving in. You have to, I don't know — I guess, implode, and that's very difficult. Anyway, my eyes are watching the puck on his stick. If I'd had more time, I might have tried to see where he was looking, but a player like Brind'Amour is tricky enough that he'll skate with his head down and only look up quickly, or barely raise his eyes."

I called Brind'Amour, and he said, "Once I had the puck on my stick, I took a quick look but mostly I kept my head down. I can see what I'm looking for — how far out of the net he is, whether he's leaning one way or the other, or maybe leaving more space to one side, if he's got his arms close to his body, or if there's any room between his legs — but I don't want *him* to know that. All I could tell as I got closer was that no one else was with me, and that there wasn't much available. Richter was where he wanted to be, and he wasn't giving much away."

Richter: "Brind'Amour has a clear lead on everyone else, no one is going to catch him, and he must have realized that, because about twenty-five feet from me he changes from having his arms extended and the puck out in front of him to carrying the puck on his forehand, close to his body with his arms relaxed, which means that he can either shoot now or throw a fake. As long as his arms are extended and he's skating hard, he can't shoot — he has no force available to propel the puck."

Brind'Amour: "I'm going forward, trying to find the first hole I can, but I don't see one. I know he doesn't very often make a first move, and he's quick to recover, so I thought I'd probably only get one chance."

Richter: "What he wants is for me to move first. If I lean one way or the other, or move my feet, or respond to any gesture of his head or his hands or his shoulders or his stick, then I've committed my body, and he will have a fraction of a second to act before I can move in another direction."

Brind'Amour: "Sometimes you don't even think about what you're going to do — you just trust your body to come up with something — and sometimes you plan. It depends on how you feel, and it depends on the goalie. If you know he has a weakness, you might try and take advantage of it, but I didn't know of any weakness with Richter. I made up my mind to walk in and cut wide to the forehand once I got close to him, which would make him open his legs to stay with me, and then try to slide the puck between them."

Richter: "Brind'Amour's feet are planted and set apart, and he's gliding, but he hasn't yet dipped his shoulder or turned his blade to fake a shot, or moved the puck to either side to try and draw me with it. I'm lined up with the puck in front of him, and it looks to me like he is going to his left, because he's traveling in that direction and, as fast as he's moving, I don't think there is room anymore between him and me for him to reverse himself. I have to honor every one of his possibilities, though, because he's flying — if I go down too soon, he'll just chip the puck over me — and how I'm doing it is by taking little tiny steps, so that I'm not thrown off balance or caught leaning to one side or the other, which opens up holes. Also, you take small steps because it's very difficult to move a leg you have put your weight on. By cutting wide, Brind'Amour's trying to make me open my legs, but I'm making sure my stick is in place to protect the space between them."

Richter turned around and picked up the fireplace tongs to use as a goal stick. Then he moved a wingback chair to a position a few feet in front of him and a little to his right, to represent Brind'Amour. "Brind'Amour got to the net," he said, facing the chair, "and I remember it seemed like he almost came to a stop and faded to the left, because he ran out of room, which is ideal; it means that I gave him nothing to exploit, that he used up his chances, and the advantage suddenly began to shift toward me. When he cut wide to the forehand, I had to explode my right leg out in case he was going to shoot, and that was how I ended up in a split. The momentum threw my left arm behind me. And then I fell over backwards. Before I did, he shot the puck toward the space between my legs, but I had my stick blade in front of me so that he had only a couple of inches between the top of the blade and my body, and if he's good enough to fit the puck through that slot he gets the goal."

Brind'Amour: "I didn't have anything, so I tried to make something."

Richter: "Instead he hit me with the puck."

Brind'Amour: "If you're going to write that he stoned me, you better put in that I got two goals on him later in the game."

Richter doesn't return phone calls. It is something he says he is working on. His tolerance for talking on the phone is limited anyway. A phone call to him usually ends by his abruptly invoking some variation on the theme of urgency. "OK, buddy, I'm running a little late. I was supposed to be at the gym/meet a guy/be at the airport an hour ago." Richter lives modestly, especially compared with his teammates. He is the only Ranger who does not have a fancy car; he drives a Honda several years old. Usually, the first purchase a hockey player makes is the best showcase car he can afford. Richter is frugal. He puts his money in the bank. There is a joke among his teammates that if you want to find Richter you announce that you are buying lunch. He was paid approximately seven hundred thousand dollars to play hockey last season, and he managed to save most of what didn't go to taxes and rent. He bought his mother a trip to Ireland, where her family is from, and over the summer he took a trip to France. One of his sisters works for a man who has a chateau in the country south of Paris, and he offered Richter the use of it. It took him a while to make up his mind to go. Visiting France meant giving up summer school — he has been attending Cornell during the summers — and resigning himself to making it up later; it will take ten years of summer classes to complete the year and a half he has left. His father conveyed to him the feeling that a person is hopeless without a college degree.

There are stories of Rangers wearing lampshades, and stepping from limousines in funny costumes after the team's Halloween party, and livening up the atmosphere of this or that club, but except for a little sing-along two years ago in an obscure Irish bar on the Upper East Side, I don't know of any such episodes that involve Richter. After games, his teammates head for bars where models gather. Richter, though, is often on his way home early, in order to have sufficient rest for practice the next day and the game on the day after that. Richter's adherence to sensible policies of diet and rest give him the air of an ascetic, or a priest. Without any difficulty, I can imagine Father Richter superintending a parish among the leafy precincts of suburban Philadelphia — not dynamic, perhaps, but admired for his deliberateness and reserve — which his parishioners read as wisdom — and beloved for his tenacity and humor. I see him as never insisting to his flock on the need for moral behavior but striving by example to convey its advantages. I do not see him as entirely comfortable with sympathy calls — shyness would restrict his natural feelings. I see him living in a small parish house, his light on late into the night, writing sermons on the subject of what might be said to be the goaltender's creed: Only the most rigorous vigilance can see a person safely through this life.

(1992)

Part Two

An American Original

WHEN I WAS a child, William Maxwell and his wife, Emily, lived down the road from my parents, and Maxwell was my father's closest friend. My father was the art director of the magazine *Woman's Day.* Three days a week, Maxwell edited fiction at *The New Yorker.* My father drove to the train station in northern Westchester County in a Jeep he'd bought for twenty-five dollars from a dealer in army surplus. On the mornings when Maxwell also took the train, my father stopped at the end of Maxwell's driveway and pressed on the horn. They were so comfortable with each other that if they spoke at all during the ride it was about the furnace not working properly, or the poison ivy taking over a stone wall, or how to keep a pipe from freezing, or whether a woman who lived up the road was as pretty as my father insisted she was. Their intimacy was of the kind that excludes other people; a man who sometimes rode with them once said dismissively, "They're like an old married couple." When my father's first wife sat up late sewing a ruffle around the edge of the bed my father was trying to sleep in, Maxwell used it in a story, and when my mother, standing in his flower garden, remarked, "Children and roses reflect their care," he used that, too. My father read Maxwell's books and was proud of their inscriptions to him and my mother, but he wasn't literary. He was impatient and earthy and impulsive. His opinions were bluntly expressed, and he was indifferent to social conventions — I doubt whether Maxwell has ever said anything pointed without considering its effect on the feelings of the person he's talking to. My father was also unhesitating in his friendship. If the phone rang and it was Maxwell saying that a storm had blown down a tree across his driveway or that his car wouldn't start, my father would stop what he was doing, find a saw or a gas can, and head down the hill to the Maxwells' house. I was aware of Maxwell among my father's friends: he was quieter than the rest of them, and his face tended to give away his feelings.

In 1976, at the age of twenty-four, I decided that I would try to become a writer, because things weren't going so well for me as a rock-and-roll musician, and I thought that by being a writer I could get rich. Then I could go back to being a musician. What I planned to write about was a year I had spent as one of nine policemen in Wellfleet, Massachusetts. I had not read many books as a child, and I'd read only a few in college. One of them was *Look Homeward, Angel,* from which I retained only the phrase, "The night was a cool bowl of lilac darkness." I thought that if such a description was writing I couldn't be a writer. Either you regarded the world poetically or you didn't. Nevertheless, I sat down at a typewriter and began describing the things that had happened to me as a policeman, and the remarks that I'd heard people make, and after I had been at it for a while my father asked Maxwell if he would read what I'd done.

One afternoon following another, over the course of years, as it turned out, one piece or one book succeeding another, we sat side by side at a table — sometimes at Maxwell's apartment in New York, sometimes at the house in Westchester, and sometimes in the woods surrounding a rented house in Wellfleet — and he suggested cuts or changed a word I had learned recently into plain English. "Write as if you wish to be understood by an unusually bright ten-year-old," he said, or, "Henry James said, 'Dramatize, dramatize, dramatize,' not 'Generalize, generalize, generalize.'" Or he took out scissors and cut up my sentences and rearranged them and pasted them back together. Or he leaned back from the table and asked, "Isn't there a simpler way to say that?" and I explained what I had been trying to convey, and he wrote my explanation in the margin and said, "That's it," and I was surprised to see that words I had just spoken could be writing. During the forty years that Maxwell edited fiction at *The New Yorker,* he handled such writers as Vladimir Nabokov, J. D. Salinger, John Updike, John Cheever, John O'Hara, Sylvia Townsend Warner, Eudora Welty, Shirley Hazzard, Mavis Gallant, Frank O'Connor, Larry Woiwode, and Harold Brodkey, none of whom needed his help as much as I did. He shares the dedications of three of my books, and I share one of his.

I know that Maxwell and I are very different people, but we have spent so much time together, and been so intimate in our conversations, and I have relied so heavily on him and without realizing it have modeled certain parts of my behavior on his, that I sometimes feel as if we were nearly alike. Proof that such thinking can be carried too far came to me about ten years ago in a dream in which I went to a tailor to order my writer's coat. In the logic of the dream, having such a coat was a privilege given by a guild to an apprentice it was ready to admit. When I picked up the coat a week later, the tailor gave me a baseball jacket made from strips of colors arranged like a hand of cards. I told him it wasn't my coat. He said it was. I said that writers' coats are blazers made of green or brown corduroy. Maxwell has a closetful of such coats.

Maxwell is ninety-one years old. He was born on August 16, 1908, in Lincoln, Illinois. His father was the state agent for a fire-insurance company. His mother died in 1919, during the epidemic of Spanish influenza. Two years later his father remarried, and two years after that, was promoted to a position that required him to move to Chicago, where Maxwell finished high school. He went to the University of Illinois and did a year's graduate work in English at Harvard.

From photographs kept in a cabinet in the study of Maxwell's house in the country, I know that his features when he was a boy were so finely drawn that he looked almost like a girl. As a young man, he had a narrow face, with a long nose, full lips, and a wide, thin mouth. He had brown hair, and his eyes were dark and liquid and expressive to the point of radiance, and they still are. At parties, which he isn't especially fond of, he tends to find one person he can talk to. His voice is almost a whisper, and in order to be heard he sometimes draws a breath and pauses or hunches his shoulders and leans forward. His posture is slightly stooped from years of sitting at the typewriter. He is about five feet eight inches tall and so thin as to be nearly delicate. His skin is like paper. His health has always been robust, and he has surprising strength.

In the way a baseball player might regard himself as a participant in a tradition involving Gehrig and Ruth, Maxwell thinks of himself as engaged in an occupation that goes back to the blind old man at the crossroads — the professional storyteller, led around by a boy, addressing whoever will listen and using his skill to hold the attention of his audience as the light fades and all of them have a good reason for being home. Somewhat subversively, he believes that the patterns of ordinary life, acutely observed, provide more drama and structure and emotional resonance than purely imagined events are likely to. This is not the same as suggesting that a writer's imagination ought to surrender itself to the outward patterns of actual happenings, only that — as he writes in his novel *So Long, See You Tomorrow* — "too many conflicting emotional interests are involved for life ever to be wholly acceptable, and possibly it is the work of the storyteller to rearrange things so that they conform to this end. In any case, in talking about the past we lie with every breath we draw."

Since 1934, Maxwell has published six novels, two volumes of stories, a book of literary improvisations somewhat in the style of fables, a book of essays and reviews, a family history, two children's books, and an edition of collected stories. The fables, in *The Old Man at the Railroad Crossing*, are imaginary and were mostly written for family occasions — for a birthday or at Christmas, for his wife and two daughters. He wrote them by sitting at his typewriter in an attitude of receptivity until something, he says, was handed to him, as if from his unconscious. Often it was the phrase "Once upon a time," and from that everything else followed. "A person I didn't know anything about," he writes in the book's introduction, "and had never known in real life — a man who had no enemies, a girl who doesn't know whether to listen to her heart or her mind, a woman who never draws breath except to complain, an old man afraid of falling — stepped from the wings and began to act out something I must not interrupt or interfere with, but only be a witness to: a life, with the fleeting illuminations that anybody's life offers, written in sand with a pointed stick and erased by the next high tide." The only one of his novels that is almost entirely imagined is *Time Will Darken It*, which unfolded as a series of conversations among his characters. As he began each chapter, he determined which character had not spoken to another in a while, and put down what they had to say to each other.

An autobiographical writer is often trying to deliver himself from an experience that haunts him. In several stories and two novels, Maxwell has described the death of his mother. As far as the novels are concerned, he approached the subject first in *They Came Like Swallows*, published in 1937, and again in *So Long, See You Tomorrow*, published in

1980. In the first book he writes about the experience directly. In the second, his way of treating it is more oblique — what he is writing about really is his mother's absence from the family and the permanent shadow such deprivation cast over the household. In the narrative the consequences of his mother's death are combined with the description and aftermath of the murder of a tenant farmer by his lover's husband. The love affair that led to the murder, and the effect of the killing on the life of the boy who lost his mother, Maxwell was obliged to imagine. The facts were no longer retrievable.

They Came Like Swallows was recently included in the Modern Library, and in the introduction Maxwell says that he wrote the last part in ten days:

> Much of the time I walked the floor, framing sentences in my mind and then brushing the tears away with my hand so I could see the typewriter keys. I was weeping, I think, both for what happened — for I could not write about my mother's death without reliving it — and for events that took place only in my imagination. I don't suppose I was entirely sane.

In presenting to Maxwell in 1995 the Gold Medal for Fiction of the American Academy of Arts and Letters — that body's highest award, which is given only every six years — Joseph Mitchell said, "William Maxwell's principal theme, like James Joyce's, is the sadness that often exists at the heart of a family. . . . He is as aware as any novelist who ever lived of what human beings are capable of." Maxwell's prose is precise and understated. His stories and novels are meticulously crafted; sentences, he says, are moved around until they stick. Even so, the finished work is without any self-consciousness or sign of effort. He never strives for effect. He never performs what he used to describe scornfully to me as pirouettes on the page. Mitchell also said, "Nevertheless, in his pages one often reads with surprise descriptions and observations that seem truer and more revealing and more powerful and more memorable and more shocking than the deliberately shocking scenes and observations found in the pages of many of his contemporaries."

Maxwell says that he no longer has the inclination for sustained literary efforts, for holding the pattern of a story or a novel in mind for the time it would take to complete it. He sometimes says that he seems to have lost touch with the place where stories and novels come from. He still loves, he says, to write sentences. His disengagement from the source of his work is not something he feels reconciled to. He sometimes says that when people ask him what he is writing, even though he knows they only mean to be polite, he wants to pick up something and throw it at them.

When Maxwell's older brother died, about ten years ago, he realized, he says, "that no one any longer remembers the things that I do." A few years ago, Knopf published a volume of letters exchanged between Maxwell and Frank O'Connor. It is called *The Happiness of Getting It Down Right.* Maxwell talks about being awakened in the middle of the night by his daughters when they were children or the difficulty he was having making a piece of writing come out or a trip he made to his in-laws on the Oregon coast, and I read the letters with a kind of fascination, because, except for the material about his childhood which appears in his books or which he has described in interviews, I knew hardly anything about his life when he was young. He was a figure from my childhood, and whatever daydreams I had then didn't include imagining what older people I actually knew were doing when I didn't see them, or who they might have been when they didn't look exactly as I was accustomed to having them look.

I now know that in 1933, after finishing his first novel, *Bright Center of Heaven,* Maxwell came to New York from Illinois. The dust jackets of the period often said that the author had been to sea, and Maxwell hoped that if he found a ship in the harbor that would take him aboard, it would give him something to write about. He was twenty-five years old. At a party, he met a man who wrote popular sea stories. The man gave him a letter of introduction to the captain of a four-masted schooner that had belonged to J. P. Morgan and was anchored off Brooklyn. Maxwell hired a rowboat to take him out to the ship, where he found that the man his letter was addressed to was leaving the next day. The crew consisted of one sailor chipping rust, with a police dog beside him. The captain read Maxwell's letter and explained that the ship had not left anchor for four years and was not likely to anytime soon.

Maxwell was living in the Railroad Men's YMCA, on East Forty-seventh Street, and in its library he came across a book from 1890 by Lafcadio Hearn which discussed the beautiful city of Saint-Pierre, Martinique. Maxwell decided to go there and then discovered that it had been destroyed by a volcanic eruption in 1902. Even so, he thought, there must be some vestiges of it, and so he booked a passage on a small, dingy freighter, in February. He got off the boat at Trinidad and stayed several days. On one of them he went to the races. In the evening, when the races were over, immigrants from India set up card tables all around the track and gambled by candlelight.

From Trinidad he took a boat to Martinique, where there was a double rainbow over the harbor at Fort-de-France, and the purser gave him the name of a good pension. In an effort to gather material he wandered through the streets. The women wore the costume Hearn had described — a madras turban and a dress with a small bustle — but nothing else was recognizable. It was carnival time, and he was sometimes stopped by two or three towering young black men dressed in baby clothes, who demanded small sums of money. And there was a man with a lion's mane with bells in it who roamed the streets, followed by fifty boys chanting antiphonally. At nine o'clock, the light went on in the kitchen of the pension, and at ten food began to appear on his table, in an open courtyard. It was better food than he had ever known anywhere. At midnight, he drew mosquito netting around him as he fell into bed, drunk from the wine in his carafe. In the crotches of the trees orchids bloomed, and sewage ran down the gutters. He sometimes stood in the door of a dance hall. The music consisted of a single phrase repeated endlessly. The dancers, without moving their feet, ground their pelvises together. The book he had hoped to write eluded him.

He sat on a bluff looking out to sea. For the first time in his life he was homesick. A month in Martinique, where he went days at a time without speaking to anyone, seemed like a year anywhere else. One night when he sat down to dinner, he found a letter telling him that Harper & Brothers was seriously considering publishing *Bright Center of Heaven*. He went back on the same freighter he had arrived on.

When the novel appeared, in 1934, Maxwell was hoping the newspapers would carry large ads. Instead, Harper's publicity director took him to lunch and said, "Now we must pray." The reviews said that the book was promising, and the first printing of a thousand copies sold out; the second printing didn't. The central character is a flighty woman who in her incessant pursuit of order induces disorder. She is reduced to taking paying guests, and when she invites a distinguished black man for the weekend it is more than the social fabric can bear, and there is an unmanageable and partly comic situation. Maxwell has never allowed the book to be republished.

Maxwell had just turned twenty-eight when he came to New York a second time, in August of 1936. "My father had given me a hundred dollars, and I had another hundred I didn't tell him about," he says. "I went to a friend of his, the president of an insurance company, to get the check cashed. He had always before been friendly and fatherly to me, and this time he surprised me by being harsh and telling me I had no business trying to get a job in New York, that I wouldn't make it here and had better get back to my longhaired friends in Chicago. About whom he actually knew nothing. I had been given letters of introduction to the *New Republic* and to *Time,* and my editor at Harper's, who published E. B. White, had called Katharine White at *The New Yorker* and asked if she would see me. I went first to the *New Republic,* and it took them only a few minutes to realize that I didn't have a political thought in my head. And it took three weeks to receive an appointment with the personnel office at *Time.* Meanwhile, my father's friend had made me so furious that I talked myself into a job reading novels for Paramount Pictures. Then I went for an interview with Katharine White.

"I hadn't been reading *The New Yorker* at all. Mrs. White was a small, handsome woman, with a Bostonian accent and a confident manner. At the end of the interview, she asked how much I would want in the way of a salary. I had been told by a knowledgeable friend that I must ask for thirty-five dollars, that they wouldn't respect me unless I did. So I took a deep breath and said thirty-five dollars, and she smiled and said, 'I expect you could live on less.' I could have lived nicely on fifteen dollars. I couldn't make out whether the interview had been favorable or not. The thought of reading manuscripts for the movies didn't make me cheerful.

"I was living on the top floor of a brownstone rooming house at Lexington and Thirty-sixth Street, or thereabouts. I remember the mattress was lumpy, and there were bedbugs. I went down to the Village and wandered around and decided to eat dinner at a Chinese restaurant on Eighth Street, and though there were empty tables they made me sit with another person. In a bottomless depression I said to myself, There is no place for me anywhere in the world. And after dinner came home and under my door was a telegram from Mrs. White that read, COME TO WORK ON MONDAY AT THE PRICE AGREED UPON."

Eventually Mrs. White encouraged Maxwell to submit stories to the magazine. From his reading of the opinion sheets accompanying the manuscripts, Maxwell felt he understood the sort of material the magazine was looking for, and he was able to give its editors what they wanted — "valentines that arrived on the wrong day, that sort of thing," he says. "Something trivial but amusing." When he felt that the subject was too slight, he published the story under the pseudonym Jonathan Harrington.

"Somewhere along in the first three months I felt I was going to be fine, and I sent back my father's hundred dollars," Maxwell says. "When he got it, my stepmother said, he wept. He was a businessman. The concept of literature was outside his experience and beyond his understanding and so he had no idea, really, what I was up to. If my books had sold to the movies, he would have been reassured and thought I was engaged in a worthwhile occupation. In any case, he tried to understand. It had been the great fear of his life that I would be financially irresponsible and sponge off other people."

Not long ago I said to Maxwell, "You seem so untroubled," and he said, "I am now." In his early thirties, he lived as a solitary bachelor. "Working at *The New Yorker* five days a week was so consuming I had no other life," he says. "I lived in Patchin Place, in the West Village, in a very small two-room apartment, and I didn't have a telephone until the magazine insisted on it. And when it did ring I wouldn't answer it. I had been with people all day long and couldn't stand any more." What he wanted was a home and a family, but he felt shut out by his temperament from the part of the world where he might find them.

At the suggestion of a friend, he began seeing the psychoanalyst Theodor Reik, who had studied with Freud. "I had too great a sense of my own difference from other people," Maxwell says. "After spending a year talking with him, five days a week, though, the whole first part of my life fell away and I had a feeling of starting again. When I stopped talking to him and felt the need for it, I sat down for two days at the typewriter, and what came out was very strange. I decided that I was so angry at my parents for having another child — why weren't they satisfied with *me?* — that I thought they should die and then be brought back. I damn near accomplished it with my father, who caught the flu and recovered, but I had lost my mother. So I was a murderer. And what do you do with murderers, you put them in a cell. I was in a cell — no wife, no family. I was in a prison cell, and there was Reik saying, 'You're in a prison cell, but the door's not locked.'"

In the meantime, Maxwell had moved to the house in Westchester, where, a few months later, he woke up in the middle of the night remembering a young woman who had come to his office a year and a half earlier hoping for a position in the poetry department. "She wore her hair on top of her head," he says, "and she had a hat trimmed with fur — it was winter, I suppose — and I thought I had never seen anyone so beautiful, but I did nothing about it. It was as if I'd been in a deep sleep." He tried to find her name — Emily Noyes — in the phone book, and it wasn't there, but she had left her number with the magazine's personnel office, and on the disingenuous pretext of wanting to talk to her about her poetry he asked her for a drink at the Algonquin. She was from a prosperous family in Portland, Oregon. She was teaching at a nursery school on the Upper East Side and lived on the top floor of the building. Maxwell was thirty-six, and she was twenty-three, with black hair and a wide face and eyes so lively that people later often took her and Maxwell for sister and brother. It was the fall, and he asked her to a party at the house of a friend. They talked all evening, and when he took her home he asked her to marry him. He hadn't planned on saying it — the words simply came out of his mouth. She said that she didn't want to get married and that she wouldn't be able to see him again until after the first of the year but in the meantime he could telephone her at the nursery school between four-fifteen and four-thirty.

At four-fifteen each day, Maxwell closed the door of his office and began dialing. More often than not, the school line was busy, but sometimes he got through to her. In January he closed his house, rented a one-room apartment in New York, and began courting her. She had grown up on horseback and liked to play the faux cowboy song "Don't Fence Me In" on the jukeboxes in Third Avenue saloons. They were married in May, in the chapel of the First Presbyterian Church at Fifth Avenue and Twelfth Street. For more than forty years, they have divided their time between the house in the country and an apartment on the Upper East Side, over by the river.

·   ·   ·

Maxwell quit *The New Yorker* twice. He quit the first time in the thirties, because he was indignant at having been passed over for a promotion and decided that he would be a writer instead. He went to Santa Fe for several months, and when he came back Gus Lobrano, the head fiction editor, said that he missed him and asked if he could send over manuscripts for his opinion. After about a month, it became easier to read the manuscripts at the office.

He left again in 1947. "I thought I would write more and better if I did nothing but write," he says. "I was selling enough stories to live on, and I had some savings and I thought we could skid by, but the first thing that happened was we needed a new refrigerator, and the second thing that happened is that the stories I wrote weren't being taken. It helped to know what the magazine wanted, but not infallibly. Also, even though I saw what they wanted, I didn't necessarily want to give it to them. I had more serious things on my mind. But then I looked at the bank balance and my approaching fortieth birthday, and I thought I ought to insinuate myself back onto the staff."

When Maxwell was young he was strongly attracted to Virginia Woolf's elaborate and lyrical prose, but as he got older he began to prefer writing that was formed on the writer's habitual way of speaking and was simple and to the point. He is fond of a remark by the poet John Hall Wheelock that writing involves the imposition of a line of words on a line of feeling. As an editor, he was particularly good at saving stories that didn't quite work. He would suggest possibilities for the development of a character or a line of narrative, or for compressing a scene or combining one scene with another, or for moving several sentences or a paragraph from the beginning of a piece to nearer the end or from the end to the beginning, so that the emotional tone of the story was changed, and the story was brought to life and made to reverberate in a way that it hadn't before.

What suggestions he made he offered unobtrusively, and he qualified them by saying that if the writer didn't agree with them he should overlook them. "I wanted the editing to be such that when the writer reread the story ten years after it was published he would not be aware of any hand on it but his own," he says. While I was writing my second book, I kept hearing a voice in my head saying such things as *You don't think that sentence is any good, do you?* Sabotage is what it was, but I couldn't find any way of avoiding it until Maxwell suggested that I do my writing each day in the form of a letter I mailed him. When I had disposed of everything I intended to say, I retrieved the letters and we began going through them.

As for how other writers regarded his opinion, when J. D. Salinger finished *Catcher in the Rye,* he drove to the Maxwells' house in the country and in the course of an afternoon and evening read it to them on their porch.

To mark the occasion of his ninetieth birthday and his fifty years as a member of the club he belongs to in Manhattan, Maxwell wrote an essay describing two old men, both of whom he had known when he was in his forties: Austin Strong, a playwright, whose grandmother married Robert Louis Stevenson, and Rodman Gilder, a publisher. Last fall, he read what he had written at a dinner held at the club in his honor. Nearly four hundred people turned out to hear him, several hundred more than had been expected. Strong and Gilder were a generation older than Maxwell, and in describing the end of their lives he wrote, "The following winter when Austin did not appear at the club for a week or so I inquired of the doorman about him and was told that he had been unwell but was better and that Mrs. Strong had said visitors would be welcome. I went looking for Rodman, who said soberly, 'Heart attack.' When I was led upstairs to Austin's bedroom I found him sitting up in a four-poster. Except for his poor color he was his usual self. He said he would be back in the club soon. Instead I found myself attending his funeral."

Something about the way Maxwell said this made people draw in their breath quickly.

"Shortly after that," he went on, "Rodman sat back in his chair, with one arm behind his head, to think about something, and never finished the thought. That made two funerals. I said, I will never again love an old man. They die on you."

I have persuaded myself that he will not do this to me.

(2000)

Fatherhood

ROMANCE

MY FATHER held himself aloof from our family in a way that was common for the period, the 1950s and '60s. We lived in the suburbs of New York City and he had a job in Manhattan; he was the art director of the magazine *Woman's Day*. He was a charming, bluff, and somewhat insensitive man, and he was a philanderer, too, so a part of his attention was always somewhere other than in his household. I held him, though, in high regard, as children tend to do, and imitated his example, which was only intermittently appropriate, and so I had a lot of flawed experiences, and when enough of them had piled up, I sat in a leather chair in the office of a Jungian analyst once or twice a week for a number of years and, staring just to the left or right of him or at the row of small fetishes on the bookcase above his head, described my difficulties with my mother, while he replied, "I think you have more issues with your father." Son of a bitch isn't even listening to me, I thought, until I had a dream in which I was a teenager about to take the ice in a hockey game and I discovered that my father had put me in skates with broken blades. After that I began to carry him a little bit less glamorously in my mind and eventually some kind of balance within me shifted, and somewhat unexpectedly and a little bit late — I was forty-two — I arrived at a point where I felt that I was prepared to raise a child. Prepared in the sense that I imagine the poor holy loser who died in the bus in Alaska felt he was prepared, with his rifle, his books, and his bag of rice, to wait out the weather.

Before we leave Confession Gulch, I would like to add that I have been married twice. The first time, my wife and I both picked wrong and the marriage ended sadly after seven years. In truth, it had been over for some time, so it also took a few sessions in the leather chair to see why I had made such a piece of bad judgment, why both of us had engaged in it, and what I could do to make sure I would marry again happily, if I was lucky. When I did, I used sometimes to wake in the middle of the night and think, Please, God, let me live out my natural life in the company of this woman I love. Our son was born six years ago, and it is not that my feelings for my wife ever changed, except to deepen, but I was aware that when he had been in the world only a short time, I had begun thinking, Please, God, let me live to see as much of his life as I can.

What has followed between us cannot truly be described as a love affair, unless your version of one includes tests and dismissals and reversals and forbearance and an awareness that whatever you had thought the affair might be, had hoped or imagined it might be, is precisely what it won't, or even can't (apparently), ever be.

WATERWORKS

I did not expect to cry when my son was born — it seemed a silly and conventional and trivial thing to do, weep for joy, like a figure in an advertisement — but I did, quite suddenly and without warning, as if it were a reflex. He was delivered in the morning by a midwife in a hospital in Manhattan and I felt embarrassed, slightly, to be weeping among women, to be weeping when no one else was, as if trying to emphasize that the strength and capacity to bear pain that my wife had demonstrated was laudable but I was *sensitive,* so I looked toward the floor and wiped away the tears. When his face had appeared, I had seen his eyes and the instant in which consciousness lit them. He was examined briefly by a doctor and then lay with his mother and I watched them for a while, then went to get some coffee and bagels for our breakfast. When I got back, Sara, my wife, was in her room with Sam, our son, who was wrapped up — a small bundle with a cap on, a face about the size of a softball — and she handed him to me, and I held him for the first time. He felt like a piece of china in my hands. I held him the way you would hold a fragile and tiny creature whose existence depended entirely on the lightness of your touch. There was a nurse with us. She said, "You'll scare him if you don't hold him tighter. They need to know they're being supported."

I spoke his name. I looked into his eyes, which had the luminance of polished stone. What I felt mainly was the absence of what I expected to feel — that is, I thought his arriving in my arms would somehow stimulate an awareness I had never felt toward anything before, a resonance that was primitive and universal and private, a code shared between us that couldn't possibly be stirred by any other form of contact, the kind of experience that would appear in a movie. Instead I heard a voice in my mind saying things such as, This is my son — my son. Yes, this is my son. And at the same time asking, Shouldn't something else, something more, be happening? Pay closer attention.

I have never asked any other man if he had an experience such as mine, but I don't think mine is singular. How could it be? I can imagine men holding their son or daughter for the first time and having feelings regarding the child's destiny or place in the family and among his or her ancestors or the traits he or she appears to display, but such feelings are sentimental, and sentimental feelings are a lie concocted to cover the feelings you might more straightforwardly have. You hate your brother who tormented you, but persist in feeling that your upbringing with him as your comrade and sergeant at arms was fortunate; it made you tougher. I am capable of insensitivity, as my father was, but I am not an insensitive person. I would mistrust the account of any man who told me that the first time he held his child he felt profoundly attached to him. Attached to what, really? Someone you're meeting for the first time, who is incapable of returning your feelings, who has only a peripheral awareness of you and none really of who you are, or of his relation to you, or that you might intend for him or her to be a fireman as you have been, or a union man or a doctor, or preside over a commercial empire, or replace Wayne Gretzky or Willie Mays or James Taylor or John Coltrane or Billie Holiday? I do not mean that the moment of first embrace is not significantly charged, only that its import is elusive, and the elusiveness is the first signal that the process of caring for a child is fraught with ambiguity and things you can't know. A child is a territory, a landscape, a region, an outpost, a republic and island of worry.

ILLUSION

Y ou forget a lot of it. The first year is hell, I remember that. You don't sleep. The fatigue accumulates. Your child goes to bed, you have a little bit of fun, then you realize he has a two-hour head start on you. You see in your wife's face a concern, a preoccupation even, that you never saw before. The carefree look is gone, anyway. The emotional balance of your household is altered. Your wife and child have formed an alliance that at times excludes you. They spend so much time together and are so intimate with each other that it was bound to happen. My sense of my son as an enigma was reinforced during the first year because there was little I could provide for him. So far as I could tell, he liked dimly lit rooms, tranquil surroundings, breast milk, and the company of his mother. Because I had read about studies concluding that an infant prefers to his father's voice the higher, softer tones of his mother's speech, I tried for a while talking to Sam in a womanly voice, then worried that I had confused him in some essential way about the properties of masculine life, so went back to my own voice, to which he seemed only occasionally to respond. Sometimes he appeared to enjoy himself when I whistled.

A child's personality hardly emerges before he is seven or eight months old. During most of his or her first year, what you are aware of really is the child's temperament: his capacity for frustration, whether he is cautious or extends himself toward the world. It is easy to imagine who he is — that is, to make up an identity for him, as if he were a screen on which to display the images you have always intended for your son or daughter — and to persuade yourself that he or she is moving toward becoming some version of those images, and to do it all without really even being aware of it, to think that really you are occupied simply with his development, with his becoming, say, someone who will be accomplished at math because you played Mozart for him as he lay in his crib, overlooking that probably what you were doing was making it difficult for him to sleep, overstimulating him, making him nervous, and depriving him of rest. You meant well, and you can tell him that thirty years down the road when he confronts you, although it is very difficult to know what will prey on the minds of the adults who are small children now — certainly not what bothered us, it was a different time, the fifties and sixties and seventies, and people behaved differently and felt differently about what was proper in the way of raising a child. In any case, the slow appearance of his character has perhaps to do with the design of childhood. (Certainly in the past, and in cultures where women were not sufficiently valued and babies were killed for being of the wrong sex, a boy who disappointed his father might also be left in the forest.) So they emerge slowly. You become attached to them and to your version of them, and then they begin perilously to become themselves, someone different from your idea. This calls for a great deal of restraint, to let a child develop according to his nature. To give him sufficient guidance that he becomes equipped with the virtues and judgment he needs to preserve himself and to flourish but not so much that you cause him to repress parts of himself out of fear that they will not be accepted.

Children are utterly dependent. If they meet with disapproval, they will assume that something is wrong with them. Their security, their lives, depend on keeping their mothers and fathers interested in them. If a mom is taken with the bottle or drugs, or the dad is emotionally withdrawn or unconsciously hostile to the child's well-being, the child will build an explanation for why he has brought such an existence on himself. The alternative — mother or father is unreliable — is a story by Stephen King, your well-being in the hands of people who are capricious about your welfare, who have their own plans for your future, who reward you for certain behavior that might make you uncomfortable and punish you for behavior you find fulfilling. Making a mess, for example.

We are only a few generations removed from the Victorian idea of the child as a little adult, which gave way to the child as a small being with instincts for sex, a devious and slothful package, which gave way to the child as a being engaged in behaviors and activities designed for his pleasure to oppose and thwart the interests of his parents, one who needs to be subdued, to be broken the way a horse might require it — spare the rod and spoil the child, and the advice current in my parents' generation of letting a child put down for the night lie in his crib crying; if you pick him up you'll only give him the impression that the world is a compassionate place interested in seeing him protected. Then he'll manipulate you mercilessly the rest of your life.

EVANESCENCE

My wife and I haven't been to a movie since my son was born, in 1993. I have seen movies on airplanes and I have rented them, but none longer than an hour and a half, because that would keep us up too late. A year ago, I walked past a restaurant on Broadway that has a big window facing the street and saw the people at the tables and in the instant before my mind focused I thought, So how does that work, you go in there and ask for food and they prepare it and you pay them; how do you know what you can ask for?

Before I had a child, I had no interest in children; I had thought it was possible I might never have one. I didn't think children were amusing, sometimes I thought they were scary, and I was always on the side of the people on the airplane who crane their necks to stare at the mother unable to calm her child's crying.

I was not aware before Sam was born of the circumstance of feeling hostage to the unfolding of the universe, to the things that lie in wait for your child, the torments and hardships and assaults. I now know that there are disasters lurking everywhere for a child, many of them simple and commonplace. The threat of dehydration for the infant who throws up for too long — a day without water is all it seems to take — so that his eyes may roll back into his head, even while you are waiting in the doctor's anteroom, and you will have to be rushed to the hospital, carrying your child in your arms with people ahead of you kicking doors open, as on TV. Then the children's ward and children walking around with eyes that seem to have no light in them.

I am convinced that one needs to live beside one's children with the feeling that they might not be there at the end of the day, or that you won't, or your wife won't. There are accidents and illnesses, there are divorces. The cemetery is always waiting.

DISCLAIMER

I should probably announce that I have an eccentric child, and that his eccentricities have influenced my feelings about childhood and being a father. What afflicts him, his mother and I only partly know. He appears, from tests and the opinions of various people with diplomas on their walls, to have great difficulty with sensations. Sounds are too loud, touch is often too abrasive or hard or ticklish or startling, something impedes his speech, he has no peripheral vision, and he has trouble organizing the elements of visual images — photographs and paintings and the movements on a television screen. I am not sure exactly how he views images, but it puts me in mind of the natives of whatever territory it was who were shown photographs of their faces and saw in them only areas of black and white.

My son began crawling when he was supposed to, but he dragged one leg. The world, though, has an abundance of people who tell you when your child has trouble, say, speaking, that their great-uncle so-and-so didn't say a word until he was four and then he framed perfect sentences, or in our case they say, "Did you ever meet anyone who didn't learn how to walk?" so you think, Well, that's unusual, the leg dragging, but they're right, and there isn't much you can do with the diagnosis of a child that young anyway, unless the difficulties are severe. So my son has grown into a radiant child who is a little clumsy and has a list of experiences he can't tolerate. My friend William Maxwell, the novelist, says, "Don't worry about him, he has the soul of a poet." Like a lot of poets, then, he isn't much socialized, because his excitement at the appearance of other children overrides what social patterns he might have collected by observing the way other children act, and instead of restraining himself, he races up to them and stands too close and waves his arms while he talks loudly, and this scares them. Some children it doesn't bother at all, but the majority don't cotton to it. Moreover, he doesn't have an older brother or sister whose manners he can imitate. If your attention is distracted by the imminence and immensity of the world and its lights and textures and sounds, if you are constantly alert to voices from the other side of the room or the movements of other children and adults in order to assess whether they contain some threat to you and so that you can keep some distance between yourself and them, your mind is occupied and hasn't got time to address the muscular patterns necessary for speech or movements. You fall behind. And once you are behind, what is measured is how far behind you are and whether you have fallen so far behind that you might not catch up. If you are a five-year-old with the capacities of a four-year-old, do you become a twenty-year-old with the capacities of a sixteen-year-old, or does the equation change? No one knows.

If you are father or mother to such a child, you might think that you have been wronged. You might, as I have occasionally done, feel resentful of the simple commonness, the uncomplicatedness, on display in the lives of garden-variety children; and then something, the sight in the newspaper of a child separated from his parents in Kosovo, say, might cause you to reflect that if this is the worst thing that happens to you and your child, among the catalog of grievances and disappointments and tragedies and unfair happenings in life, you will be lucky and you should probably shut up about it so that the Almighty doesn't hear you and send something else your way with the note, *You thought that was bad.*

A child such as my wife and I have needs extra care. You know what he doesn't like — loud places, places where there is a great deal of activity, especially chaotic places, especially loud, chaotic places, and you avoid taking him to any such places. You try to give him what he likes. The seashore, the wide-open beach, with no avenues of ambush for any adversary, with room for everyone, with the sounds of the waves and the games of running from them and into them and having them tumble you over and the dunes to climb and the sand to dig tunnels in and build cities on that you can destroy. You try to make him happy, to make his life, since it includes so much torment, a pleasure. The longer I can make him happy, the better I feel. The world with its thousand and one things is always waiting there to disappoint him, to bruise his feelings, to exclude him, and I figure that the more capital my wife and I give him in the form of solid fun, the more likely he is to spin off from the distasteful experience into another that pleases him and not to become stuck brooding on the insufficiencies that have made him a figure of sport or rejection for the moment.

One important thing a parent can do for a child, I think, is provide him with a sense of safety.

IRONY

An irony of raising such children is that, if you are like me, you spend your life trying to get away from the small-minded and conventional people, the gym teachers and guidance counselors and spinster penmanship instructors who have a hold over you when you are young, and finally you're shed of them and then you have a child and they get their claws into you all over again. In order to obtain from the state the money to help pay for a portion of some of the therapies my son receives, he had to submit to examinations conducted by people who work for the government. The most indignant I have ever been made as an adult was when I learned that one of them, a psychologist, had asked my son, my heartbeat, my household angel, who was then four, "Have you ever wanted to kill yourself? Have you ever wanted to kill anyone else?"

Then it becomes time to get your child into school, which, if you intend it to be a private school, is not simple. When we went for an interview at one school, a woman with a clipboard said, "Is yours the child who also speaks Russian?" No three-year-old speaks Russian as a second language, a few words of Russian, some phrases perhaps, but a couple desperate enough to place their child had had the nerve to describe their three-year-old as a speaker of a complicated foreign language. I wasn't so surprised at that; people are always willing to make fools of themselves. What surprised me was that, so far as I could tell, the school had taken them seriously.

Schools do not like an eccentric or lively child. Schools — any school, a public school, the most prestigious private school, the school with the reputation for having great concern for the inner life of the child — are all interested in the same thing: tractability. None of them want a child who does not do what he is told. It is nice if your three-year-old plays the cello or speaks Hebrew or can ride a horse, but if he can't perform according to commands, if he is willful or resistant, you will have difficulty placing him in the school you might most wish he would attend, unless of course you are fortunate enough to have sound public schools in your neighborhood. Such a child makes the lives of everyone involved, the teachers and the administrators, more difficult. Other parents resent an obstreperous child. A child who is aggressive. During the interviews of three-year-olds, which are enveloped in mystery, only one assessment is taking place. Absent the variables of whether yours is a child of minority parents or not, prosperous or not, absent the consideration of how many spaces are available for siblings and boys and girls, only one judgment is taking place, indeed only one is possible, since the range of behaviors for children that age is so limited. Your child arrives and plays with two or three other children, then, having been told to, he puts the toys away and sits down for juice and a cookie, perhaps while a story is read. If your child plays nicely, fine, that's nice, nice child. The only gesture that matters is whether, when he is instructed to, he puts away the toys and sits down with the others. If he decides that he is having fun playing with the toys and wants to continue and resists, if he cries in frustration, he has failed his interview and has no chance of being accepted. He has displayed what the school will regard as difficulty with transitions, or, in the language of bureaucracy, he will be said to have difficulty transitioning. They will thank you for coming and you will receive in the mail a letter saying that the school is disappointed not to be able to admit your child, but that there were an unusual number of siblings this year. His future at that school is likely hopeless, unless you are in the position to make a donation of astonishing proportions.

ANOTHER IRONY

For a couple of years, before I knew anything in my son was compromised, I thought that he was more interesting than the boys I saw in his classroom, more able to concentrate, more diverse in his reactions to play, more inventive, and more avid in his joy. The other boys seemed ordinary, a little mean, a little sneaky, a little quick to gang up and exclude, a little taken with aggression. The first time I began to feel something was amiss with Sam, I was watching him in his classroom and noticed that when he was moved toward an aggressive gesture, when another boy, say, had taken a toy he was playing with, Sam tried to get the toy back. There was a struggle. Once the matter was handled, he let it drop. If he had a conflict, he pushed or pulled in plain view. The other boys, I noticed, usually waited until the teachers were looking the other way and pushed or pinched or slapped the other child and impersonated innocence when the teacher looked in their direction. This, I thought, was cowardly. Because my son was open in his behavior, he was more often caught at it. I told one of the teachers that I was proud of him for not misbehaving behind their backs, that the other boys often struck me as angry and mean-spirited and were rarely brought to account because they were sneaky about it. The teacher was nearly as fond of Sam as I was. It pained her to say, "Yes, and you wonder why they have learned not to get caught and Sam hasn't."

My son's difficulties make simple coordination a problem for him. He could not ride a tricycle as a toddler because he could not alternate the actions of his feet without thinking about it. Among my own meager accomplishments are the kind of tennis game and skating style you can have only if you began these activities very early in life and practiced them intensely, so I had imagined that my son and I would go skating together and play tennis, but his difficulty controlling his excitement, which gives him at tranquil times the air of an ecstatic, means that he can't really yet concentrate on an activity as intricate as a tennis swing, or as relaying to his brain the myriad signals involved in maintaining your balance on ice skates. He is a terrific climber, and although he often looks as if he is about to lose his balance, he never does. I was pleased to realize that I would not likely be spending his adolescence in a car traveling between Providence and Boston and Philadelphia to take him to hockey tournaments, but I was concerned that he would not have the protective coloration of an athlete — being accomplished at tennis and captain of the hockey team had gotten me a lot of free passes.

I have no interest in being the kind of parent whose child takes lessons in cello and horseback riding and French and modern dance. Too great an involvement in these activities suggests parents who are social climbers or who have too little time to spend with their children. What I didn't realize was that there is an alternative version of this circuit of activities in which you have a child who takes speech therapy twice a week and has occupational therapy on the other three days.

A PLAN FOR THE FUTURE

Children are made uncomfortable by eccentricity, because it suggests mysteries they know intuitively they are not equal to. They will set upon children who are sufficiently different from them to cause them anxiety, or who seem to be made for their sport. I have no idea how my son will do as an adolescent, whether he will escape harassment or be the object of it, but if he is a target of it I will tell him to try to find ways to avoid the person who bullies him, or to talk his way out of a confrontation, to outsmart his adversaries and leave them looking for easier marks. If he is unable to do one of these things, or if the schoolyard constantly throws him and the bully together, if the bully can't be escaped and he is making my son unhappy, I might also try to tell my son that the world is not built for our happiness and that we have to accommodate some degree of misery and ride it out the best we can.

If I feel that the bully might harm my son, I plan to visit the bully. I will pretend to be interested in something he is engaged in, perhaps. I am Sam's father, I might say. How are you? Those are terrific arms you have, you must lift weights, wonderful. Listen, are you busy, could we go sit over on that bench and talk for a moment? All right, here's fine, sure, listen, what I have to say is, I understand from Sam that you make him unhappy, you seem to like to tease him, and I just wanted to suggest that you find someone else, would that be hard? A little? All right, that's fair. Well, here's what I'm thinking: I'm thinking, if you don't quit, I will find you somewhere, when you really aren't thinking about me or Sam, of course, and I or someone representing my interests will beat you within an inch of your miserable, worthless little life, you understand? One more time I hear from Sam that he had any trouble from you of any kind, and those are the consequences for you. Everything in your life at one moment will be as good as it ever has been, and the next moment you will wake up in a hospital room, with double vision and your head hurting and you unable to take solid food. If you think I am not serious about this, try me. Go ahead, tell your father.

When the father calls me, I will say that his son, who makes things up, might need psychiatric help. If you think that this behavior is discreditable of me, I would suggest that we are all immortal in our souls, not in our characters.

LOVE

The physical pleasure, the intimacy, the smell of their hair, their bodies, their closeness, their acceptance of you as their sheltering presence, the way they look when they sleep, their breathing in the night, the light in their eyes, is intoxicating to the point of exquisiteness. Throughout my son's life I have now and then thought of him as a household divinity — that is, as an uncorrupted presence of joy. Like any idol, he is susceptible to vanity and solipsistic behavior, he is interested in his acceptance as a majestic being, and he grows jealous and intolerant whenever the attention of his subjects is divided. Sometimes he hurts me so deeply by what appears to be indifference that I think I will refuse to look at him for the rest of his life, I will give him up. I hope that he will have none of my smaller and undesirable qualities and all of my better ones. I want him to grow into a man who is unplagued, regarded affectionately for his sensitivity and intelligence and candor and steadfastness and a tranquillity at the heart of his being that comes from knowing that he has been loved, that he has no obligation to carry forth a family myth, that he is unencumbered. And that he will value the company of his mother and father because he feels it is uncomplicated by any insistence that he abandon his identity for one we need him to embrace.

Perhaps nearly every observation I've made applies only in my case. I know one thing: A moment arrives when your child leaves your lap, and you realize he isn't coming back.

(2000)

At Home Outside the World

WHEN LIZZIE GOTTLIEB began interviewing her brother, Nicky, on camera, three years ago, she was twenty-seven and he was twenty. She was the director of a theater company in Manhattan, and she had also made a short film. She had been thinking of making a movie about Nicky, but she was uncertain how to turn his life into fiction. "Nicky is always on my mind," Lizzie says. "I suppose a reason for the film is that I don't have the answer to how I feel; so many emotions, really, are involved." One morning she woke up and thought that there was no need to make him a character in a story; she could make a documentary. She borrowed a friend's camera and had Nicky sit for a few hours of questions.

"He rose to the occasion," she says. "He was very formal. He refused to acknowledge that I was his sister. He would say, 'As I've often said to my sister, Lizzie . . .'" Lizzie had always regarded her brother as the most interesting and original person she had ever met. As a small boy, he had been taken by his parents to Italy, where their mother's family is from — Nicky and Lizzie are the children of the actress Maria Tucci and Robert Gottlieb, the former editor of *The New Yorker*. Nicky was just learning to talk, and a doctor told the Gottliebs not to let him hear too much Italian, because it might confuse him. At the end of two weeks, he spoke Italian fluently. Lizzie felt that in making a movie about him all that would be necessary would be to turn on the camera and follow him around, although it didn't turn out that way. "We got some nice moments," she says, "but they didn't stand on their own."

As formidable as Nicky's intelligence was, he had always seemed somehow disengaged from the world and without sufficient resources to find his way in it. Clearly, he was smarter than many of the people around him, yet as he says, "Little children are like me; I am still a child." No one knew why. Everyone his mother and father had turned to for an opinion said that they had never been presented with anyone like him.

Not long before Lizzie began interviewing him, his parents had enrolled him in a program in Florida that was meant to help him live on his own. He attended a community college, but the first day he talked out of turn so often that he was asked to leave. He spent hours by himself in an apartment near a highway, eating Pop-Tarts, Lizzie says. One morning around two he was found walking along the highway, on his way to the mall, he said. He came home to New York for a few days and Lizzie said, "You don't seem yourself," and he said, "I don't?" She went to Florida to visit him. "I spent a week with him, and he was obviously unhappy. He had nothing to do, maybe two activities a week. He grew up in Manhattan and was free to move around, and now he's stuck in this condo by the side of the road in Fort Lauderdale. He had always been this cheerful person, but he wasn't now. He wanted to be in Beverly Hills, having a glamorous life. Florida was the first failure."

The second took place shortly after he moved back into his mother and father's house. An employment agency found work for him in the mailrooms of two banks in Midtown. One job began immediately, on Madison Avenue, and the other began in three months on Park Avenue. Without hesitating, Nicky took the position on Park Avenue. In his mind, Park Avenue represented power, style, forceful and brilliant men and women, and the pleasure and privilege that attached to such people. A friend of his mother took him to buy suits. Lizzie and his parents told Nicky that he didn't need suits, he could wear jeans — it was, after all, only the mailroom — but he insisted on wearing a suit. On the first day, he kept appearing in the doorway of his supervisor's office and asking when he would be allowed to go upstairs, where the executives were. He also asked a number of times if he could have a break. On the second day he was fired. "From television he had these images of what life should be like," Lizzie says, "and it didn't measure up. He said he was so surprised at how boring sorting the mail was. He thinks of himself as the star of the show, and the star didn't work in the mailroom. When Florida didn't work out and the bank didn't work out, he wasn't a quirky child any longer; he was a strange young man."

As a baby Nicky began having seizures, two of them serious. He was given various tests, including two spinal taps, and eventually doctors decided from the results of EEGs, which discovered irregular rhythms in his brain, that he suffered from a rare neurological disease. They told his parents that 90 percent of the children afflicted with it regress, and that they would know that he could walk when he walked and that he could speak when he talked. The next day he took his first steps. Usually the condition leads to retardation; when it turned out Nicky was so bright, no one knew what to make of him. Periodically his parents wondered whether autism might be responsible, but he seemed far too sociable to qualify as autistic.

"He didn't know how to talk to people in any conventional way," Lizzie says, "so he would go up to people at parties my parents gave and ask how old they were and when they were born. When they told him, he would giggle and say, 'Oh, you were born on a Tuesday.' I used to play a game with him where I would make up a number, say, 59,657, and ask him, 'Is that a prime?' and he'd laugh and say something like, 'No, Lizzie, thirteen goes into it 4,589 times.' When he wanted to learn French, he picked up my copy of *501 French Verbs* and memorized them, and he put them between Italian nouns and adjectives, and the result sounded sort of French and sometimes was exactly French." (Nicky: "I taught myself French when I was nine years old. I memorized pluperfect subjunctives. Not an easy thing for a nine-year-old. Even a nine-year-old Frenchman.")

A couple of years ago a young woman who had worked for the Gottliebs as an au pair and had become a child psychologist suggested a diagnosis of Asperger's syndrome, a condition so recently recognized that it has been included, as Asperger's disorder, only in the most recent version of the *Diagnostic and Statistical Manual of Mental Disorders,* the book on which all psychiatric diagnoses are based. Even so, the Gottliebs were reluctant to accept the description.

"At first we thought there couldn't be a diagnosis, because everyone's always told us that they've never seen anyone like Nicky," Lizzie says. "We went to an Asperger's meeting, and a boy walked in who was so much like Nicky that we knew. My mother then went to a lecture by Tony Attwood, a clinical psychologist who is an authority on Asperger's, and she said that he described Nicky totally. This was a relief for us because in twenty years we had never imagined that there was anyone like him in the world. And we didn't exactly live a sheltered life."

· · ·

Asperger was a pediatrician in Vienna who, in 1944, published a post-doctoral thesis in which he identified a collection of behaviors, occurring far more often in boys than in girls, that included a lack of empathy, not much ability to make friendships, conversations that offered little opportunity for another person to take part, and obsessions with subjects that were scientific or technical — types of trains and their routes, for example. In addition, these children tended to be clumsy. Asperger's paper, published in German, was noted but not widely influential. In the 1980s, a British researcher making a study of children in London described them in terms of Asperger's findings, and the condition the researcher called Asperger's syndrome, or Asperger's, has since been more widely observed. Now it is thought to afflict one out of 250 to 500 people, which is to say perhaps half a million Americans.

The habits and manners of someone with Asperger's are likely to be eccentric. Often they stand too close to people when they talk to them, and bear in as they speak. They easily become overstimulated, and throw their hands up or jump up and down and shout or fail in other ways to contain their excitement. Their remarks are often candid to the point of being blunt. Seeing someone who is overweight, they might say, "Look at how big that woman is," and then not understand why they shouldn't say so, their observation being, after all, only the truth. That it might be hurtful to someone else is not within their capacity to understand. They often appear to be selfish or self-centered, but they aren't. They are merely, obdurately, intact within themselves. They have no interest in pleasing anyone else.

The way that we use our hands when we speak, or shrug our shoulders, or widen our eyes, especially the way we cut our eyes to one side or the other without perhaps realizing we are doing it — the import of all these gestures is lost on someone with Asperger's. Looking a person in the eye does not come to them easily. "I was born not knowing that you have to look at somebody when you talk to them," Nicky says, "but I'm learning. I'm trying to look at people without staring."

I am more aware of the condition and its attributes than I might otherwise be because I have a son who is eight and while not being a classic case of Asperger's has a number of its characteristics. The expression in his eyes is often apprehensive and bewildered. He knows that there is a reason to look someone in the eye, else why would his mother and father tell him to do it so often, but he doesn't know why they tell him, or what is to be found there, or what he is missing that might cause him trouble later. Attwood describes a boy whose habit it is to close his eyes when he becomes anxious. When a therapist interviewing him said that it was difficult to have a conversation with someone who had his eyes closed, the boy said, "Why would I want to look at you when I know where you are?"

Someone with Asperger's is as if blindfolded, taken to a strange territory, spun three times, and told to remove the blindfold. The words he hears mean one thing to him and something else to other people. In *Asperger's Syndrome,* a popular handbook, Attwood writes that to someone with Asperger's it seems as if the rest of us willfully obscure our intentions. By means of gestures we conceal parts of a conversation. Whatever it is that attaches us to one person and not another is opaque. "Sometimes I understand how people feel," Nicky says, "and sometimes I don't. You're told that people are sad when they cry, but people can be sad without crying. That's been confusing to me."

The minds of people with Asperger's tend to be inflexible and to favor rituals. In describing Nicky one day, Lizzie made use of a metaphor that circulates among people familiar with the syndrome. Most people have minds that are like cars, she said, and can travel over a landscape. People with Asperger's have minds that are like trains and are confined to the tracks. Rituals bring order. Attwood observes that most children like to break rules, whereas a child with Asperger's seeks to enforce them.

For someone with Asperger's, existence is abrasive. The world with its lights and intensities bears down on them with terrific force. Many of them are extravagantly sensitive to textures and sounds and tastes. Attwood mentions a child who was reluctant to play in his parents' garden. When they asked him why he avoided the garden, he said he couldn't stand the *clack-clack* sound the butterflies made with their wings. When my son was five, he was sitting in our living room. My wife had put a Mozart quartet on the CD player for him and left the room for a moment. When she came back, he was weeping. She asked what had happened and he said, "The music, it's so sad."

It is perhaps difficult to have a sense of how conventional the world is and how narrow its tolerance for eccentric behavior until you see your maverick child try to find a place for himself, or how indifferent, even hostile, most of us are to those among us who disregard rules. Having such a child changes your life. You give up seeing people to whom you have to apologize when your child does something they don't care for, and seek out people who are sympathetic. You avoid places that might be stressful for him — anywhere loud, or with too many people. Your life becomes devoted to nurturing and protecting this child who is vulnerable to so much, and the things you did that might disturb him fall away from you. Such children are not much given toward independence. They are not easily left with other children to play; too many difficulties arise. Other children, aware of their limitations, often spurn them or tease them. School is particularly fraught. No child with Asperger's has an easy time in school; indeed it is difficult to find any school that will accept them at all. My son travels two hours a day and sometimes more to a school on the outskirts of the city. The two he attended that were closer to home both asked us to leave.

I sometimes observe conventional families with a feeling that we live on separate sides of a sheet of glass. I suppose occasionally I feel envious that their lives seem so simple by contrast. In an earlier marriage I took part in the raising of a stepson, who is now a young man, and the endeavor by comparison was effortless. Nor did it offer, time and again, unbidden, the opportunity to have my heart broken on behalf of my child.

Nicky is tall and big-boned and heavyset. He has brown hair. He walks with his feet splayed, as if he were a dancer, and his progress is stately. He is not especially graceful, but neither are a lot of people who grew up in New York City and didn't spend their childhoods playing sports. He tends to be either emphatically interested in a person or aloof. Interviewing him is like interviewing someone famous. The way that he turns his head from side to side, staring to one corner or another rather than meeting your eye, the impression of restlessness, as if he had more interesting claims on his attention but is deferring (briefly) to yours, the sense of forbearance, all remind me of the way movie stars behave. If he weren't compromised by other limitations, such a manner would be alluring, even charismatic.

He spends hours a day watching television. He describes his relationship to television as a "one-sided friendship." In Lizzie's movie he says, "TV is what I do. It's what I love to do most of all. Not only do I love the

TV shows, but since I've been watching the shows for the last eight years, TV is like home to me. Like a second home. I sometimes wish that the characters in the TV shows could come out and talk to me. I wish the people could know that I am a big fan and that I personally exist. They say that TV can be really catching. You don't learn a lot about the real world through watching TV, but I would be literally crushed if TV were taken away from me. It would be as if my sister were taken away from me."

A truly original person is usually a burden at close hand — insistent, demanding, self-absorbed. Children with Asperger's are often gifted. Frequently their memories of childhood are more complete than those of other children. Memories of the remote past tend to begin with the arrival of language. Children with Asperger's often recall episodes from before they could speak. They characteristically display abilities in math and science and in music and art. Asperger believed that some measure of the syndrome he identified — the ability to absorb oneself in a task, to regard a subject in a novel way, to bring all of one's talents to bear on a problem — was necessary for success in science or art. The complication, of course, is whether the child's social eccentricities will isolate and overwhelm him before he can apply his talents. The six-year-old boy with the maps of the New York subway system and the London Underground and the Paris Métro committed to memory and the bus routes superimposed above them may become an engineer with an apparently intuitive understanding of transportation design, or a train-spotter people avoid at a party, if he is invited to a party at all.

My son is deeply engaged by construction cranes and by lizards. He makes drawings of them that are imaginative and resourceful and complex. One of them portrays a lizard driving a construction crane. In another one, the lizard is spread over the page, and above his head, attached by a thin line, is a small drawing, enclosed in a bubble, of the crane, with the lizard's head a notation of color in the cab — the lizard remembering driving the crane. He makes figures with pipe cleaners that have an eerie sense of liveliness, as if out of the corner of your eye you might catch them moving. I can imagine his becoming an artist. He also loves animals, and I can imagine his becoming a veterinarian. I can also imagine his becoming a shut-in with a library of videotapes and books, and pictures torn from magazines and newspapers, of lizards and cranes.

Nicky is disarming and articulate in talking about himself, and through his observations I gain understanding of my son's preoccupations. When I asked Nicky once how he felt different from everyone else, he said, "Well, I've been told, really, and I've observed society, and I just feel so different. I have no socialization, really, and no world knowledge. Other people are less smart than me at math and technical material, but as for the real world, other people — both older and younger — seem more sophisticated. And I am really at the bottom of the totem pole."

Lizzie was aware as a child of her brother's differences from other children, but she also thought that he was immensely entertaining and a great companion, and that no one else had a brother like hers. With all children of this kind, as with Nicky, one wonders how much distress the affliction causes. Surely someone whose behavior is sometimes grating and for the most part unresponsive to discipline becomes accustomed to having people turn away from him. "He seems impervious to shame," Lizzie says. "He seems to be impassive, but as a result of these problems, we yell at him a lot, and he keeps going, barely notices, although my mother thinks, and I tend to agree, that at some level it must be affecting him deeply."

Nicky says, "I feel like I've been deprived of joy, of the friends I can make. I feel outside the world. I don't want to go around having to be friends only with kids and little children. What I'm hoping for is to have a lot of friends who don't know about my tendencies, or who know about them but it's secret, or on the side. I would like to have spunky people for friends, spunky gals, ones full of pizzazz, full of life. I just want them to love me. And guys I can look up to. Good, modern American guys. They're aware of the world, they know who Shakespeare is, they're educated, but they also know the modern-day lingo. Making people upset, though, is something I do too much of. And the real thing I'm worried about is that Asperger's could cost me a lot of friends, because of not being able to interpret feelings."

While he talked, Nicky was sitting in a restaurant in TriBeCa near his sister's apartment. He'd arrived by himself on the subway. Before long he was due at a class in number theory he was taking at NYU. In a notebook he was writing pages of numbers, his homework, he said. I asked if he knew what a Möbius strip was. He said he didn't. I said it was a circle in which a twist had been made, so that instead of having two sides it had only one. Then I made one for him out of a napkin. He began tracing the side of the strip with a pen, following its route, while he talked. I asked what would make him happy.

"My fantasy would be to have my childhood with me always," he said, "available to me whenever I need it. Like a rerun. It would incorporate the taste and smells and feel, everything as if it were," and he paused. "A certain feel in the air is what's missing," he went on. "I can't describe it. There's a feeling of happiness; there's a feeling of no pain. A fun moment would be to have it all back."

He traced the napkin over and over with his pen.

I asked if anything frightened him. "Around the time I turned twenty I thought of death," he said. "I was lying in bed one day — I was in Italy, with my parents — and it just occurred to me that people die and there was nothing I could do about it, and I had morbid thoughts and panic attacks about death and nothing has felt the same since."

He held the Möbius strip nearly in front of his nose, as if he were a jeweler examining a watch.

"I'm also afraid of coming to a point in a relationship where I don't know what to say," he continued, "because I have only a limited number of topics. I worry that other people may be saying something to me to be polite, but not meaning it."

In the movie he says, "I'm scared of being scared, I'm scared of fighting the fear." And "I would like to come up with an Aspergian-like solution: a somewhat technical way to learn when and how to get rid of certain crazy emotions I get. . . . I mean, I know that everyone is scared. And that's a great thing to know. But everyone who is scared, I know, knows how to deal with their fears. And move on. Not just because they have to but because deep down they want to. So I have to find the secret."

I watched him absorbed with the Möbius strip. I felt as if he were somehow imperturbable, as if the only way of reaching him were through some deep code I had only part of, a way I sometimes feel with my son. After a moment he said of the strip, "An amusing game." He put it down abruptly and looked right at me and said, "Ask me more questions." Then he lowered his eyes to the page and began writing columns of numbers.

Lizzie expects her movie to be completed shortly. She has seventy hours of footage, which she intends to reduce to an hour or an hour and a half. I have seen only parts of the film, but a love story is what it has always struck me as being, one suffused with complications. "I had to try to find the answer from interviewing everyone else — my parents, Nicky," Lizzie says. "But Nicky is always changing, and I came to realize that I was never going to make the film that defines him. There is, at some point, a kind of letting go."

As a small boy at parties, after he told a person the day of the week on which the person had been born, Nicky went immediately to someone else and repeated the question. When I asked how he had been able to compute the dates, he said, "I just looked at the calendar, and I had a kind of system in my head. I had a kind of picture of it, like Monday the first had its own image and an abbreviation of the date in a certain style of writing. It felt natural. I know the rules of the calendar — there are 365 days in a year and every four years it's a leap year so you can imagine every twenty-eight years the calendar repeats itself. Three hundred and sixty-five days times four, plus one, that's 1,461 days, times seven, whatever that is, 10,227. I know the way the dates flow by. It's as if I see them."

"Like little signs passing?"

"Yes."

"A parade."

"That's right."

"It makes you happy, doesn't it."

He looked to one side, and his eyes seemed to brighten, and he smiled broadly.

"It does," he said softly.

(2002)

My Mentor

NO ONE I LOVED had ever died until William Maxwell died last summer. Sitting up in bed one morning, he had something to eat and drank a cup of coffee; then he lay down and fell back asleep, and his heart stopped beating. He was ninety-one.

Sixty years ago, Maxwell and my father met on a commuter-train platform. My father was a magazine art director in New York City, and Maxwell was a novelist and short-story writer who also edited fiction at *The New Yorker*. Maxwell eventually married and raised two daughters, but at the time he and my father were introduced by a neighbor, he lived by himself in a cottage that had been delivered to its site on a flatbed truck and he grew roses, and my father and his first wife lived up the hill in a house with a horse barn and horses. My father understood anything he could put his hands on. He knew how machines worked, and he was an accomplished carpenter. I can imagine him and Maxwell in a scene that Maxwell described to me. It is evening and darkness has already fallen. In my father's workshop in the barn, Maxwell stands beside my father while he cuts on his jigsaw the façade for the dollhouse that Maxwell is building for his daughters at Christmas.

My father was robust, and Maxwell's frame was slight. My father spent hours on the weekends in the fields and the barn, attending to chores, while Maxwell sat at his typewriter. If he accepted an invitation from a neighbor to dinner, he always rose from the table in time to be in bed by ten-thirty so as to be rested for the next day's writing.

My father was charming and blasphemous and subversive by nature, and Maxwell took pleasure in the way he embraced life. Whereas Maxwell's emotions tended to show on his face, my father had a tendency to say whatever was on his mind. He was indifferent to whether anyone cared for his opinions. If the company he was among disappointed him, he sought new company. Maxwell's nature was sedentary. He disliked change. He didn't especially care for new experiences or all that much for travel, which is unusual in a writer, but Maxwell was a profoundly original writer and didn't feel obliged to look around in the world for his material. Except when he was a young man and had the idea that he might find something to write about if he went to sea, he drew almost entirely for his writing on his childhood in a small town in central Illinois, the relatives and neighbors and acquaintances who surrounded him, and the impressions he gathered — what he described as "the natural history of home."

Maxwell's dependence on my father was practical, and my father's dependence on Maxwell was emotional. He knew no one else like Maxwell — so receptive, so quick to respond to gestures of friendship. My father could say wounding things, and he was capable of insensitive behavior, but it was in reaction to, even alarm over, an element of his nature that was gentle and feminine. Maxwell's company was a comfort to him, and they were kind to each other, and my father was affectionate with Maxwell in a way that I never saw him be with another man. On the other hand, none of his other friends that I was aware of offered the opportunity. It was possible with Maxwell because he was unafraid of emotion. What people felt is what drew his interest, and he was uncommonly sympathetic. The gentleness my father was able to express in Maxwell's company was balanced, I think, by his feeling that he bore some responsibility for Maxwell's well-being as a householder, the way one farmer might feel toward another the kind of masculine affection that involves a deep acceptance of the other's nature while also being concerned that his friend didn't know enough to come in out of the rain.

I inherited the dependence my father and Maxwell shared. At twenty-four, when it appeared that my hopes of becoming a rock-and-roll star weren't going to fly, I decided to try to become a writer. My father asked Maxwell if he would read something I'd been working on. I didn't know the regard that serious writers had for Maxwell's work and his opinions. I saw his name on the spines of his books on my parents' bookshelves, but I hadn't read the books. I read books quickly and promiscuously then and without much appreciation for what the writer was up to. I was protected by my innocence from feeling self-conscious about the writing that I was showing to Maxwell, and he was not the sort of person who felt the need to impress people, to have an audience or acolytes; there was nothing in him of the self-inflater. A few years earlier he had retired from *The New Yorker* and was devoting all his working time to writing, and except occasionally, when a friend asked him to read a draft of a novel, no one was asking for his help. The writers he had edited sent him their work in the hope that he would buy it, not that he would show them how to make it into something that they might be able to publish. Anyone who wrote as poorly as I did then and sent Maxwell a story at *The New Yorker* would not likely have received an encouraging letter in return.

Time and again over the years, we sat side by side at a series of tables — at the Maxwells' apartment or at their country house or in houses they took for the summer in Wellfleet on Cape Cod — while he patiently showed me what a writer needs to know. Not that much, it turns out: when to compress and when to go on at length; the order in which to present things; how to arrive at a style that resembles one's habitual patterns of speech; knowing what is and what isn't sensible to ask the reader to be a witness to. He took me on out of affection for my father, but he continued to help me because we became friends ourselves.

Having my most intimate friend be nearly twice my age did not seem unusual to me, partly because I am not so much captivated by things that younger people are interested in. I attribute this to having been the youngest by far in a family of four brothers. Every privilege, every opportunity, every adventure, and every pleasure appeared to be reserved for people older than I was. When I arrived at a landmark I had seen on the horizon, my brothers had given it up for another that was just as remote. What was behind me didn't seem valuable. I am also not so much engaged by what younger people are interested in, because I was young and I remember what it was like. I have no desire to have the same experiences or to reenact them at second hand through the experiences of people who now are young. Popular culture relentlessly celebrates the same characteristics — excess, outrage, and adolescent beauty. For me to have too close an interest in the lives of young people at this point in my life would amount nearly to a perversion. Furthermore, it seems unnatural to me to be unwilling to get older. It takes courage, of course, but the pleasures only deepen, and the most fortunate of us achieve some sort of wisdom.

If my father and I had been more comfortable with each other, I wouldn't have sought someone to replace him. About fifteen years ago, in order to arrive at some understanding of my growing up, I occupied once or twice a week a leather chair in the office of a Jungian analyst in the Village, and after a few years of talking about other subjects, I began to wonder how I would feel when my father died. I had once considered myself close to him but had come to believe that we hadn't been very well suited to each other and that I had concerns and grievances I wasn't sure how to take up with him, if I could take them up at all, since by then he was elderly. It seemed unreasonable to hold him to account for the way he had behaved thirty years earlier, and if he said he regretted it, what difference would it make? Except in memory, I couldn't recover my childhood, and certainly I could change nothing that had happened; I could only change how I regarded it. Moreover, my relations with him were, after all, what had left me open to an intimate friendship with someone of his generation, and if he had done nothing else than make a close friend of Maxwell, then allow me to transfer my feelings for him to his friend, he had set in place some way of my being looked after.

When Maxwell was elderly, he once told me, "Of all my friends, as I look back on it, your father had the truest heart." The charming, amiable, and eccentric man who delighted Maxwell and whose friendship toward him was unstinting was not the aloof and temperamental man I knew as my father. What I ended up feeling toward my father is sadness for the relationship I wish we had had. I felt we had failed to make some fundamental connection when we should have, and after that nothing that ought to have happened between a father and his child had gone right. I never thought that I had exactly replaced him with Maxwell — for years I thought of Maxwell as my godfather — but I had. Which is to say that when my father died, in 1995, I missed him but I didn't feel shipwrecked, or even much thrown. What I began then to be apprehensive about was how I would feel when Maxwell died.

I am sorry that I was not present when Maxwell passed away. I am sorry I did not get to see him with his eyes closed, departed, free of all concerns, the never again facing a bank statement or an income tax form or someone who wants something from you that you don't want to give them or someone you resent or who intends you harm, someone you dislike, any kind of violence, any suffering. No pleasure anymore, but it's not my impression that his life was short on pleasure. For fifty-five years he was married to an exceptionally beautiful woman — the painter Emily Maxwell — and they were deeply in love. They were like two trees whose roots have grown together. Their daughters were gifted, and although they felt the need when they were younger to assert their independence, their devotion afterward was sustaining to their parents. Maxwell once said, "When I die, I hope people won't grieve for me. I've had a very happy life."

I intended not to grieve. I resolved instead to feel only gratitude for his friendship, for all the things he did for me, for having taught me to be a writer, for providing me when I was young with a model of masculinity that was sensitive and appealing and courtly and had great dignity and was graceful. (If you wonder what kind of graceful, I can tell you that John Updike once described Maxwell as a figure resembling Fred Astaire.) Any reaction other than resignation seemed unrealistic. The world can't go on forever as it is; the future is never an extension of the present. I felt thankful that he had lived as long as he had. A man who dies at, say, sixty-eight or seventy is not generally thought to have died too early. Many men of Maxwell's generation died within years of having retired, at sixty-five. Maxwell was privy to every decision of any consequence that I made during the past twenty-five years, and who I would have been in the absence of his influence I am the last person who could say.

I had the impression for days after he died that I hadn't paid close enough attention, that I should have written down everything he said at dinner parties and teas and over bottles of champagne. I felt I hadn't seen him often enough. I have read that there are stages to grief, and I suppose that they are conventional and can't be avoided, like stages of an illness, but nonetheless I had hoped to escape them.

It turns out that such a resolution appears not to be within my control. The deeper layers of memory are indifferent to time — it is why we can feel ourselves to be several ages at once, or in succession — and they are also resistant to being dominated by simple intention. Everyone knows this, and I can't help wondering how I could have expected such rules not to apply in my case, except to say that it seems to me most lessons in life are learned by means of experience, and I hadn't been exposed to this one.

In a state that is something like a reverie, I can hear Maxwell's voice.

Sometimes I can make out what he is saying, and sometimes it is simply the sound of him talking. Once since he died, he has appeared in my dreams. As an old man who embraced me and said, "I'm glad I had you for a father." I am aware that Maxwell had grown fatigued by the effort of existence — by having outlived his body, that is — and was not much interested in going on without his wife, who died eight days before he did, and these are sufficient reasons to be grateful that his end was peaceful and without suffering. Even so, I do not feel resigned to his being gone. This is the contradiction at the heart of grief — there is no point at which I expect to be able to say I am happier than I was when he wasn't in the cemetery. We simply arrive eventually at a state of existence in which we are better able to bear the sadness. I keep a picture of Maxwell on my desk, and sometimes I forget it is there and raise my eyes from what I am doing and wonder how it is possible to feel so strongly about someone who isn't here anymore.

He often said that when someone you love dies you incorporate parts of their personalities into your own, so that you never lose them. He said it was in his mother's nature to be interested socially in the lives of other people and that when he found himself talking to strangers at parties he was aware the impulse came from her.

Six or eight years ago, when a woman I cared a great deal for died while she was still in her thirties, I used to feel for nearly a year that I saw her on the streets of the city. Out of the corner of my eye. Or her face reflected in a store window. Or her back as she turned into a doorway. Partly this was a result of how I felt about her, and her dying, which took place without my knowing of it and during a period when I hadn't seen much of her. Partly it was also the result of there being other women who have her sleek figure, or red glasses like hers, or her short black hair, which she sometimes colored with henna. There are not that many old men on the streets in New York. Who move slowly but with resolve, who might pause to take in the sight of a group of schoolchildren coming toward him, or to watch a young man break suddenly into a run to chase a bus. With a coat on even though it's spring, and a hat. And maybe a scarf wrapped around his neck. A brown raincoat and a red scarf and a brown felt hat. So I don't have that experience. Ten years ago, when I was walking through Grand Central on my way to the Lexington Avenue subway, I came to the top of the long stairs that lead to the turnstiles, and just as I arrived, Maxwell placed a foot on the top step, as if he had come as a guide from the underworld, as if he had materialized from my unconscious, because I had been thinking of him, perhaps, or had needed him just then. "How did this happen," I said. It was an occurrence to be grateful for, to rest my mind on — the way he was smiling, his radiance — even now. To meet your protector in a crowd, in the subway especially where one expects nothing.

Thirty years ago, my father gave up his job in the city and he and my mother moved to their summer house in Wellfleet. My father began cultivating an oyster bed in the harbor. Every Christmas, he sent the Maxwells two dozen oysters. One winter Maxwell wrote to my father:

"They were — there is no other word — exquisite. The best oysters I ever tasted. Twice in one year this has happened to me. Emmy's father served us a bottle of Château Margaux 1961 that had been given to him seven years ago on his eightieth birthday, and there is no better year or better wine for that year, and I realized that, alas, I have a palate for wine even though I don't know a bloody thing about it. And now the Wellfleet oysters. I also thought, as champagne glasses were raised to you, of what it meant trudging through the icy cold to get them for us, and who else would do it? The answer is nobody. There is no adequate way to thank you. It isn't even very sensible to try. I mean, you don't thank people for being your friend, you thank God for your good fortune in having them as a friend."

(2001)

Part Three

Mr. Apology

Personal stories or myths that impose a sense of meaningfulness to life exist in every individual at various levels of abstraction and consciousness. . . . [They] modify and are themselves modified by such existential issues as religious belief and philosophical outlook, the nurturing quality of relationships, the state of "good" and "bad" internalized objects. In every individual, the story is fashioned and refashioned and combined with more complicated stories.

   — David M. Berger, in the *Canadian Journal of Psychiatry,*
   vol. 30, February 1985

M R. APOLOGY began the Apology Line in 1980 by taping posters to the walls of buildings in Manhattan:

ATTENTION
AMATEURS, PROFESSIONALS,
CRIMINALS
BLUE COLLAR, WHITE COLLAR
YOU HAVE WRONGED PEOPLE. IT IS TO THE
PEOPLE THAT YOU MUST APOLOGIZE, NOT TO
THE STATE, NOT TO GOD.
GET YOUR MISDEEDS OFF YOUR CHEST!
CALL APOLOGY (212) 255-2748

He connected a phone in his apartment to an answering machine and recorded the calls he received. A lot of criminals called. Some confessed ("Uh, hello, I'd like to apologize for something I did last night"), and some asked who was Mr. Apology to suggest that they had anything to feel ashamed of. Some provided descriptions of how Mr. Apology would meet his end, which preyed on his mind until it was borne in on him that the pleasure for these individuals lay in delivering the threat, and that the rest — the business of finding out who he was and where he lived — was work.

Mr. Apology intended to collect confessions until he had enough to play at museums. He did this for the first time at the New Museum, in SoHo, in 1981. The New Museum was concerned that criminals might appear at the opening, so they asked Mr. Apology not to announce the show in the message he played to callers of the Apology Line. He was a little concerned himself, so he wore a costume beard to the party. Because he believed that the tapes should be heard by the people who had contributed to them, and these people didn't strike him as the kind to scan the museum-listing columns of whatever papers or magazines they read, he thought of playing the tapes over the telephone (a found object). Someone who calls the Apology Line can listen to apologies, make his own, or leave his opinion of the ones on the tape. If his apology is novel or moving or especially dramatic, he may hear it later on one of the programs Mr. Apology assembles from the calls he receives. Or he may read a transcript of it in *Apology,* the magazine that Mr. Apology has begun publishing.

Initially, calls to the Apology Line were brief: I want to say I'm sorry to so-and-so for this and that. They became extended. A certain sort of lonely person began to call. Errant husbands called. A man called who had given his wedding ring to a prostitute in Vietnam and for years had told his wife he had lost it. A man called to shed feelings stirred by an erotic dream he had about his mother. A woman called and said she was the sort of person other people confided in. She had found this "thrilling," but lately someone had confessed to her a violent crime and had sworn her to silence. She had always felt that someone who knew the truth about a harmful deed and concealed it was despicable, but now that she was doing that, she found herself unsettled about what sort of person she actually was.

Mr. Apology is in his forties. He has the strong, square frame of a man who builds stone walls. He has a thin beard and small, broad hands. As a younger man he often engaged in shoplifting, usually of art supplies. He began to feel uncomfortable about it, though, and providing a forum for confession is partly a penance. He had expected to disconnect the Apology Line and go on to other work once he had gathered enough material for his museum shows, but he didn't. A number of people seemed to have become dependent on it, and besides, Mr. Apology was still interested.

Many calls to the Apology Line involve coarser, earthier, and more intimate subjects than the ones I have described, and it is not uncommon for them to involve violence. Mr. Apology figures that a third of the confessions he hears are true, a third are not, and a third are a mixture of truth and invention. People leave messages asking him to call them, and sometimes he does. He tries to be helpful. One man believed that Mr. Apology was Satan because his poster said that it was not necessary to confess to God. The man thought that his brother, who was in prison, had been claimed by the Devil, and that he could reach him through Mr. Apology. In apologizing, someone is "making an attempt to turn his life into a moral tale," Mr. Apology feels: "a beginning, a middle, and an end; I did this, I learned this, and the moral is this. A confession becomes a story."

What was on the mind of Jumpin' Jim, who called the Apology Line on several occasions over the summer, Mr. Apology has no idea. He confessed to a murder, which Mr. Apology first doubted, then believed, then came to learn the truth of, but more than once during the summer Mr. Apology felt as if a character from Dostoyevski were living in an outer borough of New York.

"This is Jim," the caller said. "Jumpin' Jim. OK. This is the story. It happened last night. Well, anyway, I meant to tell you exactly what happened from a period of time, a year I would say. My mother, who is, was, sixty-six years old, kept nagging me and nagging me. Told me that I was nothing but a waste of life, I would never amount to anything. I'm twenty-three years old, and pretty much she'd been telling me this for, approximately, I would say four years now, and I've been hearing it every single day. I can't move out on my own right now, because — well, I'm on my own, but in the past I couldn't move out on my own, because, financially, I wasn't stable, so I had to stay home with my mother, and I had to put up with this shit of the nagging, and nagging, and nagging. So one day, I just, just — I, I was with a couple of my friends and I figured out a plot, you know, to, um, terminate my mother off the face of the earth, because of the fact that she was driving me up the wall.

And I was just, it was just — more or less, I was just thinking about it, and, and I had no real intentions of killing my mother, but it quickly went through my mind, so, um, the reason I'm calling is to tell you, because I want to apologize, to myself, and to my mother, and to whoever, if there's a God or whatever, for taking my mother's life, last night. And, um, it's quiet now, and there's no screaming or nothing, but uh, just the noise outside, which it is New York City, so I got to expect that, so — don't, you know, if you're going to bother tracing this, there's no need for you to trace this, because, uh, you're just going to wind up with a possibly pay-phone car-service number anyway, and, uh, the only thing I don't, I just don't understand, it's just, it came over me, and I just couldn't take any more, and I had to do it, I just want to tell my mother and myself, and whatever, I'm apologizing for, I guess you could say killing my mother, and, uh, I don't know, maybe perhaps I'll go for help. Uh, right now. I'm just thinking how am I going to dispose of the body. And I'm sure, if anybody listens to this, you'll be thinking, What a crazy bastard, there's no emotions or nothing, but, see, if you were, if you were in my shoes and you heard every single day nagging and telling you that you'll amount to nothing, and you'll be nothing, and constantly nagging about every tiny little thing, you would also get pissed off, too. Maybe not to the length that you would kill somebody, but myself, I'm the type of person who, not exactly, uh, I don't know — I'm not the kind of person who, who forgets things and I just let things build up until they explode, you know, and, uh, I'm fairly a nice guy, but uh, you know, if you push me to a limit, I'm going to explode, and I just, uh, it's really, I don't know. So, anyway, I'm apologizing for doing that, and, uh, I don't know, maybe I should have some emotions or something, or, you know, I should feel *bad* or — but then again, I did it, so why should I feel bad, you know what I mean? So, Mom, I know you nagged me, but I had to do it, and this is the only way for you to stop nagging me. I'm apologizing. That's it. Bye."

Mr. Apology thought that Jim might be telling the truth but he also might not. He decided to assemble a program featuring Jim's call along with one from a man who described a violent sexual escapade and one from a woman who had been forced as a child into sex with her brother, and the program began playing on July 9. Anyone who called the Apology Line from anywhere in the world heard Jim tell his story. Mr. Apology hoped that people would have something to say about Jim's message, and that when he played those responses over the line, Jim would hear them and leave a message of his own. The first person to respond was a man I will call Trevor, who was familiar to Mr. Apology and other callers to the Apology Line. Trevor calls regularly and has plenty of opinions, and he often works people's nerves. He lives at home with his mother, who drives him crazy, and he frequently broods about this in the messages he leaves.

To Jim, Trevor said, "Up until the point where you said that you killed your mother, I was thinking to myself how totally I can relate to what you're saying. I don't know if — I didn't catch your name, whoever you are — I don't know if you've heard the statements that *I've* felt concerning my family life, but I totally can relate to what you felt and the feelings that led up to your actions, and I won't say that I haven't thought about killing my mother. I mean, I've never been serious about it, I'm never going to do it, but I won't say that I haven't sat and thought to myself, Could I get away with it? How would I go about it? You know, just daydreamed about it. I won't deny that. I have. But, uh, well, I don't know, Mr. A. generally likes to hear some kind of documentation of murders, some kind of evidence, before he'll believe that you killed somebody. Mr. A. didn't ask for it from you, but by all means — I hope this doesn't sound insensitive, but if you, you can show us that you killed your mother, if you can kind of prove it to us, I'd appreciate it. I realize you have no need to prove anything to me, and, in fact, proving it could, if you don't go about it slickly enough, cleverly enough, put you in a dangerous situation, but, uh, whatever, if you feel like you'd be comfortable doing it, if you feel like you could get away with doing it and not put yourself in jeopardy, then by all means."

The tone of the messages left for Jim by other callers involved mainly pity or contempt.

Mr. Apology collected these comments for several weeks, as he usually does, and he began playing them on the Apology Line on August 4. Jim called the same day.

"How you doing, Mr. Apology?" Jim said. "This is the Unknown Caller. To all the other callers who said that they have no pity for what I have done to my mother, I personally don't know who you people are, and I really don't care. If you had lived with her as long as I did and hear every single day her tell me how no good I am, and how I wasn't going to amount to nothing, and put me down constantly and say that I'll never make any women happy, and I'll never get married, and I'll just be a waste of life, and vermin, people may say, 'Oh, you're psychotic,' or, 'There's something really wrong with you,' but I feel that I'm just as normal as everybody else, but just one time too many she upset me.

"I would like for you, Mr. Apology, to call me at this number, which is a friend's number, and you can leave a message, whatever, and tell me how to get in touch with you."

The first time Jim spoke to Mr. Apology, he said, "See, it goes way back in my household. I have two other — actually, I *had* — two other brothers, and one had ran away when he was young, and the other one died, two years ago. Ever since then, I feel, or I *felt*, that my mother kept taking it out on me, and every day of my life, since all this happened, she'd been telling me how no good I am, and I'm going to amount to nothing, and I'll never make anybody happy. A couple of times, I've been seeing a therapist, but that hasn't been helping, so I figure I'll solve things on my own. And, uh, I — it's funny, I, I, I have no regrets. And I don't feel that I'm crazy, or anything like that, because I know I'm not — a crazy person actually wouldn't know if he was crazy anyway, and, uh — I'm kind of edgy right now, because I don't know who I'm speaking to, I could be speaking to the law, I don't know. I don't know who you are, I just know your number — that's about it. I didn't go to any trouble checking you out or anything, so, uh —"

"Yeah, well, I'm not the law," Mr. Apology said.

"She humiliated me in front of everybody, and I lost a couple of relationships off of her, and one day I just couldn't take it anymore, and, uh, I'm going to have to hang up now. I'll call you back in three minutes."

"The only reason I'm doing this hanging up is because of my safety, because I really don't trust anybody anyway," Jim said. "OK. Well, anyway, when I was younger, I had thoughts, you know, like kids usually have thoughts of doing things but not exactly carrying them out, and I thought about what it would be like to be God for the day, and it was just thoughts, I didn't really think I could actually do something like that, because who am I to judge anybody? But, like I said, when you live with somebody for a long period of time and they constantly get on your horse and then constantly scream and put you down, after a while that gets to you. Either you move or, if you're not financially stable — you can't move — then you have to just live with it. And our house isn't that big, and there's not many places I can go except outside, which I'm antisocial, I don't like to be with anybody, I don't have many friends in New York, anyhow. And there's day after day listening to this, and just one day, I just woke up, I said to myself, I am going to make her shut up, because I cannot go another day like this. So what happened is, I just woke up one morning and I said if she says one more thing to me, maybe I'll just scream, but screaming to her is like talking to a wall, because the more I screamed at her, the more she would scream at me and things just wouldn't get anywhere."

Jim let out a long breath.

"See, now, this is kind of hard for me telling you this," he went on. "Because I don't know you, you know, but, it's like — oh, man — uh, OK, it was like, oh, man, it was like Thursday, I think it was a Thursday evening, and uh, she went one, one, one word too far with me, and I hit her. That was the first thing I did, I hit her. And she seemed to shut up, and I said, 'Wow, this is good.' So I went into my room, and I heard her go on the phone and start talking to her friend about what I'd done, and her friend's suggestions and she should call the cops — you know, take me out of the house. So I heard *that*, because we have a speaker phone, so I took the scissors and went in there and I cut the wire to the outlet, and I said, 'This is enough.'

"When I hit her again, I felt like, Wow, now I'm in charge. And she's not going to say anything, and I must have hit her several times. So she passed out, and I thought I killed her. OK. I have to hang up now. I'm sorry."

He called back several minutes later.

"OK, this is the last call," he said. "This is —"

"All right."

"I hear in your voice that you find something amusing, which is kind of disturbing to me."

"No — I'm sorry," Mr. Apology said. "I don't find it at all amusing. I think sometimes I have a nervous laugh in my voice, but no, I don't find it amusing."

Jim paused. "Because I'm not calling to amuse anybody," he said.

"I'm calling to be serious with you, and I'm not exactly, like, *apologizing,* but, like I said earlier, I had to get this off my chest.

"Basically, what happened is, I took her and I put her in the closet. Now, our closet is a walk-in closet, and I put, like — I can't explain it — a broomstick to hold from the doors to move, because the doors move outward. So I put a broomstick in. And I, I left for the weekend, I went to a friend's house for the weekend. I came back and to my surprise she was still *alive.* And, uh, I said to myself, 'Now, if she goes out, she'll tell somebody,' and at that point I was saying, 'Well, she's very weak and obviously she hasn't ate anything,' and I just —

"You see, let me just explain something to you. My relationship with my mother is very, or *was,* very bad. Extremely. It was more like an acquaintance type of relationship, and this is why I had no exact feelings. So I figured that I can't let her go out and tell people this, because for sure I'll go to prison, and I don't want to go to prison — I don't want to be with no population or nothing, I just want to be by myself, I just want people to basically leave me alone. And by being in prison I'll be surrounded by people, and I really don't need that. And even if I would go to prison I would just commit suicide anyway, because not one day goes by that I don't think about it.

"Anyway, what I did is, I basically suffocated her —"

"With clothing or —"

"With a pillow. And I may sound like an evil bastard, but I had no feeling, and, to be honest with you, with somebody I don't care about I wouldn't hesitate in doing it again if somebody would keep harassing me for periods of years. But obviously I'm never going to let that happen again. So, right now, I'd really rather not say, or can't exactly remember quite well, where I did place her body at, because for the fact I've been going in and out of blackouts a lot — faints and cold sweats and stuff — and just blacking out and forgetting things that happened the night before and — it's in the New York area. I know that.

"And now I'm going to be moving upstate, or possibly California. And I'm going to leave my New York past behind. And basically that's it. I just had to get all that off my chest, that's all.

"I will call back one more time, if you don't mind."

"You're laughing," Jim said, "and to make this sound like a game, it's not. This is a serious matter to me, and I feel that, you know —"

"I'm not laughing," Mr. Apology said.

Jim seemed to consider this; then he said, "It's my own conscience. I don't know, I hear snickers and it's really disturbing. I'll call back."

"All the anger," Jim said. "Finally, that wall, I knocked it down, and just put all my anger out in that way, and, like I said, I have no regrets. I can just live my life the way I want to now, you know? But, um, I want to know: how do you feel about speaking to somebody who committed a crime like I have?"

Mr. Apology cleared his throat. "Well, it, it puts me into kind of a bind," he said, "I mean, you can imagine, because I collect what people leave on the tape recorder and most of the time you don't know one way or another if what someone says is true, you just feel like this person is making it up and that person is telling the truth, and this other person you don't know if it's true or not —"

"I figured that would be running through your mind," Jim said. "That this would all be false. It's off my chest now, which you could take it as you wish, but long as I feel better. I just wanted to tell people that I'm not crazy, and to inform your callers that I heard them say that I was a sick bastard or I'm a waste of life, I just wanted to clear that up, to tell them that I'm not. I'm just your normal, to myself, your average Joe. But, you know, if somebody does something to you for your whole life, and it feels just like killing you, then to me it feels like you just might as well kill me, because torturing me this way is not helping any. What I done, I think, was the right thing to do for myself and it's *quiet*. It is very quiet. And that's how I want it."

"If you go away to California or someplace far away like New York," Mr. Apology said, "and you start over again, get a job, an apartment, do you think you'll be able to really leave it behind?"

"I'll block it out," Jim said. "Like I am doing now. If I wasn't able to do that, I wouldn't be talking to you right now. I'd be very nervous. I'd be in my room sweating, constantly drinking. That's why I know I can block this out. It really doesn't hit me, maybe it's not hitting me now, maybe it'll hit me in twenty years down the line from now, but as of right now I don't feel no regrets."

"Couldn't you have just moved away? Left New York and your mother behind?"

"But don't you understand? The hurt is still there. All the relationships that she screwed up on me — if she'd have left me be, things would have been fine, but it wasn't like that. And when my father left her, that's when all hell broke loose."

"How long ago was that?"

"Five and a half years ago. He couldn't take it."

"How old are you approximately? Are you like in your twenties?"

"Yeah. . . . Is there a reason you're asking me all these questions?"

"I'm trying to get some kind of mental picture of the whole situation."

At the end of another long pause, Jim said, "I'm twenty-five, to be exact." Then, "I've been getting a little nervous. I guess that's normal, to get nervous. It's usually like if somebody thieves something, they get that little nervousness after they do it, it's just like that." Then, "Do you have a name besides Mr. Apology?"

"If you want to, call me Chris."

"OK, Chris. Ah, Chris, do you meet these people off this line?"

"Face to face?"

"Yes."

"Almost never have."

"Would you feel intimidated in any way by meeting me at some place in Manhattan, in a public-area place?"

"I'd be nervous, but I'd probably do it, I guess. Why would you want to do that?"

"I just want to show you what I am, and how I am, so you don't think that I am an evil, devilish person — because I'm not. And I just have this feeling about you — about hearing what you say on these lines, and I feel a certain distance bond there that I can trust you. I don't know what it is, but that's the only reason that I'm speaking to you about this."

Jim suggested a bar called Alcatraz, on St. Marks Place at Avenue A. "It's a very dim atmosphere," he said. "Very dark, it's small, just a regular bar, and I can concentrate there, and think about the future, and everything. Is there any way that we can make an arrangement to meet there?"

Mr. Apology said that the idea of meeting Jim made him very nervous. What if, having confessed, Jim wanted to kill him?

"I can understand that going through your mind," Jim said. "I wouldn't kill somebody inside a public place where I was going to get caught." Mr. Apology could bring someone with him, Jim said, if he was nervous.

Mr. Apology said he would think about it.

"I have this strange but very positive trust in you," Jim continued. "Like if I knew you for a certain period of time, but I don't. It's very, very complicated. I can't explain this right now, because I've been on the phone for a long time, and I would say I would like to meet you at Alcatraz. I'll be there till morning, more or less. I usually arrive around ten, and I don't leave until closing."

Mr. Apology said it was possible that he would come, but he didn't want to get hurt.

"You're not going to get hurt," Jim said. "And if you don't believe me — I know this is really sick and twisted — I would take pictures, and I would show you, because all my life, Chris, they call me 'liar.' People've been calling me 'liar,' they call me everything to degrade me, to make me feel humiliated, and just this once, just when I feel that I'm on top of — practically on top of the world —"

"You feel like you have this great weight off your shoulders," Mr. Apology said.

"I feel like I was a ruler," Jim said. "I actually did something where I was in control, and that's all I wanted. To be in control."

"All right, let me think about it."

The next day, August 5, Jim left a message on the Apology Line for Trevor, the man who lives with his mother. "Trevor," Jim said, "the reason I'm calling is because I listened to the comments. And I found yours very interesting. You have this voice that makes the most gulliblest, happiest, peacefulest person angry, and it's really annoying. If you want evidence, how about giving me — or, as you put it, Mr. *A.* — your address, and I will deliver it before I leave town, *personally,* to your house. Because you're the kind of people in society who makes me angry, and I just wanted you to know that, Trevor."

On August 6, Mr. Apology left a message for Jim on the Apology Line to say that he had decided not to meet him. That night, Mr. Apology went to a birthday party for a friend in the East Village, and afterward, about three in the morning, he went into Alcatraz, which turned out to be a heavy-metal bar. Mr. Apology had it in mind that if he saw a young man on his own, "staring into his beer," he might watch him for a while, but the bar was crowded, and there was no way of telling which of the patrons might be Jim.

Mr. Apology left the city for the weekend. Most of his time away, he was absorbed by thoughts about Jim, who he now thought was likely telling the truth. A person who had invented a fiction about murdering his mother did not seem to Mr. Apology the sort of person who would want to talk about it. Moreover, from the sound of Jim's conversation, he did not seem like someone with the resources to concoct such a compelling account. A few times before, people had confessed to murders on the Apology Line — the murders had taken place a long time ago, and no one had ever said that he had killed his mother — but something about the tone of many of their voices had seemed unnaturally dramatic. Also, their stories had not stood up to questioning. The most convincing element of Jim's conversation was the anxiety in his voice. Mr. Apology felt that Jim was living under an exhausting burden of pressure.

On August 9, a woman named Pearl called the Apology Line to reprimand Trevor for having asked for proof from Jim. "I'm sorry," she said, "but that sounds like the most insensitive thing I have ever heard."

Mr. Apology returned to New York on Tuesday, August 10, and that night he stayed up late preparing his conversation with Jim for callers of the Apology Line. Mr. Apology has no idea who most of his callers are. Over the years, the number for the Apology Line has been passed around by word of mouth, and calls arrive now from all over the country. He assumes that the police dial the line from time to time, so in the message that precedes the playing of the tapes he tells callers to make their apologies from pay phones, so that they cannot be traced afterward. He had decided that if Jim was telling the truth his call should be heard as soon as possible.

On August 11, Jim left a number where Mr. Apology could reach him. His voice sounded strained. "I just want to ask you another question," he said. "How come, when I call, you have a deeper voice? Do you have a voice modulator? Or do you change your voice? I don't understand this. I don't know who I'm exactly speaking to, because you sound different from the lines when we call and we hear you speaking. When you're advertising *Apology* magazine, your voice is much deeper. I just don't understand why you sound different."

A few hours later, Jim left another message for Trevor. "I have nothing really to prove to you, Trevor, out of anybody on this whole line. I spoke to, as you prefer to call him, *Mr. A.*, as I guess I prefer to call him

Mr. Apology. We are working something out here, so I can prove, or show him evidence, because you are nothing to me, and what you say to me I really don't care. You don't know what I'm going through, and you say you can sympathize, but I really, really don't think you can, because you haven't, or I doubt it if you had a mother like mine."

Mr. Apology called Jim on the morning of August 12, and Jim said that he was having nightmares. While he and Mr. Apology talked, Jim thought he kept hearing clicking noises on his telephone. "There's something wrong here," he said.

Mr. Apology thought it might be his tape recorder.

"If there is anybody tracing me at this point, I made plans to be leaving," Jim said. "So if any cops plan to come to this place, I won't be here."

Jim mentioned Trevor's request for evidence. "You want evidence," he said. "I, I, I, I, I have evidence. I don't know how well the rest of your life will possibly be after the evidence, but you want evidence. I, I'll, I'll, I have it."

At the end of a long pause, Mr. Apology said, "I sort of decided that proof is kind of a secondary issue, because, whether it's true or not, obviously you've got a very — or, you know, *had* a very — terrible relationship with your mother, and it's really tearing you up, and that's really the key thing here. But yeah, I guess so. I mean, if it's all the same to you."

"Right."

"I listened to the recording of our conversation about two or three times, and I finally decided that I believe you. Because emotionally it sounded real. It just doesn't sound like something you'd make up. Of course, someone could make up a story like that, but on the emotional level it sounds real — the sound of your voice and the kind of things you said. If it wasn't real, why would you be so worried about something like how when I played the recording back my voice sounded higher than it normally sounds? Why would anybody even worry about that? You probably are because you're in a high state of paranoia. So that makes me tend to believe you. If you were just making it up, you wouldn't be paying much attention to little details like that."

"I'm starting to feel a little bit — like, when I go to the grocery store I think that people are talking about me. It's getting me on the edge."

Mr. Apology suggested that Jim get a lawyer and plead insanity.

"I didn't call this line for you to tell me to surrender or find a lawyer," Jim said. "I called so I could be at peace with myself and say that, I, I told somebody. These cautions that you're throwing at me, it sounds like somebody's asking you to tell me this, you know? I told you, I have some certain — well, I *had* some certain — trust in you, but these questions are like, you know, kind of iffy questions. To me they are."

Mr. Apology said that he was simply concerned about Jim. Jim had said that he was thinking of killing himself. Mr. Apology suggested that at least jail offered a second chance.

"I don't believe in neither God or the Devil," Jim said, "and, from what I understand, the Bible says Hell is a forever-burning pit. Now, to myself, that I'm an atheist, I believe once you die, you're dead and that's it, it's over and there's no Limbo or anything like that, you're just in the ground and you're gone, that's it. If I'm alive and I go to jail, that means I'm going to be in living Hell, you understand what I mean? I don't want to be living in Hell."

That night, Jim left a message for Mr. Apology saying that something had prevented him from leaving New York City. The tone of his voice was uneasy. "You say you don't have my address," he said, "but there's a lot of detectives' cars going around my neighborhood, and maybe because it's Thursday and payday for the police, or something, but the traffic of detectives is heavier than it usually is, and it's making me a little bit nervous." Then he asked Mr. Apology to call him.

The possibility of receiving proof of the murder had begun to suggest to Mr. Apology that Jim had never got rid of the body at all.

When Mr. Apology called Jim on Friday, August 13, a woman answered the phone.

"Hello, is Jim there?" Mr. Apology said.

"Who's calling?"

"This is Chris."

"Who's Chris?"

"A friend of Jim's. . . . Is this, is this Jim's mother?"

"Yes, it is," the woman said.

"What?"

"Yes. This is Jim's mother."

"Uh-huh. Well, uh, is Jim there?"

"Yes, he is."

In the conversation that followed, Jim said that he would be sending Mr. Apology pictures to confirm the murder. "I don't know when they're going to arrive, but they're going to arrive," he said. "By the time you get them, I'm probably not going to be here anyways."

Mr. Apology did not say anything about what the woman had told him.

Very late that night, Mr. Apology put his second conversation with Jim onto the Apology Line. Over the next few days, several people listened to the conversation and left messages.

A man who called himself Option said, "I was thinking about people who do strange things and why. In my own mind, I thought of their personality, and it came to mind, 'deformed personality,' and it's funny that when I went to the dictionary there was something listed as 'deformed personality.' I thought I had thought that up myself."

A guy with a Southern accent called and said, "I can't conjure up much sympathy for the guy. If all of us whose parents had ruined our lives went out and killed our parents, it might not be too bad of an idea, because it would pretty much get down the population and solve a lot of problems, but it's not very practical."

Another man who called said, "Uh, don't visit that guy."

A woman named Margo called and urged Mr. Apology to betray Jim to the police. "God, I hope you know what you're doing," she said. "I mean, there is a guy out there, I think, who really did kill his mother, and he's blacking out, and he doesn't know what he's doing, and I think he's lying to you when he says that he doesn't know what he did with the body, because he's ready to send you pictures. Pictures of what, you know? The body, I suppose. So he knows right where the body is, he's just not saying. And, I don't know what you hope to accomplish with these conversations. I honestly think this is maybe the one time in all the years I've listened that you may be way over your head. What are you playing with here? Jesus Christ, be careful."

A man who called himself Bird left a message for Jim. "All these voices and things in your head, we call it a story," he said. "So this story in your mind about you and your mom and bah, bah, bah, all of that will not have to run your life anymore. You're going to say, 'Yes, my life was run by this story and set of experiences with my mom, up until this point in time,' and I don't know when you're going to reach that point, but when you reach that point, you're going to live your life different.

Up until then you were living your life as whatever your name is and whatever your past history was, and when you reach this point that I'm talking about you're going to start living your life from a different place: 'Here I am, I'm alive on this earth and I can contribute.'"

On August 19, Mr. Apology called the number Jim had given him. Jim wasn't there, but the woman answered. Mr. Apology asked again if she was Jim's mother, and she said she was. Mr. Apology persuaded her to talk. She seemed eager to. Trouble in the family, she said. Jim a hard boy to control.

"It's just the two of you," Mr. Apology said.

"Yes. His father's in the nursing home."

"What happened?"

"They operated on him and crippled him, and he got bedridden and wasn't no way I could keep him, so they put him in the nursing home."

There was also a sister in Connecticut, the mother said, married to a doctor; a brother who was a psychologist; another sister on Long Island. Calling "900" numbers on his mother's phone, Jim had run up a bill in one month of thirty thousand dollars. The phone company excused her from all but five hundred dollars of it. Then he did it again. The phone company cut off all but her local service, she said. Some time ago, Jim had been in a car accident, and now he received disability payments, but he would not give any portion of them to his mother. Instead he often spent his check in one day on his friends. On the theory that she would rather write checks to a landlord than to the phone company, his mother agreed to pay for an apartment Jim had found, but then he changed his mind and refused to live in it, saying it was dirty. Her landlord had told her that Jim was rough with his girlfriend. The girl's father had even brought a charge against him. Jim had skipped the court appearance, and now there was a warrant for him. His mother said that she felt sorry for him. Her own mother had died when she was twelve, and she had been left on her own. "I had nobody, and maybe that's one reason I'm still holding on to him," she said. She asked Chris to tell Jim that he thought it would be a good idea if he helped out his mother with the rent and the phone bill.

"Does he ever hit you, or do anything violent?" Mr. Apology asked.

"Well, he threatens to hit me sometimes, or he might grab my arm or something like that, but as far as hitting me, no, he's never really hit me, but he's grabbed my arm. Everybody tells me his temper, I should watch out, because one of these days he might just do it, you know. My daughters want me to just give up the house and come live with them. But I don't want to, because I keep thinking the worst is going to happen to him, and they tell me stop feeling sorry for him. For some reason, I don't feel afraid of him. I don't know."

That afternoon, Mr. Apology called Jim. His mother answered and gave him the phone. His voice was low, and he sounded anxious and tired and distracted.

"There've been detectives by my house," he said.

"Really?"

"Do you have anything to do with that?"

"Sure don't."

"They're asking questions about why isn't my mother around, and stuff. You say you have nothing to do with that?"

"I definitely didn't contact the police. But what about this woman that's there that says she's your mother?"

"This one here?"

"Yeah."

There was a pause. "She's not my mother," Jim said.

"OK, but I'm glad if your mother's still alive."

"What?"

"I'm glad if your mother's still alive."

"She's not my mother."

"She *sounds* like she's your mother."

"You can doubt it, whatever you want. I'm going to show you proof, and that's it. You're *assuming* she's my mother. You're assuming from what somebody told you."

"I'm assuming from what you told me, and I'm assuming from my conversation with her."

"Well, you had a very *short* and brief conversation with the woman. You had a very *long* conversation with me. She tells you one thing, and suddenly it's the truth?"

"Well, why don't you put her on the line and I'll ask her."

"What's the *point?* You're calling to talk to *me*. The line has nothing to do with my grandmother, it has to do with *me*. You talked to her already. Would I go through all what I been going through just to make this up?"

"Well, last night I was transcribing some of our second conversation, and I was totally convinced that what you were telling me was true, so I think there is an *emotional* truth there. There's something really true about it, but it might be a very strong fantasy."

"You think this is all mentally a fantasy? What kind of fantasy is that? To me a fantasy is something nice, or 'My fantasy is to have three women at one time.' You're saying this is my *fantasy?* To kill my mother? That's not a fantasy, that's a *nightmare*. I just don't understand how you can say, 'Well, I'm really convinced,' and now you're saying because you just spoke to somebody for two minutes —"

"More than two minutes."

"Two minutes, three minutes, five minutes — whatever."

"Well, I call up and this woman says she's your mother, and she sounds real, and I'm thinking, This guy probably didn't kill his mother."

"See, I don't want you to be like that. I want you to say, 'Yes, he did kill his mother.'"

"But what I'm thinking is, whether you did kill her or you didn't, you must have some strong problems with your mother, living or dead, and the best thing you can do, for you and for her, is to put some distance between yourselves."

"Would you want me to bring you to the site?"

"No, I'll pass."

"I'll do *that!* How about that?"

"No, thanks."

"What can I possibly do to convince you that I am telling the truth?"

"Why don't we just end this conversation, and we'll just talk another time, if you want to talk."

"Why do you want to end it now?"

"Well, I'm not interested in proof. Proof is not important to me."

"So now you'll say to your wife, 'Wow, honey, I can sleep better tonight, because I know that guy's — wait, maybe because you *want* it to be the truth, because you'll *feel* better. Because, maybe — I have a feeling — this is the whole thing, that, knowing that you're speaking to a guy that murdered his mother, that's really *bothering* you, and you probably never spoke to anybody like that before. And you can't sleep, it's disturbing the hell out of you, and now that somebody told you, 'Oh, I'm his mother,' it's a kind of relief to you, and you're saying, 'Wow, I feel much better now.' That's what you wanted to hear. You wanted to hear some kind of hope thing like that. Deep down inside, I think in the back of your head that you do believe me in a way, but you just don't want to be — I don't know if you're having nightmares, whatever the hell's going on with you. You just don't want to go through this no more, so you figure, Well, it's more of an easier way out. But I still can't understand after a couple of minutes talking to somebody, you're saying it's the truth automatical. Chris, I'm going to show you proof. That's it. I'm so determined to show you proof now. Even more than ever."

"Then the only thing I have to say is, I don't need proof and I don't want you hurting anybody to create proof."

"I'm going to show you it anyway. I don't care what you say, I'm going to show it to you anyway. Just for the fact that you called me a liar."

"I don't need proof."

"So what are you going to do, just take the box and throw it in the garbage?"

"If something shows up, I'll look at it, but I don't want to motivate you to create harm to someone to create some proof."

"What do you mean 'create'? You already created something when you called me. You already started something when you returned my call. So the damage, or whatever you want to call it, has been done. There's no stopping that."

"It's not important to me whether you killed anybody."

"Well, listen, fine, I understand, fine, that's good, but when you see a strange man standing by your PO box you'll know it's me, because when you come up to it, then I'll tell you it's me. Like I said, you're the one who started this. You're the one who returned my call. You didn't have to. If somebody told me they killed their mother and said they wanted to speak to me about it, I'm not going to call them back. This guy's nuts, you know, whatever, which I'm not crazy or anything like that, but, you know, I just wouldn't call them back. Provoke them more. No."

"It's not important to me."

"I'll direct you to it. I'll take you there. I'll meet you at where you pick up your mail at. I'll be there, I don't have a job right now. I can go to Manhattan."

"Suit yourself. But proof is not the issue."

Jim left a message a few minutes later saying that he hadn't heard Mr. Apology's last words. Mr. Apology called him back. Jim was still upset that Mr. Apology had taken his mother's word over his own.

"What is this, a game?" Jim said. "To me it's not a game. Somebody talked to you for two freaking minutes, whatever the hell long you talked to her, and you're taking her word over mine?"

The conversation turned in circles for some time. Then Jim said, "Listen, I'm getting pretty bad heartburn here, I'm really getting myself upset."

"We'll figure it out," Mr. Apology said. "Don't worry."

"I'm not worried," Jim said. "You're the one who should be worrying. I have nothing to worry about. I have nothing to worry about. The only thing right now really to worry about is this damn proof, and I don't know how the hell I'm going to do it, but I'm going to do it."

"Well, don't worry about that, either."

"I *am* going to worry about it. I have to prove this now. The candle's been lit."

"Well, if you called back six months from now and said, 'I got my own apartment, I got a job,' that would definitely prove something to me."

"Or, 'Oh, yeah, I just killed three other people because I was doing some thinking.' Would that prove anything to you?"

"No. I'd like to hear that you'd got your life together a little bit more."

"Sure, all right, Chris. So we'll talk in the future. I have this smile — I don't mean to be smiling, or anything — I am just smiling because this is definitely a strange, strange conversation I'm having here. It's blowing my mind."

"Well, it's good to get your mind blown occasionally. It blows out the cobwebs."

"Well, believe me, my mind is not empty," Jim said.

"I know that."

There was a pause; then Jim said, "So in the future, I hope you have success with this, ah —"

"Weird project?"

"This project that you have."

"And same to you."

"And I guess I bid you goodbye," Jim said.

(1993)

Allan Bridge, Mr. Apology, died in a scuba diving accident off Long Island during the summer of 1995.

Conversations with a Killer

J OHN WAYNE GACY is obsessively fond of defending his innocence, which is imaginary. On March 12, 1980, he was convicted in Chicago of killing thirty-three boys. The murders took place between 1972 and 1978, when he was caught and arrested. No one else in America has ever been convicted of killing so many people. Twenty-seven of the bodies were buried in a crawl space beneath the house where Gacy lived, in a neighborhood out by the airport. About many of the murders there was a suggestion of sexual torture. Twenty-one of the murders were committed before Illinois had enacted a death penalty, and for those Gacy was sentenced to twenty-one terms of life in prison. For the others, he was sentenced to death. He is to be killed on the tenth of May. On the night he was arrested, he gave the police an account of the murders; his lawyers asked him not to, but he insisted. He told them more the next day and more on the day after that. Then he began saying that he knew nothing about any of the murders except one, that of a boy he brought home from a Greyhound bus station and had sex with, then killed after the boy attacked him with a knife from his kitchen. On occasion, he has said that the only crime he is guilty of was operating a cemetery without a license.

When Gacy says that he knows nothing about the murders, it's impossible to tell if he really has no memory of them or is just saying that he doesn't. He says that twelve people — a cleaning woman, some friends, a bookkeeper, and some carpenters who worked for the small contracting company he owned — had keys to his house and could have buried bodies in the crawl space while he was traveling on business. All the murders took place in his house, nearly all between three and six in the morning. A neighbor said that now and then she heard screams from the house in the middle of the night; she called the police, but whenever they knocked on Gacy's door he told them that nothing was wrong. They never heard anyone screaming. After Gacy was arrested, he said that he had paid 150 boys for sex. Sometimes he only brought them to his house and took off his clothes and talked to them and gave them advice and drinks and something to eat. He killed the ones who raised their prices after striking an agreement, and those who he thought might tell his neighbors how he obtained his sexual satisfaction. Boys who seemed to feel bad about having had sex with him fell into the second category. The boy from the bus station was stabbed, the others were strangled. Some were hustlers from an area of Chicago called Bughouse Square, some worked for Gacy, and some had run away from home to Chicago and encountered Gacy and agreed to service him for money. Saying that he was going to show them a trick, he persuaded them to allow him to loop a rope around their necks. He tied three knots in the rope and inserted a stick between two of them, then tightened the noose by turning the stick. Once, as he was turning the stick the phone rang. When he left the room to answer it, the boy was still standing. The person on the other end of the line was a contractor calling about a job. Gacy discussed the job, and when he returned the boy was dead on the floor and had lost control of his bladder. A few times, Gacy killed two boys in one night. Sometimes he kept a boy's corpse in his closet for a day before burying him. He poured acid on some of the corpses and lime on others, then buried them in graves about a foot deep. He buried one of the boys in his yard and another beneath the floor of his garage. The bodies in the crawl space were buried so close together that when the police dug up the first one they found the head of another at its feet. In some of the graves, the bodies were buried on top of one another. When no room was left in the crawl space, Gacy thought for a while about keeping corpses in his attic. The last four bodies he dropped at night off a bridge above the Des Plaines River, about seventy-five miles south of Chicago. He thought that one of the bodies might have landed on a barge. On the way to the bridge with a body in the trunk, he once picked up a hitchhiker. The hitchhiker said that he would exchange sex for money, but Gacy decided not to.

Gacy lives on death row at the Menard Correctional Center, near

Chester, Illinois. Chester is on the Mississippi River, about eighty-five miles southeast of St. Louis. The part of the prison where Gacy is confined sits on a hill above the river, but he cannot see the river; he has no windows in his cell. He was thirty-six when he was arrested; he is fifty-two now. He is five feet eight and weighs 230 pounds. Confinement has left his skin pale. His hair has turned white. His face is broad and round. He had a mustache when he was arrested, but he doesn't anymore. His eyes are small and remote and measuring. His hands are delicate. He has no tattoos. The guards call him JW or John Wayne or Gacy or, sometimes, Chester Molester.

For twelve years following his conviction, while his lawyers filed appeals, Gacy said no to anyone who asked for an interview. The requests were constant. Oprah Winfrey sent a handwritten letter. So did Truman Capote. Two years ago, Gacy spoke with a television reporter from Chicago, and then fell silent again. His reticence has mainly to do with his feeling that the press has portrayed him as a monster, and that the bulk of what has been written and broadcast about him is "theory and fantasy." He often says that he has "no ego for fame." He is, however, by no means reclusive. Since he arrived at Menard, he has answered approximately twenty-seven thousand letters. He talks on the phone with a number of people, whom he calls collect, and he receives visitors more often than any other inmate of the prison. Some of the people who visit have written to him for a while and believe from the avuncular and benevolent tone he strives for in his letters that he cares about them; some are law students interested in his case; some are opponents of the death penalty; some believe that he is a great man; some are curious about him for sexual reasons; some feel themselves to be outcasts and think that they have something in common with him; some have read about him or seen his picture and believe that he resembles the sympathetic idea they have formed of him in their minds; and some think that he is innocent, and are trying to help him prove it.

Over the winter, I received a call from an acquaintance who said that Gacy was willing to be interviewed. She asked if I was interested, and I said I guessed so. What I hoped was that I would meet someone who had arrived by reflection at an acceptance of his past and was preparing to meet his end with dignity.

Visiting Gacy is like spending time with a person who is pretending to like you in order to separate you, violently, if necessary, from something you possess. A haughtiness in his manner suggests that he thinks he is smarter than anyone he is talking to, but it is unlikely that if he were not also capable of charm in the service of deception so many of those boys would have got into his car in the middle of the night. He appears to have no inner being. I often had the feeling that he was like an actor who had created a role and polished it so carefully that he had become the role and the role had become him. What personality he may once have had collapsed long ago and has been replaced by a catalog of gestures and attitudes and portrayals of sanity. In support of his innocence, he often says things that are deranged in their logic, but he says them so calmly that he appears to be rational and reasonable. He has concealed the complexity of his character so assiduously that a person is left to imagine the part of him that carried out the murders. Three other killers had visitors on days when I was talking to Gacy, and they gave me an impression of anxiety and violence. Compared with them, Gacy seemed tranquil. If I saw him among a crowd, I might take him for a truck driver or an autoworker, or maybe the warden of a prison.

Talking to Gacy requires patience. He doesn't listen to what you say, and consider it, and then respond. He merely defends himself. It is difficult to ask him a question that a detective or a prosecutor or a defense attorney or a psychiatrist has not already asked him and that he does not have an answer for. He goes over the same ground again and again. His voice rarely changes pitch; when he is excited, it is the result of uneasiness or apprehension, not enthusiasm. He is fond of the phrase "knowingly knew," as in "He knowingly knew I was out of state at the time." He uses it when he wishes to emphasize an injustice he believes he has suffered: "He knowingly knew I was innocent, but he still claimed I killed the boy."

He seems to have no capacity for intimacy or friendship. Another person makes no impression on him at all. One day, he and I looked through a scrapbook of photographs. There were pictures of his father and mother, his two sisters, his two wives, his son, his daughter, and people who visit and write letters, but there was not a single image of anyone he described as a friend. He says that he has no friends in the prison, either. A doctor who interviewed him after he was arrested wrote that he "conducts his life as if he possessed a complete and sensitive emotional capacity, which he has not."

After it had been arranged for me to visit Gacy, I began to feel obscurely anxious about what effect he might have on me. He struck me as someone who was overwhelmed by his interior life, and since I have never felt anything like control over my own, I was afraid that spending time alone with him might cause something damaging to rise from my unconscious. The night before I met him, I dreamed, in a motel in Perryville, Missouri, that I was being chased at night across a desert by a huge hooded figure riding a black horse. The figure had a crossbow. Once I had met Gacy, I realized that I was nothing like him, and my fears subsided, but I continued to have dreams in which he seemed to figure as a violent and malevolent presence.

I saw Gacy on six occasions during February and March. Two visits lasted a little more than an hour, and the others lasted five or six hours — more time, he pointed out, than any other writer had ever spent with him. He said this to flatter me, so that I might write favorably about him. Occasionally his company was so dreary that I would take off my watch so I couldn't see how slowly the time was passing. Now and then, he struck me as being like someone you start a conversation with in a bar and then realize you can't get rid of. Other times, the context of our conversation was so peculiar that I didn't know how to respond. Gacy seemed unaware that he was in prison because he was a criminal. He seemed to think that I had come to see him because he was famous. I never had the feeling that he heard voices or saw things that I didn't, but he was delusional in that he believed himself to be someone else: an innocent person. He seemed to feel that if he behaved as if he were, then I would have no choice except to take him as one.

If Gacy is executed on the tenth of May, he will die on the anniversary of the first time he was arrested — in 1968, for sodomy, in Waterloo, Iowa. He was twenty-six. He and his wife had moved to Waterloo not long after Gacy graduated from Kentucky Fried Chicken's KFC Chicken School, in Louisville. In Waterloo, Gacy helped run three Kentucky Fried Chicken franchises owned by his father-in-law.

The following account of Gacy's background is based on conversations with Gacy and with his lawyers, and on his confessions, the records of his psychiatric interviews, newspaper stories, Gacy's writings, his correspondence, the record of his trial, and the books *Buried Dreams*, by Tim Cahill, and *Killer Clown*, by Terry Sullivan. A grand jury in Black Hawk County heard testimony from two boys. One, a sophomore in high school, said that he had been spreading gravel in Gacy's driveway the summer before when Gacy asked him into his house. Gacy's wife was visiting friends in Illinois. Gacy showed him blue movies, then persuaded the boy to let Gacy go down on him. Then the boy did the same for Gacy. Gacy, he said, had also tried to bugger him. On a few occasions during the fall, Gacy paid him for sex.

The second boy washed floors and cleaned up in the kitchen at one of the restaurants, and sometimes he cooked. He said that after work one night Gacy offered to drive him home. They ended up at Gacy's house. Gacy's wife was in the hospital, giving birth to their second child. Gacy served the boy whiskey. They watched stag films, then Gacy attacked him and strangled him until he nearly passed out. When the boy revived, Gacy said that he hadn't meant to hurt him. He drove him home, and a few days later he fired him.

Word of the boys' stories spread through town in the days before the indictment was returned. The County Attorney's office found other boys who said that they had been to Gacy's house and that Gacy had asked them to go down on him or had tried to convince them to allow him to go down on them. Gacy asked to be given a lie detector test, and he failed it. He asked to be given another, and he failed that one, too. In the County Attorney's office it was said that the only answer he got right was his name.

In August 1968, Gacy engaged a high school senior to intimidate the boy who had been spreading gravel, and keep him from testifying at his trial. The senior drove the younger boy into woods outside town and sprayed Mace in his eyes, then beat him up and told him not to testify. The boy broke free and hid in a cornfield. When he got back into town, he went to the police and gave them the name of his attacker. The senior told the police that Gacy had provided the Mace and had promised to pay off his car loan.

Gacy pleaded guilty to sodomy. He expected to receive probation and to be allowed to move back to Illinois. Instead he got ten years at the Iowa State Reformatory for Men at Anamosa. The judge said that the severity of the sentence was intended to make certain that "for some period of time you cannot seek out teenage boys to solicit them for immoral behavior of any kind." While Gacy was in the reformatory, his wife divorced him. His father died. Gacy wanted to attend the funeral, but the warden wouldn't let him.

Gacy proved to be an exceptionally cooperative prisoner. After serving eighteen months of his sentence, he was paroled in June of 1970 and went to Chicago. There he moved into his mother's apartment and got a job in a restaurant as a cook. He often told people he met there that his ex-wife was the daughter of Colonel Sanders, the founder of Kentucky Fried Chicken.

When Gacy was a child, his father spent hours by himself in the basement of the house where they were living, in Chicago. His wife and son and two daughters were prohibited from going down there. Through the floor they sometimes heard him talking in different voices. When he emerged, he was often drunk and likely to be violent. One evening, he struck his wife so hard that he knocked out some of her teeth, and then he chased her into the street and beat her some more.

As a teenager, Gacy was preoccupied with his health. He had fainting spells, and he believed that he was born with a defective heart. He was not particularly attracted to girls. He considered becoming a priest. His father thought that he was effeminate. Occasionally, late at night, Gacy would have thoughts of embracing his friends. He believed that his father could tell what he was thinking. When Gacy was arrested for the murders, his mother told the police that if her husband had known that his son had had sex with men he would have killed him.

Gacy ran away from home when he was twenty. He wrote the following account, for his own purposes, a few years ago. It is part of a manuscript composed of a series of entries, usually a page or two long but sometimes longer, covering nearly every year of his life. He gave it to me one day as I was leaving the prison. I have made a very few changes for the sake of clarity.

"In the first three months of 1962, I hadn't been working and I had my dad on my back about everything. There wasn't nothing I could do that was right to him. I had to pay him $100.00 a month as part of the money he put up so that I could get a car and by March I had fallen one payment behind. By April, he was threatening to take away the car, so on the sixth or ninth of April, I decided to run away. I knew I had a cousin out west; the last known place where she lived was Las Vegas. She was a high priced hooker, not married but with a child. She had run away from home two years before me. Uncle Ray made an attempt to talk her into coming back by making a trip out there, but she refused, since she enjoyed what she was doing and had a home of her own, with a maid. She became the black sheep of the family. In any case, I watched enough TV to know that Route 66 went out west, and that's all I had going for me when I left.

"One morning after everyone was gone from the house, I loaded the car with the personal things that I was going to take with me. Then the phone rang — mother was calling, to ask me to pick her up from work at noon, as she wasn't feeling well. I went out to Dor-O-Matic and brought her home, dropped her off, and told her I was going to get the car gassed up. Then I just left. Irving Park to the Tollway, then south to Route 66, towards Springfield, Illinois. That first evening I got as far as 100 miles north of St. Louis. I pulled over to the rest area and slept in the car. The next morning, I took off across the rest of Illinois, all of Missouri, stopping to see some caves on the way, then the southeast corner of Kansas and into Oklahoma, where I spent the night in a motel. I had to watch my money, as I left home with $136.00, all I had to my name. The next morning west out of Oklahoma City, down 66 across Texas, upper part, to New Mexico. I stopped for the night in Albuquerque, again sleeping in a motel. Then across the rest of New Mexico, into Arizona, through Kingman, and on to Nevada. By late afternoon I hit Hoover Dam and was in time to go on the last tour of the day. After that Las Vegas. It's a great sight to see all those lights coming in from off the plains. There were so many motels. I couldn't believe it.

"I was so tired from the driving all I could think of was finding a place to shower and go to bed. I paid for one night at a place, and it left me just a little more than $35.00. I woke around noon, checked out, and went sightseeing, ending up in a downtown casino. Whereby, I went through $25.00 with no luck on my side. In three short hours, I had gone through two-thirds of all I had. I walked to my car, which was parked in the sun. Of course, coming from Chicago, I had the windows up and no way for the air to get out. I had a lot on my mind, wondering what I was going to do next, where could I get more money, wondering what was going on at home, since this was the first time I had thought of my family since leaving three days before. I got in the car, closed the door, and just sat there with the windows up; the heat got to me so fast I didn't know that I had passed out. The next thing I remember was a police officer pulling me out of the car, and hearing an ambulance coming up the street. I kept saying that I was all right, but he said that I had to go to the hospital (another expense I did not need). I told the doctors I didn't have any money, couldn't afford it, but they said the county would pay their bill. The ambulance ride cost $34.00 and wasn't covered. I got back to my car around 10 that night, had about $7.00 to my name, so drove north out to the desert, pulled off the road, and sleeping in the car again.

"Next morning I stopped in a gas station and after cleaning up in the restroom got a city map, as I wanted to know where the ambulance company was. I had decided I would just go and be honest, telling the owner I would work it off, had no money. I went into the office and told him my problem and that I would wash his ambulances, or anything else he wanted to pay the bill. He said that he liked my honesty and wondered if I would want a steady job. I told him I would, but had no place to stay. He said I could grab one of the bunks in the ambulance room. I agreed and had a job.

"The first day off I got, I found my cousin's name in the phone book and went looking for her. The third time I went to her house, I happened to pull up just as she was just going into her driveway. She was surprised to see me and asked me in. She talked honest and frank about her business in front of the maid and her little girl. She talked about the money, $200 a trick, and wondered if I was offended by what she was doing. I told her, hell it was her body and I guess she could do what she wanted. She had a new home, new Cadillac convertible, a maid full time, and she would get up at noon and have breakfast. It was a new enlightenment to me, so open about sexual conversation, as if nothing was wrong with anything. She worshipped the child and wanted the best of everything for her, and by the way she was living was doing all right. I would meet many of her friends, and she said that she would fix me up with any of them I wanted, meaning sexually, but I turned her down. I told her I would find my own. I felt funny doing that with her knowing.

"After working nearly two months, I was told that I would have to get a work card, since the ambulance company had city contracts. In order to get a work card in Las Vegas you have to be 21, I was not. The owner said that he thought he had a job for me at a mortuary, being their night man and picking up remains from the hospital and sometimes from the homes.

"Again I was able to live right there. The room where I stayed was known as the call room, right next to the embalming room. During May the mortuary had 86 funerals and over two months I was pallbearer for some 75, never knowing the person or family."

Gacy told me that he grew homesick and went back to Illinois in the beginning of July. Other accounts say that one night in the mortuary he climbed into a coffin containing the body of a boy whose manner of death had left him with an erection, and arranged the body on top of him. He grew frightened and jumped out and, the next day, called his mother and asked if she thought that his father would allow him to come home.

In Chicago, Gacy took classes at a business college. Then he got a job as a shoe salesman. The company he worked for sent him to Springfield, Illinois, to superintend the sale of its shoes in a department store. He traded shoes for clothes with salesmen who came into the store. "The Jockey man would come in and get a pair of $40 shoes at cost," Gacy wrote in a letter he gave me a copy of. "I would get a dozen briefs and Jockey T-shirts, sometimes more. It was the same with shirts, nothing but the best. Manhattan French cuff white shirts, some silk, some the finest cotton Van Heusen shirts the same way — shoes for shirts. . . . You talk about men's jewelry, hell again I had the best of Swank cuff links, tiepins. I had a collection of stones of the world in cuff links. I liked large flashy cuff links, as women would always remark about my dress. Psychologically, I got recognition from the customers, always remarking about my cuff links, or ties, and never the same. I enjoyed the attention . . . and it made a good impression on the customer, not only would they know I was the manager, but just by looking at me, you knew I had to be the boss. . . . I dressed and looked like an owner or a millionaire even when I was young. . . . I never wore brown because a man from Hart Shaffner and Marx said I didn't look good in brown. . . . I liked rich dark blues, blacks, burgundy, grays, olives; some wool but I stayed with sharkskins and silks because of the richness."

In Springfield, he lived with an aunt and uncle. He met Marlynn Myers, and they married in September of 1964. Around that time, he had his first homosexual experience. He was drinking at a friend's house and he passed out, and when he woke up the friend had Gacy's penis in his mouth. Gacy felt that he couldn't ask the man to stop, and, besides, he enjoyed it. For months, though, recalling the experience depressed him.

In February of 1971, eight months after Gacy was released from the reformatory, a boy in Chicago told the police that Gacy had picked him up and tried to force him to have sex. Gacy was arrested for assault. He said that the boy had been hitchhiking and had propositioned him and that he had thrown him out of the car. In any case, the boy did not show up to testify. The charges were dropped; the parole board in Iowa never learned of them.

While cooking at the restaurant, Gacy double-jobbed at painting and renovation, mostly for people who lived in his mother's building and occasionally for people he met at the restaurant's bar. He and his mother came up with a name for his sideline: P.D.M. Contractors, for Painting, Decorating, and Maintenance. He needed a place to store the lumber and paint cans and ladders he used, and his mother's apartment was too small. She sold the apartment, and she and John bought a house on West Summerdale Avenue, in Norwood Park, a suburb near the airport. They moved in during August of 1971.

The first boy Gacy killed was the boy he picked up at the Greyhound bus station during January of 1972 and brought back to the house. His mother was spending the night at her sister's. He made the boy a few drinks with grain alcohol. He and the boy went down on each other, then the two of them went to sleep, in separate rooms. Early in the morning, he woke and saw the boy in the doorway of his room with a kitchen knife in one hand. Gacy charged the boy. They wrestled. Gacy got control of the knife and stabbed him several times. For a while, the boy made a sound as though he had fluid in his windpipe. Gacy left the room and did not go back until the sound had stopped. He dumped the body into the crawl space through a trapdoor in the floor of his closet, and a few days later he buried the boy there. For years after Gacy's arrest, no one learned the boy's name. Whenever the police spoke of him, they referred to him as the Greyhound Bus Boy.

In July of 1972, Gacy married Carol Hoff. As a teenager Carol had been a friend of Gacy's sister Karen and had often been at the Gacys' house. She and Gacy had gone on a date when she was sixteen. Carol felt that Gacy was like a brother. Toward the end of 1971, after Carol and her husband divorced, she often visited Gacy and his mother. Gacy was kind to her two daughters, and she liked listening to him talk. When Gacy's mother heard that Carol was having trouble paying her rent, she suggested that Carol and her daughters move in with her and John. Before Carol and John were married, he told her about the trouble he had been in back in Iowa, and he also told her that he was bisexual, but she thought he was kidding. A few months before the wedding, Gacy's mother rented an apartment and moved out of the house.

Carol and John were married on the first of July. Nine days earlier, Gacy had been arrested again. Somehow, he must have kept her from knowing about it, or convinced her that it was a mistake and he was innocent. The police said he had told a boy that he was a deputy sheriff and ordered the boy into his car. He forced the boy to go down on him. Afterward the boy jumped out of the car and Gacy tried to run him over. For some reason, the charges were dropped.

Throughout the summer of 1972, Carol noticed a smell that seemed to come from something decaying in the crawl space. In a back room was a swarm of flies, which she thought might be feeding on whatever was down there — maybe dead mice. Gacy said the odor was the result of a runoff from a broken sewer pipe, and he spread lime in the crawl space to try and control it, but the odor got worse. Carol left on a trip, and when she got back Gacy told her that he had poured concrete over a section of the crawl space to get rid of the smell. The flies disappeared, but the smell remained, only fainter. Sometimes she saw Gacy drop into the crawl space carrying a fifty-pound bag of lime to spread over the damp ground.

In the summer of 1973, Gacy took over the garage for his contracting business and told his wife and stepdaughters to stay out of it. He was often gone most of the night. When Carol asked where he had been, he said visiting stores and construction sites that he hoped to bid on, and talking to people about work he might do. Late at night, he said, he could see more places and have more conversations than he was able to during the day. Beneath the sink in the kitchen, Carol found some magazines featuring naked men. One of the pictures was of a young man who appeared to have blood on his body. She and John made love less and less often and finally not at all.

Early in 1975, Gacy's mother moved to Arkansas to live with her daughter. During the summer, she broke her hip and Carol went out there to help care for her. While she was away, Gacy strangled a boy who worked for him, and buried him beneath the floor of his garage. In October, Carol told John she wanted a divorce. They lived together, though, until the following February. Gacy continued to pick up boys and pay them for sex, but he did not kill any of them until April. By the end of 1976, he had killed six more.

Around this time, Gacy began performing at hospitals and parades and store openings as Pogo, a clown. Pogo had a white face, bat-shaped red lips, and wide blue eyes in the shape of beehives. "I took up the name Pogo," Gacy wrote in the account he gave me, "and the reason was based on, one, that I was Polish, so that's where the Po, for Poles, and since I was on the go all the time, I took go and added it to it."

In 1977, Gacy was briefly engaged. His fiancée moved into his house in April. They argued often, though, and after a few months he told her he was leaving for a week on business and wanted her gone by the time he got back.

In January of 1978, a nineteen-year-old boy told the police in Cook County that he had been walking a little after midnight when Gacy pulled his car to the curb in front of him. Gacy pointed a gun at him and said he was a cop, and told him to get into the car. Then he handcuffed him. At his house, Gacy raped the boy. He held a gun in front of his face and, spinning the chambers as if he were playing Russian roulette, pulled the trigger a number of times before a blank cartridge fired. He caused the boy to lose consciousness several times by choking him and by holding his head underwater in the bathtub. The boy said that he had been in such pain that he begged to be killed. In the morning, Gacy drove him to work. Gacy told the policeman who arrested him — for kidnapping and deviate sexual assault — that he had picked up the boy and made a deal for sadomasochistic sex. He implied that the boy had gone to the police because he had not paid him. The assistant State's Attorney decided that in court Gacy would appear more believable than the boy, and the charges were dropped.

In May, a civil warrant was issued for Gacy. A twenty-six-year-old man said that Gacy had offered him a ride to a bar. As he was driving, Gacy suddenly covered the man's face with a rag soaked in chloroform, and the man passed out. He said that Gacy took him home and tortured and raped him for several hours while he drifted in and out of consciousness. He woke the next morning at the base of a statue in a park near where he'd been picked up. His pants were unzipped, his rectum was bleeding, and his face was burned from the chloroform. In the hospital, he learned that the anesthetic had worked severe damage on his liver. The man identified Gacy's picture among a collection the police showed him, but the police didn't pursue a charge. Gacy settled with the man for three thousand dollars.

No one testified that they had ever seen Gacy with any of the boys he was about to kill. Since most of their bodies were under his house, no one could be sure what had happened to them. On the few occasions when a parent reported to the police that his son was missing, and said that the boy had a job with a contractor named Gacy, the police would visit the Summerdale house, and Gacy would shrug and say that he would do anything he could to help but he hadn't seen the kid for several weeks. Runaways are what the police assumed they were dealing with. Gacy was finally caught when he killed a boy who had told someone that he was on his way to see Gacy about a job. This was on the evening of December 11, 1978. When the boy didn't come home — it was his mother's birthday, and the family had planned a party — the police turned their attention to Gacy. Eventually they got a warrant to search his house. While one of the policemen was using the bathroom, the hot-air furnace forced air from the crawl space through the room's heating vent. A day or so later, it was borne in on the policeman that the smell was the same as the one he recalled from the morgue.

Of the thirty-three boys Gacy is convicted of killing, only twenty-four were identified. The names of some became known from dental records brought to the police by parents who had heard about the excavation and thought that their son who was missing might have crossed paths with Gacy. The nine boys who were unidentified were buried in various cemeteries under headstones with the inscription WE ARE REMEMBERED.

In June of 1978, Gacy was found to be syphilitic. Not long before, he'd had the idea that he would fill in the crawl space completely with concrete, and that he and Carol could get back together and leave Chicago for a small town where he could open a fried-chicken franchise. One night, a few days after his arrest, he wrote a letter to his mother and family that began, "Please forgive me for what I am about to tell you. I have been very sick for a long time."

At night, I would take Gacy's manuscript to the Park-Et Restaurant, in Perryville, and sit in a booth and drink coffee and eat pie and read. Here is the first of two entries concerning his childhood:

"Background incident, age 5, John W. Gacy, sexual bewilderment, 1947.

"Back then, in the summer, after dad was off to work, and mother had things in order at the house she would visit some of the neighborhood woman friends with children. Anyway, this particular time we had all went down to another family's house which was in the next block south on Opal. We would usually stay for lunch, and get back home by 3 P.M.

"The family's kids were all older than the three of us, and except for two which were our age. From what I could remember several of their children were slow learners, and one was mental retarded, so she stayed close to home. While the rest of the kids were either playing or taking a nap after lunch, this older girl said that she would watch over me and we went upstairs. She was mentally retarded, and 15 at the time. While playing house in one of the bedrooms she took off all my clothes and was fondling me and tickling me, me being too young to know what was going on. Downstairs, both their mother and Mom thought that the kids were too quiet and went to investigate, and starting to account for them. When they came upstairs, walked into the room where we were, they saw her playing with my ding a ling. And their mother while yelling came in and grabbed the girl, and hit her several times, while yelling about what she was up to. My mother came over to me, asked me what I was doing with my clothes off or something to that nature, and got me dressed and took me downstairs. I was scared, as I thought that I would get hit, too. I was told not to be taking my clothes off with girls and to sit down there by them until they left. I had told them that the girl said it was all right for her to take my clothes off.

"While I never did understand what we were doing that was so wrong at the time, it left a profound feeling on me in my thinking about taking off clothes in front of others, even my sisters, thinking that I was going to get hit for doing it. As at the time I was told that what we were doing was dirty and wrong. I think now all it was was curiosity, me not knowing, and her for her age, even being retarded."

The second entry reads:
"1950, age 8, Sexual incident with contractor.
"In the late spring of 1950, we lived at 3536 North Opal, in Chicago, Ill., at that time there was an empty lot next door on the right. And word was that a new house was to be built. After the foundation was poured, a contractor came around and was looking at the lot, since it was a Saturday my dad was in the yard trimming hedges. The contrac-

tor spoke with my dad and one thing led to another and dad offered him a beer, and they sat in our yard and talked. Mother came out so he met her, too. I was playing in the yard, and was interested in the conversation about building. Several weeks passed, and the contractor was back to see how progress was going on his building (weekday). He seen me in the yard as we kids were home for spring vacation. He asked me if I would like to go and see some other building sites, and have some ice cream. I asked mom and she said it was all right. (I must add at the first visit with my parents, they talked about wrestling on TV.) I went with the man in his car and after the second stop, he asked me if I had seen last week's wrestling show, I said yes, and then he said he wanted to show me a new hold in the car. He moved out from behind the steering wheel, closer to me, and told me to bend down and put my head under his leg, which I did, he held me between his legs for several minutes, tightly so that I could not move, and in fact I had tears in my eyes. When he seen that, he let me go, and said let's go get that ice cream I told you about. After that I returned home, never mentioning anything about it. Couple weeks went by, he came back, seen me and asked if I would like to go again with him to get ice cream, again went. After several stops he was talking about wrestling, and again he wants to show me a new hold, so we did it again in the car, only it was the same hold, with a little more grabbing of me between the legs. Ice cream again and I was dropped off at the house. After a fourth time of the same thing each time when I seen him coming down the street, I ran and hid from him. Later mother in the yard told me that the contractor was looking for me. I told her I didn't like that man, and didn't want to go with him. She said he wanted to take me for ice cream for watching over his building. I told her I didn't care. When my dad came home that night, mom told him what happen, and dad came to me and asked me about it. I told him what was happening each time, and he told me that he didn't want me going with him no more. The next time he came around on a Saturday, my dad was home, I stayed in the house. Dad went over and talked with him, and from what I can understand from hearsay, Dad told this man to stay away from me or he would call the police. With that he was around a few more times to see his building finished, but never came near our house again. That's all that happen, but I have never forgotten it from the age of 8½. I still remember the man wasn't too tall, middle aged, semi bald, dark heavy glasses, with a mustache, a little overweight, two-door car, light blue, I think it was a new Chevy, it was newer than my dad's, as in 1950 he had a '46 Chevrolet four door."

Gacy and I would meet in the prison in a room that was small and had no windows. Against one wall were a table with a Formica top and three chairs. On the other side of the wall was death row. To arrive at the room, I would first take off my shoes and my coat and pass them across a counter to a guard, who put them in an X-ray machine. I asked him if anything interesting had ever appeared on the screen, and he said not really, but that he was hoping to find a cat to examine. Nothing can be taken into the prison except twenty-five dollars, to buy food from the vending machines in the visitors' lounge, so I would empty my pockets of everything. Then I would be patted down, and then I would walk through a metal detector. The metal detector was sensitive enough so that one morning it registered the metal in the buttons on the fly of my bluejeans; to get into the prison that day, I had to drive to the Dollar Store in Chester and sit around in the parking lot waiting for it to open, then buy a pair of sweatpants. Sometimes other visitors arrived at the same time I did, and we were signed in and searched and taken into the prison together. One day, I went in with a short, heavy woman who was making a sympathy call on behalf of a local church. The next time, I went in with a tall, thin man wearing glasses. While we were waiting for a door to be unlocked, I asked if he had a ministry of some kind. "I know the Lord," he said, "but I don't have a ministry." He asked if I knew the Lord, and I said, "Not as well as you appear to," and he said, "Yeah, I guess I should be more humble."

That day, Gacy said, "I go to bed and say three Hail Marys and the Our Father. I dream about the life I used to have. I dream about being in construction. I dreamt one night that my daughter was getting married and of all the things that I would do for her. For a while, I would tape newspaper pictures of the victims to the wall beside my bed and go to sleep seeing if I would dream about them or if I could recall if I ever met them. I would look at them and say, 'Who the hell are you, and how did you die?' I don't have fantasy-type dreams, and I don't ever have nightmares.

"I arrived here March 14, 1980, nine-fifteen in the evening, with a five-car caravan and a helicopter overhead. (You can move your chair over here, I won't bite you.) State car in front, I'm in a van, and then there's another state car behind me. Both cars had Thompson machine guns. I didn't see them — this is from what I was told, maybe to scare me. Behind us was two troopers' cars, and the whole caravan doing seventy-five down Interstate 55 from Chicago. Instead of pulling into the prison where I thought they would, they turn off the lights and go down this gravel road. And I'm thinking, Oh, no, they're going to kill me now. But they brought me around to the back of the prison. They couldn't bring me in the front, because there was a whole stack of reporters. And there were a whole bunch down at the main prison, too, because they were waiting for me there, also.

"I'm the first man to arrive on death row at Menard. I opened the place up. There was nobody else here. Now there's sixty-one of us, twelve on my cell block — three black and nine white. At the time, there was nineteen men on death row in Stateville, the other prison in Illinois where they have executions. The State decided that the first guy who got the death penalty after the beginning of the year in 1980 they were going to send here, and that was me. When they brought me down here, the press came out with how I was scared to be with the prison population, so they put me here by myself. Like the State was going to be concerned with my feelings.

"I was greeted by the warden and the assistant warden, who's a big monster dude. They walked me up to the third floor and marched me down the tier to the last cell. Not a sound in the place except what the chains on my feet were making. Everyone had white shirts. I didn't even *see* any gray shirts until the second week. Everyone had white shirts, because they were all lieutenants. I was supposed to be superhuman — I was supposed to be some kind of monster — so they gave me all lieutenants.

"The first thing one of them did was bring me two ham sandwiches, an apple, and a pitcher of orange juice, because I had been on the road all day and hadn't had anything to eat.

"They assigned a guard to watch me, because I'm the only one here. Every fifteen minutes, he has to write down what I'm doing — Gacy's on the toilet, Gacy's lying down, Gacy's pacing the floor, talking to an officer, Warden So-and-so was here. Every time somebody came near the cell, he had to make a note. How'd you like to have that job? Some people would just come by and look at me. They wouldn't say that — they'd pretend they were giving a tour or had to check on something — but there's only nine other cells and they were empty, and I'm in the tenth one down at the end of the hallway, and they walk all the way down there, what the hell you think they were looking for? They wanted to see what Gacy looked like. Three times a week, they'd put handcuffs on me and walk me down to the shower with a towel around my waist.

"Prison life has been the doldrums, same goddam thing day after day. You can have a cell six and a half by seven and a half, which has a window, so you can see the barges going up and down the river, but you only get let out an hour a day, or you can have a cell eight by nine, with no window, and you are let out only three days a week but three hours at a time. I have one of the larger cells, so no window. I don't know if it's night or day. I can't tell you if it's raining. Being in prison is like being in Las Vegas, where you're gambling and you don't know what's going on outside. I was a workaholic outside anyway, so time meant nothing to me then, either.

"I go to bed late — two-thirty, three o'clock, four. I get up at five and look at the food they're serving for breakfast — who the hell wants to eat at five in the morning? I don't sleep much. I like to make my time work for me. I don't believe in that macho thing of lifting weights and getting all muscular — I've got strong legs and a tight ass, and I carry all my weight on my chest and in front of me. When I get out of my cell, I go to the rec room and play cards. Otherwise I answer my mail. Personally, if I was on the outside I'd *never* write someone in prison. I've had people send me paintings of clowns, figurines of devils, T-shirts — all declined. You're not allowed to receive anything except books, but no novels on homosexuality, bestiality, or incest. They say it stimulates you. They allow photo books like *Penthouse* and *Playboy*, they show lesbian films on the late-night in-house channel — two women getting it on, that's not supposed to incite you. The other stuff, I guess they think it might incite you to attack guards. We're not on the farm down here, so I can't understand where the bestiality comes in.

"When I first walked in here, I was scared to death. I didn't know how to think like a con: it wasn't part of my nature, and I still can't do it. I didn't realize men could be bitches. Women sit at home and gossip, but in prison I've learned that as soon as you walk away they'll talk about you. Everybody who doesn't say a word when you're standing there will put in his two cents when you're gone. They get bigger balls when you're not around.

"If somebody threatens you, that's not the guy you have to worry about, because he's warning you — it's the rattlesnake theory. The guy who's dangerous is the one who asks about some small thing he heard you told someone, and you say you don't know what he means, and he says, 'You're lying to me, you're making me look like a fool.' Now you're in trouble. People say the worst weapon in prison is a homemade shank. That's not the worst weapon in prison. You know what the worst weapon is in prison? A pen. Or a regular No. 2 lead pencil. You got one of those, you hear someone's got a visit, you arrange to have a visitor at the same time. We could be friendly, he could have his arm around my shoulder, we're talking, and he jabs me in the eye and says, 'That's for stealing my pack of cigarettes two months ago.' The other day, we were playing cards during rec time. One of the guys at the table got up to get something. A few days before, another guy had overheard him make some remark about him in the cells. He came up now and said, 'What you say about me, motherfucker?' and beat him and slapped him around and kicked him until he felt he had had enough, and meanwhile another guy just sat down at his place at the card table and everyone looked out the window. Then somebody said, 'Your deal.' When the guards asked the guy who had got beat what had happened, he said he slipped on a wet place on the floor. Even if someone came in now and stabbed you while we're talking, even if the security camera above us showed me looking straight at you, no way I would ever say I saw anything. 'I don't know, it all happened so fast, I didn't see nothing,' I'd say.

"Down in the Pit, the main part of the prison, you're on tiers, and, even though you're assigned a cell and don't come out, it's gang territory. They'll take everything you got, and when you're out of everything they'll say you got to pay them rent. They know you have money, because they know what you have on account at the commissary. And even if you're in for just, say, car theft — a year and a half, simple — they'll rape you, do all *kinds* of things to degrade you, and you might think you'll fight off one guy, but how you going to fight off three or four? They'll have you giving blow jobs up one side of the tier and down the other. You've only got a year and a half to serve, but you're not going to let yourself get killed over something like that — you have to put up with it. Sooner or later you'll have to give it up. When I got here, my attorneys said it would take three years for an appeal, and I said, 'I don't know if I can take it.'"

Gacy insists that he never confessed to the murders. He has written an account of his trial, called *A Question of Doubt,* which has been privately published. In it he says there are two sides to every story. He describes himself as "the thirty-fourth victim." After he finished *A Question of Doubt,* he wrote a manuscript called "A Questionable Case and Conviction," which contains his answers to 147 questions. Toward the beginning of the manuscript he writes:

> The following is some of the many unanswered questions with answers as factually as I know them.
>
> But first to be fair, I will give you the states version of the case which is mostly their theories.
>
> According to the State over a six year period 1972–78, John Wayne Gacy stalked the streets of Chicago and suburbs, and kidnapped at gunpoint or manipulated young men and boys to come to the Summerdale house. Some on the pretexts of a job. According to the State, once there they were tricked into handcuffs, forced to have sex, beaten and tortured, then all killed by ligature strangulation and buried (27) under the house, or in the crawlspace, two others found on the property, and four additional were found in the Des Plaines river. According to the State, John Wayne Gacy went back to running his construction business during the same years, working seven days a week, 12–14 hours a day.
>
> The State wants you to believe this fantasy theory based on their scenario and that the motive was for sex and that they were killed so that they could not tell anyone or blackmail me and that I confessed to the whole crime.
>
> 1. PEOPLE SAY THAT YOU CONFESSED TO THE CRIME THEN LATER RECANTED IT?
>
> JW: That is what has been said in the media and trial. Yet to this day nobody has produced one. There is NO written confession, no tape recorded confession, NO police stenographer typed confession, and no videotaped confession.

It is true that there is no copy of Gacy's confession. The State's Attorney decided that he would not have the confession taken down by a court reporter; doing so might have offered Gacy the opportunity to put on record aspects of the murders which he might call on in his defense. Also, the police were afraid that Gacy might become uneasy at the sight of a tape recorder or someone taking notes, and stop talking. His confession exists only in the form of accounts the officers wrote afterward of what they heard Gacy say.

A signal document of Gacy's claim of innocence is the Victims Book, a collection of newspaper stories, interviews, photographs, and legal papers. A few years ago, Gacy began exchanging letters with a man, who has asked me not to use his name because he is still gathering information and doesn't want to alert the people who are the subject of his interest; I will call him Chris Lewis. Gacy wrote Lewis that he didn't know who had murdered thirty-two of the boys he had been convicted of killing, nor did he know who most of the boys were or where they had come from.

"I wanted to know who the hell these guys were," Gacy says, "because, keep it in mind, at the trial they were all Boy Scouts and altar boys, and I was the monster that came along and swatted them like flies. Jesus, I didn't even want to run into myself the way they described me.

"My idea is, if I didn't kill them, and I had no knowledge of them, then who did they know? If I didn't do the murders, then we have to find out who did them by finding out about the victims and cross-referencing them. Did any of them know each other? If you can't find the who, what, and why, where are you going to go with it?"

Every time Lewis found the name of a relative of one of the victims, or someone who knew one of them, he wrote to the person or called him. When he learned of a place where one of the boys had worked, or a club where he was known, he went and took a photograph of it. The information he has collected he put between the covers of a folder, and then gave a copy of the folder to Gacy. It is now larger than the Manhattan telephone book. On the cover are the words

VICTIMS

RESEARCH

CONFIDENTIAL

The Victims Book has thirty-three sections, one for each victim; the victims are numbered according to the order in which their bodies were discovered. When Gacy leafs through the book, he refers to the victims as "Boy No. 12" or as "Victim No. 26" or as "Body No. 7." He never refers to the victims by name.

Each section begins with a photograph of the boy. In some cases, the photograph portrays the reconstruction that the police made of the victim's face from the structure of his skull. Beneath the picture is a description of how he was killed and where his body was found. In at least one case, there is an autopsy report. Then there is a description of what Lewis has been able to learn about the boy's past. He has included photographs and excerpts from the high school yearbooks of some of the victims. One entry includes the names of pets that the boy's family owned. There is a color photograph of the house or apartment building where a victim lived, and in many cases there are color photographs of the graves. "We know where they lived," Gacy said, "and we know where they are now." There are newspaper pictures of the parents of some of the boys, and in one case there's a story about how the murder of their son caused a couple's marriage to dissolve. A hand-drawn design in the form of a red spoked wheel on the first page of a boy's report means that Gacy was out of town on the day the authorities selected as the approximate one on which the murder took place.

The Victims Books includes charts labeled "Victims Calendar Breakdown." The charts record the days of the week on which the boys disappeared. They are compared with days when Gacy was out of town. When Gacy explained the charts to me, he began speaking of himself in the third person. "Gacy went out of town," he said. "When did Gacy leave? Gacy generally went out of town on a Sunday."

When some of the families found out that Gacy was collecting information about them, they were indignant.

One day, Gacy placed the book between us on the table. When I asked if I could look at it, a smile crossed his face and he said, "If you're so interested, maybe we'll have to save this for later." He started to put the book aside, but then he gave it to me. "This isn't a toy," he said as I opened it. "This is years of solid research, chasing down leads. Everybody wants this. I'm not leaving it to anybody. I'm giving it to my sister with instructions to destroy it."

He went on, "People ask what would I do if I got free, and I tell them I'm still obsessed with this case. They say, 'What the hell, why do you care what happened to them?' and I say, 'Because I want to know what happened as much as anyone else. If I don't get justice, then how will the victims?'"

When I had read some of the entries, Gacy said, "How can a guy who is family-oriented kill somebody, anyway? There's no motive here. I figured if I was going to be put to death for killing somebody, I'd like to know something about them, thus we did the research. God damn, if you're going to kill me, let me know what it's for. Even if I didn't kill somebody, I want to know what the hell happened. If I'm going to kill somebody, why did I kill them? The *why,* the *when,* and the *how.* What happened on Summerdale? Right now, we don't know what happened on Summerdale."

In assembling the book, Chris Lewis turned up a coincidence that Gacy believes proves he is innocent. Gacy mainly suspects two young men who worked for him, David Cram and Michael Rossi, of killing the boys and burying their bodies under his house. Cram and Rossi were questioned by the police when Gacy was arrested, but the police found no reason to believe that they had taken part in Gacy's crimes. In 1977, Cram and Rossi had asked Gacy to hire a friend, a young man I'll call Tom Peters. (Lewis asked me not to use his real name.) Peters had an alliance with a man I will call Lester Tompkins, who operated a business that supplied boys to older men. Lewis says that Tompkins is now in prison in Colorado for molesting a child. Gacy says that the boys were killed because they were members of Tompkins's prostitution ring and wanted to quit, or had become involved in drug deals that soured. He says that movies were made of some of their murders. It does not seem to occur to him that Peters was hired after a number of the boys had already been killed.

Before I met Gacy, I exchanged a couple of letters with him. He asked me to fill out a form he had drawn up. The form had "Bio Review" written at the top of the page, and underneath were questions asking where did I live and was I married, did I have brothers and sisters, and what kind of car did I drive. Then there were questions such as "Childhood Hero," "Most Treasured Honor," "Favorite Song," "Favorite Singers," "Perfect Woman or Man," "Nobody Knows I'm . . . ," "I View Myself As . . . ," "Friends Like Me Because . . . ," "If I Were an Animal I'd Be . . . ," "Behind My Back They Say . . . ," "I Consider Myself (Conservative, Moderate, Liberal)," and "Thoughts on Sex."

He mailed me a copy of his answers:

Perfect Woman: Independent, thinker, self-starter, mind of her own. . . .

I View Myself As: A positive thinker, self-starter, open minded, nonjudgmental.

My Biggest Fear: Dying before I have a chance to clear my name with truth.

If I Were an Animal I'd Be: A bear or an eagle.

My Biggest Regret: Being so trusting and gullible, taken advantage of.

Favorite Song: "Send in the Clowns," "Amazing Grace."

I Consider Myself: Liberal, with values.

Thoughts on Sex: Liberal, whatever the will of consenting adult people who are in control of their own well-being and lives.

In the prison, on the first day, he had my answers in front of him. I had written that I considered myself liberal.

"How liberal?" he asked.

I assumed he was asking about my political views, but I wasn't sure. I said, "What do you mean?"

"Any homosexual experience?" he asked. "None as a child? No fondling? You have any brothers? Three? Nothing there? No masturbation? No circle jerking? What about when you were in school? Gym class? Anything in the showers? You ever see other boys naked? I didn't. I never took gym classes, because of my health, so I never saw boys naked. No ever thinking about men when you masturbate? *Nothing?* You never get hit on? What did you say when that happened? You never took anyone up on it? *Never?* Not even once? Damn, I hate these handcuffs; I'm used to talking with my hands. I've been married twice, engaged two other times, and shacked up a few times, but they always try to portray me as homosexual. I'm bisexual. I never turned down a chance to take part in a threesome, and I never passed up the opportunity to get a blow job, but no man has ever got anything from me above the waist. So why do they call me a homosexual? I think sex is overrated. My mother told me about sex, my father never did. She said try to make it an act of love and never force yourself on anyone. And I never have."

Another day: "I was stabbed on February 12, 1983," Gacy said. "By Henry Brisbon, the I-57 killer. He killed a number of couples on the interstate — shoot the man and take the woman into the woods and rape her, then shoot her, too — then he killed another inmate, so they gave him the death sentence.

"Henry was going to the law library with two or three other guys, and he got out of his cuffs. You used to be able to take a pop-top from a soda can and file it down so it fit into the keyhole of the cuffs. He was on the first floor and he pushed the guards out of the way and went running up to the third floor and down the tier and stabbed this inmate he had a grudge with. He had taken the bar off a typewriter that holds the paper in place and sharpened it. Then he took a swipe at the officer on the tier. I was on the second floor, picking up trash, for my work. Henry came down the stairs and ran into three officers and he said, 'You can move or get stabbed, your choice' — Henry's a bodybuilder — and they backed away, so he came running toward me through the tier. He and I had just been talking about betting on a football game fifteen minutes before. He pushed me up against the wall, and when he did he hit me on my arm with the shank. Then he ran over to one of his buddies and said, 'Get rid of this.' They never did find the weapon. Meanwhile, I was kind of sliding down the wall, because I was off balance, and one of the other inmates standing there said, 'John, you're bleeding.'

"The newspapers make it up like it was something between me and Henry, him making some kind of statement about my case. Within two months after, though, him and me were talking. He said, 'You know, John, I never meant to stab you.' I was an afterthought. But it taught me never to trust these guys.

"Last time I seen Henry was 1988. I don't know what they did with him, if he's dead or still in prison. They took him somewhere else, I know that."

Gacy turned then to look at a black man in leg irons and handcuffs being led past the door of our room.

"That looks like Henry now," he said.

"Bring me some of those prison cigarettes," the man said to a guard. (One of the industries at Menard is making cigarettes sold in the prison.) "I don't want no menthol, now. I want the kind with the red label. Hurry up."

"That *is* Henry," Gacy said.

He looked down at the table and shook his head. Then he raised his voice and said, "Henry, where you been?"

"I was up north enjoying myself," he said. "Pontiac. Till I wore out my welcome."

A guard unlocked a storeroom in the hallway and gave Brisbon several packs of cigarettes. Brisbon went and sat in a room across the hall with his visitor, a big white man in a coat and tie. Gacy started talking again. When I turned to see if Brisbon was still in his chair, Gacy said, "Are you worried about him? I got your back covered."

I said I wasn't worried. I didn't say that it was slim comfort to hear Gacy say he had my back covered.

"He'd kill you anyway," Gacy said. "Even when he's friendly with me, like now, I still remember 'You stabbed me for no reason.'"

The next day, Gacy said, "I've been thinking about your answers to the Bio Review. They bothered me. You never had *any* homosexual experience? Nothing at all? Kinsey says that eighty percent of all men have had some kind of homosexual experience. The way you look, you know, and me in here for what I am, the guards are thinking you're a homosexual. If I was to lean over and lick your ear, or put my cuffs around you, they'd be in here fast to kick me out."

"What difference would it make if you *were* a homosexual?" I asked. "No one cares about that kind of thing anymore."

"It wouldn't be fair to the victims," he said.

I asked what he meant.

"It would portray them as sexual," he said, "and that wouldn't be fair to their reputations."

I asked about his father.

"My dad has been butchered," he said. "The media made an image out of him like he was an alcoholic monster. OK, my dad drank, and he was Jekyll and Hyde when he drank. If he came up from the basement and said the walls were pink, you said the walls were pink, but you learned to stay away from him and keep your mouth shut at the dinner table."

I said that as far as I could tell, the description of his father as crude and menacing seemed accurate.

"This is my first pair of Levi's," he said. "When I grew up, my father always said that corduroys and khakis were the proper way for a man to dress. If you were wearing jeans, you were making sexual gestures. I went to school in flannel shirts and corduroy pants. But I never hated my father. He was a strong man, an immigrant born in Poland. He married my mother when he was forty-one. We didn't get along. I thought I could never please him, but I still love him. If we went fishing, though, like we did for a week every summer, and I rocked the boat, or my line got tangled, or it happened to rain, Jesus, it was all my fault."

His father, I said, struck me as a coward and a bully, a drunk who beat his wife and terrorized his children.

"I learned values from my father," Gacy said.

I said that you could learn values from a book. Gacy said that it pleased him that flagstones he had hauled on his bicycle were still in place in the yard at the house where he lived with his parents, and that a tree he had planted still stood, whereas nothing was left that his father had done. "My way to remember my dad is not to be like him," he said. "That's my way of getting back at the son of a bitch."

Some days when I was driving to and from the prison, I would hear on the radio a country song with a refrain that made me think of Gacy. It went:

> That's my story,
> That's my story.
> I ain't got a witness, and I can't prove it,
> But that's my story, and I'm sticking to it.

Gacy told me more than once that he couldn't have buried any of the bodies in the crawl space, because his heart was weak and he weighed too much to maneuver in such a close space, especially with a corpse.

"It was thirty-eight inches in the crawl space," he said one day. "That's about how much room there is under this table." He got on his knees. "Then don't forget the floor joists." To demonstrate the amount of room they took up, he held a piece of paper against the edge of the table. "Right now, I weigh two thirty; when I was arrested, I was from between two thirty to two thirty-five. If you look at where the edge of that paper is to the floor, can you imagine me bringing a body down there, in that little space, with my bulk, and being agile with it?"

"You're forgetting one thing, John," I said.

"What's that?"

"You did it once before, when you buried the first body." He stood up.

"Very true statement," he said without resentment. "But you're going back six years earlier. You're talking about 1972, and what was my weight then? A hundred and seventy-six pounds. So it's not a contradiction."

I didn't mean to argue with Gacy, but I didn't seem able not to. When I asked about the confession he gave at the police station, he said that he remembered nothing about talking with the police on the night he was arrested or on the days after. "I was arrested on December 21," he said, "and I took a hundred and thirty milligrams of Valium, and I woke up on December 26 wondering why I was tied to the bed." Another time, he surprised me by saying, "I remember them asking me the night I was arrested, 'Are you a night person or a day person?' Simple question. What would you answer?"

"Night person."

"Well, how would you feel if they said then, 'Do you always stalk the streets at night?' That's what they said to me."

"You're describing moments of your interrogation," I said. "You can't have it both ways. Either you remember nothing or you recall confessing."

"You're getting semantical with me about the words."

"What do you mean?"

"I read it in the court transcripts."

One day, he said something that remained in my mind. He had been talking about how he couldn't have murdered anyone, because he was nonviolent, a coward, someone who would walk away from a fight. Furthermore, he said, he had had all the sex he needed, so there was no reason for him to have sex with the boys he was said to have killed.

"Why would I want to kill these boys, anyway?" he said then. "I'm not their father."

The next day, when I asked what being the boys' father had to do with murdering them, Gacy didn't say anything. He just looked at me. Then he said, "I didn't say that."

"You did, John."

"I didn't say it."

"I wrote it down."

"We covered so many things," he said. "I don't know if I said it or not." Then, "If I said it, I was saying it because I feel like a father to these boys."

"Even so, fathers don't kill their sons."

Another pause. Then he said, "I wasn't afraid of anything in the basement of the Summerdale house. If I was afraid of something, how come when the basement flooded three times I called the plumber in there? How come I would have had boys digging drainage trenches for me down there?" Gacy had once had Rossi and Cram dig trenches in the crawl space — for drainage, he told them. The prosecution said they were graves. "If I was afraid of being caught, don't you think I wouldn't have wanted anybody down there?"

"What if I said you had Rossi and Cram dig trenches in the basement so they'd find the bodies?"

"Why would I want to do that?"

"Because then the nightmare would be over."

"What nightmare?"

"The killing. Finally it would stop. The part of you that was horrified by what had been going on could then find some kind of peace."

For a moment, he said nothing. Then he said, "I'd like to know what we were talking about yesterday." Then, "I didn't believe in the State's theory of the case, but the more we started studying the victims, the more I started feeling like a father. Just like what I do with people I write letters to. I feel like a father to them. What am I always doing — you've read some of my letters — I'm always giving them advice." Then he closed a folder he had opened on the table. The folder, he said, had more information to prove his innocence. "I think you've got your mind made up," he said, with a sudden sharpness, "and I don't think you want to see where we're coming from."

I was going to say that wasn't true, but a guard in the hallway called, "Gacy," and John got up and went to see what he wanted. When he came back, a few minutes later, we talked instead about Robert Piest, the last boy he killed.

"The State tried to assemble this case against me," he said. "They tried to say, 'You were in the store, Piest was in the store.'"

Piest worked at a drugstore. Gacy had stopped in to see one of the owners about some renovations. He told the police after he was arrested that he had spoken to Piest in the store about a job. As he was pulling away from the curb in front of the store, he said, Piest ran up to his car and asked about work. Gacy told him to get into the car and took him to his house. Piest was the boy Gacy was strangling when the telephone rang.

"All right, I'll give you all of that," Gacy went on, "but you show me one person who puts me in the car with Piest. That saw him coming to my house."

I said that it didn't really matter whether someone actually saw the boy in his car. The boy's jacket and a receipt that someone who worked in the store had put in one of the jacket's pockets were found in his house.

"That's the State's story," he said. "But you show me one person who says they saw me with Piest."

"Forget the State's story, John. Let's say Robert Piest took a taxi to your house, he hitchhiked to your house, he walked to your house, a guy in a helicopter gave him a ride to your house, and no one saw him do it. It doesn't make any difference how he got to your house — that's irrelevant. That's not part of the story, don't you see? He was in your house, that's all that counts. He was in your house the night he died, and no one ever saw him anywhere else again."

Gacy said nothing for a moment, then, "Michael Rossi brought him there."

"You're telling me that by chance, out of all of Chicago, Michael Rossi, your employee, happened into *that* drugstore at *that* moment and met the same boy you are convicted of killing and brought him to your house and *he's* the one who killed him?"

"Rossi got his prescriptions there."

"So?"

"Don't you think that's strange? He didn't live anywhere near there, but he still went to that drugstore to get his prescriptions. We found this out."

"So what?"

"We were going to meet there to talk about a job," Gacy said. "We had jobs on opposite ends of the city, and the drugstore was halfway in between, so we decided to meet there."

"Did you ever tell Rossi that you had buried a body under your house?"

"No."

"Then you mean to say that there happened to be a house in Chicago — well, actually, let's say anywhere in the world — where two different people were burying bodies, neither of them aware of the other doing the same thing?"

"I know I didn't put those bodies there. In my heart, as God is my witness, I never killed anyone."

"Two different people?"

"Yeah."

I started laughing. "That's crazy, John. That's the craziest thing I ever heard. That's a lunatic idea. Do you understand the probability of something like that happening?"

"It was the perfect place for him and Cram to bury them."

"What are you talking about?"

"It wasn't their house. They weren't going to get caught."

"That's ridiculous. They wouldn't bury bodies there, because they couldn't have any control over who might find them, they didn't control who came and went from your house."

"If anybody found those bodies, who's going to get blamed?" he said. "Me."

"It makes much more sense that you would do it."

"I told Rossi I buried the bodies there."

"*What?*"

"I got drunk one night and told him, and that's how they were able to do this — he had this holding over me. People say, 'Why didn't you fire the guy?' and I say, 'I couldn't, because he knew about that first body.'"

I gave him a skeptical look.

"How come the body I buried is under concrete and the others are not?" he said. "It breaks the pattern."

I thought of saying that this was absurd. Then I realized that it wouldn't make any difference. He would have a reply.

"Talking to you is like talking to a wall," I said. "You never actually answer a question."

"I answer."

"You're being disingenuous."

"What's that mean?"

"Not straightforward."

"Just because these things fit, it don't mean that I'm the one that fits them together," he said. "Because I own the house, I have to take responsibility, sure, but how the hell am I supposed to know what's going on there when I'm in fourteen other states? The police found that receipt from Piest's jacket in my trash. Michael Rossi probably went through his pockets to rob him and found the receipt and threw it in the garbage. I had nothing to steal from him. I made seventy grand that year. I didn't kill the kid. What do I have to do, give a pound of blood to prove it?"

I made no reply.

"It looks bad for me, I know," he said. "I'm not trying to simplify it.

But I'm not their father, why do I have to be responsible for them? If I've left you confused, then that's the way it's got to be, but we are going to continue to look at all the avenues."

"Tell me something," I said.

"Yes?"

"What do you think of the people who committed these murders?"

"I can't even begin to fathom how they thought," he said. "Even to try to think of how they could do something like this is completely foreign to me."

Leaving the prison that day, I said to the guard who walked me to the gate, "May I ask you a question?"

He nodded.

"Do all of them swear that they were somewhere else?"

"I never heard one of them yet say that they done it," he said.

"They all say they want to know as bad as anyone else who's responsible?"

"Yup."

On the river, a tug was pushing a line of barges against the wind.

"Tell you what," the guard said. "I believe he don't even know himself he did it."

"Same with the others?"

"Yes, sir." He took a cigarette from his pocket and spit on the ground and said, "I believe it's a *syn*drome."

On the next-to-last day that I saw Gacy, he said, "If I was to confess to you, you know, they could make you a witness against me, if I ever got a new trial."

Most people feel that Gacy should die. Even people who feel ambivalent about the death penalty often feel that the kinds of ambiguities and complexities that give them pause are absent in Gacy's case. Or they simply relax their concerns when Gacy is the subject. He is sometimes cynically referred to as the poster boy for the death penalty.

Gacy is an outcast, a lonely and isolated man who has had experiences unlike those of a civilized person. He has failed again and again to restrain homicidal impulses that might occur to other people but that they manage to stifle or defuse. He has caused profound suffering and harm and sadness. He lives with the knowledge of having done something horrible by refusing to live with it. He is like someone who inhabits a parallel world, which is unreality. At his trial, his lawyer defended him by entering a plea of insanity. Psychiatrists who examined Gacy for the defense were prevented by legal maneuvering from describing the afflictions and disturbances he suffers. In the reports that the psychiatrists wrote of their interviews with him, they most often described him as a paranoid schizophrenic, but the prosecution portrayed him as a man who ran a profitable business; if he was insane on the thirty-three occasions when he murdered, the prosecution said, then it was a convenient form of insanity.

Gacy resents any suggestion of psychiatric complications in his personality, and he especially resents being described as insane. The more firmly he can maintain an impression of sanity, the more firmly he can dismiss the suggestion that he is a killer. He never endorsed the plea his lawyer entered for him, and he particularly didn't care for it when he learned that it contained an admission of guilt. Gacy's case strikes him as uncomplicated. He is not guilty. He wasn't there. He has been too trusting. Other people have taken advantage of him. What the doctors say about him has no meaning for him. "I'm like a chess game they played," he says. "Thirteen of them, and they couldn't come to an agreement about me."

I went one afternoon to a print shop in Perryville to have a copy made of the manuscript Gacy had given me. The young man working there saw Gacy's letterhead, which says, "Execute Justice . . . Not People."

"You should have talked to my dad," he said. "He died a few months ago, but I guess he knew Gacy as well as anyone. He was thirty years a guard at the prison, the last fifteen of them on death row a lot of the time."

I asked if his father had ever talked about Gacy.

"My dad would say how much it cost to keep him there," he said, "and he thought maybe him and the other guards should have just left his cell door open and turned their backs for fifteen minutes. Save everyone a lot of money."

I asked Gacy one day what he believed the end might be like. He said that he never thought about it. He was on a "positive mental kick," he said, and he refused to consider anything negative. Then he said that people often ask if he's scared, and he tells them he'll start worrying when the needle is put in his arm — he is to die by lethal injection — because then he'll know that the State is serious.

"If I'd been a hell-raiser — if I'd killed a guard or another inmate, or if I was a threat to the world outside — I could see it," he said. "But what is to be gained by killing me, except revenge? There's not a thing I can do about it, though. If I get off somehow, I get sent down to the Pit to do the rest of my time, and I don't want natural life in that animal kingdom."

Another time, he said, "I'll tell you what — I'm not going to make no damn Ted Bundy last-minute confessions. None of that shit. I'm not going to put my family through the media circus. And I'm not going to be buried with my mother and father, like some people have written, because I don't want no one desecrating their graves.

"The prison won't let me have my family there — I hear the victims' families can come, but I can't have my own family. I don't know. And I'm not going to invite anyone else, either. I got all these people that tell me they want to be there, and they say, 'I've known you for eight years, you've got to let me come,' but I spent my life as a workaholic and a loner and I'll go out that way, too."

A few weeks before I began visiting Gacy, my wife gave birth to our first child, a boy. The last time I saw Gacy, he asked how my son was doing. "When he's about a year old, get him a turtle," he said. "Put the turtle down on the floor, and he'll chase it and that's how he'll learn to crawl — it'll make him crawl faster — but you have to watch out, because if you don't get there in time he'll put the turtle in his mouth. That's what we did with my son, and we think it made him walk sooner."

I shook his hand and said goodbye. When I reached the end of the hallway, I turned and looked over my shoulder, expecting to see him. The hallway was empty; he had disappeared back into his obsession.

(1994)

The Archive of Stopped Time

ONE WINTER MORNING about twenty years ago, shortly before daybreak, I sat on my bed looking into a mirror I had leaned against the back of a chair, and held a gun to my right temple. The gun was loaded, and I had my finger on the trigger. I was a policeman in a small town. I had worked until two and had come home and played some records and drunk two beers. The gun was my work gun, and I used to unload it each night and put the bullets in a desk drawer and the gun under a blanket at the top of a closet. Feeling its weight against my temple, I thought, I wonder what makes people pull the trigger. I had not been despondent. I was just interested to know what the components of such a moment were, the way a friend of mine who wanted to be a poet had walked across the campus of his college in Iowa one night in the snow, in bare feet, so he would know how to describe being cold.

I was a policeman in Wellfleet, Massachusetts, on Cape Cod. I was twenty-three. Most of the things I was seeing as a policeman I had never seen before. The husbands and wives who fought so bitterly that their children called the station for help. The women who met their lovers while their husbands or boyfriends dragged fishing nets on boats whose lights you could sometimes find at night on the horizon. The solitary, intoxicated figures walking home in the cold after the bars had closed. The woman who had to be removed from the house she had occupied all her life, because she had become susceptible to hearing voices and seeing figures that weren't there, and the imploring way she looked at me — that is, into the eyes of another human being — for an explanation.

One evening, the dispatcher sent me to a house by the bay where an old man was lying on a couch with a blanket drawn up to his chest. His wife stood beside him, wringing her hands. "We were watching television," she said, "same as every night, and he made a sound in his throat, like he was choking, and he wouldn't wake up. I tried to wake him, but I couldn't." Sherman Merrill, my partner, gave him oxygen from a tank that was kept in the trunk of the police car. The man's mouth had gaped open and his cheeks had turned blue. Out of consideration for the woman's feelings, Sherman held the mask in such a way that she couldn't see them. It was the business of the medical examiner, who had been called, to say that he was dead. Having heard that a doctor was coming, the woman assumed that her husband would be revived. "No point giving this man oxygen," the doctor said as he walked through the door. "He's dead — can't anybody see that?" The woman brought her hands to her face and began sobbing. I went outside and walked a circle on the lawn to compose myself, and when I came back through the door she was on the phone and I heard her say, "Your father died tonight."

A woman from a town at the other end of the Cape called the police station one afternoon and asked if we would deliver a message to her husband, who was visiting the house they were building for their retirement; the house had no phone. I was in the station when Charles Berrio, another patrolman, who was known as Chickie, found him. The man had attached a length of yellow nylon cord to a water pipe in the ceiling of the basement and tied the other end around his neck. Since Chickie had one of the town's two police cars and the Chief had the other, I asked Lori Kmiec, a dispatcher, who was leaving for the day, if she would take me there, but she said she wouldn't go near a house with a dead body in it. Someone else took me, I forget who. I walked through the front door. In a chair by a picture window looking over the marsh was an old man sitting with his hands folded in his lap. He paid no attention to me. The man hanging from the rope in the basement had his back to a sliding glass door that framed an inlet of the marsh. His knees were bent, and his feet were touching the cement floor. He had taken his shoes off. The ceiling was so low that there had been no tension to the rope; he had brought about his end simply by letting his body go slack. He could have stood up anytime he lost his nerve. In the shadowy basement, Chickie, his eyes not yet adjusted from the daylight, had walked into him. Months later, when the subject of the man's suicide came up, Chickie said that the figure of a hanging man still appeared in his dreams.

The county man arrived and took photographs, and then Chickie applied the blade of a pocketknife to the yellow cord. None of us looked into one another's eyes as we lowered him. It felt as if we were performing an ancient gesture. The man from the funeral home showed up and poked at the dead man's swollen neck and said, "I don't know how I'm going to get that down for an open casket."

I asked Chickie about the man upstairs. "Guy's brother," he said. "Deaf. Never heard a thing."

I stood for a while looking at the piece of rope and the water pipe and the view out the window. I felt the way I remembered feeling as a child when, rising early, I could hear the voices of my parents through the walls of their bedroom — my father's low and rumbling and my mother's high, the combination like a piece of music — but I couldn't make out what they were actually saying, and I had the feeling that the substance of their conversation was important and that if I could understand it I would be in possession of something profound.

Because the eight other officers, including the Chief and the Sergeant, had been on the police force much longer than I had, I worked from midnight to eight more than anyone else. In the winter, after two, I was the only policeman on duty. Approximately two thousand people lived in Wellfleet, and there wasn't often much to engage me. Arrest drunk drivers on the state road. Travel the sand roads through the woods. Visit the ocean. I was supposed to stop at each business in town and determine whether the doors were locked, which didn't take long. I would drive the drunks home from the bars, or watch the fishing fleet leave the harbor in the darkness before dawn, or park in the woods and sleep — what was called "cooping." When all other forms of amusement failed me, I would open a drawer in one of the file cabinets that contained the department's records and look through the narrative of misfortune, poor behavior, envy, suspicion, and spite that they formed. If I found a file marked "Accidental Death" or "Suicide," I would read it and look at the photographs. In one such file were two photographs of a young man lying on a stretcher in a hospital hallway. He had been standing like a surfer on the roof of a car that was moving and had fallen off. He is looking into the camera in one of the photographs, and in the next one his eyes are closed and he is dead. The shock registered in the faces of the people standing beside him makes them look angry. In another file I found a photograph of a teenage boy who had been drinking with friends in a car and had passed out. What I heard happened is that when his friends realized he was dead they stopped the car and pushed him out. In any case, he is on his back on the pavement. His knees are bent and his legs are in the air, as if he had been sitting. In the file of the man who hanged himself I found the note he had written to his wife, on the stationery of a cottage colony. It said:

My Love,
    I have no excuses or explanations — I never have been able to give you all you deserve. Maybe this will all work out for the better for you.
    Don't stay here, sell all and get out — raise your dogs. This place will drag you down.
    I want no viewing services, the cheapest burial. . . . Tell the kids I love them and to hang in there with you. Tell Dad I can never thank him enough for all he has done.
    Your loving husband.

During the year that I spent as a policeman, three people killed themselves and two others tried. One of the unsuccessful ones took an overdose of drugs and had her stomach pumped. The other put the barrel of a gun in his mouth and pulled the trigger. The bullet came out the back of his neck. Of the two remaining suicides, one was a young man who drove his car deep into the woods and ran a hose from the tailpipe through one of the windows. The other was a young woman who hanged herself a few days before Christmas from a rafter in her house.

I saw the young woman the next day in the funeral home; I was a witness to the autopsy. She was lying on her back, naked, on a metal table, and there was a block of hard rubber underneath her neck to support her head. She was slim and she had long blond hair, a narrow face, and high cheekbones. Whoever cut her down had found her just after she died, so her neck was not swollen. It wasn't only because her hands were raised slightly that she seemed about to wake up. It was also her blue eyes. And her mouth's being open. When the doctor spoke her name, it seemed indiscreet — that is, it was hard to persuade myself that she didn't exist somewhere, that she wasn't listening.

All people probably share some impulse to self-destruction. What one person can bear another one can't. A few years ago, I was brooding over circumstances that had come to feel like an inescapable collection of obstacles in front of me. I felt sure that my affairs couldn't get better, that it was hopeless to try to improve them; even when I tried, the effort didn't seem to make any difference. As if a door had opened then or a curtain had been pulled back, I realized that if I killed myself these difficulties would end. I immediately felt the ease that I imagined I would feel if I opened an envelope and unexpectedly found a check, an inheritance, say, that left me free from ever worrying about money again. I had never thought of suicide before. No one in my family had ever killed himself. But I now felt that I knew how to manage everything. For months, I had not felt any respite from my anxieties, and now they were gone. Nothing could deflect or oppress or overwhelm me anymore. My spirits lifted so dramatically that I felt almost exalted. I had the answer and it was up to me and no one else to decide when to employ it. I had a power that I hadn't had before. I could choose the moment, and I could say goodbye and do whatever else I cared to and feel sure that everyone would remember me.

The suggestion had arisen from my unconscious, and I had entertained the thoughts that arrived after it in a state of mind that was something like a reverie. When I realized what I was thinking, I became frightened. Not because I had thought of killing myself — only the pure extroverts, who are capable of being in despair without knowing it, go through life without ever having such thoughts — but because the suggestion had brought about such a feeling of resolution and tranquillity, because I had embraced it. I knew that it was genuine, and not at all like sitting on my bed with the gun pressed to my temple and wondering what made people pull the trigger.

What it might have been like had I not turned back is something I thought I could only imagine until, reading *Voices of Death*, by Dr. Edwin Shneidman, I found an account of a woman who had unexpectedly survived an attempt to kill herself. She had begun by taking barbiturates and had been found and brought to the hospital. When she recovered, her husband was unwilling to let her come home, because he was afraid that she might try again. The hospital set about finding a place where she could be kept safely for a while. "And I thought to myself, there's only one thing I can do," she told Dr. Shneidman. "I just have to lose consciousness. . . . The only way to lose consciousness, I thought, was to jump off something good and high. I just figured I had to get outside, but the windows were all locked. So I managed to get outside. . . . I just slipped out. No one saw me. . . . And I just walked around until I found this open staircase. As soon as I saw it, I just made a beeline right up to it. And then I got to the fifth floor and everything just got very dark all of a sudden, and all I could see was this balcony. . . . And the horribleness and the quietness of it. . . . Everything became so quiet. There was no sound. And I sort of went into slow motion as I climbed over that balcony. I let go and it was like I was floating. I blacked out. I don't remember any part of the fall. Just . . . just going. I don't remember crying or screaming. I think I was panting from the exertion and the strain of running up all those stairs. And then, when I woke up, I was having a dream, which seemed very weird. At that point I was in an intensive care unit and I was looking at the patterns on the ceiling."

I became interested in suicide notes. I thought that they might convey a sense of what it is like to reflect on one's past in the company of death, that they might have a grandeur and clarity and contain revelations about the end of life that couldn't be found anywhere else.

From studies of suicide notes — especially those of Antoon Leenaars, Edwin Shneidman, Charles Osgood, Jacob Tuckman, James Conway, and Jerry Jacobs — I know that of any five people who kill themselves only one is likely to leave a note. Immigrants to America are more likely to sign their notes than people who were born here. Sometimes a person leaving a note for someone he is intimate with begins by writing Dear Mary, or Dear Michael, and ends by signing his full name — William H. Thompson, say — as if he were inscribing his tombstone. The reason that many notes are not signed may be that the dead person assumes that whoever finds him will know who he is, or it may be that someone about to end his life is unable or disinclined to comprehend a future in which he no longer exists.

Notes written on matchbooks, scraps of paper, receipts, pages torn from books and calendars, pieces of cardboard boxes, and the backs of grocery lists are as common as notes written on stationery. They are written with crayons or markers or lipstick almost as often as they are with pens or pencils. Typewritten notes are uncommon. A priest once wrote a note on the wrapping of the rope he hanged himself with. A young woman wrote in the mud with her toe. A hunter wrote on the back of a shell box. A mechanic wrote on the wall of the garage where he worked. Sometimes the note is found with the body. Sometimes it is left on a table nearby or in a desk drawer or on a chair. People who asphyxiate themselves in a car sometimes leave a note in the glove compartment. Someone who has thought about suicide for a while might send a note through the mail.

More notes are written, perhaps, than are found. No one knows how many are suppressed to protect the standing or the feelings of someone mentioned in the note, to avoid a scandal, to interfere with the suicide's wishes concerning the manner in which he wants his possessions dispersed or the messages he wants delivered, to allow someone who has committed suicide to be buried in a churchyard, or to make a suicide appear to be a natural death for the purpose of defrauding an insurance company.

Notes are most often written by people who kill themselves by taking drugs. Sometimes a person writes a note after taking the drugs, and from the way that the shape of his letters deteriorates you can see when he began to lose consciousness. The handwriting of someone composing a suicide note doesn't usually resemble his regular handwriting. From the writer's anxiety and agitation, the characters in a suicide note tend to be made larger and on more of a slant. Homicide detectives know that someone concocting a fraudulent suicide note to conceal a murder is likely to imitate the dead person's handwriting exactly.

The tersest notes are written by people who choose the most violent means for their death. No one knows the difference between people who write notes and those who don't, but it may be simply that those who write them care more about being remembered.

A letter written early in the second millennium B.C. by a man in Egypt discusses suicide; if he went ahead and killed himself, it is the earliest suicide note anyone knows of. A copy of it, on papyrus, is in a museum in Berlin. A translator working in the nineteenth century gave it the title "The Dispute with His Soul of One Who Is Tired of Life." The letter is in two parts. In the first part, a man is talking with his soul. The Egyptians believed that a man's soul lived in his tomb and depended on his relatives for offerings. The soul appears to be persuading the man toward suicide. When the man agrees, the soul reverses itself and says that suicide would be a disaster, because no one would make offerings to such a contemptible person. Better times might lie ahead, the soul says. The man then describes how he feels now that his soul has abandoned him. The second part of the note contains four poems. One of them includes the stanza:

> Death is before me today
> As a man longs to see his house
> When he has spent years in captivity.

While there are agreements on the form and the elements of every other kind of writing, there are none on what a suicide note should express or contain. One might expect that a suicide note, being in some sense the description of a compulsion, would be dramatic and original, but it usually isn't. Most suicide notes are rather flat in tone. The writing they contain is as compressed as the writing on postcards. It has taken years for the suicide to arrive at the point where he decides to kill himself, and now there seems nothing left to say, except whatever absorbs him at the moment, often simply an explanation of where some cash is to be found and whom it should go to, or an admonition such as "Don't let that rotten son of a bitch so-and-so get his hands on my car." The narrowed state of mind necessary to eliminate all possibilities except suicide is probably incompatible with a thoughtful consideration of one's circumstances. It is as if, shortly before writing, the writer had disengaged himself from his past. What he appears to remember are only slights, disappointments, failures, and grievances. He is no longer the person he was — a catalog of memories, gestures, habits, and accomplishments. He is now a collection of feelings and intentions collaborating on his demise. He is a version of one dimension of himself. Why he has decided to kill himself is straightforwardly plain to him — the irrefutable answer to a complicated equation that he believes no one else can understand. Perhaps for the only time in his life, he feels superior to the people he believes have thwarted him.

Norman Farberow, a doctor who has studied suicide notes, believes that there are five kinds: notes that blame someone, notes that deny that an obvious reason is the cause ("I did not kill myself because my wife left me"), notes that blame and deny ("My wife is to blame, but I did not kill myself because she left me"), notes that contain an insight ("Perhaps I gave her reason to leave me"), and notes that contain no explanation at all and have only instructions for the dispersal of property.

When I was describing my surprise at the notes' being so ordinary to an elderly friend of mine who is a novelist, he said, "If you were collecting love letters, you would have the same difficulty. Because people can't express their feelings. They go through life not being able to explain themselves, so it's no wonder that they can't at such an extreme. It's the absence of dignity that's the tragedy. They're behaving nobly under the weight of their concerns, but they can't see it. If they could only view themselves that way, they wouldn't be able to go through with it."

Not long ago I found a reference to a collection of suicide notes held in Windsor, Ontario, by Antoon Leenaars, a clinical psychologist. Windsor is on the south bank of the Detroit River, and it is about as close to Detroit as Brooklyn is to Manhattan. If you lived in Detroit, you might go to Windsor to gamble at the casinos by the river or to buy Cuban cigars.

Dr. Leenaars is forty-eight. He came to Canada with his parents from the Netherlands when he was a teenager. His archive, which he began in the eighties, is the largest of its kind: it includes about two thousand notes. The shortest is "Happy Father's Day," and the longest is four pages — a man's complaint over how shamefully he felt he was treated by the company he worked for. Most of the notes were obtained from coroners. Typists whom Dr. Leenaars engages to transcribe the notes are often able to complete only a few notes at a sitting before they require consolation.

One morning, while he was occupied, I sat in a room in his office and copied the following notes in my notebook. Then later I changed the names:

> Actually I already died on Sunday morning. What will die tonight is only (finally) my body and my damned heart will finally stop beating like mad.
>
> Since Sunday my heart seems to be saying to me Mary you're still alive, but I have been thinking for a whole while, damned heart, why don't you stop beating so wildly?

· · ·

Mother, I know the words that I am about to write will never answer why or relieve any sorrow you may feel. These last 13 months of my life have been the most painful of my 30 years. I've been through so much that along the way I lost myself. This is the way I want it; if that will help. Unfortunately I must once more be faced what to do about loose ends.

Most importantly Mom I want you to understand I must be cremated, not buried, and I do not want any kind of service! . . . No mourning or sadness. If you like, on my one year of being gone have a mass for my soul to be found. . . .

Tender words only make matters difficult. I would like to say I love you and thank you for your love. Theresa.

Life isn't worth the bother. I know I am a coward for taking the easy way out, but it isn't easy to kill yourself. About a month ago I told James that I was going to kill myself. I was drunk at the time. I am slightly drunk now. He talked me out of it. I gave him my army ring mainly so I would remember that he had a worse life than I have had so far. It is too late. I know I didn't say much, but I am in a hurry.

I can't stand the thought of going to the hospital and dying by inches. . . . This was done by my own hand.

My dearest Andrew, It seems as if I have been spending all my life apologizing to you for things that happened whether they were my fault or not.

I am enclosing your pin because I want you to think of what you took from me every time you see it.

I don't want you to think I would kill myself over you because you're not worth any emotion at all. It is what you cost me that hurts and nothing can replace it.

I can't begin to explain what goes on in my mind. It's as though there's a tension pulling in all directions. I've gotten so I despise myself for the existence I've made for myself. I've every reason for, but I can't see, to content myself with anything if I don't do this or some other damned thing. I feel as though I'm going to have a nervous collapse.

May God forgive me and you too my parents who have always tried so beautifully to understand me. It was futile for I never quite understood myself. I love you all very much. Ellen.

I'm sorry but I'm possessed by demons.

Lucy. Please don't come in. I suicide myself. Call the police. From Nancy's house.

Would you please put my blue suit on me with a white shirt and Susan's dad has my butterfly tie. . . . Also I would like to be smiling. And would like to have them play two songs for me. They are first the Marine Hymn. And play "A Dozen Roses." This one is the most important and has meant a lot to me. I will hear those songs and also see everyone.

I would like to be in Park View Cemetery as it is close to all my happy days and would like to have the same minister as Susan's mother had. My past should speak for itself so I don't believe they will have to ask for any forgiveness to get me into the next world.

Give my ring and watch to Tom. Sign the station over to Joe Wilson and be sure Susan is at my funeral, she at least owes me that much. I would like to lie beside Susan's mother, she did so much for me. I'm not a coward to do things this way. I am not ashamed and hope no one else will be ashamed of me. . . .

I hope you are never allowed to forget what you've done to me. I can write this now and know that my last words will be (you know what?)

(I love you angel.)

I no longer live here. I am farther beyond than you can reach.

The young man who asphyxiated himself in Wellfleet left a note. I have remembered it all these years. It was four pages long. On the first page was a drawing of a cross he designed for his grave. At the top of the cross he wrote "Behold." Along its arm he wrote, "The Prophet Is Coming." He drew a line through "Prophet" and wrote "Messiah." Underneath he wrote his name, the date of his birth, and "Died." He was thirty years old.

After he had been missing for several days, his parents came to the police station. His father was an oysterman. They lived in a large white Victorian house with scrollwork and green shutters in a back part of town, beside the filling station where the police department bought its gas. Several of the policemen had grown up in Wellfleet — I had not — and had gone to school with the young man, and one of them, Paul Francis, remembered that he was fond of a part of the woods by the back shore. Before daylight on the morning after the oysterman and his wife had come to the station, Paul shone the spotlight on his cruiser up a sand road that was overgrown with oaks, and saw the taillights of a car. He waited until the sun rose to see if anyone was in it. "I wasn't going in there in the dark," he told me. "I saw the car and I went up to talk to him. Course he's dead, I knew it — I figured he was. I talked to him anyway, in case his spirit was still around."

The young man died in the spring. Since I had spent the fall and winter working mostly from midnight to eight, I had been given the day shift. By the time I arrived for work, his body had been delivered to the funeral home and his car had been towed to a garage. For some reason, no one told me about it. As far as I knew, the young man was still missing. I rode with Chickie to the gas station. He told me to fill up the tank. Meanwhile, he walked across the parking lot to the oysterman's house. The oysterman and his wife were standing in their yard. I assumed that Chickie, who knew them, was saying that we were still looking for their son, or was asking if they had heard anything from him. After a moment, the woman's knees seemed to give way.

There weren't many oystermen left in town, and the father had been one his whole life and so was a figure of some stature, at least for me. A few years later, his car was found one morning after a snowstorm near a beach by the ocean. The car had broken down, and he'd left it and wandered into the woods and froze.

What I have remembered in particular since I read his son's note was one line: "Bury this body in the ground that I have suffered on."

(1999)

A Changed Version of God

MRS. IM CHEANN went blind in Cambodia for reasons that no one can explain. So did Mrs. Lar Poy, and so did Mrs. Long Eang. This took place in the late 1970s, during the rule of Pol Pot and the Khmer Rouge. Mrs. Im Cheann feels that she lost her sight because of smoke from the cooking fire in the hut where she lived. Mrs. Long Eang feels that hers was ruined when she was forced to carry dirt in baskets on her shoulders while a prisoner in a labor camp, and the dirt got in her eyes. She also sometimes says that her sight first failed when she learned of the execution of her brother and his family by soldiers; she began to cry, and her eyes swelled up and got red, and when the swelling subsided everything she looked at was blurred. Mrs. Im Cheann sometimes recalls that she was forced by soldiers to watch a man they had beaten, then thrown onto a fire, moan and "shiver like a fish," and that for a long time afterward she was not able to see anything except areas of light and dark. Mrs. Lar Poy watched soldiers in a rice field beat her daughter with clubs and the butts of their rifles; they beat her to death. When Mrs. Lar Poy came to America, in 1982, in addition to having trouble with her eyes she had virulent headaches. To distract herself from the pain that they caused her, she would scratch above the bridge of her nose with the point of a knife until she bled.

Between 1982 and 1989, nearly a hundred and fifty Cambodian women in middle age presented themselves to doctors in California, and said that they couldn't see. The majority arrived on the arms of relatives. The women were small, and they shuffled and stood hunched over and rarely spoke except to answer a question. The ones who were worst afflicted could see nothing at all. Those whose vision was clearest could make out shadows, and some could count fingers on hands held a few feet from their faces. All had been victims of the Khmer Rouge, but none had known any of the others or been aware when she lost her sight that the same thing had happened to anyone else. Some were permanently blind, and some had periods when their vision improved, but even then none could see as clearly as they had before the war. Most had been beaten or subjected to torture; many had contracted disease or had drunk tainted water; and all had been given so little to eat that they had lived on the edge of starvation. Any of these circumstances can cause blindness, but if one of them had done so, the women could have recovered their vision, or at least had its loss explained once they had visited doctors in America; all diseases that cause blindness are detectable. A number of the women had applied for disability payments, had been examined by doctors, and had been refused. The tests the doctors gave them found that nothing was wrong with their eyes. Most of the doctors described their difficulties as resulting from hysterical blindness, or psychosomatic blindness, but none of the doctors could tell the women why they had lost their sight or what they could do to get it back.

I first learned about the Cambodian women from an article written by Lee Siegel, an Associated Press reporter, and published in the *Los Angeles Times* in 1989. Dr. Patricia D. Rozée, a psychologist at California State University at Long Beach, had interviewed a number of these women and thought that they might have gone blind from being unable to absorb the suffering and death they had witnessed. "Their minds simply closed down, and they refused to see anymore," she said. Rozée had been working with an electrophysiologist named Gretchen B. Van Boemel at the Doheny Eye Institute, in Los Angeles. Van Boemel examined many of the women. One of them, she said, "saw her four children and husband killed in front of her, then lost her vision right after." Soldiers took the husband and three children from another woman, and they never returned. The woman said that she had cried every day for four years, and that when she stopped she had been unable to see. Rozée's and Van Boemel's impressions were not the only ones the reporter described; some people thought that the women might be faking in order to receive sympathy or money, and some thought that they might have gone blind under the pressure of flight from their country to one where they were frightened and lonely and couldn't speak the language.

Mrs. Im Cheann and Mrs. Long Eang live in the Cambodian community of Long Beach. Each prefers the Asian custom of preceding her first name with her family name. Mrs. Lar Poy used to live in Long Beach and may still; I don't know. I have never met her. What I know about her comes from the translator I employed, a young woman named Kolvady Men who had known her, had lost touch with her, and then met her by chance on the street one day and spoke to her on my behalf.

Mrs. Long Eang and Mrs. Im Cheann do not even slightly resemble each other. Mrs. Long Eang is squat and robust. Mrs. Im Cheann is slight and skittish. Mrs. Long Eang is trusting and inquisitive. Mrs. Im Cheann is vigilant. Mrs. Long Eang's voice is throaty and a little nasal, and it trails off softly when she concludes what she is saying. Mrs. Im Cheann's voice is thin and trembly, and sometimes it sounds as if it has been stripped of all elements except grief and anxiety. Mrs. Long Eang enjoys company. She receives a visitor on the sofa in her living room and chews betel leaves and spits the juice into a can she keeps beside her on the floor. Mrs. Im Cheann is solitary. She rarely looks in the direction of someone she is talking to, and while she speaks her hands often rise from her lap and make startled, fluttery gestures in the air before her, as if they had escaped her control. Her manner is anguished, and she is constantly fearful. Over the last year, she has lost enough weight so that people who know her often remark about it, but she has not been able to put any back on, partly because she does not feel much like eating. She and Mrs. Long Eang both have straight black hair cut short, like schoolgirls' hair, and both have soft dark-brown eyes. Both women own pairs of thick glasses. Mrs. Long Eang rarely takes hers off; sometimes she wakes in the night and realizes that she still has them on. Mrs. Im Cheann rarely wears hers; she apparently believes that they wouldn't do her any good. The impression Mrs. Long Eang makes is mannish and bossy, and Mrs. Im Cheann's manner is so frail and submissive that she seems like an echo of Mrs. Long Eang.

Mrs. Im Cheann rarely leaves her apartment, and when she does, it is usually to go no farther than her porch. Above her living room mantel is a portrait in oil of her mother and father. It was painted in Long Beach, from a photograph, by an artist at a flea market. Her father died in Cambodia, but her mother came to America with her; she died in the apartment. In Cambodia, before the Khmer Rouge, Mrs. Im Cheann sold food in the marketplace of a town in the province of Battambang. By her account, it was a small town in the forest with a lake and a fishing fleet and many ox wagons and rickshaws and bicycles.

To subdue the villagers, the Khmer Rouge soldiers made them attend executions, which were frequently of people the villagers knew. Often the offenses were imagined or trivial. Mrs. Im Cheann was responsible on these occasions for gathering everyone. After the beating, or the disemboweling, or the beheading, or the hanging, or the shooting, or the incineration, the villagers were given salted water with some grains of rice or the stalks of some vegetables in it and sent back to the fields to work. To keep from starving, Mrs. Im Cheann ate leaves she found in the forest. When she lost her sight, she did not tell the soldiers, because she was afraid they would think that she was mentally ill and kill her. In her small, dark apartment, she sometimes wonders if she is really alive or if she died in the rice fields; that is, she believes that the beatings she received drove her soul from her body, and she sometimes thinks that it is back there.

Mrs. Long Eang was born in 1931, in a village about thirty-five miles south of Phnom Penh called Khet Kandal, and she lived there for thirty-eight years. She grew up on a plantation belonging to her parents. The plantation had been in her family for several generations, and it was given to her when she got married. She says that she wasn't a mischievous child but she was lazy. Instead of doing the work her parents expected of her, she was always running off to play with her friends along the bank of the river that ran past the village, or at the edge of the forest behind it, and then sneaking home in the hope that she hadn't been missed and wouldn't be punished. When her father wasn't occupied in the fields, he built oxcarts and wagons and plows, and on the occasions when one of his neighbors was ready to be buried he made coffins. He arranged Eang's marriage to a young man named Eng Theap Kuoch. Theap (pronounced "Tep") lived in a village nearby. He was visiting his older brother one day in Eang's village when the brother pointed to Eang and said, "Do you like this girl?" Theap said that he had no feeling one way or the other, but his brother decided that they should be married. Theap's parents had been dead for many years, his brother had raised him, and Theap's feelings for him were such that he did whatever his brother said he should. Eang and Theap met for the first time on their wedding day. Theap's brother and Eang's father had seen to all the arrangements, and the wedding was the biggest and most festive the village could recall. For two months then, Eang and Theap avoided being alone with each other, and neither looked the other in the eye. Eang was so nervous in Theap's presence that she could hardly swallow her food, so she was constantly hungry. Little by little their feelings of shyness dissolved.

To begin a house for himself and his wife and her parents, Theap walked into the forest behind the village with an ax and cut down seven hardwood trees. The house took two years to build. Most of the houses in the village had walls made from the long, braided leaves of a reed that grew by the river, and roofs woven from palm fronds; every three or four years, the walls and the roofs had to be replaced. The plantation had enjoyed several good harvests, so Theap bought cement in Phnom Penh for the foundation and the pilings and the walls, and tile for the roof. Everything else — the floor, the altar, the staircase that descended from the porch to a landing and then divided toward opposite points of the compass — came from the forest. The house faced the water. During the dry season, the family received guests on a sofa in the shade beneath the porch. The village followed the curving banks of the river. Through lanes among the houses ran children and stubby-legged, shorthaired dogs. Along with Theap's house, the houses of the other more fortunate families stood on the higher ground and, except in remarkable years, escaped being flooded when the river overflowed its banks. Profuse schools of fish arrived in the river during high water. As the river withdrew, they were confined to ponds in the fields; the villagers caught them in buckets. Eang says that the plantation was big enough so that "if you were to look at it, it would almost go out of sight." What she means is not that it ran to the edge of the sky, like a farm on a prairie, but that the crop rows crossed lengths of cleared land until they reached the forest, which closed the view as abruptly as a wall.

The days were always hot, and in the air was the damp, fertile smell of the river. The year had two growing seasons, the length of each depending on the condition of the waters, which rose and fell in accordance with the rains and the melting of the snows on the mountains in China. After Eang married, she got up each morning between three and four, because it was easier to work in the cool darkness than to be in the fields during the heat of the day. She had inherited land along the river-bank, which was especially productive. For themselves and to share with their neighbors and sometimes to trade, she and Theap grew mainly rice and corn and beans and bananas; tobacco was their only cash crop. The families of the village hung the leaves to dry from the beams beneath their porches. Buyers appeared at the conclusion of the harvest, and the day that Eang and Theap were paid for their crop was the only time all year that they had money.

In 1969, Eang and Theap decided that the living they made from the plantation was no longer sufficient for them and their children — a boy and two girls — and that having cash in hand only once a year made their lives too difficult, so they leased the plantation to a relative and moved, with Eang's parents, to a town called Svay Sisophon, in north-western Cambodia. Eang's mother opened a stall in the market, and Theap and her father went partners as carpenters. They built for the family a small house with a tin roof, near the town's movie theater and the place where the road delivered travelers from the provinces. Each morning before leaving for work, Theap made several pots of porridge from rice and chicken and, occasionally, dried shrimp, and sometimes he also fried noodles and made flour cakes, and each day Eang sat in a corner of the marketplace, behind a bamboo stand with a green cloth strung above it like an awning, and sold what he had made. When it rained, she tilted the cloth to let the water run off it. The most trouble-some customers were boys recruited by Lon Nol and his government for soldiers. Carrying rifles almost as tall as they were, they appeared before her, saying "Grandma, I'm so hungry," and reached their hands out for porridge, for which they never paid. More than once, because of them, she ran out of money and had to borrow from her mother to start the porridge business again.

Before long, Theap began to have difficulty working. He would climb to the roof of a house and get dizzy and begin to shake, and when he looked down he was afraid he would fall. He decided he was too old to be a carpenter, and finished what work he was obliged to and did not accept any more. His father-in-law, whose contribution had been to read the plans, retired, too, since he no longer had someone to carry them out and was too old to do it himself.

The first Khmer Rouge soldiers to arrive in Svay Sisophon came on a truck from the forest, with other soldiers running behind them. It was about eleven o'clock on a hot, windless morning in April of 1975. From her stand, Eang watched the truck race through the marketplace. Dogs barked. Other trucks arrived. The soldiers were boys, yelling "Mother!" and "Father!" as greetings of triumph and celebration to the women and men they passed. Over a loudspeaker on the roof of the first truck, a soldier told the people to throw down their weapons. The people were also excited. Eang and her neighbors believed that Lon Nol and his government were corrupt and given to acts of brutality, and that Pol Pot and the Khmer Rouge were patriots. She assumed that the soldiers' arrival meant that the war had been brought to an end.

The trucks came to a stop in the marketplace. Eang watched soldiers stride onto the porches of the houses and knock on the doors and ask the people who answered if they had any guns. "We are here now to protect you," the soldiers said, "and no one has a need for a weapon anymore." People who said that they kept no weapons were made to stand aside and allow the soldiers to look for themselves.

A man on a bicycle said something to the man who sold cloth in the stall next to Eang's, and the merchant began packing up his wares. Eang asked where he was going, and he said that the statue of the Buddha in the temple was weeping. Eang put the money from her cash drawer in her pocket and ran to the temple. Outside was a crowd too large to allow her to see the statue, but everyone was saying that it was no longer smiling and that there were tears on its cheeks.

That evening, Theap stood in front of his house and talked with his neighbors. Some were worried that the future would not be peaceful. One neighbor left that night with his family for Thailand, where he had relatives. He asked Theap to go with them, but Theap didn't know anyone in Thailand or what he could do there to make a living or how he would feed his family.

The next morning, when Eang arrived in the marketplace it was empty. Birds wheeled above the river. A dog trotted up the street and disappeared around a corner. She decided that someone must have told the other vendors not to open their stalls, but no one had said anything to her, and she grew afraid and went back home.

A few days before, Eang and Theap's son, Thong Bun, had left with Eang's mother, in the hope of finding a province where there was no fighting and where it would be safe to settle until the war had run its course. Once they had found such a place, Eang and Theap and the rest of the family would join them. By that morning, Thong Bun and his grandmother had reached a village about twenty-five miles away, but the arrival of the Khmer Rouge in the province had disrupted communication among the villages, and there was no way for Thong Bun to send word to his parents of where he was.

For a week, Eang and Theap mostly stayed in their house. The market never opened. It was the dry season, and the skies were blue and cloudless, and it was hot all day. From her window, Eang saw no one but soldiers, raising dust as they passed. A few people collected their possessions in bundles that they carried on their shoulders and tried to walk away from the village, but they were turned back by guards at the place where the road from the country arrived.

A number of men who had retired from Lon Nol's army lived in Svay Sisophon. When the Khmer Rouge announced that everyone who had a weapon must deliver it to them, many of the ex–military men formed a line in the field that had been the marketplace and handed over rifles and pistols and boxes of ammunition, which the soldiers tossed on a pile. Some of the ex–military men were fearful of revenge. With the arrival of the soldiers, they had begun pretending that they had always been civilians, and now they were afraid to turn in their weapons and risk being identified, so they buried the weapons in their yards or waited until darkness and threw them in the river; months later, when the soldiers ordered prisoners to begin cultivating land in the town, the prisoners turned up the guns with their plows. The roundup of weapons took nine or ten days, and once the soldiers had concluded that the villagers were no longer armed they dropped their pretense of friendliness.

Over a loudspeaker one morning came the voice of a soldier calling everyone in Eang's part of town to a meeting in the marketplace. The soldiers stood in the shade of a canopy strung between the beds of two trucks. The people sat on the ground. They wore scarves and palm hats, and some unfurled black umbrellas. The soldiers told them that each person would be expected to perform the job he had held under Lon Nol. Those who had occupied positions of status or authority — doctors, men in the military or the police, anyone with an education —

were asked to sit, with their families, at the front of the gathering; these people, a soldier said, would be essential to the task of building the country again. Tricycle-taxi drivers and laborers who had bought shirts from Lon Nol's soldiers as they fled, and hoped by wearing them to pass themselves off as more important than they were, took seats among them. Eang and Theap, with no hope of impersonating educated people, found seats at the back, with the farmers and fish sellers. The soldier said that everyone would have to leave the village so that the troops could search for weapons; when the search was finished, they could return. He told them that in the meantime they should go back to the towns where they were born, and set about work in the fields to help restore the country. He ordered the people at the back to leave the meeting, and the soldiers began to form the others into ranks. It was said that they were to be taken to another part of the province and given work. Two of Eang's brothers were among them. One of the brothers sensed that disaster awaited them, and tried to leave with the farmers and the other unfortunates, but a soldier blocked his way.

Eang and Theap felt that the plantation was too far to reach by walking, so they joined a group heading east. They had no idea of their destination; a soldier had simply told them to travel ten kilometers. Eang put her daughters in the wagon that Theap had built to carry her porridge. In addition, she put in it a few clothes and some photographs of her father and her mother and her brothers. All the money that she and Theap had went into a bag, and that also went into the wagon, along with all their pots and pans, and some blankets and pillows, and enough rice to last them the week that they expected to be gone. Theap brought his motorbike. Now and then in ditches by the edges of the road they saw corpses. Occasionally, someone recognized the face of a corpse and word passed quickly through the crowd — "Oh, he used to be a general of the military," or, "He was the head of the bank" — but Eang and Theap never knew the names of any of the people. They were just shocked into silence by the sight of the bodies, some of which clearly bore signs of torture. Some people wheeled motorcycles or hauled wagons or swatted cattle, urging them to move faster. Once in a while, a car passed with suitcases tied on the roof and children staring out the back windows. Everyone was careful not to meet the eyes of any soldiers they passed. From time to time, a soldier would pull from the line of travelers a person whose progress was slowing everyone down, or someone who reacted hotly to being harassed, and took him away. More than once, Eang and Theap and their companions heard rifles being fired behind them but were too afraid to turn around and see why.

The village they arrived at was far from the main road. There was no river. The land was flat and under rice on small farms against the edge of the forest. Theap walked up to a shed by the border of a field and pulled the door open. Light came through cracks in the walls but not so much through the roof, and he and Eang moved their few clothes and their rice and their children into it. The next day, Theap went back to Svay Sisophon on his motorbike to get a lantern and some salt and more food, and it was like a ghost town. He left as quickly as he could. The family stayed two nights in the shed, watching processions of people arrive. Then a soldier banged on the side of the shed and told them that they would have to move closer to the center of the village. That afternoon, Theap met an old friend who knew of another empty shed, near one where he had settled, on the grounds of a disused mill, and Eang and Theap took up residence there. Within a few days, word passed among the villagers that the soldiers had executed the men and women who had not left Svay Sisophon. At night, shadowy figures could be seen among the dead, searching for jewelry.

The soldiers took Eang and Theap's daughters to live in a camp called the Little Children Labor Camp. The camp was close enough to the shed where Eang and Theap were living so that the girls could occasionally visit them at the start of the day and again at the end, but they could not spend the night, and they could not have visitors. Eang never asked why this was so, but the soldiers' explanation was known throughout the village: they have their work, and you have yours.

The days became an alternation of work and insufficient rest. Eang and Theap rose in the dark to the sound of a bell rung somewhere in the village by a soldier. Holding a leaf in the palm like a plate, each accepted a portion of rice being served from a huge pot. Some days, they carried water from one field to another, and on other days they joined crews digging ponds. A soldier would stake out a piece of ground, and Eang or Theap would be told to remove all the rocks by the end of the day. Each was given a shovel and two buckets, hung from a pole carried across the shoulders. Not finishing the task meant that they would be given more work the next day, and finishing also meant that they would be given more. They worked under the eyes of collaborators from the village. The collaborators reported anyone who talked as a plotter, and anyone who had trouble keeping up they reported as a shirker. The punishment for either was death. Sometimes Theap or Eang could look up and see the other tilling or planting or working on a ditch across the field, but mostly each worked through the day with no idea of where the other was. In the past, on the plantation, they would have left the fields at noon and had something to eat and slept beneath a coconut palm before working again, but the soldiers made everyone labor without rest. Every two or three days, the soldiers called the villagers to meetings and told them that those who shirked or fell behind would be turned into fertilizer.

One day, as Eang worked in the field, it was borne in on her that she would never go back to her plantation, or even to Svay Sisophon. She had exchanged one life for another, and even though there seemed no explanation for how this had happened, it had, and there seemed to her no point in not believing it.

Eang was assigned to haul dirt from the fields to the base of a mountain not far from the village. She carried the dirt in a basket on her shoulder, and under the weight she often grew weary, and the basket collapsed toward her cheek and spilled dirt into her eye. She recalls rubbing her eyes with clean hands, then finding dirt at the ends of her fingers. Her only relief from the irritation the dirt caused was to squeeze juice from betel leaves into her eyes. The juice washed some of the dirt from them, and then she could see a little better.

Around this time, the soldiers learned that a brother who was with her in the village had been a policeman, and they added him and his wife and their four children to a group they were sending to another province. Eang tried to persuade her brother to attempt an escape to Thailand. He told her that he was being given an important job. Eang said that if he escaped she would do her best to look after his wife and children, and he said that he had done nothing wrong and that he didn't believe that the soldiers would kill a person for no reason — especially a person who was blameless. To carry what belongings the brother had, Theap gave him Eang's porridge wagon, and a few days later he left early in the morning, with his wife and their children and the rest of the group.

The next day, while Theap was carrying water, he saw the wagon outside a temple. Then, in a rice field several days later, the woman who was the leader of the group of workers that Eang was assigned to called her from her work and told her that she had seen her brother and his family depart. When the family entered the forest, the woman climbed a tree and kept them in view. One of the children asked for water. Eang's sister-in-law stopped to get some from a ditch, and the soldiers began to beat her. Eang's brother knelt before them, saying, "We are innocent, we are good people," and the soldiers began to beat him, too. A soldier then took hold of the smallest child by his ankles and swung him so that his head struck the trunk of a palm tree.

The woman walked Eang to a clearing among trees at the edge of the field. On the ground Eang saw packages of rice with the label of a brand she knew her brother to favor. She had heard that the soldiers liked having their victims stand in front of them naked. Beside the packages of rice were the shirts and pants that her brother and his wife and their children had been wearing when they left. Over the clothes and the labels and the leaves on the ground, blood had dried hard and black. Eang wanted to cry out but was afraid to. She put her hand inside her shirt and stroked her racing heart. Then her knees gave way, and when she recovered she realized that everything had gone dark and she couldn't see. The workers' leader told her that the bodies of her brother and his wife and their children had been thrown into a pit with those of many other people. Then she led Eang back to the field and told her to finish her task. Eang couldn't hold the tools she had been given. She could barely move her arms. The woman told her that she had better work hard, and Eang said that she had no strength. The woman turned and walked away.

The women in the rows beside Eang said that the soldiers and their spies would be watching to see whether she showed any anger or sadness or otherwise gave any impression that the death of her brother and his family meant more to her than her allegiance to the state. If they thought that she did, they would kill her. Thereafter, whenever anyone said anything to her, she would laugh. At night, she would crawl under her mosquito net and bury her head in a cloth and sob as softly as she could manage. If she heard the steps of a soldier outside, she would make herself stop.

Eang remained blind for many days. Whenever she was afraid, she could see only a brightness that was like a concentration of stars. She fell ill with a fever that lasted for months and left her without the strength to rise from the place where she slept on the floor. When the soldiers came to examine her, they said she was sick like a rabbit, meaning that she was pretending. For a while, she was afraid of what they might do to her, and then she gave in and began to welcome her death.

After I had sat with Eang in her living room on a few occasions and observed her solemn way of speaking, and the gravity with which she conducted herself, and the way it tired her to recall her past, and the way her small grandchildren returned to her lap every chance that they got, and the careful way she held them despite being upset, I began to wonder if it wasn't inapt to describe the affliction she suffered as hysterical blindness. The description I find of hysteria in "Hysterical Personality Traits," by Seymour Halleck, published in the *Archives of General Psychiatry*, and in "The Clinical Management of Hysteria," by George E. Murphy, published in the *Journal of the American Medical Association*, and in "The Hysterical Personality," by Martin G. Blinder, published in the journal *Psychiatry*, suggest the nineteenth century. A hysterical patient, they say, is expected to be a woman, probably younger than thirty, who describes her troubles flamboyantly. If she has a headache, she may say that it feels as if someone were banging on the inside of her head with a hammer, or as if her head were caught in the grip of a tightening vise. She is likely to be high-strung, vain, and self-absorbed, not much capable of interest in other people, seductive, emotionally dependent, demanding of attention, given to lying and short-lived enthusiasms, impulsive, impressionable, mercurial, and inventive. She gets bored easily. She craves novelty and becomes frustrated by the slightest obstacle. The turmoil of her inner life she might display as a series of physical problems, sometimes intentionally — by means of a limp, say — and sometimes unconsciously, by means of difficulties whose origins are obscure. Her symptoms are often thought to be the result of a nature exquisitely responsive to suggestion; that is, upon finding herself in distress and recalling, say, a blind aunt who was looked after, she might invent blindness as an affliction in her unconscious mind and actually become blind, with the result that she must be taken care of.

It happens sometimes that a boy is drawn by provocative sounds to the doorway of a room and sees his parents making love and goes blind. This would be an example of hysterical blindness. The child is threatened by sexual and violent impulses within himself; he has managed to stifle them. A psychoanalyst might say that the child, having experienced potent and ambiguous feelings at the sight of his coupled parents, must invoke a stronger defense. Perhaps the child has seen his father in bed with a woman the child knows — one his father works with, who always says hello to him — and has recognized the scent of her perfume, or he has seen his father in bed with a friend of his parents', his mother's sister, or his own, and goes blind. The blindness is explained as the boy's possession of an unbearable secret. His body has volunteered a solution that will keep from his awareness the turmoil he feels when he is reminded of what he has witnessed. This is what Freud calls a conversion reaction: the anxiety that the boy feels about what he has seen has been converted into a physical symptom.

A person consulting a psychoanalyst today is more likely to say that he is unhappy in his marriage or feels an obscure dissatisfaction in his life than he is to report that he feels fine except that he no longer has the use of his legs, or that he has no idea who the woman is who brought him to the doctor's office and who insists that she is his wife. Some people believe that hysterical symptoms and conversion disorders are seen less often nowadays because the twentieth century has less patience with them than the nineteenth did. Other people think that, whereas hysteria was once thought to reside mainly among the upper classes, it is found now among poorer people, and especially in the wards of public and military hospitals.

An object held before the eyes of a hysterically blind person can often be described by the person once he is hypnotized. In earlier times, a doctor might cure a patient of hysterical blindness by saying that the image her eyes were registering wasn't reaching her brain, and that he could correct the problem by surgery. If fear of an operation did not bring about a cure, he might give her ether or some narcotic and attend to other business and, when she recovered, tell her that the trouble was corrected, and often it would be. A doctor once saw a girl cured of blindness when a frog was thrust in her face. The miraculous cures performed by faith healers and visits to shrines are believed by many doctors to be the work of suggestion on the minds of hysterical patients. The supposition that by going blind Eang and the other women were responding in terms of repressed childhood dilemmas seems absurd enough to dismiss.

Since Eang no longer had the strength to work in the fields, she was assigned to care for the two young sons of the officer in charge of the village. She was able to find her way around, but everything looked to her as if it were dissolving, as if she were seeing it through water. Theap would leave in the morning, before light, to dig irrigation ditches in the camp garden. He knew how sick his wife was, but the soldiers made him work and wouldn't allow him to stay home to care for her.

One evening, Eang made a fire in the shed and placed on it, one at a time, the photographs of her family. She feared that the soldiers might kill her for cherishing mementos, especially of people they had executed. Behind a board in the wall she concealed a picture of her father, who had died, so that she could pray to him.

When her eyes got a little better, she was sent back to the fields to transplant seedlings, even though she couldn't really see what she was doing. She would feel with her hand for the last seedling in the row and then move her fingers along the earth to the place where she thought the next one ought to be. Sometimes juice from betel leaves cleared her eyes, but never very much. Whenever she wept for the death of a friend or another relative, or from fear, her eyes seemed to swell and everything looked blurred.

Another villager told Eang that the soldiers knew she had learned of her brother's death and how it had happened. She began to be oppressed by the feeling that the soldiers were waiting for her to make a mistake that would allow them to take her away.

A month after her brother was killed, he appeared to her in a dream. He was naked, and he said, "I am going to live in Phnom Penh." She woke Theap and described the dream, but he did not know what it meant.

A few weeks later, Eang collapsed in a field from a fever and was carried to her shed by people who had been working beside her. The soldiers gave her medicine in the form of a ball of dried leaves, which tasted bad and did not make her any better. All the Western medicine from before the war — mainly from France — the soldiers kept for themselves. Soon her legs grew numb and would no longer support her. The muscles began to lose their tone. A medicine man made splints for her legs from bamboo and applied a concoction of herbs to her muscles. Her legs swelled, and the numbness spread to the lower half of her body, and she lay on a mat on the floor of the shed for a number of days before she was able to rise.

Along any trail that someone might take to escape from the camp, the soldiers dug trenches and planted bamboo stakes cut to sharp points. Sometimes they concealed the stakes and sometimes they left them in sight and hid others where they believed that someone might step to avoid the ones he could see. Around the borders of the camp they buried land mines. "For almost all of them who tried to escape, their escape was only as far as the bamboo stakes," Eang says. Those who succeeded were believed to have had the protection of a god. Theap had a friend who planned to escape and wanted Theap to come with him. The friend was from the province and knew the forest; an escape undertaken without knowledge of the forest was sure to fail. Theap knew that once he was discovered to have gone, the soldiers would kill Eang and their daughters: it was their habit to kill the wife and children of any man who escaped, even if he ended up impaled on the bamboo stakes. Theap resolved that he and Eang would meet their death in the camp together. His friend slipped away deep in the night. Years later, after the war ended, Theap learned that by the morning his friend had made it to Thailand.

Sometimes Theap was sent to work in fields so close to the border that he could hear chickens in the yards of houses in Thailand. One day when it was raining, the soldiers sent Theap to mind cattle, because he had become too frail to dig ditches or carry heavy loads. He saw some nuts at the top of a tall tree and climbed up to get them and fell. When he came to, he was lying on the ground and he could not see his left arm: it was pinned behind him, and his hand was joined to it at an angle that made him sick to look at. He had also broken his left ankle, and the left side of his body was numb. He crawled through the mud to a shed at the edge of the field. After a few hours, a boy on a bicycle passed by the shed, and he carried Theap on his bike to the camp. By the time they arrived, it was dark. Eang had been waiting for him all evening. When she saw him, she began to cry and said, "This is the end. There is no more." What she meant was that Theap had always managed to find food for them in the forest or by hiding vegetables in his pockets when he was working in the garden, and she was sure that with him crippled they would perish. While his body was numb, he set his bones. There was nothing to be done later for his pain. The only medication available was the kind that the medicine man made from roots he ground and mixed with sugar, but that was intended for fevers and infections and had no anesthetic qualities. Eang was certain that the soldiers would kill Theap for no longer being useful, but all they did was allow him less food until they judged that he could go back to work and earn what he ate.

The cloth of the villagers' shirts and pants grew thin and frayed, and there was no fabric in the camp to patch them. The women became embarrassed by having intimate parts of their bodies revealed. The soldiers worked everyone so hard and gave them so little food that no one looked anymore as he had in the past. Their heads and their knees had become the biggest parts of them. "Mothers couldn't recognize children," Eang says. "Sons couldn't tell their mother, daughters couldn't tell their father." To divert herself, Eang sometimes recalled meals she had eaten before the war. A man in the village crawled to a potato field and began to dig and died before he reached anything. "People were dying like falling fruit," Eang says.

Often the only thought in Eang's mind was of when the soldiers would bang on the door of the shed and tell her and Theap to pack and report for transfer. Obedience preserved her, she felt — she did everything the soldiers said to do as quickly as she could — but she also felt that it only deferred the end that she was certain awaited her and Theap. She had seen people taken from the fields for a dispute with a guard to a place just inside the forest and shot, so that everyone heard the report. A man she knew came down with an illness and was confined to a storage room where rice had been kept. He collected grains he found in the cracks in the floor and concealed them in his pants and brought them back to his family when he recovered. A spy betrayed him, and the soldiers shot him. When, as a means of discipline, the soldiers wanted the villagers to see the dead, they sometimes assigned villagers to gather leaves for fertilizer from just inside the edge of the forest, where corpses were strewn. A person the soldiers planned to kill might be assigned to drive a wagon of rice under escort through the forest. The soldiers who returned would say that he had tried to escape and they had shot him. Or, more cynically, they would simply say that he had escaped. Often Eang was too afraid to eat, and that struck her as ironic, since there was no food to speak of anyway.

In the shed at night or in the morning, or in the fields under the scalding sun, with buzzards turning slow circles above her, Eang prayed vigilantly, always in silence. The men and women had become so ashamed of their sunken faces and scrawny bodies that they pulled the brims of their palm hats forward or draped their faces with scarves. The scarves and lowered brims also let them hide the dismay that crossed their faces in response to what they saw and the things they heard the guards say. Even if no guard stood at hand to observe how someone reacted to hearing that his or her mother or father or child or husband or wife had been beaten or tortured and then killed, spies carried word from the fields to the soldiers in no time. Beneath her scarf, Eang kept up a plea to her ancestors and the angels and the gods of the fields and the forest and the trees to shield her from Pol Pot's soldiers.

"Block my enemy from seeing me," she would say. "Block their minds from noticing me."

People at the social agencies in California who saw Eang and Lar Poy and Im Cheann and other blind Cambodian women often tended to think that the women were either exaggerating their symptoms or inventing them. Malingerers, though, are less likely to be women. They tend to be men who invent problems with their backs after an accident on the job, or people who have been in car accidents, or young men trying to avoid the draft or an assignment to a battlefield. Hysterics adore examinations, but malingerers tend to resent them. They aren't sure what they are being tested for, particularly as the procedures become more arcane. If they are pretending to be blind, they sometimes refuse to look at charts, or they blur their eyes by putting substances in them such as pepper or tobacco or lime or lye. If they detect anything painful in the course of an exam, they are quick to object and refuse to continue. The Cambodian women submitted to tests without resistance. Malingerers who say they are blind often walk toward walls and stop just short of them. If they are asked to sign their names, they frequently trace a scrawl or a series of loops; blind people have no difficulty signing their names. A malingerer who is asked to look at his hands will often pretend he can't find them, though the request is not a test of vision but of sensation in one's hands.

Physicians trying to expose a malingerer will sometimes place chairs in the path he is likely to take through their waiting rooms and then surreptitiously watch him arrive. They abruptly make faces in front of his eyes. They might watch from their windows as he leaves the office, to see how he makes his way on the street. Doctors who heard that the Cambodian women spent a considerable portion of their lives crying, or sitting by themselves and staring into space, or lying on their sides on the floors of their houses with their arms curled toward them and their knees drawn up to their chests, often thought that the women were terribly depressed. No doctor believed that any of the women had invented their troubles.

Eang's sentence of death arrived early one morning, in the form of a soldier who banged on the door of the shed and told her and Theap to pack their belongings. In the camp it was said that among the first people the Khmer Rouge had killed were Chinese who had been in Cambodia for trade and were stranded when Pol Pot took over. The soldiers worked their way down the list until they arrived at the category of people with Chinese blood. As it happens, Theap is half Chinese, but the soldiers didn't know this. He and Eang had received their summons because somebody in the camp had informed the soldiers that Eang was Chinese. She pleaded with the officer in charge of the camp to be allowed to stay. One of the soldiers recognized her as the porridge seller from Svay Sisophon, so the officer struck her name and Theap's from his list.

Anxiety over Theap's well-being and her own often made Eang feel as if her head were swelling and her eyes filling with smoke. After that, everything would break into patterns of light, as if someone had struck her in the face. Sometimes she felt as if a needle were piercing her eyes. Mostly, she arrived home from the fields and slept without dreaming. She felt no better when she woke, but at least she had been able to forget for a time where she was. There is an account of a survivor of a Nazi concentration camp being awakened by a man beside him having a nightmare. The inmate started to wake the dreamer, then thought that whatever was happening to the man in the nightmare was less awful than the life he would wake to. On the days when Eang had been unable to work, she fell asleep less easily. She spent her nights worrying about which relative would be taken next and what would happen to her and Theap and their children. "What day, what hour were they going to kill us?" she says. "That was our only thought. That constantly ran through our minds."

Making his way back from the outhouse one night, Theap perceived a shadowy form, dressed in black and wearing a black hat, lying under the shed, where he could listen to anything that Theap and Eang said. Theap waited several days to tell Eang that they had been deprived of one of the last comforts left them. From then on, they returned to the shed from the fields and said nothing. They just lay down and went to sleep. If they had anything to say, they would contrive to cross each other's path in the fields. They would look all around them, and only after they had assured themselves that they were alone and couldn't be seen would they whisper.

Eang occasionally saw her daughters at work in the fields. She could never get close to them. They worked from early in the morning to the end of the day. Sometimes they carried burdens on their shoulders that were bigger than they were. Eang cannot read or write Cambodian, because her parents could imagine no circumstances under which she might need to, and it pained her to think of how hard she had worked before the war to insure that her daughters could go to school. One of her daughters was asked to be a group leader. She didn't want the position, because leaders were expected to work harder than everyone else, as an example, and also because there was a good deal of cruelty involved in the position. She cut her gums with a knife. The cut became infected and swelled her cheek, and the swelling allowed her to say that she was sick and couldn't attend the meeting where she was to be proposed for the position.

Eang's daughters and the others in the Little Children Labor Camp would sometimes be sent to work in a far province, and she would hear nothing of them for weeks, until they returned. These periods were among the hardest for her. When her children were away, she felt as if her soul were disengaged from her body and had traveled with them wherever they had been taken. She performed her work and went about the rest of her life with no feeling, as if she were a machine.

Thong Bun, Eang's son, who had gone with his grandmother to find a safe haven, appeared to his mother in a dream. He was naked, his face was black, and his body was pale. She woke Theap. She was so worried about Thong Bun that she didn't care whether there was a spy under the shed or not. Theap said that the message of the dream was that Thong Bun was very sick. Eang put her hands together and inwardly asked the gods and all the angels who possess and watch over the earth to please care for her son as if he were their own.

Someone from Svay Sisophon told the soldiers about the porridge that Theap used to make, and the fried noodles and the flour cakes, and they assigned him to be a cook. This happened during a time when the soldiers were harassing Eang by reducing her rations. As she arrived one day at the place in line where she was to be given her portion, the servers ran out of gruel. A soldier told Theap to make more. When it was ready, Theap stood beside the pot, facing his wife, but he did not serve her, because he was aware that the soldier hadn't given him the order to. Once the soldier had, Theap was careful not to serve her more than he had given anyone else. The soldiers came to value Theap, because he could prepare the villagers' food and at the end of the month still have rice left over. When he began, they told him that if he ran out of rice before the month was through they would know that someone was stealing and they would blame him, so he substituted leaves and plants and creatures he found in the forest.

One day a few weeks after Eang had dreamed about Thong Bun, she went secretly to a fortuneteller to see if he could divine anything of her son. What it may have been beyond his measure to know was that recently Thong Bun had been sent to cut bamboo in a province notorious for a fever that afflicted nearly every outsider who entered it, and that this was the sickness that Thong Bun was suffering. Eang was careful to enter the fortuneteller's hut when she thought that no one could see her. He told her that Thong Bun had recovered and was being protected by a guardian spirit, who would keep him from any more harm.

At night, Eang lay on her mat and thought, If I live through the night to the morning, I will live one more day. That was because in her camp the soldiers usually came for their victims at night. To illuminate the shed, she and Theap made a torch by wrapping cotton around the end of a bamboo stalk and smearing the cotton with tree sap. Sometimes she hoarded salt with other women, and they fried it and mixed it with pepper and used the mixture to place a curse on Pol Pot and the soldiers for starving them and causing them such harm. *Let them live in poverty and suffering a hundred years* is what they would ask for. Or, thinking of a particular soldier, *May you die and suffer in fire just like the fire in this pan.*

The soldiers encouraged children to listen to the conversation of their parents and observe how they behaved, and betray them. Eang was aware that boys and girls were searching among their elders in the fields for people without calluses on their hands. The children would report them as shirkers. Sometimes, when a child's testimony led to a sentence of death for an elder, the soldiers let the child perform the execution.

One day, Eang and Theap heard that a young man who was trusted by the soldiers had seen their older daughter in the camp — she was now about sixteen — and had asked the soldiers for permission to marry her, and that they had given it.

After Eang had been living in the camp for four years — and had given up hope that any of the circumstances of her dismal life would change — she was working with a group of old women spinning cotton into thread, which was a task she could do without having to see, when one of the women said that a number of young men and women with pale complexions had been caught in the forest near the village and killed. The woman wondered whose children they were; they all had foreign suitcases, she said. Everyone in Eang's family had a pale complexion. She thought immediately that one of her brothers, who was a doctor and would have a suitcase, had come looking for her, or that Thong Bun had been among them. The woman told her where in the forest the corpses had been left, but she was too frightened to go and look at their faces. For several days, she felt dizzy, and whenever the subject of the young men and women was brought up she thought she might faint. Her vision grew cloudy, and she could see nothing except changes of light; she had to follow the movement of the dark outlines of the people in front of her to find her way around.

At a meeting one evening, she found herself walking toward a soldier and unable to stop, as if she were in a dream. Aware that everyone was watching her, she asked the soldier if he knew what had become of her son. The meeting fell silent. The soldier stared at her. She expected that he would kill her.

"Mother, why do you wish for your son?" he said. "I am your son. Your former son is in another village. He has other mothers. I am here with you now." The look that he fixed on her before walking away was haughty and taunting.

She was able to contain herself, but she wanted to reply, "You can't be my son. My son could never be that cruel and that dark-skinned. He had light skin and was kind."

Eventually the day arrived when the forest seemed full of gunshots and soldiers running, and the villagers knew that Vietnamese troops were close at hand. Someone said that the officer in charge of the village had been shot. As the Khmer Rouge fled, they ordered the villagers to come with them, to serve as shields between them and the enemy. A soldier told Eang to follow him. She said that she was waiting for her husband and would leave as soon as he arrived. The soldier said not to delay, but he left without her. Several days after the Khmer Rouge left, one of the villagers turned up a document in the building the soldiers had used as their headquarters. It said that as soon as the harvest had been brought in, the soldiers intended to kill the whole camp. A ditch that the villagers had begun digging by the edge of the forest was where their bodies were to be thrown.

Eang and Theap collected their daughters and their son-in-law and walked back to Svay Sisophon. Thong Bun and his grandmother also left the village where they had been stranded when the Khmer Rouge arrived, and returned home. When Thong Bun got to Svay Sisophon, he walked toward the market. He saw a small, shrunken woman coming toward him, and stopped and told her his name and asked if she had any idea of what had become of his family. He had been so altered by starvation that Eang, standing before him in the road, did not recognize him until she heard his voice; and he did not recognize the emaciated woman as his mother until she began to weep and threw her arms around him. She told him the dream she had had of his being ill, and he said that at that time he had been so sick that he expected to die.

Thong Bun was appointed by the Vietnamese to superintend the village. He was quick to learn, and they considered him to have sufficient promise to be sent to Vietnam to study. Eang and Theap feared that Pol Pot could return. They wanted to escape to Thailand but didn't know the way through the forest and were afraid of the land mines and thieves along the way. A few weeks before, their married daughter and her husband had reached the border only to meet some Thai soldiers, and the soldiers had beaten her and then chased them back into the forest. After the two returned to Svay Sisophon, the husband continued to seek a route through the jungle. Eang asked why the rush, and he said, "The new government is the same truck — they are just switching the driver." He would leave after nightfall and return before morning until, one night, he didn't come back. Two stories reached his widow to explain his disappearance. One was that he had stepped on a land mine and been killed, and the other was that he had been killed in the forest by bandits among the group he had set out with, for the gold that they believed he was carrying.

Eang suggested to Thong Bun that he marry his girlfriend, a nurse;

the Vietnamese would give him a day off to celebrate, and the family could use the holiday to escape. Eang and Theap and their daughters and Thong Bun and his wife and Eang's mother and an elderly aunt left one morning before dawn. To conceal Thong Bun from soldiers who might know him, they threw a cloth over his head and pretended he was sick. Eang entered the forest with her hand on Thong Bun's arm, as if she were a debutante with an escort; anxiety over the escape had caused her vision to fail completely. They fell in with a group of about thirty villagers also heading for the border. Each person set his foot in the print of the person in front of him, in order not to step on a mine. No one knew how long they would have to walk. The Vietnamese soldiers they met along the way they bribed with dried fish. They carried rice for themselves, and when they ran out of water they bought more with gold. As the day wore on and they got farther into the forest and beyond areas where there were likely to be mines, they began to spread out, according to the speed at which each person was able to travel. Sometimes Thong Bun carried his mother; sometimes he pulled her in a cart; sometimes he wheeled her on a bicycle he had borrowed. Other times, Eang walked with her aunt; the two of them kept falling behind. Eang urged the old woman to walk as fast as she could, because thieves were more likely to set upon stragglers. The forest grew dark and quiet and cold. Sometime during the night, the aunt sat down and told the others to leave her behind, but Thong Bun ran back and picked her up and carried her.

"We walked one whole day and night," Eang says. "I thought we were so tired that we would go back, but we knew that nothing would be waiting for us there except thieves and land mines and soldiers who would shoot us for leaving. Along the road, there were no houses — just big, tall trees and pitch-dark. My eyes were almost totally blind, day and night.

"When we got near the border, there was only a small clearing in the forest, but there were a lot of people. We just collapsed anywhere, just slept on the ground. I was relieved but not happy. When I woke up, night was almost falling again. We were about to build a fire, but we were told not to, because thieves might see it, or Thailand soldiers in the forest, or planes from the air that might bomb us. This was just a camp for food and sleep."

Theap was too anxious to sleep, so he wandered around the camp watching gambling games. Eang's foot had a blister that had swelled up "like an egg," and she was so tired by the time they arrived at the clearing that when she tried to sit, her body seized up on her and she froze halfway, her knees bent and her legs spread, and she was unable to stand or sit. Thong Bun saw her stuck that way, her face grim, and he said, "Is this the face that wanted to go to a foreign country?" and she started to laugh. With that, something in her relaxed, and she was able to reach the ground. The next morning, they set out for a refugee camp across the border.

"When we arrived, they measured a piece of land and tossed me a stick and a piece of plastic, and they told us, 'You build your home,'" Eang says. "My husband got some bamboo to hold the plastic, but a storm with wind took our plastic away, so that night we used the sky as our cover."

They couldn't light a fire, because it was raining, so they couldn't get warm, and they couldn't cook anything, either, so they were hungry. They wrapped blankets around their heads to keep the rain off their faces and tried to sleep. In the morning, they looked for their plastic to start again. "It was difficult," Eang says. "But I was very happy, because they gave us food. And I had the feeling then that I would live again."

An American woman helping evacuate refugees saw Eang and decided that she needed to go to the hospital. To load Eang onto the truck that would take her there, the woman picked her up as if she weighed no more than a child, and that was when Eang realized how shrunken she had become from starvation. A little while after she left, her aunt died.

The doctor noticed Eang squinting. He put drops in her eyes and shone lights in them, and he asked her to read letters from a chart, but she couldn't see the chart. For a month, she made weekly visits to the hospital, a one-room concrete building in a clearing with bamboo benches. By her third visit, she could see the chart, but the letters were so blurred that it looked to her as if they were all stuck together. Sometimes she sat next to women on the benches who did not look in the direction of the person who was speaking to them, and she asked the nurse what was wrong with them. "The same thing as you," the nurse said. When Eang asked one of the women what had happened to her eyes, the woman said that she had been forced by the soldiers to work too hard.

o buy him what h
ays later, when
s that he looked pai
leaving Ohio.

ean buildings of Salt Lake Ci,
nought that it looked new and ru
vith Ohio, and he was a little sorry that
family join Eang and Theap there. He
g, Theap, her brother, her older daugh-
hemselves in an old Buick that someone
. The car broke down for the first time
ins. There was no heat in the car, and
mb. She held her grandchild close. The
the daughter to the hospital to recover
p and the rest of the family spent the
f a church. The trip took three days and
roke down, they had nearly reached the
es "Ohio" "Oh-hi-*yo*," as if she were a
other than "*Oo*-ta" that I can ever make

om the window of the car, she was dis-
eafless trees and the snow. Everything
ick her as colder than Utah and as hav-
es were too old, the streets were too nar-
the color of the sky was oppressive.

n his ABCs, but he found it difficult to
ed a new word, he tried to fix it in his
1 as anyone spoke to him, the word van-
ften spent hours memorizing Buddhist
recall nearly entire books. Sometimes,
name, his hand shook so badly that he

ing again, to a place with a sympathetic
ould do, but they always came back to
1 without any money. None of their rel-
noney to lend them. And there was no
lace wouldn't be just as severe and un-

Then began a period of waiting for word of when Eang and her family could leave the camp. Her life still resembled the life of a prisoner. Thai soldiers beat the Cambodians whenever they felt like it, and at night they roved the camps raping women. Women in the camps often said that rape was as common as the night. The soldiers allowed peddlers into the camp, but sometimes when the Cambodians bought the food and jewelry they offered, the soldiers beat them. Not infrequently, they beat people to death. The meat that Eang was given was not sufficient to feed her family, so she would have to trade it for chicken, and the chicken for enough fish. Eang's eyes were sometimes clear and sometimes not. Mostly, her sight depended on how frightened she was. At times, her eyes would water uncontrollably.

Thong Bun had been writing to his in-laws, who had escaped to Salt Lake City before the war, in the hope that one of them would act as the family's sponsor. Eang had no special desire to live in America, but she knew she could not go back to Cambodia, and life in the camp was too harsh. Each day, she would visit a board on which was posted the list of names of the people who had sponsors and could leave. Unable to read — or, usually, even to see — the list, she asked others to help her. Day after day, she heard, "Your name is not there," and she returned to her family feeling tired and defeated. Watching others pack made her wonder what would ever happen to her.

Three years passed. Now and then, Theap made a little money building beds of bamboo. Eang's daughters wove thread into fabric and made clothes, which they sold. In the camp were missionaries attached to a schismatic Christian sect. Eang had been raised a Buddhist. The missionaries told her that Christ and Buddha both taught one how to become a good person; they taught you how to walk the same road, the missionaries said. The idea that all gods were the same appealed to Eang, and so she became a convert.

One day, an acquaintance of Eang's pointed out a man in a crowd of people buying fish from a peddler. Everyone in the camps knew that among them lived Khmer Rouge soldiers who had fled the Vietnamese. Most of the soldiers tried not to draw attention to themselves, because when they were exposed people sometimes beat them to death or stabbed them while they slept, but occasionally someone recognized them from their former life or they got drunk and bragged about what they had done. Eang walked up to the man and narrowed her eyes and

stared hard at him — so hard that he stopped what he was doing and turned and faced her — because what the acquaintance had said was, "That is the man who killed your brother and his family." The rest of his fate she left to the gods.

On the day that the name of Eang's family appeared on the list, her neighbors came to watch her pack. They wept and embraced. Happy as Eang was, she also felt sad for the people she was leaving, who still had no idea of their future. She and Theap and the two girls left with all they had in the world — two changes of clothes and two hundred dollars borrowed from the American woman.

Eang had never been in an airplane before, and when the plane took off and she watched the ground fall away beneath her, she felt as if she were going to Heaven. She was excited by the sight of the forest from above and of the ocean, which looked like stone. The stewardess served her a whole chicken. It was the first time in seven years that she had eaten until she was full. Her destination was Salt Lake City. She had never seen a picture of Utah, or heard it described, and she had no idea what to expect. She imagined the landscape of the United States as a safer and more bounteous version of the Cambodian jungle. From the air, it didn't look that way. She arrived in Salt Lake City in the winter and was very surprised by the cold. Since no one said anything about how long it would last, she assumed that it was permanent.

A doctor put drops in her eyes, and this time they made her go completely blind for several days. He also gave her glasses with thick lenses. When the effects of the medicine wore off, her sight remained blurred, but the glasses helped her focus slightly.

For a month, she lay awake at night while the family slept. She hardly ever left the apartment, because of the cold, and because she could think of no destination where she would feel comfortable or where anyone would be happy to see her. To her, the city was distant and indecipherable. At night, it was still and aloof and as hard as metal, as if anything a person might say would echo, and nothing in it felt like home. Preparing lunch and dinner were the events of her day, but she was happy, because she felt that no one was going to kill her and that she would have enough to eat. She was nearly always hungry. Alone in the apartment after Theap had left to look for work and the kids had gone to school, she would eat bowls of cereal, and before long she noticed

stamps. The man voluntee he gave him the stamps. T the bus, Eang's first though out that he had not eaten s

When the brother saw t mountains behind them, promise, especially compar he had not proposed that stayed two nights, and then ter, and a grandchild arrang had given them. It was Janu during a snowstorm on the Eang's hands and feet grew police rescued them, and to from exposure. Eang and T night on cots in the basemer nights. The third time the ca Ohio state line. Eang prono cowboy, and it is the only wo out in her conversation.

When Eang first saw Ohio appointed, because of all th seemed dull and gray. Ohio s ing much more snow. The ho row, there was no sunshine, a

Theap went to school to le concentrate. Whenever he lea mind by repeating it, but as so ished. Before Pol Pot, he had scriptures, and had been able when he tried to eat or sign h had to give up.

The family talked about mo landscape or with work they wondering how they could tra atives were prosperous or had way to be sure that any other welcoming.

It became an increasing effort of will for Eang to resist an idea that came to her sometimes late at night — that she could solve her difficulties by waiting until everyone was gone from the apartment and then looping one end of a belt around the shower rod and the other around her neck. She dreamed one night that she was wandering in the forest looking for her mother's house and was set upon by wolves, which chased her. Then she was building a fire from corncobs and was about to step into it when her father appeared and told her to be careful. Theap said that the fire was a symbol of anger, and that her father was warning her not to let matters go too far. Theap himself had grown despondent. He could not find work or any way to occupy his time except for his studies, and he, too, was worried about not having any money. A few weeks after the dream, he told Eang that if they did not leave Ohio he was going to hang himself.

One day, in the office of a doctor where Eang was having her eyes examined, a woman told her that the climate of Long Beach, California, was a lot like that of Cambodia, and that many Cambodians lived there. The woman also said that old people often went there to be cured by the weather.

Asking, "Please keep us safe, and don't let the car break down or bad luck overtake us, and please protect us from harm," Eang made an offering to the gods and her ancestors of fruit she had bought with part of a hundred dollars in food stamps that her daughter had saved. Then seven of them — she and Theap, their two daughters, a son-in-law, and two grandchildren — climbed back into the Buick and put Ohio behind them. What Eang could see of the landscape from the windows seemed all plains and low hills, and she kept up a prayer the whole time for safe passage.

They arrived in California, having spent nearly all their money, and moved in with a Cambodian family her brother had written to, asking if they would help his sister. The family had an apartment with two bedrooms, and now there were ten people in it. At night, they all slept on mats on the floor. During the day, everyone left. Eang had no money to contribute to the rent, and her brother had had none to lend her to find an apartment. She sought to borrow money from a neighbor, but the interest he demanded was more than she could afford. She gathered all her jewelry and her daughters' earrings and took them to a pawnbroker, but he said that there was not enough value in them to pawn. She was afraid to tell people she met why she and her family had come to California: because they had failed to find a place for themselves in Utah or in Ohio. One way and another, over the next few weeks, she collected enough money to rent an apartment. A church group filled the refrigerator with chicken and vegetables and bought the family fifty pounds of rice. After a few months, Eang's younger daughter took her to a clinic at a state hospital. Eang told the doctors that she couldn't see, but they were unable to tell her why. They gave her some medicine, and they told her not to worry so much and to be happy.

In the annals of war, no other descriptions occur of a number of people isolated from each other losing their sight for reasons that no one can explain. A warrior in Homer goes blind on seeing the enemy. Soldiers have gone blind on the eve of a battle, or on hearing that they were to be transferred to the front, but they have recovered. It is a curiosity of the women's situation that no one can say what caused them to go blind or what they can do to get better. No doctor has ever seen more than nine or ten of them, over the course of several years, and few have seen even that many. The biggest difficulty facing anyone who hopes to learn what happened to the women to make them go blind is finding them. They move often and suddenly, and rarely leave addresses behind. They have, in a sense, disappeared.

Another curiosity of their situation is that nothing can be done for the women to remove the anxiety they feel when the subject of their experiences arises. Before Freud, the elements of the mind that form the personality were believed to be able to repair any damage they suffered. Disease might alter the structure of a person's brain and deform his nature, but it was not thought possible that a harrowing experience could harm his sense of well-being or the pleasure he was able to take in life, or turn a person who had been vigorous into someone who was fretful and retiring. People who sat in rooms with the shades pulled or flinched at sudden noises were considered to be feckless or to be exaggerating their circumstances or to be victims of hysteria. Given rest and support, a man or a woman of even the most fragile nature was expected to recover from any setback.

Psychoanalysis assumed that a child could only imperfectly protect himself from distress, and that things that overwhelmed him might take up an active, if shadowy, residence within him and influence and

Then began a period of waiting for word of when Eang and her family could leave the camp. Her life still resembled the life of a prisoner. Thai soldiers beat the Cambodians whenever they felt like it, and at night they roved the camps raping women. Women in the camps often said that rape was as common as the night. The soldiers allowed peddlers into the camp, but sometimes when the Cambodians bought the food and jewelry they offered, the soldiers beat them. Not infrequently, they beat people to death. The meat that Eang was given was not sufficient to feed her family, so she would have to trade it for chicken, and the chicken for enough fish. Eang's eyes were sometimes clear and sometimes not. Mostly, her sight depended on how frightened she was. At times, her eyes would water uncontrollably.

Thong Bun had been writing to his in-laws, who had escaped to Salt Lake City before the war, in the hope that one of them would act as the family's sponsor. Eang had no special desire to live in America, but she knew she could not go back to Cambodia, and life in the camp was too harsh. Each day, she would visit a board on which was posted the list of names of the people who had sponsors and could leave. Unable to read — or, usually, even to see — the list, she asked others to help her. Day after day, she heard, "Your name is not there," and she returned to her family feeling tired and defeated. Watching others pack made her wonder what would ever happen to her.

Three years passed. Now and then, Theap made a little money building beds of bamboo. Eang's daughters wove thread into fabric and made clothes, which they sold. In the camp were missionaries attached to a schismatic Christian sect. Eang had been raised a Buddhist. The missionaries told her that Christ and Buddha both taught one how to become a good person; they taught you how to walk the same road, the missionaries said. The idea that all gods were the same appealed to Eang, and so she became a convert.

One day, an acquaintance of Eang's pointed out a man in a crowd of people buying fish from a peddler. Everyone in the camps knew that among them lived Khmer Rouge soldiers who had fled the Vietnamese. Most of the soldiers tried not to draw attention to themselves, because when they were exposed people sometimes beat them to death or stabbed them while they slept, but occasionally someone recognized them from their former life or they got drunk and bragged about what they had done. Eang walked up to the man and narrowed her eyes and stared hard at him — so hard that he stopped what he was doing and turned and faced her — because what the acquaintance had said was, "That is the man who killed your brother and his family." The rest of his fate she left to the gods.

On the day that the name of Eang's family appeared on the list, her neighbors came to watch her pack. They wept and embraced. Happy as Eang was, she also felt sad for the people she was leaving, who still had no idea of their future. She and Theap and the two girls left with all they had in the world — two changes of clothes and two hundred dollars borrowed from the American woman.

Eang had never been in an airplane before, and when the plane took off and she watched the ground fall away beneath her, she felt as if she were going to Heaven. She was excited by the sight of the forest from above and of the ocean, which looked like stone. The stewardess served her a whole chicken. It was the first time in seven years that she had eaten until she was full. Her destination was Salt Lake City. She had never seen a picture of Utah, or heard it described, and she had no idea what to expect. She imagined the landscape of the United States as a safer and more bounteous version of the Cambodian jungle. From the air, it didn't look that way. She arrived in Salt Lake City in the winter and was very surprised by the cold. Since no one said anything about how long it would last, she assumed that it was permanent.

A doctor put drops in her eyes, and this time they made her go completely blind for several days. He also gave her glasses with thick lenses. When the effects of the medicine wore off, her sight remained blurred, but the glasses helped her focus slightly.

For a month, she lay awake at night while the family slept. She hardly ever left the apartment, because of the cold, and because she could think of no destination where she would feel comfortable or where anyone would be happy to see her. To her, the city was distant and indecipherable. At night, it was still and aloof and as hard as metal, as if anything a person might say would echo, and nothing in it felt like home. Preparing lunch and dinner were the events of her day, but she was happy, because she felt that no one was going to kill her and that she would have enough to eat. She was nearly always hungry. Alone in the apartment after Theap had left to look for work and the kids had gone to school, she would eat bowls of cereal, and before long she noticed that her waist was expanding. She missed her friends, but she didn't miss the war. She would think of the machines for farming that existed in America and of all the food that she and Theap would be able to grow.

The weeks passed. As the elation she felt at being safe from harm began to fade, she came to realize that she and Theap were in a country whose language they did not speak, and that even though they were fed, other people had jobs, and she began to grow afraid. She expected from what she had been told about America that the government would give her and Theap land, and now she realized that it wasn't going to, and she wondered where they would ever find another plantation. When she looked around Salt Lake, she didn't see any land that was useful for farming, and the climate was inhospitable anyway. She and Theap were willing to work for anyone and do anything they were asked, but no opportunity presented itself, and they had no idea of how to find one.

Sometimes Eang could see reasonably well, with the help of the glasses, and at other times she saw nothing but bright lights or smoke. During those periods, about the best she could do was make out the shape of someone's hand passing in front of her eyes. She took medicine for headaches and to help her sleep, and it sometimes calmed her and made it easier for her to see.

The despair she felt is such a common human feeling that it is not difficult to imagine her at the window of her apartment, watching the blurred shapes of cars driving by and of city buses and of strangely dressed people going here and there with no sense of leisure about their movements, and to imagine her wondering where she and Theap would ever fit in.

A year passed. One of Eang's brothers called from Ohio. He had been a preacher in Cambodia, and now he was living with their mother and working as an interpreter at a church. Theap told him their difficulties, and the brother suggested that they come to Ohio, where the rest of the family was. He said that Ohio was fun. Theap said that Utah was fun, too, but he agreed that it would be better for all of them to be together. At a bus station in Ohio, Eang's brother bought a ticket to Salt Lake. His wife gave him thirty dollars' worth of food stamps she had saved, and told him to be careful with them. Waiting for his bus, he met a man who asked if he had any money, and the brother showed him the food stamps. The man volunteered to buy him what he needed for the trip if he gave him the stamps. Two days later, when the brother stepped off the bus, Eang's first thought was that he looked pale and sick. It turned out that he had not eaten since leaving Ohio.

When the brother saw the clean buildings of Salt Lake City and the mountains behind them, he thought that it looked new and full of promise, especially compared with Ohio, and he was a little sorry that he had not proposed that his family join Eang and Theap there. He stayed two nights, and then Eang, Theap, her brother, her older daughter, and a grandchild arranged themselves in an old Buick that someone had given them. It was January. The car broke down for the first time during a snowstorm on the plains. There was no heat in the car, and Eang's hands and feet grew numb. She held her grandchild close. The police rescued them, and took the daughter to the hospital to recover from exposure. Eang and Theap and the rest of the family spent the night on cots in the basement of a church. The trip took three days and nights. The third time the car broke down, they had nearly reached the Ohio state line. Eang pronounces "Ohio" "Oh-hi-*yo*," as if she were a cowboy, and it is the only word other than "*Oo*-ta" that I can ever make out in her conversation.

When Eang first saw Ohio from the window of the car, she was disappointed, because of all the leafless trees and the snow. Everything seemed dull and gray. Ohio struck her as colder than Utah and as having much more snow. The houses were too old, the streets were too narrow, there was no sunshine, and the color of the sky was oppressive.

Theap went to school to learn his ABCs, but he found it difficult to concentrate. Whenever he learned a new word, he tried to fix it in his mind by repeating it, but as soon as anyone spoke to him, the word vanished. Before Pol Pot, he had often spent hours memorizing Buddhist scriptures, and had been able to recall nearly entire books. Sometimes, when he tried to eat or sign his name, his hand shook so badly that he had to give up.

The family talked about moving again, to a place with a sympathetic landscape or with work they could do, but they always came back to wondering how they could travel without any money. None of their relatives were prosperous or had money to lend them. And there was no way to be sure that any other place wouldn't be just as severe and unwelcoming.

It became an increasing effort of will for Eang to resist an idea that came to her sometimes late at night — that she could solve her difficulties by waiting until everyone was gone from the apartment and then looping one end of a belt around the shower rod and the other around her neck. She dreamed one night that she was wandering in the forest looking for her mother's house and was set upon by wolves, which chased her. Then she was building a fire from corncobs and was about to step into it when her father appeared and told her to be careful. Theap said that the fire was a symbol of anger, and that her father was warning her not to let matters go too far. Theap himself had grown despondent. He could not find work or any way to occupy his time except for his studies, and he, too, was worried about not having any money. A few weeks after the dream, he told Eang that if they did not leave Ohio he was going to hang himself.

One day, in the office of a doctor where Eang was having her eyes examined, a woman told her that the climate of Long Beach, California, was a lot like that of Cambodia, and that many Cambodians lived there. The woman also said that old people often went there to be cured by the weather.

Asking, "Please keep us safe, and don't let the car break down or bad luck overtake us, and please protect us from harm," Eang made an offering to the gods and her ancestors of fruit she had bought with part of a hundred dollars in food stamps that her daughter had saved. Then seven of them — she and Theap, their two daughters, a son-in-law, and two grandchildren — climbed back into the Buick and put Ohio behind them. What Eang could see of the landscape from the windows seemed all plains and low hills, and she kept up a prayer the whole time for safe passage.

They arrived in California, having spent nearly all their money, and moved in with a Cambodian family her brother had written to, asking if they would help his sister. The family had an apartment with two bedrooms, and now there were ten people in it. At night, they all slept on mats on the floor. During the day, everyone left. Eang had no money to contribute to the rent, and her brother had had none to lend her to find an apartment. She sought to borrow money from a neighbor, but the interest he demanded was more than she could afford. She gathered all her jewelry and her daughters' earrings and took them to a pawnbroker, but he said that there was not enough value in them to pawn. She was afraid to tell people she met why she and her family had come to California: because they had failed to find a place for themselves in Utah or in Ohio. One way and another, over the next few weeks, she collected enough money to rent an apartment. A church group filled the refrigerator with chicken and vegetables and bought the family fifty pounds of rice. After a few months, Eang's younger daughter took her to a clinic at a state hospital. Eang told the doctors that she couldn't see, but they were unable to tell her why. They gave her some medicine, and they told her not to worry so much and to be happy.

In the annals of war, no other descriptions occur of a number of people isolated from each other losing their sight for reasons that no one can explain. A warrior in Homer goes blind on seeing the enemy. Soldiers have gone blind on the eve of a battle, or on hearing that they were to be transferred to the front, but they have recovered. It is a curiosity of the women's situation that no one can say what caused them to go blind or what they can do to get better. No doctor has ever seen more than nine or ten of them, over the course of several years, and few have seen even that many. The biggest difficulty facing anyone who hopes to learn what happened to the women to make them go blind is finding them. They move often and suddenly, and rarely leave addresses behind. They have, in a sense, disappeared.

Another curiosity of their situation is that nothing can be done for the women to remove the anxiety they feel when the subject of their experiences arises. Before Freud, the elements of the mind that form the personality were believed to be able to repair any damage they suffered. Disease might alter the structure of a person's brain and deform his nature, but it was not thought possible that a harrowing experience could harm his sense of well-being or the pleasure he was able to take in life, or turn a person who had been vigorous into someone who was fretful and retiring. People who sat in rooms with the shades pulled or flinched at sudden noises were considered to be feckless or to be exaggerating their circumstances or to be victims of hysteria. Given rest and support, a man or a woman of even the most fragile nature was expected to recover from any setback.

Psychoanalysis assumed that a child could only imperfectly protect himself from distress, and that things that overwhelmed him might take up an active, if shadowy, residence within him and influence and unsettle him for the rest of his life. It also assumed that when he was grown the only events that could cause him persistent anxiety were ones that stirred feelings from childhood which he hadn't been able to master and so had repressed. What dismantled this supposition was the effects of adult experience on the men and women who survived the Holocaust. Disturbances in the realm of infant experience and childhood sexuality fell short of explaining the suffering the survivors felt even after they were free. Psychoanalysis had been a hopeful discipline before the Holocaust. Whereas surgeons sometimes had to tell someone who had broken his leg that he might not walk again, psychoanalysts believed that of the afflictions of the mind which could descend on a person only schizophrenia and the most severe forms of melancholia were beyond the capacity of psychoanalysis to reverse or correct. The example of the survivors showed that it was possible to meet trouble in adult life which could work permanent damage on the way one thought of oneself, and that whatever strength one might summon to resist the dismantling of one's personality would in the end make no difference at all. The stronger, more confident, more resourceful man or woman might hold out longer than the one who was fragile, timid, and conflicted, but the nature of the experience was such that, in the end, both would collapse.

Suffering of the kind endured by survivors of the Holocaust or by the Cambodian women belongs either to antiquity or to periods of the distant past. Galley slaves, peasants in the Thirty Years' War, Jews awaiting a pogrom, and victims of the Holy Inquisition are examples that Freud cites in *Civilization and Its Discontents*. Today, such suffering is mainly an experience of wartime. The trauma it causes is more formidable and thuggish than the emotional result of an earthquake or a flood or an accident or a kidnapping, or even a beating or a rape. I am obliged to Erwin K. Koranyi, the author of "Psychodynamic Theories of the 'Survivor Syndrome,'" which appeared in the *Canadian Psychiatric Association Journal*, for a description of the differences between severe trauma and "'civilian' trauma or natural disaster." In more ordinary trauma, "the damaging event" lasts a few seconds or days, whereas in severe trauma it continues for years. Someone harmed by more ordinary trauma is rescued by people sympathetic to his distress, and afterward is cared for by doctors or hospitals or other benevolent hands. A victim of severe trauma is a prisoner with no hope of rescue. Someone is constantly looking for an excuse to kill him. If he is injured or falls sick, he will receive no care, only further persecution. A victim of ordinary trauma is someone who was intact until the frightful event took place. A victim of severe trauma suffers attacks while he is "already damaged" and has lapsed into a numbed and regressed and hopelessly apathetic state. The anxiety that pursues him is relentless and indefatigable.

The changes worked by severe trauma are beyond the ability of psychoanalysis or psychiatry or any other form of psychotherapy to repair. Seeking a connection between one's difficulties and one's experiences of childhood which have been repressed is irrelevant. What is responsible for how Long Eang and Im Cheann feel is things that happened to them as adults and were far too powerful for them to manage or deflect or somehow absorb, and were disfiguring. Their suffering is independent of any childhood reference. They have undergone an alteration of their personalities, a setback, a regression, that cannot be reversed.

Moreover, it is a hallmark of people who have survived a severe trauma that their experience is resistant to being diffused by means of recollection. Talking about what happened to them causes the experience to return, undiminished in its clarity and accompanied by the feelings they had while it was happening. Afterward they often have dreams of persecution in which no detail is different from the details in scenes that actually happened.

It strikes Eang as strange that no matter how many things she forgets and how much difficulty she has remembering, she never forgets the things that happened to her in Cambodia. The images that arrive in her mind without invitation are so clear that they seem almost as if they were happening again. Sometimes they seem so real that her life appears wan by comparison; it is as if the visions were real and her life were imagined. When she has a nightmare, Theap shakes her awake, and it is a moment before the impression of being in danger in Cambodia dissolves and she realizes where she is. It is mysterious to her that despite what she considers the relative good fortune of her present life, despite having met and become fond of many people who have helped her since she came to America, she never sees the faces of those people when she closes her eyes but sees only the faces of the Khmer Rouge soldiers, or scenes of hardship and suffering. Reflecting on happier times from before the war eventually turns to sadness over the unlikelihood of her ever seeing her plantation again, and such thoughts lead her back to Pol Pot. If she has a dream that is set during that time, she is always working and feeling the pain of being starved.

The disturbance that Mrs. Im Cheann feels when she wonders in California whether she died in Cambodia suggests that at least part of the injury to these women resides in their memories and the way these now work. By means of repression, one confines to distant parts of one's memory things that it would distress one to recall. What happened to Im Cheann and Long Eang in the war happened too recently, the experience of it is too clear in their minds, it was too horrific, and it went on too long ever to reside peacefully within them. Their relation to their memories has turned antagonistic. They are pursued by their memories; their memories harass them, and they cannot get rid of them except by the most contrived and mechanical resolve to forget, which takes all their energy and leaves them feeling cheerless and drained. They also feel differently about time. Whereas most of us believe that the future will be a continuation of the present, or perhaps a more or less favorable variation, Long Eang and Im Cheann fear that it will resemble the past. A part of them came to a standstill in the war, and they are drawn back to it with a frequency that is punishing. Time is mainly repetitive for them — not linear anymore. Their recollections of deprivation and suffering are a barrier between them and the people they were before the war.

Eang and Theap live on the second floor of a run-down, two-story, flat-roofed, concrete-and-stucco building that looks like a motel. You walk down an alley, past windows and doorways in which somber, dark-haired Mexican children sometimes appear, to watch you climb the staircase to the landing outside Eang and Theap's door. If Theap has not got one of his tapes of Cambodian music turned up too loud, he usually hears the doorbell and answers. He wears a sarong at home, the way he would in Cambodia, but puts on pants when he goes out. Their home is one of the cleanest I have ever been in. It has two bedrooms. Eang and Theap's widowed daughter and her children live with them. A line of photographs of Asian men and women hang high on two of the walls of the living room, like images in a temple. Mainly, the photographs are of ancestors and of Eang's and Theap's brothers and sisters. Eang collected them from relatives to replace the pictures she had fed into the fire. Many of the people they portray, of course, are dead, most of them murdered by soldiers. Over the kitchen sink is a window from which you can see the walls and rooftops of other houses and some telephone wires and, in the distance, the tops of hotels and office buildings down by the ocean. Above the kitchen table is an altar, where Eang makes offerings to her ancestors, in the hope that they will visit her dreams. She has not seen any of them except her father since she was baptized in the refugee camp. She thinks that the other ancestors no longer visit because "they consider Christ to be a higher authority than they are," and are afraid of him. She feels betrayed by the missionaries, who told her shortly after her baptism that she must give up her attachment to Buddha and follow only Christ. After brooding on this, she decided to follow both and to try to live the most exemplary life that she could. In her dreams, she occasionally finds herself at her plantation, sometimes during the dry season, when the family would sit on the sofa under the porch and receive guests, and sometimes in the rainy season, when the river flooded and everyone would go from place to place in canoes. In her favorite dream, her brother who was killed and his wife and children are present, and everyone is having dinner together the way they did before the war. No one is talking, but among them is a feeling of contentment at being together.

When you ask Eang about the war, she often shakes her head and says, "It was so long ago."

The last time I saw Mrs. Im Cheann, I hoped to ask her to explain something she had told me which I hadn't understood. In talking to the young woman who was my translator, Mrs. Im Cheann hung a few feet back from the door, one hand on the frame — a fragile, harmed figure as small as a child. I was acquainted with the way anxiety often caused her to run out of breath before she reached the end of a sentence, which made her voice rise in a way that was unintentionally coy, but as I listened to her I also heard a flatness, which I took to mean that it wouldn't be possible to talk, and I felt relieved, because she was defenseless and I didn't want it on my conscience that I had added to her tribulation by asking her to recall her shipwreck. I had the impression as her voice grew softer and the conversation appeared to be coming to a close that she had withdrawn into the shadows of the room. In any case, the sun behind me was strong, and I could no longer see her. The door closed softly. When I asked what Mrs. Im Cheann had said, the translator told me, "She said, 'I remember nothing.'"

(1994)

The Enormous Monitor

HERE IS A CAUTIONARY TALE about loneliness and modern appliances. The other night, my wife and I were having dinner at the apartment of friends who have a baby. The child was asleep. Beside the table we were sitting at, our friends had one of those monitors that allow parents to hear their child if he or she wakes. I have no idea when people began using these devices, but I think that by now everyone is sufficiently familiar with them to know that they are just as likely to broadcast a gypsy-cab driver's radio call as a child's crying. Once, late at night, over the monitor that my wife and I have for our son, I heard a woman sobbing and a man's voice saying, "If you don't quit drinking, I don't think there's much hope for our marriage."

After dinner, we were talking — there were five of us — and a woman's voice came over the monitor. "Well, what time, then?" she said peevishly. We could hear a man's deep voice at the other end of the line, but we couldn't hear what he was saying — when he talked we mostly heard static. What we gathered was that he was in a car in New Jersey, heading toward the Lincoln Tunnel.

"Where am I supposed to meet you?" she asked.

" . . . "

"Port Authority!"

" . . . "

"You want me to wait in the cold in a doorway?"

" . . . "

"I can't believe this. All right. Wait a minute. All right. South side of Forty-second Street, between Eighth and Ninth Avenues, halfway down the block. How am I going to recognize your car?"

" "
. . .

"Jesus Christ. I asked for a gentleman, and they sent me you."

I think he offered to pick her up at her building, because she said, "No, I don't want anyone seeing us."

About then, it dawned on us that the woman had called an escort service, and that this was the date they were sending. He must have asked how he would recognize her. "I look like Lady Godiva," she said. "With brown hair."

" "
. . .

"All I can say is, you better not keep me waiting."

" "
. . .

"And you *better* be romantic." Then she hung up.

It can have been only a few seconds before we heard her again. She called a friend, a woman, I'm guessing — we couldn't hear that voice either — who seemed to believe that standing on Forty-second Street late at night to meet a prostitute was an insufficiently considered idea. "Listen, honey," the woman said, "I'm looking for love. I'm old enough. I'm allowed."

I don't remember what she said next. What I remember instead is one of our friends saying, "That's the woman in 8-C! The paralegal with the cocker spaniel! I knew I recognized that voice!"

"I'm dressed like a cheap hooker," the woman said morosely, and then she said that it was time for her to leave.

Our friends' apartment is on the fourth floor. I ran down the stairs. The building has a self-service elevator, which was in the lobby when I arrived. Nothing happened for what seemed so long that I was about to walk back upstairs. Then the elevator rose. I heard it pause and descend. The lobby is very small. When the elevator doors opened, she walked toward me. She was perhaps fifty. Her face was long and thin and a little tense. She had on a fur coat held tightly closed with one hand at her neck, and she had thin legs and was wearing black stockings and heels. The color in her cheeks and around her eyes had required some time before a mirror. I thought it would be funny to say, "Going to Forty-second Street?" and then realized that it wouldn't be. She walked out the door and called a taxi and got in and rode away.

I watched the taillights disappear and felt the strange, thrilling (and totally one-sided) sense of intimacy around me dissolve. I imagined the woman stepping out of the cab, wrapping her fur coat more tightly around her, then climbing two steps, turning toward the street, and waiting in the doorway for a car to pull to the curb. I did this a number of times. Each time, her face became more and more difficult to recall, until finally I couldn't picture it anymore, and then I went back upstairs to the party.

(1996)